W9-DBN-263

CCDA: Cisco Certified Design Associate Study Guide

Designing for Cisco Internetwork Solutions Exam (DESGN 640-861)

OBJECTIVE	CHAPTER
Analysis	
Gather and evaluate information regarding an organization's existing social requirements.	4
Gather and evaluate information regarding a network owner's current data network and future needs.	4
Gather and evaluate information regarding a network owner's current voice network and future needs.	4
Identify possible opportunities for network improvement.	1, 4
Validate gathered information.	4
Document relevant findings.	4
Modeling	
Given a network design or set of requirements evaluate a solution that meets IP addressing needs.	3, 7
Given a network design or set of requirements evaluate a solution that meets routing protocol needs.	8, 9
Given a network design or set of requirements evaluate a solution that meets network management needs.	11
Given a network design or set of requirements evaluate a solution to incorporate equipment and technology within a Campus design.	2, 6, 12
Given a network design or set of requirements evaluate a solution to incorporate equipment and technology within an Enterprise Edge design.	12
Design solutions to meet network owner needs applying the Enterprise Composite Network Model.	5
Evaluate solutions addressing the issues of delivering voice traffic over a data network	13
Evaluate solutions for compliance with SAFE architecture.	12, 13
Planning	
Develop an implementation plan.	4
Develop a prototype testing plan.	12
Develop a verification plan.	12

Exam objectives are subject to change at any time without prior notice and at Cisco's sole discretion. Please visit Cisco's website (www.cisco.com) for the most current listing of exam objectives.

SYBEX

CCDA: Cisco Certified Design Associate Study Guide

Designing for Cisco Internetwork Solutions Exam (DESGN 640-861)

OBJECTIVE	CHAPTER
Analysis	
Gather and evaluate information regarding an organization's existing social requirements.	4
Gather and evaluate information regarding a network owner's current data network and future needs.	4
Gather and evaluate information regarding a network owner's current voice network and future needs.	4
Identify possible opportunities for network improvement.	1, 4
Validate gathered information.	4
Document relevant findings.	4
Modeling	
Given a network design or set of requirements evaluate a solution that meets IP addressing needs.	3, 7
Given a network design or set of requirements evaluate a solution that meets routing protocol needs.	8, 9
Given a network design or set of requirements evaluate a solution that meets network management needs.	11
Given a network design or set of requirements evaluate a solution to incorporate equipment and technology within a Campus design.	2, 6, 12
Given a network design or set of requirements evaluate a solution to incorporate equipment and technology within an Enterprise Edge design.	12
Design solutions to meet network owner needs applying the Enterprise Composite Network Model.	5
Evaluate solutions addressing the issues of delivering voice traffic over a data network.	13
Evaluate solutions for compliance with SAFE architecture.	12, 13
Planning	
Develop an implementation plan.	4
Develop a prototype testing plan.	12
Develop a verification plan.	12

SYBEX

CCDA:
Cisco Certified Design Associate
Study Guide
Second Edition

CCDA™:
Cisco® Certified Design Associate
Associate
Study Guide
Second Edition

Todd Lammle

Andy Barkl

San Francisco • London

Associate Publisher: Neil Edde
Acquisitions Editor: Maureen Adams
Developmental Editor: Heather O'Connor
Production Editor: Susan Berge
Technical Editors: Patrick Bass, Michael Woznicki
Copyeditor: Sarah Lemaire
Compositors/Graphic Illustrators: Rozi Harris, Bill Clark, Interactive Composition Corporation
CD Coordinator: Dan Mummert
CD Technician: Kevin Ly
Proofreaders: Emily Hsuan, Laurie O'Connell, Nancy Riddiough
Indexer: Nancy Guenther
Book Designer: Bill Gibson
Cover Designer: Archer Design
Cover Photographer: Tony Stone

Library of Congress Card Number: 2002116887

ISBN: 0-7821-4200-1

SYBEX

To Our Valued Readers:

Thank you for looking to Sybex for your Cisco exam prep needs. We at Sybex are proud of the reputation we've established for providing certification candidates with the practical knowledge and skills needed to succeed in the highly competitive IT marketplace.

It has always been Sybex's mission to teach individuals how to utilize technologies in the real world, not to simply feed them answers to test questions. Sybex is committed to providing professionals with the means for acquiring the skills and knowledge they need to meet Cisco's tough standards, and Sybex has already helped thousands of CCNA, CCNP, and CCDA certification candidates prepare for their exams over the years.

The Sybex team of authors, editors, and technical reviewers has worked hard to ensure that this Study Guide is comprehensive, in-depth, and pedagogically sound. We're confident that this book, along with the collection of cutting-edge software study tools included on the CD, will meet and exceed the demanding standards of the certification marketplace and help you, the CCDA certification exam candidate, succeed in your endeavors.

Good luck in the pursuit of your CCDA certification!

Neil Edde
Associate Publisher—Certification
Sybex, Inc.

Contents at a Glance

Contents

Introduction

This book is an excellent step in your Cisco certification. If you are reading this, you are most likely a CCNA, and perhaps even a CCNP. This book is designed to introduce you to the world of network design and prepare you to pass the DESGN exam and achieve certification as a Cisco Certified Design Associate (CCDA).

 WARNING If you have not yet achieved your CCNA certification and do not have at least equivalent experience, you should start with the CCNA before going on to CCDA.

Cisco—A Brief History

A lot of readers may already be familiar with Cisco and what they do. But those of you new to the field, or maybe even those of you with 10 or more years in the field wishing to brush up on the new technology, may appreciate a little background on Cisco.

In the early 1980s, a married couple who worked in different computer departments at Stanford University started up cisco Systems (notice the small *c*). Their names are Len and Sandy Bosack. They were having trouble getting their individual systems to communicate (like many married people), so in their living room they created a gateway server to make it easier for their disparate computers in two different departments to communicate using the IP protocol.

In 1984, cisco Systems was founded with a small commercial gateway server product that changed networking forever. Some people think the name was intended to be San Francisco Systems, but the paper got ripped on the way to the incorporation lawyers—who knows—but in 1992, the company name was changed to Cisco Systems, Inc.

The first product they marketed was called the Advanced Gateway Server (AGS). Then came the Mid-Range Gateway Server (MGS), the Compact Gateway Server (CGS), the Integrated Gateway Server (IGS), and the AGS+. Cisco calls these "the old alphabet soup products."

Then, in 1993, Cisco came out with the amazing 4000 router, and then the even more amazing 7000, 2000, and 3000 series routers. These are still around and evolving (almost daily it seems!).

Cisco Systems has since become an unrivaled worldwide leader in networking for the Internet. Its networking solutions can easily connect users working from diverse devices on disparate networks. Cisco products make it simple for people to access and transfer information without regard to differences in time, place, or platform.

The Cisco Systems big picture is that it provides end-to-end networking solutions that customers can use to build an efficient, unified information infrastructure of their own or to connect to someone else's—an important piece in the Internet/networking-industry puzzle, because a common architecture that delivers consistent network services to all users is now a functional imperative. And because Cisco Systems offers such a broad range of networking and Internet services and capabilities, users needing regular access to their local network or to the Internet can do so unhindered, making Cisco's wares indispensable.

Cisco answers this need with a wide range of hardware products used to form information networks using the Cisco Internetworking Operating System (IOS) software. This software provides network services, paving the way for networked technical support and professional services for maintaining and optimizing all network operations.

Along with the Cisco IOS, one of the services Cisco has created to help support the vast amount of hardware they have engineered is the Cisco Certified Internetworking Expert (CCIE) program, designed specifically to equip people to effectively manage the vast quantity of installed Cisco networks. Their business plan is simple: If you want to sell more Cisco equipment and have more Cisco networks installed, make sure the networks you've installed run properly. But having a fabulous product line isn't all it takes to guarantee the huge success that Cisco enjoys—lots of companies with great products are now defunct. If you have complicated products designed to solve complicated problems, you need knowledgeable people who are fully capable of installing, managing, and troubleshooting them. That part isn't easy, so Cisco began the CCIE program to equip people in supporting these complicated networks. This program, known colloquially as the Doctorate of Networking, has also been very successful, primarily due to its extreme difficulty. And Cisco continuously monitors the program, changing it as they see fit to make sure it remains pertinent and accurately reflects the demands of today's internetworking business environments.

Building upon the highly successful CCIE program, Cisco career certifications permit you to become certified at various levels of technical proficiency, spanning the disciplines of network design and support. So whether you're beginning a career, changing careers, securing your present position, or seeking to refine and promote it, this is the book for you!

Cisco's Network Support Certifications

Cisco has created certifications that will help you get the coveted CCIE as well as aid prospective employers in measuring skill levels. Before these certifications, you took only one test and were then faced with the lab—making it difficult to succeed. With these certifications adding a better approach to preparing for that almighty lab, Cisco has opened doors few were allowed through before. So what are these certifications, and how do they help you get your CCIE?

Cisco Certified Network Associate (CCNA)

The CCNA certification is the first certification in the line of Cisco certifications, and a precursor to all current Cisco certifications. With the certification programs, Cisco has created a type of stepping-stone approach to CCIE certification. Now you can become a Cisco Certified Network Associate by paying only $125 for the test. And you don't have to stop there—you can choose to continue with your studies and achieve a higher certification called the Cisco Certified Network Professional (CCNP). Someone with a CCNP has all the skills and knowledge they need to attempt the CCIE lab. However, since no textbook can take the place of practical experience, we'll discuss what else you need to be ready for the CCIE lab shortly.

Why Become a CCNA?

Cisco has created a certification process, not unlike Microsoft's and Novell's, that gives employers a way to measure the skills of prospective employees. Becoming a CCNA can be the initial step of a successful journey toward a new, highly rewarding, and sustainable career.

The CCNA program was not only created to provide a solid introduction to the Cisco Internetworking Operating System (IOS) and to Cisco hardware but to internetworking in general, making it helpful to you in areas not exclusively Cisco's. At this point in the certification process, it's not unrealistic to imagine that future network managers—even those without Cisco equipment—could easily require Cisco certifications of their job applicants.

If you make it through the CCNA still interested in Cisco and internetworking, you're headed down a path to certain success.

To meet the CCNA certification skill level, you must be able to understand or do the following:

- Install, configure, and operate simple-routed LAN, routed WAN, and switched LAN and LANE networks

- Understand and be able to configure IP, IGRP, IPX, serial, AppleTalk, Frame Relay, IP RIP, VLANs, IPX RIP, Ethernet, and access lists

- Install and/or configure a network

- Optimize WAN through Internet access solutions that reduce bandwidth and reduce WAN costs using features such as filtering with access lists, bandwidth on demand (BOD), and dial-on-demand routing (DDR)

- Provide remote access by integrating dial-up connectivity with traditional, remote LAN-to-LAN access as well as supporting the higher levels of performance required for new applications such as Internet commerce, multimedia, etc.

Cisco Certified Network Professional (CCNP)

These Cisco certifications have opened up many opportunities for the individual wishing to become Cisco certified but lacking the training, expertise, or bucks to pass the notorious and often failed one-day Cisco torture lab. The Cisco certifications will truly provide exciting new opportunities for the CNE and MCSE who just didn't know how to advance to a higher level.

So you're thinking, "Great, what do I do after I pass the CCNA exam?" Well, if you want to become a CCIE in Routing and Switching (the most popular certification), understand that there's more than one path to that much-coveted CCIE certification. The first way is to continue studying and become a Cisco Certified Network Professional (CCNP). That means four more tests after the CCNA certification.

The CCNP program will prepare you to understand and comprehensively tackle the internetworking issues of today and beyond—not limited to things Cisco. You will undergo an immense metamorphosis, vastly increasing your knowledge and skills through the process of obtaining these certifications!

Remember, you don't need to be a CCNP or even a CCNA to take the CCIE lab—but to accomplish that, it's extremely helpful if you already have these certifications.

What Are the CCNP Certification Skills?

Cisco demands a certain level of proficiency for their CCNP certification. In addition to those required for the CCNA, these skills include the following:

- Installing, configuring, operating, and troubleshooting complex routed LAN, routed WAN, and switched LAN networks, and dial access services

- Understanding complex networks, such as IP, IGRP, IPX, async routing, AppleTalk, extended access lists, IP RIP, route redistribution, IPX RIP, route summarization, OSPF, VLSM, BGP, IS-IS, serial, IGRP, Frame Relay, ISDN, ISL, X.25, DDR, PSTN, PPP, VLANs, Ethernet, ATM LAN emulation, access lists, 802.10, FDDI, and transparent and translational bridging

To meet the Cisco Certified Network Professional requirements, you must be able to perform the following:

- Install and/or configure a network to increase bandwidth, quicken network response times, and improve reliability and quality of service

- Maximize performance through campus LANs, routed WANs, and remote access

- Improve network security

- Create a global intranet

- Provide access security to campus switches and routers

- Provide increased switching and routing bandwidth and end-to-end resiliency services

- Provide custom queuing and routed priority services

How Do You Become a CCNP?

After becoming a CCNA, the four exams you must take to get your CCNP are as follows:

Exam 643-801: Building Scalable Cisco Internetworks (BSCI)   The BSCI exam builds on the fundamentals learned in the ICRC course. It focuses on large multiprotocol internetworks and how to manage them with access lists, queuing, tunneling, route distribution, route summarization, and dial-on-demand.

Exam 643-811: Building Cisco Multilayer Switched Networks (BCSN) The BCSN exam tests your understanding of configuring, monitoring, and troubleshooting Cisco switching products.

Exam 643-821: Building Cisco Remote Access Networks (BCRAN) The BCRAN exam tests your knowledge of installing, configuring, monitoring, and troubleshooting Cisco ISDN and dial-up access products.

Exam 643-831: Cisco Internetwork Troubleshooting Support (CIT)
The CIT exam tests you on the troubleshooting information you learned in the other Cisco courses.

If you hate tests, you can take fewer of them by signing up for the CCNA exam, the CIT exam, and then just one more long exam called the Foundations exam (640-841). Doing this will also give you your CCNP—but beware, it's a really long test that fuses all the material listed above into one exam. Good luck! However, by taking this exam, you get three tests for the price of two, which saves you $125 (if you pass). Some people think it's easier to take the Foundations exam because you can leverage the areas in which you would score higher against the areas in which you wouldn't.

At the time of this printing, Cisco is revising their four CCNP exams, and the exam numbers listed here are subject to change. Please see www.cisco.com/en/US/learning/ for the latest on all of Cisco's certifications.

Cisco Certified Internetworking Expert (CCIE)

Cool! You've become a CCNP, and now your sights are fixed on getting your Cisco Certified Internetwork Expert (CCIE). What do you do next? Cisco recommends a *minimum* of two years on-the-job experience before taking the CCIE lab. After jumping those hurdles, you then have to pass the written CCIE Qualification Exam before taking the actual lab.

There are actually four CCIE certifications, and you must pass a written exam for each one of them before attempting the hands-on lab:

CCIE Communications and Services The CCIE Communications and Services written exams cover IP and IP routing, optical, DSL, dial, cable, wireless, WAN switching, content networking, and voice.

CCIE Routing and Switching The CCIE Routing and Switching exam covers IP and IP routing, non-IP desktop protocols such as IPX, and bridge- and switch-related technologies.

CCIE Security The CCIE Security exam covers IP and IP routing as well as specific security components.

CCIE Voice The CCIE Voice exam covers those technologies and applications that comprise a Cisco enterprise VoIP solution.

How Do You Become a CCIE?

To become a CCIE, Cisco recommends you do the following:

1. Attend the GlobalNet Training CCIE hands-on lab program described at www.globalnettraining.com.

2. Pass the Drake/Prometric exam. (This costs $300 per exam, so hopefully you'll pass it the first time.)

3. Pass the one-day, hands-on lab at Cisco. This costs $1,250 (yikes!) per lab, and many people fail it two or more times. Some people never make it through—it's very difficult. Cisco has both added and deleted sites lately for the CCIE lab, so it's best to check the Cisco website for the most current information. Take into consideration that you might just need to add travel costs to that $1,250.

Cisco's Network Design Certifications

In addition to the Network Support certifications, Cisco has created another certification track for network designers. The two certifications within this track are the Cisco Certified Design Associate and Cisco Certified Design Professional certifications. If you're reaching for the CCIE stars, we highly recommend the CCDA and CCDP certifications before attempting the lab (or attempting to advance your career).

These certifications will give you the knowledge to design routed LAN, routed WAN, and switched LAN and VoIP networks.

Cisco Certified Design Associate (CCDA)

To become a CCDA, you must pass the DESGN exam 640-861. Cisco used to require candidates for CCDA certification to complete CCNA certification first. They have dropped this requirement, and you can now take the DESGN exam and achieve CCDA certification without first completing CCNA status. However, just because you no longer are required to complete the CCNA before attempting the CCDA does not mean that it would not be a great idea to do so. If you do not have technical knowledge at the level of at least a CCNA, you will have a difficult time with the CCDA. Remember the CCIE? Cisco does not require the CCNP to gain CCIE status, but you had better know the material before the exam! The same concept applies here—you will want to have the technical skills of the CCNA (whether you have the certification or not) before attempting the CCDA.

For a comprehensive list of the skills required to achieve CCDA status, look at the table of contents of this book! Topics include the following:

- Designing simple routed LAN, routed WAN, and switched LAN and ATM LANE networks

- Network-layer addressing

- Specifying routing protocols

- Filtering with access lists, and other IOS features

- Topology design issues such as security and hierarchical design

- Network management strategies

- Non-technical steps, such as analysis of the customer's existing network and responding to an RFP

- VoIP design solutions and SAFE architecture design

Cisco Certified Design Professional (CCDP)

If you're already a CCNP and want to get your CCDP, you can simply take the CID 640-025 test. But if you're not yet a CCNP, you must take the BSCI, BCMSN, BCRAN, and CIT exams. You will also need to complete your CCNA before you can become a CCDP.

CCDP certification skills include

- Designing complex routed LAN, routed WAN, and switched LAN and ATM LANE networks, building upon the base level of the CCDA technical knowledge

CCDPs must also demonstrate proficiency in

- Network-layer addressing in a hierarchical environment

- Traffic management with access lists

- Hierarchical network design

- VLAN use and propagation

- Performance considerations: required hardware and software; switching engine; and memory, cost, and minimization

What Does This Book Cover?

This book covers everything you need to become a Cisco Certified Design Associate (CCDA). You will review the basics of internetworking, then go on to discover all of the steps of network design. You will begin by taking a thorough inventory of your customer's current network and expectations. From this, you will design topology changes and specify hardware for LAN and WAN connectivity, addressing schemes, routing protocols, security features, IOS features, network management issues, and other technical details. You will learn how to present this information to your customer, both in written format and with actual demonstrations, and you will learn about Cisco's VoIP solutions and SAFE architecture design.

 This book assumes that you are already CCNA certified, or have equivalent knowledge.

Where to Take the Exams

You may take the exams at any one of the more than 3,500 Prometric Authorized Testing Centers around the world. For the location of a testing center near you, call (800) 204-3926 or visit their website for online registration at www.2test.com. Outside the United States and Canada, contact your local Prometric Registration Center. You may also take the exams at any one of the more than 3,300 VUE authorized testing centers around the world. For the location of a testing center near you, call (800) 204-3926 or visit their website for online registration at www.VUE.com.

To register for the Designing for Cisco Internetwork Solutions (DESGN) exam:

1. Determine the number of the exam you want to take. (The DESGN exam number is 640-861.)

2. Register with the Prometric or VUE Registration Center nearest to you. At this point, you will be asked to pay in advance for the exam. At this writing, the exams are $125 each and must be taken within one year of payment. You can schedule exams up to six weeks in advance or as late as the same day you wish to take it. If something comes up and you need to cancel or reschedule your exam appointment, contact Prometric or VUE at least 24 hours in advance. If you fail a Cisco exam, you must wait 72 hours before you will be allowed to retake the exam.

3. When you schedule the exam, you'll be provided with instructions regarding all appointment and cancellation procedures, the ID requirements, and information about the testing center location.

Tips for Taking Your CCDA Exam

The DESGN test contains about 75 questions to be completed in about 90 minutes. (This can vary from exam to exam.) You must get a score of about 75 percent to pass this exam, but again, each exam can be different. You must schedule for a test at least 24 hours in advance (unlike the Novell or Microsoft exams), and you aren't allowed to take more than one Cisco exam per day.

Many questions on the exam will have answer choices that at first glance look identical. Remember, read through the choices carefully because close won't cut it. If you get commands in the wrong order or forget one measly character, you'll get the question wrong. So to practice, do the hands-on exercises at the end of the chapters over and over again until they feel natural to you. Unlike Microsoft or Novell tests, the exam has answer choices that are really similar—some will be dead wrong, but more than likely, it will just be very *subtly* wrong. Some other choices may be right, but they're shown in the wrong order. Cisco does split hairs, and they're not at all above giving you classic trick questions.

Also, never forget that the right answer is the Cisco answer. In many cases, they'll present more than one correct answer, but the *correct* answer is the one Cisco recommends. A good example of this would be a question about which routing protocol is correct for a small business. The correct answer according to Cisco is RIP, even though we would personally be the last people to implement RIP in any small business!

The CCDA 640-861 exam includes the following test formats:

- Multiple-choice
- Multiple-choice, multiple-answer
- Drag-and-drop
- Fill-in-the-blank
- Mini case studies

There are no router simulator questions present in the CCDA exam at the time of this writing, and the exam does not allow for marking or moving backward.

Here are some general tips for exam success:

- Arrive early at the exam center so you can relax and review your study materials.

- Read the questions *carefully*. Don't just jump to conclusions. Make sure you're clear on *exactly* what the question is asking.

- Don't leave any unanswered questions. They count these against you.

- When answering multiple-choice questions you're not sure about, use the process of elimination to get rid of the obviously incorrect answers first. Doing this will greatly improve your odds should you need to make an "educated guess."

Once you have completed an exam, you'll be given immediate, online notification of your pass or fail status, a printed Examination Score Report indicating your pass or fail status, and your exam results by section. (The test administrator will give you the printed score report.) Test scores are automatically forwarded to Cisco within five working days after you take the test, so you don't need to send your score to them. If you pass the exam, you'll receive confirmation from Cisco, typically within two to four weeks.

How to Use This Book

This book can provide a solid foundation for the serious effort of preparing for the Cisco Certified Design Associate exam. To best benefit from this book, you might want to use the following study method:

1. Study each chapter carefully, making sure you fully understand the information.

2. Complete all of the Case Studies listed at the end of most chapters.

3. Answer the exercise questions related to that chapter.

4. Note which questions confuse you, and study those sections of the book again.

5. Before taking the exam, try your hand at the practice exams included on the CD that comes with this book. They'll give you a complete overview of what you can expect to see on the real thing.

To learn all the material covered in this book, you're going to have to apply yourself regularly and with discipline. Try to set aside the same time every day to study, and select a comfortable and quiet place to do so. If you work hard, you will be surprised at how quickly you learn this material. All the best!

What's on the CD?

We've worked hard to provide some really great tools to help you with your certification process. All of these should be loaded on your workstation when you're studying for the test.

The Sybex Test Engine

Sybex's test engine prepares you for successfully passing the CCDA exam. In this test engine, you will find all the questions from the book, plus two additional bonus exams that appear exclusively on the CD. You can take the Assessment Test, test yourself by chapter, or just jump right into the bonus exams.

Electronic Flashcards for PC, Pocket PC, and Palm Devices

After you read the *CCDA Study Guide, 2nd Edition*, work through the review questions at the end of each chapter and study the bonus exams on the CD. But wait, there's more! Test yourself with flashcards included on the CD. If you can get through these difficult questions and understand the answers, you'll know you're ready for the CCDA exam.

The flashcards include 150 questions specifically written to hit you hard and make sure you are ready for the exam. Between the review questions, bonus exams, and flashcards, you'll be more than prepared for the exam!

CCDA Study Guide, 2nd Edition

Sybex offers the *CCDA Study Guide, 2nd Edition* in its entirely in Adobe Acrobat format on the accompanying CD so you can read the book on your PC or laptop. Acrobat Reader 5.1 with Search is included on the CD as well. This can be extremely helpful to readers who fly or commute on a bus or train and don't want to carry a book. And some of us are more comfortable reading from our computers!

How to Contact the Author

Todd Lammle can be reached at his Cisco Training forum found at www.globalnettraining.com/forum.

Assessment Test

1. Which of the following best describes the function of proxy ARP?

    A. The host pings the destination site to discover which router to use.

    B. The host ARPs the router's IP address so that it can find the router's MAC address.

    C. The host ARPs the destination's IP address, and the router responds with its (the router's) MAC address.

    D. The router ARPs the host to see if it needs to communicate with the internetwork.

2. Which of the following Cisco products introduces policy-based network management?

    A. CiscoView

    B. Netsys Baseliner

    C. CiscoWorks

    D. Cisco Hub/Ring Manager for Windows

3. When gathering technical data for a customer's existing network, which sources should be considered? (Choose all that apply.)

    A. IT department

    B. Network analysis tools

    C. Company management

    D. Outside sources

4. Which of the following is true regarding VLSM?

    A. VLSM relies on providing host length information explicitly with each use of an address.

    B. VLSM relies on providing class length information explicitly with each use of an address.

    C. VLSM relies on providing packet length information explicitly with each use of an address.

    D. VLSM relies on providing prefix length information explicitly with each use of an address.

5. CiscoWorks2000 Service Level Manager includes software for which of the following? (Choose all that apply.)

    A. SLAs

    B. SLCs

    C. SLNs

    D. SLQs

6. You have an access list numbered 50. What type of access list is it?

    A. Standard IP access list

    B. Extended IP access list

    C. Standard IPX access list

    D. Extended IPX access list

    E. AppleTalk access list

7. Which of the following is usually supported at the access layer of the Cisco hierarchical model?

    A. Access lists, packet filtering, and queuing

    B. Security and network policies, including address translation and firewalls

    C. Routing between VLANs and other workgroup support functions

    D. Creation of separate collision domains (segmentation)

8. If your network is currently congested and you are using only hubs in your network, what would be the best solution to decrease congestion on your network?

    A. Cascade your hubs.

    B. Replace your hubs with switches.

    C. Replace your hubs with routers.

    D. Add faster hubs.

9. SNMP version 1 defines which of the following PDU types?

   A. GetRequest

   B. GetResponse

   C. GetBulk

   D. GetTrap

   E. Trap

10. By default, how often are IP RIP updates broadcast?

   A. 30 seconds

   B. 60 seconds

   C. 90 seconds

   D. 120 seconds

11. During which post-design phase should equipment be purchased and configured?

   A. Prototype implementation

   B. Executive summary

   C. Final testing and demonstrations

   D. Pilot implementation

12. At which layer of the OSI model does segmentation of a data stream happen?

   A. Physical

   B. Data Link

   C. Network

   D. Transport

13. Traditional voice architecture includes which of the following technologies? (Choose all that apply.)

   A. PSTN

   B. Tie-lines

   C. VoFR

   D. VoATM

14. Assuming a default mask, which two pieces of information can be derived from the IP address 172.16.25.11?

  A. It is a Class C address.

  B. It is a Class B address.

  C. The network address is 172.

  D. The network address is 172.16.25.

  E. The host portion is 25.11.

15. Which of the following should have standardized network names? (Choose all that apply.)

  A. Routers

  B. Servers

  C. Workstations

  D. Usernames

16. What does the term "Base" indicate in 100Base-TX?

  A. The maximum wiring distance

  B. The type of wiring used in the network

  C. A LAN switch method using half duplex

  D. A signaling method for communication on the network

17. Tie-lines are responsible for connecting which voice network devices?

  A. Trunks

  B. Phones

  C. PBX switches

  D. Centrex lines

18. PDUs are carried in which of the following protocols?

  A. TCP

  B. UDP

  C. SMTP

  D. RDP

19. What is the decimal and hexadecimal equivalent of the binary number 10101010?

  A. Decimal 100, Hexadecimal 3ef2

  B. Decimal 150, Hexadecimal AB

  C. Decimal 170, Hexadecimal AA

  D. Decimal 180, Hexadecimal FF

20. Which of the following are Cisco proprietary routing protocols? (Choose all that apply.)

  A. RIP

  B. OSPF

  C. IGRP

  D. RTMP

  E. EIGRP

21. Which LAN switch method runs a CRC on every frame?

  A. Cut-through

  B. Store-and-forward

  C. FragmentCheck

  D. FragmentFree

22. What WAN protocol would you use to create a WAN that provides simultaneous transmission of voice, video, and data?

  A. X.25

  B. Frame Relay

  C. ATM

  D. 56K dedicated line

23. Which of the following describes the Physical layer connection between a DTE (router) and a DCE (CSU/DSU) device?

  A. IP, IPX, AFP

  B. TCP, UDP

  C. EIA/TIA 232, V.35, X.21, HSSI

  D. FTP, TFPT, SMTP

24. When meeting with the customer to evaluate their needs and expectations, which of the following are items to review? (Choose all that apply.)

   A. Business constraints

   B. Security requirements

   C. Manageability requirements

   D. Application requirements

   E. Performance requirements

   F. All of the above

25. What is the OSPF Router ID (RID)? (Choose two.)

   A. The lowest IP address on the router (closest to 0.0.0.0)

   B. The highest IP address on the router (closest to 255.255.255.255)

   C. The loopback address

   D. The console address

26. Which of the following statements is true with regard to bridges?

   A. Bridges do not isolate broadcast domains.

   B. Bridges broadcast packets into the same domain they were received from.

   C. Bridges use IP addresses to filter the network.

   D. Bridges can translate from one media to a different media.

27. If you want to view the DLCI numbers configured for your Frame Relay network, which command or commands should you use? (Choose all that apply.)

   A. sh frame-relay

   B. show running

   C. sh int s0

   D. sh frame-relay dlci

   E. sh frame-relay pvc

28. Which of the following should *not* be included in the design solution section of a design document?

A. Business constraints

B. Topology issues

C. Hardware recommendations for LAN and WAN devices

D. Routing protocols

E. IOS software features

F. Network management solutions

29. What is the broadcast address of the subnet address 172.16.99.99 255.255.192.0?

A. 172.16.99.255

B. 172.16.127.255

C. 172.16.255.255

D. 172.16.64.127

30. When configuring IPX, which of the following are valid methods to discover existing IPX network addresses? (Choose all that apply.)

A. Ask the administrator.

B. It is not necessary since IPX automatically addresses nodes.

C. Type **show ipx** at the NetWare server console.

D. Type **config** at the NetWare server console.

E. Set the frame type to auto-detect.

31. Which of the following best describe a use for DDR? (Choose all that apply.)

A. As a backup link in case of primary link failure

B. As an additional link used for load balancing

C. As a backup link in case of excessive network traffic

D. As an additional default gateway for IP clients

32. Which of the following describes the function of the OSPF DR?

   A. OSPF routers that generate LSAs for a multi-access network

   B. OSPF routers that generate Hello packets for a multi-access network

   C. OSPF routers that generate hop counts for a multi-access network

   D. OSPF routers that generate metrics for a multi-access network

33. Which of the following are true? (Choose two.)

   A. TCP is connection-oriented but doesn't use flow control.

   B. IP is not necessary on all hosts that use TCP.

   C. ICMP must be implemented by all TCP/IP hosts.

   D. ARP is used to find a hardware address from a known IP address.

34. When gathering administrative data for a customer's existing network, which sources should be considered?

   A. IT department

   B. Network users

   C. Company management

   D. Outside sources

35. Which sections should be included in a design document or in a response to a customer's RFP? (Choose all that apply.)

   A. Executive summary

   B. Design requirements

   C. Design solution

   D. Summary

   E. Appendices

36. Which of the following best describes pinhole congestion?

   A. The router is unable to load-balance because the IPX `maximum paths` command has not been applied.

   B. Unable to load-balance because the routing protocol doesn't support load balancing.

   C. Load balancing that occurs over DDR links.

   D. Uneven load balancing when the routing protocol doesn't recognize the capacity of the links.

37. You have an access list numbered 150. What type of access list is it?

   A. Standard IP access list

   B. Extended IP access list

   C. Standard IPX access list

   D. Extended IPX access list

   E. AppleTalk access list

38. Regarding Frame Relay, which of the following statements is true?

   A. You must use Cisco encapsulation if connecting to non-Cisco equipment.

   B. You must use ANSI encapsulation if connecting to non-Cisco equipment.

   C. You must use IETF encapsulation if connecting to non-Cisco equipment.

   D. You must use Q.933A encapsulation if connecting to non-Cisco equipment.

39. What is the purpose of NAT?

A. NAT is used to convert a private IP address into a registered IP address so that connectivity with the global Internet may be established.

B. After receiving a BootP request, NAT assigns IP addresses to hosts dynamically so that connectivity with the global Internet may be established.

C. NAT resolves network addresses to MAC addresses so that connectivity with the global Internet may be established.

D. NAT resolves remote hardware addresses for local clients so that connectivity with the global Internet may be established.

40. Which of the following should not be included in your design document's executive summary?

A. Purpose of the project

B. Brief information on your design

C. Business constraints

D. Technical constraints

E. High-level topology map of the current network

Answers to Assessment Test

1. C.   Proxy ARP means that a particular machine (such as a router) responds to ARP requests for hosts other than itself. This can be used to make a router disappear from the workstations on a network and eliminate configuration of the workstations. For more information, see Chapter 5.

2. B.   Cisco's Netsys Baseliner software allows you to view a graphical representation of your network and troubleshoot problem areas by generating topologies and reports that are based on the actual configuration files. For more information, see Chapter 11.

3. A, B.   Technical data is normally gathered from the customer's IT department and network analysis tools. Technical analysis tools can provide information on protocols in use, collision rates, broadcast rates, packet flows, segment utilization, and other network-related issues. For more information, see Chapter 4.

4. D.   Variable-length subnet masks (VLSMs) help optimize available address space and specify a different subnet mask for the same network number on various subnets. For more information, see Chapter 7.

5. A, B.   CiscoWorks2000 Service Level Manager includes service-level agreement (SLA) and service-level contract (SLC) software that allows for monitoring and reporting. For more information, see Chapter 13.

6. A.   Cisco router standard IP access lists are in the range of 1–99 when configured with the IOS and can filter only on source IP addresses. For more information, see Chapter 10.

7. D.   The distribution layer of the Cisco three-layer hierarchical design model should include separate collision domains with the implementation of switches. This is also the layer where most workstation and server access occurs. For more information, see Chapter 5.

8. B.   Layer 2 switches break up collision domains and decrease congestion on your network. For more information, see Chapter 2.

9. A, B, E.   SNMPv1 only allows for GetRequest, GetResponse, and Trap messages. The latest version of SNMP, version 3, supports the security features message integrity and authentication. For more information, see Chapter 11.

10. **A.** IP RIP updates are broadcast at 30-second intervals, creating additional overhead in some cases. For more information, see Chapter 7.

11. **A.** Cisco recommends that you purchase and configure equipment during the prototype implementation phase. For more information, see Chapter 12.

12. **D.** The Transport layer receives large data streams from the upper layers and breaks these up into smaller pieces called segments. For more information, see Chapter 1.

13. **A, B.** Traditional voice architecture typically does not include the VoIP technologies such as Voice over Frame Relay (VoFR) or Voice over ATM (VoATM). For more information, see Chapter 13.

14. **B, E.** 172.16.25.11 is a class B address, and the host portion is 25.11. For more information, see Chapter 3.

15. **A, B, C.** While usernames might be standardized, it is rare for users themselves to have standardized names. For more information, see Chapter 7.

16. **D.** Baseband signaling is a technique that uses the entire bandwidth of a wire when transmitting. Broadband wiring uses many signals at the same time on a wire. These are both considered an Ethernet signaling type. For more information, see Chapter 1.

17. **C.** Tie-lines are used for interconnecting PBX switches found in traditional voice network architectures. For more information, see Chapter 13.

18. **B.** Protocol data units (PDUs) are supported by the User Datagram Protocol (UDP). For more information, see Chapter 11.

19. **C.** To take a binary number and convert it into decimal, you just need to add the values of each bit that is a 1. The values of 10101010 are 128, 32, 8, and 2. 128 + 32 = 160 + 8 = 168 + 2 = 170, so the decimal answer is 170. Hexadecimal is a base 16 numbering system. The base of hexadecimal is 0, 1, 2, 3, 4, 5, 6, 7, 8, 9, 0A, 0B, 0C, 0D, 0E, 0F—16 digits total from which to create all the numbers you'll ever need. So, if 1010 in binary is 10, then the hexadecimal equivalent is A. Since you have 1010 and 1010, the answer to this question is AA. For more information, see Chapter 3.

20. C, E. IGRP and EIGRP were developed by Cisco to meet the scalability design and multiple routed protocol needs of those protocols lacking these features—RIP and OSPF. For more information, see Chapter 8.

21. B. Store-and-forward LAN switching checks every frame for CRC errors. It has the highest latency of any of the LAN switch types. For more information, see Chapter 2.

22. C. Asynchronous Transfer Mode (ATM) provides simultaneous transmission of voice, video, and data. For more information, see Chapter 6.

23. C. EIA/TIA 232, V.35, X.21, and HSSI are all examples of Physical layer specifications. For more information, see Chapter 1.

24. F. All of the listed options must be considered when evaluating a customer's needs and expectations during a network design. For more information, see Chapter 4.

25. B, C. The OSPF RID of a router is always the highest (closest to 255.255.255.255) active IP address on a router, unless a loopback interface is used, which will always be the RID regardless of the IP address set on the loopback interface. For more information, see Chapter 9.

26. D. When a LAN switch is first brought online, it does not contain entries in its forward/filter table; they're stored in RAM. When a frame passes through the switch, the switch copies the frame's MAC address information, mapping the MAC address to the port on which the frame was received. Since the destination port is not known, the switch forwards the frame out every port, excluding the port on which the frame was received. For more information, see Chapter 2.

27. B, E. You can use the show running-config and show frame-relay pvc commands to see the DLCI numbers configured on your router. For more information, see Chapter 6.

28. A. Business constraints should be identified and specified in the design requirements section of a design document. For more information, see Chapter 12.

29. B. First start with a 256 mask or, in this case, 256 − 192 = 64. 64 is the first subnet; 128 is the second subnet. This host is in the 64-subnet range; the broadcast address is 127.255, and the valid host range is 64.1–127.254. For more information, see Chapter 3.

30. A, D. The Novell administrator defines the IPX network number when configuring the NetWare server. The `config` command displays the IPX network number along with other IPX address configuration. For more information, see Chapter 7.

31. A, C. Dial-on-demand routing (DDR) is a technique that allows a router to automatically initiate and end a circuit-switched session per the requirements of the sending station. By mimicking keep-alives, the router fools the end station into treating the session as active. DDR permits routing over ISDN or telephone lines via a modem or external ISDN terminal adapter. For more information, see Chapter 5.

32. A. The OSPF designated router (DR) is responsible for controlling and sending updates to all other OSPF-configured routers. For more information, see Chapter 9.

33. C, D. ICMP must be implemented by all TCP/IP hosts, and ARP is used to find a hardware address from a known IP address. For more information, see Chapter 3.

34. C. Administrative data is normally gathered from company management and includes such things as the company's business goals, corporate structure, geographic locations, current and future staffing, and policies and politics that may affect the new network design. For more information, see Chapter 4.

35. A, B, C, D, E. Cisco recommends that a design document or a response to a customer's Request for Purchase (RFP) include these five items. For more information, see Chapter 12.

36. D. Some routing protocols base cost on the number of hops to a particular destination. These routing protocols load-balance over unequal bandwidth paths as long as the hop count is equal. Once a slow link becomes saturated, however, higher capacity links cannot be filled. For more information, see Chapter 5.

37. B. Cisco router extended IP access lists are in the range of 100–199 when configured with the IOS and can filter on source, destination address, destination port number, and protocol type. For more information, see Chapter 10.

38. C. Internet Engineering Task Force (IETF) is the encapsulation method used when connecting Frame Relay to non-Cisco routers. For more information, see Chapter 6.

39. A.   Network Address Translation (NAT) is an algorithm instrumental in minimizing the requirement for globally unique IP addresses, permitting an organization whose addresses are not all globally unique to connect to the Internet regardless by translating those addresses into globally routable address space. For more information, see Chapter 7.

40. E.   The executive summary should be written and presented to management and typically does not include details such as a topology map. For more information, see Chapter 12.

Chapter 1

Introduction to Internetworking

CCDA EXAM TOPICS COVERED IN THIS CHAPTER:

✓ Identify possible opportunities for network improvement.

As your mom probably told you, there's really no better place to start than at the beginning. But what she likely didn't warn you is that any process—internetworking being a classic example—takes its share of rabbit trails that dead-end. Other paths flourish into full-scale systems. One thing is certain: the changes in this industry have been mercurial. One day someone has a germ of a thought, and a few days later a new field emerges from that embryonic idea. Following these trails, however, can be a bit of a challenge.

So this is your primer—a course in the ABCs of internetworks. This opening chapter will examine the history of internetworking and then establish how it evolved into the technology of today. We'll also describe the LAN and WAN equipment that's typically found in a modern internetworking environment.

A necessary prerequisite to this is to fully understand the OSI reference model. I'll show you how the layered approach to application development has created the present internetworking standards that shape how modern internetworking takes place. So relax; I'll take you step-by-step through the fundamentals you need to learn.

The main topics addressed in this chapter are

- Identify and describe the functions of each of the seven layers of the OSI reference model.

- Describe the basic process of communication between the layers of the OSI reference model.

- Describe connection-oriented network service and connectionless network service and identify the key differences between them.

- Describe the basic process of information exchange between two applications across a network.

- Define flow control and describe the three basic methods used in networking.

- Identify the major standards organizations and bodies that specify internetworking standards.

- Define multiplexing and describe its function in internetworking.

Internetworking Fundamentals

To understand internetworking, let's begin by going back to the origins of networking and following its evolutionary path. We'll look at how internetworks have developed along this path and finish with a discussion that describes the demands of a typical, contemporary internetwork.

Evolution of Internetworking

As you might recall, network communications in the 1960s and 1970s were centered on the mainframe. Machines called dumb terminals would access the mainframe over low-speed lines. This arrangement was referred to as a *centralized computing environment* because all the processing took place in one central location. A classic example of a centralized computing environment is found in IBM's Systems Network Architecture (SNA) using multi-drop lines and X.25 packet switching.

Through the dumb terminal, the user could run programs, access resources, and copy files. The mainframe would serve to authenticate or verify the user, then coordinate the user and the program. This method worked quite well and was actually very straightforward—with one computer. But relatively early on, the idea of hooking computers together to talk to one another became an obvious no-brainer. However, things become a little more complex when using multiple computers. When several machines need to be coordinated, you have to be aware of things like

- Addressing

- Error detection and correction

- Time synchronization

- Transmission coordination

Then the 1980s dawned. The PC became widely available and changed networking forever. At this point, printers were attached to PCs with serial cables that were typically shared with A/B switch boxes. This meant only two people could use the same printer. Pretty soon, boxes became available that would allow five or ten users to be plugged into and share the same printer, but since printer queuing hadn't been developed yet, it still meant only one person could print at a given time. I have a sick-minded friend who fondly remembers the days when everyone gathered around the printer waiting for their stuff—a great way to get the skinny on office gossip but a huge time-waster. And if you were on deadline, forget it! The need to have many printers to adequately service all the users' jobs was an expensive reality indeed. So *local area networks (LANs)* were born to help reduce costs. Printer queuing—which requires creating a directory on a server in which print jobs are stored and from which they are later printed in the order received—made printing more efficient. But in order to make this process possible, the printers had to be connected to a LAN with that server. Only then could hundreds of users print to a printer (or printers) simultaneously.

Early LANs were small and isolated, and it wasn't long before the need to connect them became apparent. As necessity is the mother of invention, wide area networking soon evolved. Minicomputers and shared *wide area networks (WANs)* were created to address these growing business requirements.

Today, many businesses still have mainframe and LAN technologies working side by side. The migration of applications from central hosts to distributed servers has complicated computing needs considerably, resulting in new networking requirements and changing traffic patterns. The need for instant data transfer has motivated managers to jump at new technologies to stay ahead of demand and remain competitive. MIS (management information system) jobs have become full-time positions now, where network administration was once the responsibility of whoever happened to be sitting next to the server. Both the people and equipment working in an internetworking environment must be flexible, scalable, and adaptable to remain useful and succeed.

Internetworks

Internetworks are the communication structures that work to tie LANs and WANs together. Their primary function is to move information anywhere quickly, upon demand, and with complete integrity. Today's users have become increasingly dependent on their networks—watch the chaos that results around the office when a group of users' server or hub goes offline. Remember when fax machines came out? After a while, people stopped asking if you had a fax machine and just started asking for your fax number. Now, having Internet access from your PC is as common as having a fax once was. People used to ask me if I had e-mail, but now they just ask me for my e-mail address and web page URL!

What this means is that in order for today's corporations to remain competitive in the global market, the networks they depend on now have to efficiently manage, on a daily basis, some or all of the following:

- Graphics and imaging

- Files in the gigabyte range

- Client/server computing

- High network traffic loads

To be able to amply meet these needs, your company's Information Systems (IS) department must provide to users

- Increased bandwidth

- Bandwidth on demand

- Low delays

- High reliability

- Data, voice, and video capabilities on the same media

Also, the network of today must be readily adaptable to the applications of tomorrow. In the not-too-distant future, networks will need to be equipped to handle

- Voice over IP

- High-definition imaging

- Full-motion video

- Digitized audio

In short, for an internetwork to realize its purpose, it must be able to connect many different networks together to serve the organizations depending on it. And this connectivity must happen regardless of the type of physical media involved. Companies expanding their networks must overcome the limitations of physical and geographic boundaries. The Internet has served as a model to facilitate this growth.

LAN Devices

LANs were designed to operate in limited geographic areas, such as one floor of a building or a single building. These networks were meant to be a cul-de-sac or small neighborhood of connections—everything close and within reach. LANs connect PCs together so that they can access network resources like printers and files. A LAN connects physically adjacent devices on the network media or cable. Typical LAN devices include repeaters, bridges, hubs, switches, routers, and gateways.

Repeaters

Repeaters regenerate and propagate signals from one network segment to another. They don't change the address or data; they only pass the data on. Repeaters can't filter *packets*, which are bits of data in a package. Even though a repeater helps to extend network reach by regenerating weak signals, be aware that using one will result in combining multiple network segments into a single network. In other words, it may connect pieces of your network that you don't want to talk to each other. Figure 1.1 shows what a repeater in a LAN looks like.

FIGURE 1.1   Repeater in a LAN

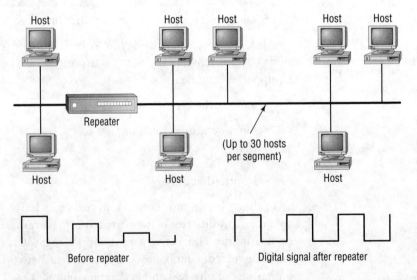

Sometimes repeaters are placed between the source and destination hosts to help compensate for signal deterioration due to attenuation. This results in *latency*—a delay in the time it takes the signal to travel between the source and destination hosts.

Bridges

Bridges also regenerate signals, but they are more intelligent devices than repeaters. A bridge can read the destination *MAC (Media Access Control) address* or hardware address from the *data frame* and determine if the destination computer is on the local segment—the segment from which it received the frame—or on other network segments. If the destination computer is on the local segment, it won't forward the frame. If the destination computer isn't on the local segment, the bridge will forward the frame to all other network segments. Figure 1.2 shows how a bridge in a LAN works.

FIGURE 1.2   Bridging a LAN

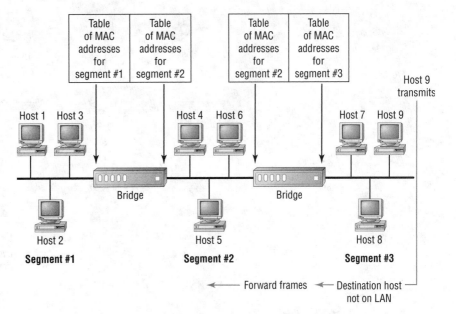

When segmenting an *Ethernet* LAN, using a bridge instead of a repeater can give you more bandwidth per user because it translates into fewer users per segment. But again, you can end up experiencing latency problems of up to 20–30 percent due to processing and filtering *frames*. Also, since bridges forward broadcasts to all other attached segments, *broadcast storms* can result from the broadcast packets propagating throughout the network.

A broadcast storm is a network segment event; during one, a broadcast packet is sent in a perpetual loop until that segment becomes overloaded.

Hubs

Hubs connect all computer LAN connections into one device or concentrator. Hubs can be considered multiport repeaters. PCs can be connected using coax or twisted-pair cable, or even radio frequency (RF). When one computer transmits a digital signal onto the network media, the signal is transmitted to all other segments that are plugged into the hub. Figure 1.3 shows a typical hub working in a LAN.

FIGURE 1.3 LAN connections in a hub

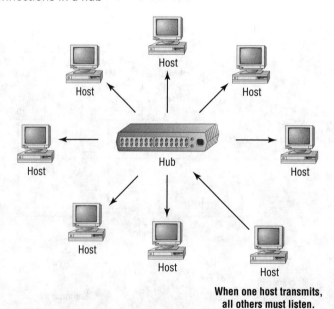

When one host transmits,
all others must listen.

Switches

Unlike hubs, *switches* can run in full-duplex mode. This means that the computer and switch can both transmit and receive simultaneously. The biggest difference between a switch and a hub is that when a computer transmits a digital signal to a hub, it's then sent to all ports attached to that hub, whereas a switch will send it only to the specific port where the destination MAC address is located. Think of each switch port as being an extremely fast multi-port bridge.

Routers

Routers are a step up from bridges. Bridges filter by MAC address, but routers can filter by both hardware and network address (*IP address*). Repeaters operate at layer 1, bridges and switches layer 2, and routers layer 3 of the OSI reference model, which I will cover at length later in this chapter. When a bridge forwards a packet, it sends it out to all segments to which it is connected, whereas a router only forwards packets to the network segment that the packet is destined for. Routers economically prevent unnecessary network traffic from being sent over the network's segments by opening up the data packet and reading the network address before forwarding it. Figure 1.4 shows a typical LAN with a router segmenting the network.

FIGURE 1.4   A router segmenting a LAN

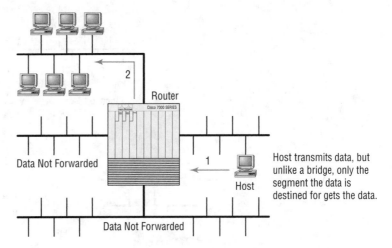

Gateways

Gateways are created with software that can be run on PCs and even routers. They link different programs or *protocols* and examine the entire packet, including the data portion, in order to translate incompatible protocols. For example, to exchange mail between a CCMail server and an Exchange server, you would have to install a mail gateway. Another example would be gateway services that run on a router. These can link an IP network to an IPX network so the users on the IP network can communicate transparently with the users on the IPX network and vice versa.

ATM Switches

ATM (Asynchronous Transfer Mode) switches provide high-speed cell switching. ATM uses a cell relay technology that combines the advantages of both conventional circuit and packet-based systems.

WAN Devices

WANs extend beyond the LAN to connect together networks located in different buildings, cities, states, and countries. WANs are typically, but not necessarily, limited to using the services of Regional Bell Operating Companies (RBOCs) like Pacific Bell, AT&T, Sprint, MCI, and others. Figure 1.5 shows a WAN connecting offices in three cities.

FIGURE 1.5   Routers connecting three cities creating a WAN

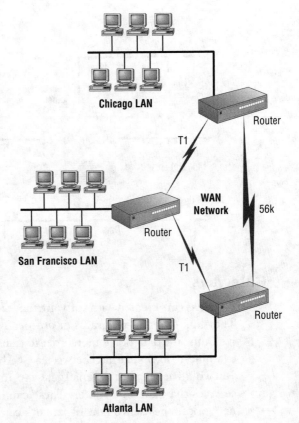

WANs are connected over links that operate at lower speeds than LANs. Typical WAN devices include

Routers   In the WAN environment, routers offer both internetworking and WAN interface controls.

ATM switches   ATM switches provide high-speed cell switching between both LANs and WANs.

X.25 and Frame Relay switches   *X.25* and *Frame Relay* switches connect private data over public data circuits using digital signals.

Modems   Modems connect private data over public telephone circuits using analog signals.

CSUs/DSUs   Components of *customer premises equipment (CPE)*, *channel service units (CSUs)*, and *data service units (DSUs)* are used to terminate a digital circuit at the customer site. These connect to a central office (CO), which is the telephone company switch located closest to the customer.

Communication servers   Communication servers are typically dial-in/dial-out servers that allow users to dial in from remote locations and attach to the LAN. Cisco's AS5300 series of communication servers are an example of devices that provide such services.

Multiplexors   *Multiplexors* are devices that allow more than one signal to be sent out simultaneously over one physical circuit. The equipment is usually referred to as a *mux*.

The OSI Reference Model

When networks first came into being, computers could typically communicate only with computers from the same manufacturer. For example, companies ran either a complete DECnet solution or an IBM solution—not both together. Unfortunately, companies that worked together or with government agencies often had equipment from different sources. So, the ability to communicate through their networks was at a dead-end, or someone had to incur the exorbitant cost of switching their equipment to their partner's manufacturer. Ouch! In the early 1980s, the *OSI (Open Systems Interconnection) reference model* was created by the International Standards Organization (ISO) to break this barrier. This model was meant to help vendors create interoperable network devices. Since each vendor's products have distinctive attributes and incorporate trade "secrets," like world peace, it will probably never happen completely, but it's still a great goal.

The OSI model is the primary architectural model for networks. It describes how data and network information are communicated from applications on one computer, through the network media, to an application on another computer. The OSI reference model breaks this approach into layers.

The Layered Approach

A *reference model* is a conceptual blueprint of how communications should take place. It addresses all the processes required for effective communication and divides these processes into logical groupings called *layers*. When a communication system is designed in this manner, it's known as *layered architecture*.

Think of it like this: You and some friends want to start a company. One of the first things you would do is sit down and think through the tasks that must be done, who will do them, in what order, and how they relate to each other. Ultimately, you might group these tasks into departments. Let's say you decide to have an order-taking department, an inventory department, and a shipping department. Each of your departments has its own unique tasks, keeping its staff busy and requiring them to focus on only their own duties.

In this scenario, departments are a metaphor for the layers in a communication system. For the system to run smoothly, the staff of each department will have to both trust and rely heavily on the others to do their jobs and competently handle their unique responsibilities. In your planning sessions, you would probably take notes, recording the entire process to facilitate later discussions about the standards of operation that will serve as your business blueprint, or reference model.

Once your business is launched, your department heads, armed with the part of the blueprint relating to their department, will need to develop practical methods to implement the tasks assigned to them. These practical methods, or *protocols*, will need to be classified into a Standard Operating Procedures manual and followed closely. Each of the various procedures in your manual will have been included for different reasons and will have varying degrees of importance and implementation. If you form a partnership or acquire another company, it will be imperative for its business protocols—its business blueprint—to match, or be compatible with, yours.

 **Real World Scenario**

Business Flexibility

"Blessed are the adaptable, for they shall not be broken" is today's business rule, meaning your business blueprint must be able to change. Suppose, after being in operation for a while, you find that many people developing your product or working on your production line have begun taking how-to-use-the-product calls, taking time away from the jobs you're paying them to do. You wisely adapt your order-taking department into a customer-service center. Of course, this means training these employees to walk customers through the "how-to" of your product. You may even find later that splitting the new call center into "order takers" and "customer service reps" gives you greater speed in handling customer calls.

Similarly, software developers can use a reference model to understand computer communication processes and to see what types of functions need to be accomplished on any one layer. If they are developing a protocol for a certain layer, all they need to concern themselves with is their specific layer's functions, not those of any other layer. Some other layer and protocol will handle the other functions. The technical term for this idea is *binding*. The communication processes that are related to each other are bound, or grouped together, at a particular layer.

Advantages of Reference Models

There are many advantages to using a reference model. Remember, because developers know that another layer will handle the functions they're not currently working on, they can confidently focus on just one layer's functions. This promotes specialization. Another benefit is that if changes are made to one layer, it doesn't necessarily change anything with the other layers.

Suppose an executive in your company in the management layer sends a letter. This person doesn't necessarily care if the company's shipping department, a different layer, changes from UPS to Federal Express, or vice versa. All the executive is concerned with is the letter and its recipient. It is someone else's job to see to its delivery. The technical phrase for this idea is *loose coupling*—though linked, they don't meddle in someone else's layer. You've probably heard phrases like, "It's not *my* fault; it's not my department!" or "So-and-So's group always messes up stuff like this; we never do!" Loose coupling provides a *stable* protocol suite. Passing the buck doesn't.

Another big advantage is *compatibility*. If software developers adhere to the specifications outlined in the reference model, all the protocols written to conform to that model will work together. This is very good. Compatibility creates the foundation for a large number of protocols to be written and used.

Let's review why the industry uses a layered model:

- It clarifies the general functions rather than the specifics on how to do it.

- It takes the overall complexity of networking and divides it into more manageable pieces or layers.

- It uses standard interfaces to enable ease of interoperability.

- Developers can change the features of one layer without changing code in other layers.

- It encourages compatibility.

- It allows specialization, which helps industry progress.

- It eases troubleshooting.

Physical and Logical Data Movement

The two additional concepts that need to be addressed in a reference model are the *physical movement of data* and the *logical movement of data*.

As illustrated in Figure 1.6, the physical movement of data begins in the top layer and proceeds down the model, layer by layer. It works like this: Someone creates some information on an application at the top layer. Protocols there pass it down to a communication protocol that packages it, then hands it down to a transmission protocol for the data's actual physical transmission. The data then moves across the model, across some type of physical channel like cable, fiber, radio frequencies, or microwaves.

When the data reaches the destination computer, it moves up the model. Each layer at the destination sees and deals with only the data that was packaged by its counterpart on the sending side. Referring back to the analogy about the executive and the letter, the shipping department at the destination sees only the shipping packaging and the information provided by the sending side's shipping department. The destination's shipping department does not see the actual letter because peeking into mail addressed to someone else is a federal offense—it's against proper protocol. The destination company's executive up on the top layer is the one who will actually open and further process the letter.

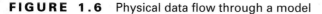

FIGURE 1.6 Physical data flow through a model

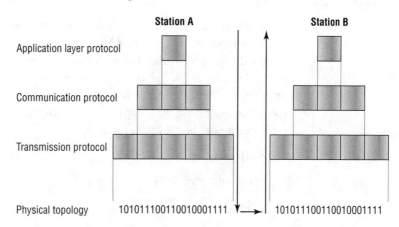

The logical movement of data is another concept addressed in a reference model. From this perspective, each layer is communicating with only its counterpart layer on the other side (see Figure 1.7). Communication in the realm of humans flows best when it happens between peers—between people on the same level, or layer, in life. The more we have in common, the more similarities in our personalities, experiences, and occupations, the easier it is for us to relate to one another, for us to connect. It's the same with computers. This type of logical communication is called *peer-to-peer communication*. When more than one protocol is needed to successfully complete a communication process, the protocols are grouped into a team called a *protocol stack*. Layers in a system's protocol stack communicate only with the corresponding layers in another system's protocol stack.

FIGURE 1.7 Logical data flow between peer layers

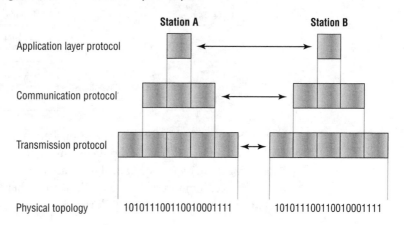

The OSI Layers

The International Standards Organization (ISO) is the Emily Post of the network protocol world. Just like Ms. Post, who wrote the book setting the standards—or protocols—for human social interaction, the ISO developed the OSI reference model as the guide and precedent for an open network protocol set. Defining the etiquette of communication models, it remains today the most popular means of comparison for protocol suites. The OSI reference model has seven layers:

- Application
- Presentation
- Session
- Transport
- Network
- Data Link
- Physical

Figure 1.8 shows the way these layers fit together.

FIGURE 1.8   The layers of the OSI reference model

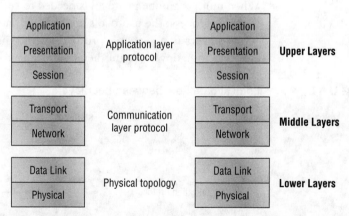

The ISO model's top three layers—Application, Presentation, and Session—deal with functions that aid applications in communicating with other applications. They specifically deal with tasks like filename formats, code sets, user interfaces, compression, encryption, and other functions relating to the exchange occurring between applications.

Figure 1.9 shows the functions defined at each layer of the OSI model. The following pages discuss the functions of each layer in detail.

FIGURE 1.9   OSI layer functions

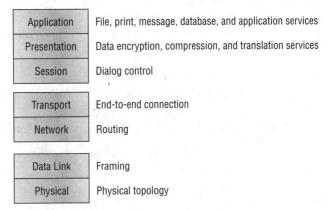

Application	File, print, message, database, and application services
Presentation	Data encryption, compression, and translation services
Session	Dialog control
Transport	End-to-end connection
Network	Routing
Data Link	Framing
Physical	Physical topology

The Application Layer

The *Application layer* of the OSI model supports the components that deal with the communicating aspects of an application. The Application layer is responsible for identifying and establishing the availability of the intended communication partner. It is also responsible for determining if sufficient resources for the intended communication exist.

Although computer applications sometimes require only desktop resources, applications may unite communicating components from more than one network application, for example, file transfers, e-mail, remote access, network management activities, client/server processes, and information location. Many network applications provide services for communication over enterprise networks, but for present and future internetworking, the need is fast developing to reach beyond their limits. For the new millennium and beyond, transactions and information exchanges between organizations are broadening to require internetworking applications like the following:

World Wide Web (WWW)   The Web connects countless servers (the number seems to grow with each passing day) presenting diverse formats. Most are multimedia and include some or all of the following: graphics, text, video, and even sound. Netscape Navigator, Internet Explorer, and other browsers like Mosaic simplify both accessing and viewing web sites.

E-mail gateways   E-mail gateways are versatile and can use Simple Mail Transfer Protocol (SMTP) or the X.400 standard to deliver messages between different e-mail applications.

Electronic data interchange (EDI)   EDI is a composite of specialized standards and processes that facilitates the flow of tasks such as accounting, shipping/receiving, and order and inventory tracking between businesses.

Special interest bulletin boards   Special interest bulletin boards include the many chat rooms on the Internet where people can connect and communicate with each other either by posting messages or by typing a live conversation. They can also share public domain software.

Internet navigation utilities   Applications like Gopher and WAIS, as well as search engines like Yahoo!, Google, Excite, and Alta Vista, help users locate the resources and information they need on the Internet.

Financial transaction services   Certain services target the financial community. They gather and sell information pertaining to investments, market trading, commodities, currency exchange rates, and credit data to their subscribers.

The Presentation Layer

The *Presentation layer* gets its name from its purpose: it presents data to the Application layer. The Presentation layer is essentially a translator. A successful data transfer technique is to adapt the data into a standard format before transmission. Of course, just like any translation, there is a cost in time. Computers are configured to receive this generically formatted data and then convert the data back into its native format for actual reading (for example, EBCDIC to ASCII).

The OSI has protocol standards that define how standard data should be formatted. Tasks like data compression, decompression, encryption, and decryption are associated with the Presentation layer.

The *Abstract Syntax Notation 1 (ASN.1)* is the standard data syntax used by the Presentation layer. This kind of standardization is necessary when transmitting numerical data that is represented very differently by various computer systems' architectures. A good example is the Simple Network Management Protocol (SNMP), which uses ASN.1 to depict the composition of objects in a network management database.

Some Presentation layer standards are involved in multimedia operations. The following standards direct graphic and visual image presentation:

PICT   This standard is a picture format used by Macintosh or PowerPC programs for transferring QuickDraw graphics.

TIFF (Tagged Image File Format)   This standard is a standard graphics format for high-resolution, bitmapped images.

JPEG   The Joint Photographic Experts Group bring this standard to us.

Other standards guide movies and sound:

MIDI (Musical Instrument Digital Interface)   This standard is used for digitized music.

MPEG   The Motion Picture Experts Group's standard for the compression and coding of motion video for CDs, MPEG, is increasingly popular. It provides digital storage and bit rates up to 1.5Mbps.

QuickTime   This standard is designed for use with Macintosh or PowerPC programs; it manages audio and video applications.

The Session Layer

The jobs of the *Session layer* can be likened to that of a mediator or referee. Its central concern is dialog control between devices, or *nodes*. Responsible for coordinating communication between systems, the Session layer organizes their communication by offering three different modes: simplex, half-duplex, and full-duplex. It also splits up a communication session into three different phases. These phases are connection establishment, data transfer, and connection release.

In *simplex mode*, communication is actually a monologue, with one device transmitting and another receiving. To get a picture of this, think of the telegraph machine's form of communication: .....--..----...---..-...

When in *half-duplex mode*, nodes take turns transmitting and receiving— the computer equivalent of talking on a speakerphone. Some of us have experienced the speakerphone phenomenon of forbidden interruption. The speakerphone's mechanism dictates that you may indeed speak your mind, but you have to wait until the person at the other end stops doing that first.

The only conversational proviso of *full-duplex mode* is *flow control*. This mitigates the problem of possible differences in the operating speeds of two nodes, where one may be transmitting faster than the other can receive. Other than that, communication between the two flows is unregulated, with both sides transmitting and receiving simultaneously.

Formal communication sessions occur in three phases. In the first, the connection-establishment phase, contact is secured and devices agree upon communication parameters and the protocols they'll use. Next, in the data-transfer phase, these nodes engage in conversation, or dialog, and they exchange information. Finally, when they're through communicating, nodes participate in a systematic release of their session.

A formal communication session is *connection-oriented*. In a situation where a large quantity of information is to be transmitted, the involved nodes agree upon rules for the creation of checkpoints along their transfer process. This somewhat resembles the many security checks for you and your luggage at the airport today. These rules are necessary in the case of an error occurring along the way. Among other things, they afford you the luxury of preserving your dignity in the face of your computers and co-workers. Let me explain. In the 44th minute of a 45-minute download, a loathsome error occurs again! This is the third try, and the file-to-be-had is needed more than sunshine. Without checkpoints in place, you would have to start all over again, potentially causing you to get more than just a little frustrated. To prevent this, checkpoints are secured—something called *activity management*—ensuring that the transmitting node has to retransmit only the data sent since the last checkpoint where the error occurred.

It is important to note that, in some networking situations, devices send out simple, one-frame status reports that aren't sent in a formal session format. If they were, it would burden the network unnecessarily and result in lost economy. Instead, in these events, a *connectionless* approach is used, where the transmitting node simply sends off its data without establishing availability and without acknowledgment from its intended receiver. Think of connectionless communication like a message in a bottle: it's short and sweet, it goes where the current takes it, and it arrives at an unsecured destination.

The following are some examples of Session layer protocols and interfaces:

NFS (Network File System)   NFS was developed by Sun Microsystems and is used with TCP/IP and UNIX workstations to allow transparent access to remote resources.

SQL (Structured Query Language)   SQL was developed by IBM and provides users with a simpler way to define their information requirements on both local and remote systems.

RPC (Remote Procedure Call)   RPC is a broad client/server redirection tool used for disparate service environments. Its procedures are created on clients and performed on servers.

X Window   Widely used by Linux, X Window is a graphical infrastructure.

ASP (AppleTalk Session Protocol)   ASP is another client/server mechanism that both establishes and maintains sessions amid AppleTalk client and server machines.

DNA SCP (Digital Network Architecture Session Control Protocol)   DNA SCP is a DECnet Session layer protocol.

The Transport Layer

Services located in the *Transport layer* both segment and reassemble data from upper-layer applications and unite it onto the same data stream. They provide end-to-end data transport services and establish a logical connection between the sending host and destination host on an internetwork. The Transport layer is responsible for providing mechanisms for multiplexing upper-layer application, session establishment, and teardown of virtual circuits. It also hides details of any network-dependent information from the higher layers by providing transparent data transfer.

Data integrity is ensured at this layer by maintaining flow control and by allowing users the option of requesting reliable data transport between systems. Flow control prevents the problem of a sending host on one side of the connection overflowing the buffers in the receiving host—an event that can result in lost data. Reliable data transport employs a connection-oriented communications session between systems, and the protocols involved ensure that the following will be achieved:

- The segments delivered are acknowledged back to the sender upon their reception.

- Any segments not acknowledged are retransmitted.

- Segments are sequenced back into their proper order upon arrival at their destination.

- A manageable data flow is maintained in order to avoid congestion, overloading, and the loss of any data.

An important reason for different layers to coexist within the OSI reference model is to allow for the sharing of a transport connection by more than one application. This sharing is available because the Transport layer's functioning occurs segment by segment, and each segment is independent of the other segments. This allows different applications to send consecutive segments, processed on a first-come, first-served basis, that can be intended either for the same destination host or for multiple hosts.

Figure 1.10 shows how the Transport layer sends the data of several applications originating from a source host to communicate with parallel applications on one or many destination host(s). The specific port number for each software application is set by software within the source machine before transmission. When it transmits a message, the source computer includes extra bits that encode the type of message, the program with which it was created, and the protocols that were used. Each software application transmitting a data stream segment uses the same preordained port number. When it receives the data stream, the destination computers are empowered to sort and reunite each application's segments, providing the Transport layer with all it needs to pass the data to its upper-layer peer application.

FIGURE 1.10   Transport layer data segments sharing a traffic stream

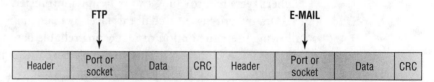

In reliable transport operation, one user first establishes a connection-oriented session with its peer system. Figure 1.11 portrays a typical connection-oriented session taking place between sending and receiving systems. In it, both hosts' application programs begin by notifying their individual operating systems that a connection is about to be initiated. The two operating systems communicate by sending messages over the network, confirming that the transfer is approved and that both sides are ready for it to take place. Once the required synchronization is complete, a connection is fully established and the data transfer begins.

FIGURE 1.11 Establishing a connection-oriented session

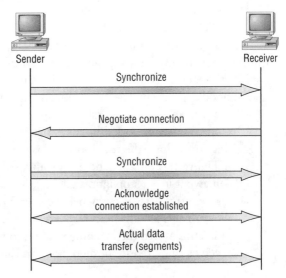

While the information is being transferred between hosts, the two machines periodically check in with each other, communicating through their protocol software to ensure that all is going well and that the data is being received properly. The following list summarizes the steps in a connection-oriented session pictured in Figure 1.11:

1. The first "connection agreement" segment is a request for synchronization.

2. The second and third segments acknowledge the request and establish connection parameters between hosts.

3. The final segment is also an acknowledgment. It notifies the destination host that the connection agreement is accepted and that the actual connection has been established. Data transfer can now begin.

During a transfer, congestion can occur because a high-speed computer is generating data traffic faster than the network can transfer it or because many computers are simultaneously sending *datagrams* (packets) through a single gateway or destination. In the latter case, a gateway or destination can become congested even though no single source caused the problem. In either case, the problem is basically akin to a freeway bottleneck—too much traffic for too small a capacity. Usually, no one car is the problem—there are simply too many cars on that freeway. And it is always rush hour when it comes to information flow!

When a machine receives a flood of datagrams too quickly for it to process, it stores them in memory (buffers them). This buffering action solves the problem only if the datagrams are part of a small burst. However, if the datagram deluge continues, a device's memory will eventually be exhausted, its flood capacity will be exceeded, and it will discard any additional datagrams that arrive. But, no worries. Because of transport function, network flow control systems work quite well. Instead of dumping resources and allowing data to be lost, the transport can issue a "not ready" indicator, as shown in Figure 1.12, to the sender, or source, of the flood. This mechanism works somewhat like a stoplight, signaling the sending device to stop transmitting segment traffic to its overwhelmed peer. When the peer receiver has processed the segments already in its memory reservoir, it sends out a "ready" transport indicator. When the machine waiting to transmit the rest of its datagrams receives this "ready" indictor, it can then resume its transmission.

FIGURE 1.12   Transmitting segments with flow control

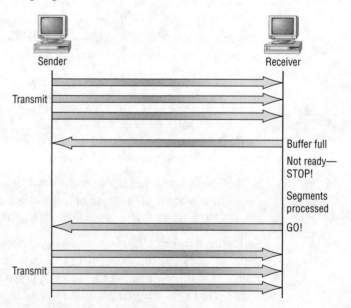

In fundamental, reliable, connection-oriented data transfer, datagrams are delivered to the receiving host in exactly the same sequence they're transmitted; the transmission fails if this order is breached. If any data segments are lost, duplicated, or damaged along the way, this will cause a failure to transmit. The answer to the problem is to have the receiving host acknowledge receiving each and every data segment.

Data throughput would be low if the transmitting machine had to wait for an acknowledgment after sending each segment. But because there's time available after the sender transmits the data segment and before it finishes processing acknowledgments from the receiving machine, the sender uses the break to transmit more data. How many data segments the transmitting machine is allowed to send without receiving an acknowledgment for them is called a *window*.

Windowing controls how much information is transferred from one end to the other. While some protocols quantify information by observing the number of packets, TCP/IP measures it by counting the number of bytes. Figure 1.13 illustrates a window size of 1 and a window size of 3. When a window size of 1 is configured, the sending machine waits for an acknowledgment for each data segment it transmits before transmitting another. Configured to a window size of 3, it's allowed to transmit three data segments before an acknowledgment is received. In this simplified example, both the sending and receiving machines are workstations. Reality is rarely that simple, and most often acknowledgments and packets will commingle as they travel over the network and pass through routers. Routing complicates things, but not to worry; we'll be covering routing later in this book.

Reliable data delivery ensures the integrity of a stream of data sent from one machine to the other through a fully functional data link. It guarantees the data won't be duplicated or lost. The method that achieves this is known as *positive acknowledgment with retransmission*. This technique requires a receiving machine to communicate with the transmitting source by sending an acknowledgment message back to the sender when it receives data. The sender documents each segment it sends and waits for this acknowledgment before sending the next segment. When it sends a segment, the transmitting machine starts a timer and retransmits if it expires before an acknowledgment for the segment is returned from the receiving end.

In Figure 1.14, the sending machine transmits segments 1, 2, and 3. The receiving node acknowledges it has received them by requesting segment 4. When it receives the acknowledgment, the sender then transmits segments 4, 5, and 6. If segment 5 doesn't make it to the destination, the receiving node acknowledges that event with a request for the segment to be resent. The sending machine then resends the lost segment and waits for an acknowledgment, which it must receive in order to move on to the transmission of segment 7.

FIGURE 1.13 TCP/IP window sizes

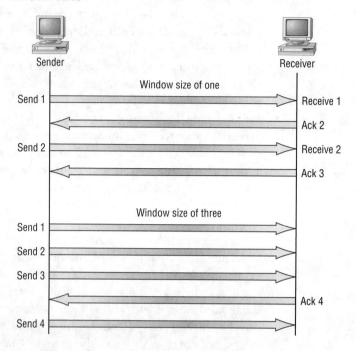

FIGURE 1.14 Transport layer reliable delivery

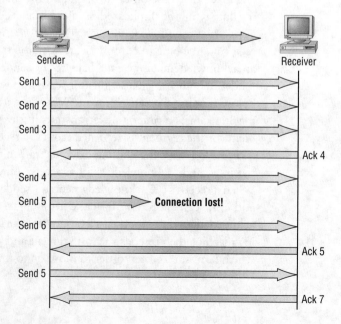

The Network Layer

In the Roman Empire, all roads led to Rome. Today, our country is a maze of interstate highways, state highways, freeways, local roadways, and the like. So, you need a map to get where you want to go and find the best route. The same holds true with the complicated cloud of networks. And the proper path through them is determined by protocols residing in Layer 3: the *Network layer*. Path determination makes it possible for a router to appraise all available paths to a given destination and decide on the best one. Routers use network topology information when orienting themselves to the network and evaluating the different possible paths through it. These network "topo maps" can be configured by the network's administrator or obtained through dynamic processes running on the network. The Network layer's interface is connected to networks, and it is employed by the Transport layer to provide the best end-to-end packet delivery services. The job of sending packets from the source network to the destination network is the Network layer's primary function. After the router decides on the best path from point A to point B, it proceeds with switching the packet onto it. This is known as *packet switching*. Essentially this is forwarding the packet received by the router on one network interface, or port, to the port that connects to the best path through the network cloud. That port will then send the packet to that particular packet's destination.

An internetwork must continually designate all paths of its media connections. In Figure 1.15, each line connecting routers is numbered, and those numbers are used by routers as network addresses. These addresses possess and convey important information about the path of media connections. They're used by routing protocols to pass packets from a source onward to its destination. The Network layer creates a composite "network map"—a communication strategy system—by combining information about the sets of links into an internetwork with path-determination, path-switching, and route-processing functions. It can also use these addresses to provide relay capability and to interconnect independent networks. Consistent across the entire internetwork, Layer 3 addresses also streamline the network's performance by not forwarding unnecessary broadcasts that would eat up precious bandwidth. Unnecessary broadcasts increase the network's overhead and waste capacity on any links and machines that don't need to receive them. Using consistent end-to-end addressing that accurately describes the path of media connections enables the Network layer to determine the best path to a destination without encumbering the device or links on the internetwork with unnecessary broadcasts.

FIGURE 1.15 Communicating through an internetwork

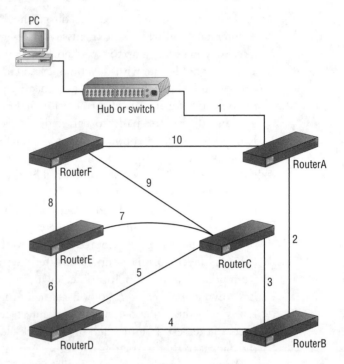

When an application on a host wants to send a packet to a destination device located on a different network, a data link frame is received on one of the router's network interfaces. The router de-encapsulates and then examines the frame to establish what kind of Network layer data is in tow. After this is determined, the data is sent on to the appropriate Network layer process; but the frame's mission is fulfilled and it is simply discarded.

Figure 1.16 illustrates the Network layer process that examines the packet's header to discover which network it is destined for. It then refers to the routing table to find the connections that the current network has to foreign network interfaces. After one is selected, the packet is re-encapsulated in its data link frame with the selected interface's information and queued for delivery off to the next hop in the path toward its destination. This process is repeated every time the packet switches to another router. When it finally reaches the router connected to the network on which the destination host is located, the packet is encapsulated in the destination LAN's data link frame type. It's now properly packaged and ready for delivery to the protocol stack on the destination host.

FIGURE 1.16   The Network layer process

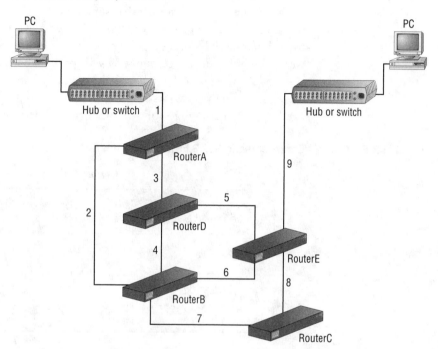

The following steps describe the Network layer process as shown in Figure 1.16:

1. The sending PC sends a datagram to a PC located on Network 9.

2. RouterA receives the datagram and checks the destination network. RouterA forwards the packet based on its knowledge of where the network is located.

3. RouterB receives the packet and also checks the destination network. RouterB forwards this to RouterE after checking to find the best route to Network 9.

4. RouterE receives the packet, puts it in a frame with the hardware destination of the receiving PC, and sends out the frame.

The Data Link Layer

The *Data Link layer* ensures that messages are delivered to the proper device and translates messages from up above into bits for the Physical layer to transmit. It formats the message into data frames and adds a customized header containing the hardware destination and source address. This added information forms a sort of capsule that surrounds the original message in much the same way that engines, navigational devices, and other tools were attached to the lunar modules of the Apollo project. These various pieces of equipment were useful only during certain stages of space flight and were stripped off the module and discarded when their designated stage was complete. Data traveling through networks is much the same. A data frame that's all packaged up and ready to go follows the format illustrated in Figure 1.17.

FIGURE 1.17 Ethernet II and 802.3 Ethernet frames

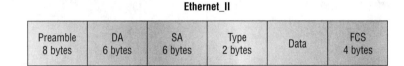

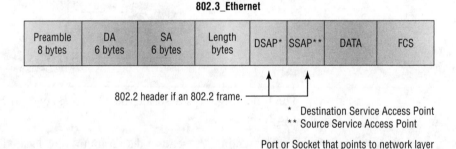

The various elements of a data frame are as follows:

- The *preamble* or *start indicator* is made up of a special bit pattern that alerts devices to the beginning of a data frame.

- The destination address (DA) is there for obvious reasons. The Data Link layer of every device on the network examines this to see if it matches its own address.

- The source address (SA) is the address of the sending device. It exists to facilitate replies to the message.

- In Ethernet II frames, the two-byte field following the source address is a Type field. This field specifies the upper-layer protocol that will receive the data after data link processing is complete.

- In 802.3 frames, the two-byte field following the source address is a Length field. This indicates the number of bytes of data between this field and the frame check sequence (FCS) field. Following the length field could be an 802.2 header for Logical Link Control (LLC) information. This information is needed to specify the upper-layer process, because 802.3 doesn't have a type field. Frame types will be discussed in detail in Chapter 3, "Network Protocols."

- The *data* is the actual message, plus all the information sent down to the sending device's Data Link layer from the layers above it.

- Finally, there's the FCS field. Its purpose corresponds to its name, and it houses the cyclic redundancy checksum (CRC). The FCS allows the receiver to determine if a received frame was damaged or corrupted while in transit. CRCs work like this: The device sending the data determines a value summary for the CRC and stores it in the FCS field. The device on the receiving end performs the same procedure, then checks to see if its value matches the total, or sum, of the sending node; hence the term *checksum*.

Logical Link Control Sublayer

The LLC sublayer of the Data Link layer provides flexibility to the protocols running in the upper and lower layers. Notice that this is a sublayer of one of the seven layers we are discussing. As shown in Figure 1.18, the LLC runs between the Network layer and the MAC sublayer of the Data Link layer. This allows protocols at the Network layer, for example, the Internet Protocol (IP), to operate without the burden of having to be concerned with what's happening at the Physical layer. Why? Because the Network layer's protocol knows that the LLC sublayer is responsible for making sure the MAC sublayer and the Physical layer are doing their job. The LLC acts as a managing buffer between the "executive" upper layers and the "shipping department" lower layers. In turn, the lower-layer protocols don't need to be concerned about what's happening above.

The LLC sublayer uses source service access points (SSAPs) and destination service access points (DSAPs) to help the lower layers communicate to the Network layer protocols.

This is important because the MAC sublayer must understand what to do with the data after the frame header is stripped off. It has to know who to hand the data to; this is where the DSAPs and SSAPs come in. Imagine someone coming to your door and asking if it's the correct address (hardware address). You respond, "Yes, what do you want?" The person (or data in the frame) responds, "I don't know." The service access points solve this problem by pointing to the upper-layer protocol, such as IP or IPX. In Figure 1.18, you can see that the 802.3 frame is not capable of handling DSAPs and SSAPs, so the 802.2 frame has to step in. The 802.2 frame is really an 802.3 frame with a DSAP and SSAP control field.

FIGURE 1.18   The LLC sublayer of the Data Link layer

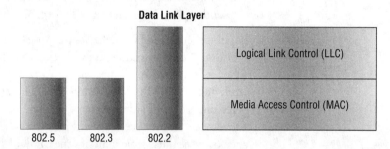

The LLC sublayer is also responsible for timing, flow control, and, with some protocol stacks, even connectionless and connection-oriented protocols.

MAC Sublayer

The MAC sublayer of the Data Link layer is responsible for framing. Again notice that this is a sublayer of one of the seven layers we are discussing. It builds frames from the 1s and 0s that the Physical layer picks up from the wire as a digital signal. It first checks the CRC to make sure nothing was damaged in transit; then it determines if the hardware address matches or not. If it does, the LLC then sends the data on to an upper-layer protocol. This layer will also accept a frame if the destination address is a broadcast or multicast.

The MAC sublayer is also responsible for media access. Through it, the workstation is allowed to communicate over the network. This is partly a hardware operation, but it is also partially a software procedure because it's defined by both the network interface card (NIC) and the network card driver. We'll cover this more thoroughly soon; for now, here is a description of the three types of media access:

Contention   A good example of contention is found in an Ethernet network where all devices communicate whenever they have something to say. It's pretty easy to imagine that in this scenario a data collision could easily occur if two devices were to "talk" at the same time. Because of this, in a contention network, the transmitting workstation must have control of the entire wire or network segment. Contention networks are great for small, bursty applications.

Token passing   Used in Token Ring, FDDI, and ArcNET networks, stations cannot transmit until they receive a special frame called a *token*. This arrangement also works to prevent the collision problem. Token-passing networks work well if large, bandwidth-consuming applications are commonly used on the network.

Polling   Polling is generally used in large mainframe environments where hosts are polled to see if they need to transmit. Hosts (secondaries) aren't permitted to transmit until given permission from the primary host.

WAN Protocols at the Data Link Layer

WAN Data Link protocols describe how frames are carried between systems on a single data link. They include protocols designed to operate over dedicated point-to-point facilities, multi-point facilities that are based on dedicated facilities, and multi-access switched services like Frame Relay.

The typical *encapsulation* standards for synchronous serial lines at the Data Link layer are as follows:

HDLC (High-Level Data Link Control)   HDLC is an MSA standard created by the ISO to support both point-to-point and multipoint configurations. It's too bad that most vendors implement HDLC in different ways, often making HDLC incompatible between vendors. HDLC is the Cisco default protocol for all serial links, and it won't communicate over a serial link with any other vendor's HDLC protocol.

SDLC (Synchronous Data Link Control)   SDLC is a protocol created by IBM to make it easier for their mainframes to connect to remote offices. Created for use in WANs, SDLC became extremely popular in the 1980s because many companies were installing 327x controllers in their remote offices for communication with the mainframe in the corporate office. SDLC defines and uses a polling media-access method. This means the *primary*, or front end, asks (polls) the *secondaries*, or 327x controllers, to find out if they need to communicate with it. Secondaries can't speak unless spoken to, nor can they speak to each other.

LAPB (Link Access Procedure, Balanced)   Created for use with X.25, LAPB defines frames and is capable of detecting out-of-sequence or missing frames. It also retransmits, exchanges, and acknowledges frames.

X.25   X.25 was the first packet-switching network. This defines the point-to-point communication between a DTE (data terminal equipment) and a DCE (data communications equipment) and supports both switched virtual circuits (SVCs) and permanent virtual circuits (PVCs). Cisco routers (DTEs) connect to modems or DSU/CSUs (DCEs).

SLIP (Serial Line IP)   SLIP is an industry standard that was developed in 1984 to support TCP/IP networking over low-speed serial interfaces in Berkeley UNIX. With the Windows NT RAS service, Windows NT computers can use TCP/IP and SLIP to communicate with remote hosts.

PPP (Point-to-Point Protocol)   Think of PPP as SLIP's big brother. It takes the specifications of SLIP and builds on it by adding login, password, and error-correction capabilities. PPP is a Data Link protocol that can be used by many network protocols like IP, IPX, and AppleTalk. See RFC 1661 for more information, as described by the Internet Engineering Task Force (IETF).

ISDN (Integrated Services Digital Network)   ISDN operates through analog phone lines that have been converted to use digital signaling. With ISDN you can transmit both voice and data.

Frame Relay   Frame Relay is an upgrade from X.25 to be used where LAPB is no longer utilized. It's the fastest of the WAN protocols listed because of its simplified framing approach, which has no error correction. Frame Relay uses SVCs, PVCs, and data link connection identifiers (DLCIs) for addressing; plus, it requires access to the high-quality digital facilities of the phone company, so it's not available everywhere.

The Physical Layer

The *Physical layer* has two responsibilities: it sends bits and receives bits. Bits come only in values of 1 or 0—a Morse code with numerical value. The Physical layer communicates directly with the various types of actual communication media. Different kinds of media represent these bit values in different ways. Some use audio tones, while others employ *state transitions*— changes in voltage from high to low and low to high. Specific protocols are needed for each type of media to describe the proper bit patterns to be used, how data is encoded into media signals, and the various qualities of the physical media's attachment interface.

At the Physical layer, the interface between the DTE and the DCE is identified. The DCE is usually located at the service provider, while the DTE is the attached device. The services available to the DTE are most often accessed via a modem or CSU/DSU.

The following Physical layer standards define this interface:

- EIA/TIA-232
- EIA/TIA-449
- V.24
- V.35
- X.21
- G.703
- EIA-530
- High-Speed Serial Interface (HSSI)

 Real World Scenario

A Real-World Use of the OSI Model

There are many reasons why you should understand the OSI reference model layers, processes, and functions. A practical reason is troubleshooting. Most network problems occur at the Physical layer. Broken connectors, bad cables, malfunctioning NICs, and bad ports are a few of the most common problems. The fact is, 90 percent of your network problems are usually related to the Physical layer.

After you have corrected the Physical layer problems, it's time to consider the Data Link layer and the processes and functions that occur there. Bridges and switches are devices that have common everyday problems such as malformed MAC address tables or bad ports.

At the Network layer, your routers can cause many different network problems, including misrouted traffic, dropped packets, and incorrect routing updates. Fixing these problems requires an understanding of the routing process, including routed traffic and routing update traffic.

> Routed traffic such as IP packets include a source and destination IP address in the network header, which are used to determine the routing path through network routers. When a router receives a packet, it scans the routing table to find the best match for the destination network port based on the destination IP address. If a route is not found, the packet is returned to the source IP address in the form of a "network destination unreachable" message.
>
> Routing traffic such as RIP or IGRP can also be a source of problems due to misconfiguration on the router or a neighboring router. On Cisco routers, your best bet is to use the show and debug commands to verify proper configuration and to watch the routing protocol updates for the correct update packets.

Now you understand why I called this a primer for internetworks. No doubt all the letters of the alphabet have become one tangled mess in your brain. If you tend toward dyslexia, I am truly sorry. Right now is a great time to take a break. You may also need to go back and review what we've discussed before you move ahead.

Data Encapsulation

Now that we have the layers and terminology defined, we'll take a look at how data logically moves through the layers. *Data encapsulation* is the process in which the information in a protocol is wrapped, or contained, in the data section of another protocol. In the OSI reference model, each layer encapsulates the layer immediately above it as the data flows down the protocol stack.

The logical communication that happens at each layer of the OSI reference model doesn't involve many physical connections because the information each protocol needs to send is encapsulated in the layer of protocol information beneath it. This encapsulation produces a set of data called a *packet* (see Figure 1.19).

Looking at Figure 1.19, you can follow the data down through the model as it is encapsulated at each layer of the OSI reference model. Starting at the Application layer, data is encapsulated in Presentation layer information. When the Presentation layer receives this information, it looks like generic data being presented. The Presentation layer hands the data to the Session layer, which is responsible for synchronizing the session with the destination host. The Session layer then passes this data to the Transport layer, which transports the data from the source host to the destination host. But before this happens, the Network layer adds routing information to the packet. It then passes the packet on to the Data Link layer for framing and for connection to the Physical layer. The Physical layer sends the data as 1s and 0s to the destination host across fiber or copper wiring. Finally, when the destination host receives the 1s and 0s, the data passes back up through the model, one layer at a time. Data *de-encapsulation* takes place at each of the OSI model's peer layers.

FIGURE 1.19 Data encapsulation at each layer of the OSI reference model

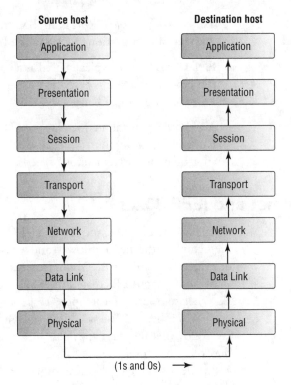

At a transmitting device, the data encapsulation method is as follows:

1. User information is converted to data.

2. Data is converted to segments.

3. Segments are converted to packets or datagrams.

4. Packets or datagrams are converted to frames.

5. Frames are converted to bits.

LAN Technologies

It's time to describe the basic characteristics of Ethernet, Token Ring, FDDI, and ATM—four LAN technologies that account for virtually all deployed LANs—and take a look at the Data Link and Physical layer details of each of them:

Ethernet Though one of the very first LAN technologies, the largest installed LANs employ Ethernet.

Token Ring *Token Ring* is an IBM creation that is widely used in a large number of corporations that migrated from mainframes to LANs.

FDDI *FDDI* was typically used as a backbone LAN between data closets. It is a popular campus LAN because it is very dependable and faster than Ethernet and Token Ring.

ATM *ATM* is taking the place of FDDI in the campus backbone arena. It's gaining in popularity because it can run in both WAN and LAN environments at tremendous speeds.

Ethernet and IEEE 802.3

In 1980, Digital, Intel, and Xerox (DIX) created the original Ethernet I. Predictably, Ethernet II followed and was released in 1984. Ethernet II is also described as *Carrier Sense, Multiple Access with Collision Detect (CSMA/CD)*. In response, the IEEE created the 802.3 subcommittee to come up with an Ethernet standard that happens to be almost identical to the Ethernet II version of Ethernet. The two differ only in their descriptions of the Data Link layer. Ethernet II has a Type field, whereas 802.3 has a Length field. Even so, they're both common in their Physical layer specifications, MAC addressing, and understanding of the LLC sublayer's responsibilities.

Ethernet II and 802.3 both define a bus-topology LAN at 10Mbps, and the cabling defined in these standards is identical:

10Base2/Thinnet Thinnet segments can extend up to 185 meters using RG58 coax at 50 ohms.

10Base5/Thicknet Thicknet segments can extend up to 500 meters using RG8 or 11 at 50 ohms.

10BaseT/UTP   All hosts connect using unshielded twisted-pair (UTP) cable to a central device (a hub or switch). Category 3 UTP is specified to 10Mbps, and Category 5 UTP is specified to 100Mbps CSMA/CD.

10BaseFL   10BaseFL is 10Mbps over fiber-optic physical medium. The advantages of using 10BaseFL over a copper medium are security, a larger network diameter, and immunity to RFI and EMI.

CSMA/CD

Carrier Sense Multiple Access with Collision Detection (CSMA/CD) was created to overcome the problem of collisions that, as mentioned earlier, occur when packets are transmitted simultaneously from different nodes. Good collision management is important, because when a node transmits in a CSMA/CD network, all the other nodes on the network receive and examine that transmission. Only bridges and routers effectively prevent a transmission from propagating through the entire network.

The CSMA/CD protocol works like this: When a host wants to transmit over the network, it first checks for the presence of a digital signal on the wire. If all is clear (if no other host is transmitting), the host will then proceed with its transmission. And it doesn't stop there. The transmitting host constantly monitors the wire to make sure no other hosts begin transmitting. If the host detects another signal on the wire, it then sends out an extended jam signal that causes all nodes on the segment to stop sending data. The nodes respond to that jam signal by waiting before attempting to transmit again. If after 15 tries collisions keep occurring, the nodes attempting to transmit will then time out.

Broadcasts

A *broadcast* is a frame sent to all network stations at the same time. Remember that broadcasts are built into all protocols. In the following example, the dissected frame of an Etherpeek (a protocol analyzer) trace is displayed so you can see the destination hardware address, IP address, and more:

```
Ethernet Header
  Destination:  ff:ff:ff:ff:ff:ff Ethernet Broadcast
  Source:       02:07:01:22:de:a4
  Protocol Type:08-00  IP
```

```
IP Header - Internet Protocol Datagram
    Version:              4
    Header Length:        5
    Precedence:           0
    Type of Service:      %000
    Unused:               %00
    Total Length:         93
    Identifier:           62500
    Fragmentation Flags:  %000
    Fragment Offset:      0
    Time To Live:         30
    IP Type:              0x11  UDP
    Header Checksum:      0x9156
    Source IP Address:    10.7.1.9
    Dest. IP Address:     10.7.1.255
No Internet Datagram Options
```

As this information shows, the source hardware and IP address are from the sending station that knows its own information. Its hardware address is 02:07:01:22:de:a4., and its source IP address is 10.7.1.9. The destination hardware address is ffffffffffff, a MAC sublayer broadcast that is monitored by all stations on the network. The destination network address is 10.7.1.255—an IP broadcast for network 10.7.1.0—meaning all devices on network 10.7.1.0.

A frame addressed in this manner tells all the hosts on network 10.7.1.0 to receive it and process the data therein. This can be both a good thing and a bad thing. When servers or other hosts need to send data to all the other hosts on the network segment, network broadcasts are very useful indeed. But, if a lot of broadcasts are occurring on a network segment, network performance can be seriously impaired. This is one very big reason why it is so important to segment your network properly with bridges and/or routers. This process is called *network segmentation*.

Fiber Distributed Data Interface (FDDI)

Like Token Ring, Fiber Distributed Data Interface (FDDI), as shown in Figure 1.20, is a token-passing media access topology. American National Standards Institute (ANSI) defines the standard (ANSI X3T9.5) for a dual Token Ring LAN operating at 100Mbps over fiber-optic cable. Copper Distributed Data Interface (CDDI) can be used with UTP cable to connect servers or other stations directly into the ring, as you can see in Figure 1.20.

FIGURE 1.20   FDDI network topology

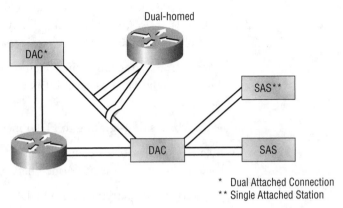

The advantages of FDDI include the following:

- FDDI can run very long distances and do so in electronically hostile environments where electromagnetic or radio frequency interference is present.

- It runs at a high speed compared with 10Mbps Ethernet and 4/16Mbps Token Ring LANs.

- FDDI employs a token-passing media access with dual counter-rotating rings, as shown in Figure 1.21. Typically, only one ring is active at any given time. The active ring, called the *primary ring*, is used for data transmission; the *secondary ring* usually is not active. That way, if a break or outage occurs, the FDDI ring will wrap back the other direction, keeping the ring intact.

- Some stations can be attached to both rings for redundancy reasons. These are known as dual attachment stations (DASs). These would be used mostly for high availability stations like servers. There are also single attachment stations (SASs), which are attached to the FDDI rings using a device known as a *concentrator*.

- Cisco routers can attach with a technique called *dual homing*. This provides fault tolerance by providing a primary and backup path to the FDDI ring.

- FDDI is both a logical and a physical ring—the only LAN that is an actual, physical ring. Like Token Ring, FDDI provides predictable deterministic delays and priorities.

- FDDI uses MAC addresses like other LANs do, but it uses a different numbering scheme. Instead of the eight-bit bytes that Ethernet and Token Ring uses, it applies four-bit symbols. FDDI has 12 four-bit symbols that make up its MAC addresses.

- Token Ring allows only one token on the ring at any given time, whereas FDDI permits several tokens to be present on the ring concurrently.

Some drawbacks of migrating to FDDI include the following:

- Relatively high latency occurs when Ethernet-to-FDDI and FDDI-to-Ethernet translation is performed between LANs.

- Capacity is still shared because FDDI dual ring is a shared LAN.

- There's no full-duplex capability in shared networks.

- It's expensive—very expensive! FDDI components, i.e., concentrators and NICs, aren't exactly bargain equipment.

Figure 1.21 shows how an FDDI LAN would wrap the primary ring back to the standby, secondary ring if a failure occurred.

FIGURE 1.21 Dual-ring reliability

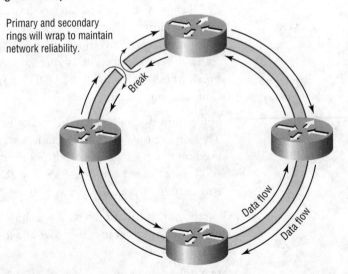

Primary and secondary rings will wrap to maintain network reliability.

When a station realizes that no tokens have been received from its nearest active upstream neighbor (NAUN) for a predetermined time period, it sends out a beacon as an alert and as an attempt to locate the failure. Once it starts to receive its own beacons, the station assumes the ring is now up and running. If it doesn't receive its beacon back for a predetermined amount of time, the primary ring will wrap to the secondary ring as shown.

Token Ring

IBM created Token Ring in the 1970s; it was popular with true-blue customers needing to migrate from a mainframe environment. It lost to Ethernet in the popularity polls because it was pricey by comparison. However, depending on what you're looking for, Token Ring is a more resilient network, especially under heavy loads. Sometimes you actually do get what you pay for.

Like Ethernet, the IEEE came out with its own standard for Token Ring, designated 802.5. This standard was so close to the IBM standard that the IEEE is now responsible for administrating both specifications.

At the Physical layer, Token Ring runs as a star topology using shielded twisted-pair (STP) wiring. Each station connects to a central hub called a *multistation access unit (MSAU)*. Logically, it runs in a ring where each station receives signals from its NAUN and repeats these signals to its downstream neighbors.

Token Ring uses MAC addresses like Ethernet does, but that's where the similarities end. Token Ring media access is described point by point below:

- Stations can't transmit whenever they want to, like Ethernet stations can. Instead, they have to wait to be given a special frame called a *token*. When a station receives a token, it does one of two things:

  - It appends the data it wants to send onto the end of the frame and then changes the T bit in the frame. Doing that alerts the receiving station that data is attached.

  - If the station that gets a token doesn't need to send any data, it simply passes on the token to the next station in the ring.

- The information frame circles the ring until it gets to the destination station. The destination station copies the frame and then tags the frame as being copied. The frame continues around until it reaches the originating station, which then removes the tag.

- Typically, only one frame can be on a ring at any given time. However, by using early token release, a station can transmit a new token onto the ring after transmitting its first frame.

- Collisions don't happen because stations can't transmit unless they have a token.

The frame in a Token Ring network is different from the frames in Ethernet. As shown in Figure 1.22, the token frame uses a priority system that permits certain user-designated, high-priority stations to use the network more frequently. The media access control field of the frame is shown in this figure.

FIGURE 1.22 Token Ring media access control field

Access Control Field

P	P	P	T	M	R	R	P

P: Priority bits
T: Token bits
M: Monitor bits
R: Reservation bits

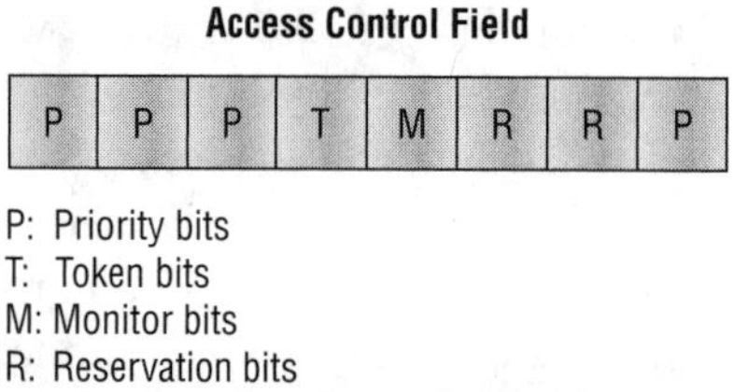

The two fields that control priority are predictably the priority field and the reservation field. If a priority token is transmitted, only stations with a priority equal to or higher than the priority of that token can claim it. Priority levels are configured by the network administrator. After the token is claimed and changed to an information frame, only stations with a priority rating higher than the transmitting station can reserve the token for the next pass around the network. When the next token is generated, it includes the highest priority for the reserving station. Stations that raise a token's priority level must reinstate the previous lower priority level after their transmission is complete.

The frame status field is shown in Figure 1.23. The address (A) bit and the copied (C) bit are used to indicate the status of an outstanding frame.

FIGURE 1.23 Token Ring frame status field

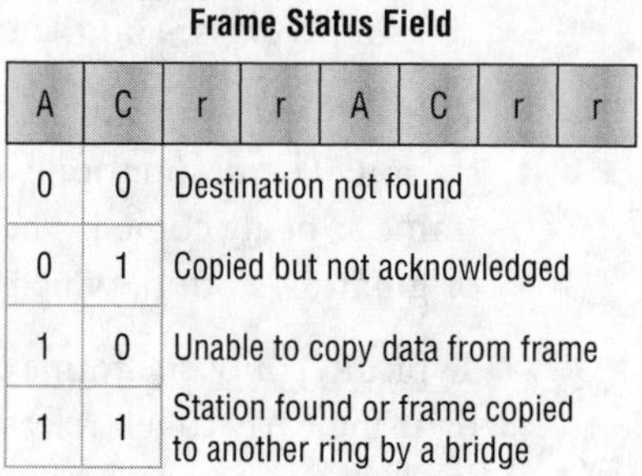

Frame Status Field

A	C	r	r	A	C	r	r

A	C	
0	0	Destination not found
0	1	Copied but not acknowledged
1	0	Unable to copy data from frame
1	1	Station found or frame copied to another ring by a bridge

Both the bits are turned off when the sending station transmits the frame. When the sending station receives the frame back again, the station reads this information to ensure that the data was either received correctly by the destination computer or that it needs to be retransmitted.

Active Monitor

One station on a Token Ring network is always an *active monitor*. The active monitor makes sure that there is no more than one token on the ring at any given time. It is the only device that can generate a new token. It also provides timing on the ring. Finally, if a transmitting station fails, it isn't able to remove the token as it makes its way back through the ring. Should this occur, the active monitor would step in, remove the token, and then generate a new one. Also, many stations on the ring will be designated as *standby monitors* (to act as backups) in case the active monitor goes offline.

ATM

The ATM protocol dictates how two end devices communicate with each other across an ATM network through switches. The ATM protocol model contains three functional layers:

ATM Physical layer   The ATM Physical layer performs Bit timing on the physical medium.

ATM layer   The ATM layer performs Generic flow control, call header generation, multiplexing, and demultiplexing.

ATM Adaptation layer   The ATM Adaptation layer (AAL) provides support for higher layer services such as signaling, circuit emulation, voice, and video.

The ATM Physical Layer

The ATM Physical layer is in charge of sending and receiving bits on the physical level. This layer also manages ATM cell boundaries and controls the cell packaging in the correct frame type for the ATM media you use. The ATM Physical layer consists of two sublayers:

- Physical medium dependent (PMD) sublayer
- Transmission convergence (TC) sublayer

The PMD sublayer sends and receives a constant flow of bits that contain associated timing information to synchronize transmission and reception. The PMD sublayer relies on the media used for transport, and thus, ATM only works on ATM-specific media. Standards include DS-3/E3, FDDI, 155Mbps local fiber, and SONET (Synchronous Optical Network)/SDH. The ATM Forum is considering proposals for twisted-pair wire.

The TC sublayer maintains several functions. It mainly extracts and inserts ATM cells within either a Plesiochronous Digital Hierarchy (PDH) or Synchronous Digital Hierarchy (SDH) time-division multiplexed (TDM) frame and passes this to and from the ATM layer. The other functions it provides are as follows:

- Cell delineation for maintaining ATM cell boundaries.

- Header error control sequence generation and verification. The TC layer creates and checks header error control to ensure valid data.

- Cell rate decoupling. The TC layer inserts or suppresses unassigned ATM cells to adapt the rate of valid ATM cells to the payload capacity of the transmission system.

- Transmission frame adaptation. The TC layer packages ATM cells in appropriate frames for physical layer implementation.

- Transmission frame generation and recovery. The TC layer generates and maintains the given Physical layer frame structure.

The ATM Layer

The ATM layer maintains the virtual connections and carries ATM cells through the network. It accomplishes this by using information contained within the header of each ATM cell. The ATM layer is responsible for the following functions:

- Multiplexing and demultiplexing ATM cells from different virtual connections. You can identify these different connections by their VCI and VPI values.

A *VCI (Virtual Circuit Identifier)* can also be called a *virtual channel*. This is simply the identifier for the logical connection between the two ends of a connection. A *VPI (Virtual Path Identifier)* is the identifier for a group of VCIs that allows an ATM switch to perform operations on a group of VCs.

- Translation of VCI and VPI values at the ATM switch or cross-connect.

- Extraction and insertion of the header before or after the cell is delivered from or to the ATM Adaptation layer.

- Governing the implementation of a flow-control mechanism at the user-network interface (UNI). UNI is basically two ports connected by a pair of wires, typically fiber.

- Passes cells and accepts cells from the AAL.

ATM Adaptation Layer (AAL)

The AAL provides the translation between the larger service data units of the upper layers of the OSI reference model and the ATM cells. This function works by receiving packets from the upper-level protocols and breaking them into 48-byte segments to be dumped into the payload of an ATM cell. The AAL has two different sublayers: segmentation and reassembly (SAR) and convergence sublayer (CS). The CS contains sublayers within itself: the common part (CP) and the service specific (SS). Like protocols specified in the OSI reference model, protocol data units (PDUs) are used to pass information between these layers.

Specifications exist for a few different ATM adaptation layers:

AAL1 (Class A)   AAL1 is used for transporting telephone traffic and uncompressed video traffic. AAL1 uses constant bit rate (CBR) service and end-to-end timing and is connection-oriented. Examples of AAL1 are DS1, E!, and nx64 kbps emulation.

AAL2 (Class B)   AAL2 does not use the CS and SAR sublayers. It multiplexes short packets from multiple sources into a single cell. AAL2 uses a variable bit rate (VBR) and end-to-end timing and is connection-oriented. Examples of AAL2 are packet, video, and audio.

AAL3/4 (Class C)   AAL3/4 is designed for network service providers, uses VBR with no timing required, but is still connection-oriented. Examples of AAL3/4 are Frame Relay and X.25.

AAL5 (Class D)   AAL5 is used to transfer most non-SMDS data and LAN emulation. AAL5 also uses VBR with no timing required.

LANE (LAN Emulation) Components

ATM networks can provide the transport for several different independent emulated LANs. This process is called *LAN emulation (LANE)*. As an attached device to these emulated LANs, the physical location no longer matters to the administrator or implementation. This process allows you to connect several LANs in different locations with switches to create one large emulated LAN. This can make a big difference, since attached devices can now be moved easily between emulated LANs. Thus, an engineering group can belong to one LANE and a design group can belong to another LANE, without ever residing in the same location.

LANE also provides translation between multiple media environments, allowing data sharing. Token Ring or FDDI networks can share data with Ethernet networks as if they were part of the same network.

LANE consists of several components that interact and relate in different ways to provide network connectivity based on the client/server model. The interaction of these components allows broadcast searching, address registration, and address caching. The LANE model is made up of the following components:

LEC (LAN Emulation Client) A LANE client emulates a LAN interface to higher layer protocols and applications. It proxies for users attached into ATM via a non-ATM path.

LES (LAN Emulation Server) A LANE server provides address resolution and registration services to the LANE clients in that emulated LAN. The LES keeps a database of all LANE servers. It also manages the stations that make up the ELAN.

LECS (LAN Emulation Configuration Server) Via a database, an LECS keeps track of which emulated LAN a device belongs to (each configuration server can have a differently named database).

BUS (Broadcast-and-Unknown Server) A BUS is used for broadcasting, sequencing, and distributing multicast and broadcast packets. The BUS also handles unicast flooding.

Notice that LEC and LECS are completely different terms and components!

Summary

The IT industry relies on a layered model rather than a flat model for design, maintenance, and troubleshooting simplicity. The OSI reference model utilizes the layered approach to define the functions of the components of each layer on the model. With each layer of the model performing its defined function, networks can operate and cooperate properly. The Transport layer of the OSI model, for instance, determines flow control and works in conjunction with positive acknowledgements and windowing to guarantee delivery of data.

The network designer must understand the client's available technology, learn to design networks using the best methods, and oftentimes justify to the customer and network engineers his or her designs.

Exam Essentials

Understand the advantages of reference models.   Using reference models, IT personnel can focus their energies on the specific functions and components of a network. For instance, making changes to one layer in an organization's network does not require changing other layers. Ultimately, the complexity of networking is divided into more manageable pieces, allowing for a logical troubleshooting approach.

Know the functions of each OSI layer.   It's very important that you understand what each of the seven layers of the OSI reference model does. The Application, Presentation, and Session layers are the upper layers. They are responsible for communication from a user interface to an application. The Transport layer provides segmentation, sequencing, and virtual circuits. The Network layer provides logical network addressing and routing through the internetwork. The Data Link layer provides framing and placing of the data on the network medium. The Physical layer is responsible for taking 1s and 0s and encoding them into digital signal for transmission onto the network segment.

Understand how the Transport layer functions.   In the Transport layer, the segments that are delivered are acknowledged and sequenced. Non-acknowledged segments are retransmitted, and data flow is maintained to avoid congestion and data loss. Windowing controls the amount of data sent from one end of the network to another end without the receipt of an acknowledgement.

Understand how the Network layer functions. In the Network layer, path determination makes it possible for routers to decide on the best route to send packets to a given destination. Network layer addressing provides the logical map used at the source and destination for communication.

Understand the five conversion steps of data encapsulation.

1. Data from the Application layer is encapsulated at the Presentation layer.

2. The Presentation layer data plus the Application layer data is then passed to the Session layer and encapsulated for synchronization.

3. At the Transport layer, all upper layer data is then encapsulated and segmented.

4. Once at the Network layer, data received from the Transport layer and routing information is added.

5. All data is passed to the Data Link layer for framing and finally to the Physical layer for conversion to 1s and 0s to be sent across the wire.

Remember the benefits of FDDI networking. FDDI includes many benefits for campus-type LANs. Using fiber-optic cabling, there is no risk of data loss or interference and higher speeds can be deployed. The primary ring is backed up by the secondary ring in case of a break or outage. FDDI uses a token-passing method that prevents collisions and provides for predictable delays.

Understand the functions at each of the three ATM layers. The function at each of the ATM layers is very much like the function of the bottom three layers of the OSI model. The ATM Physical layer is much like the OSI Physical layer and is responsible for sending and receiving bits on the physical level. The ATM Data Link layer provides for the virtual connections and carries the ATM cells similar to frames created at the OSI Data Link layer. The AAL layer provides translation services between upper layers of the OSI and the ATM layers.

Key Terms

Before you take the exam, be certain you are familiar with the following terms:

Abstract Syntax Notation 1 (ASN.1)	Ethernet
active monitor	FDDI
activity management	flow control
Application layer	Frame Relay
ATM	frames
ATM (Asynchronous Transfer Mode) switches	full-duplex mode
binding	gateways
bridges	half-duplex mode
broadcast	hubs
broadcast storms	internetworks
Carrier Sense, Multiple Access with Collision Detect (CSMA/CD)	IP address
channel service units (CSUs)	LAN emulation (LANE)
connectionless	latency
connection-oriented	local area networks (LANs)
customer premises equipment (CPE)	MAC (Media Access Control) address
data frame	multiplexors
Data Link layer	multistation access unit (MSAU)
data service units (DSUs)	Network layer
datagrams	network segmentation
de-encapsulation	nodes
encapsulation	OSI (Open Systems Interconnection) reference model

packet switching	simplex mode
packets	standby monitors
Physical layer	switches
positive acknowledgment with retransmission	token
Presentation layer	Token Ring
protocols	Transport layer
reference model	wide area networks (WANs)
repeaters	window
routers	X.25
Session layer	

Written Labs

In this section, you'll complete the following labs to make sure you understand the information and concepts contained within them:

- Lab 1.1: The OSI Reference Model
- Lab 1.2: Defining the OSI Layers and Devices
- Lab 1.3: Identifying Collision and Broadcast Domains

Lab 1.1: OSI Questions

Answer the following questions about the OSI model:

1. Which layer chooses and determines the availability of communicating partners, along with the resources necessary to make the connection; coordinates partnering applications; and forms a consensus on procedures for controlling data integrity and error recovery?

2. Which layer is responsible for converting data packets from the Data Link layer into electrical signals?

3. At which layer is routing implemented, enabling connections and path selection between two end systems?

4. Which layer defines how data is formatted, presented, encoded, and converted for use on the network?

5. Which layer is responsible for creating, managing, and terminating sessions between applications?

6. Which layer ensures the trustworthy transmission of data across a physical link and is primarily concerned with physical addressing, line discipline, network topology, error notification, ordered delivery of frames, and flow control?

7. Which layer is used for reliable communication between end nodes over the network and provides mechanisms for establishing, maintaining, and terminating virtual circuits; transport-fault detection and recovery; and controlling the flow of information?

8. Which layer provides logical addressing that routers use for path determination?

9. Which layer specifies voltage, wire speed, and pinout cables and moves bits between devices?

10. Which layer combines bits into bytes and bytes into frames, uses MAC addressing, and provides error detection?

11. Which layer is responsible for keeping the data from different applications separate on the network?

12. Which layer is represented by frames?

13. Which layer is represented by segments?

14. Which layer is represented by packets?

15. Which layer is represented by bits?

16. Put the following in order of encapsulation:
    - Packets
    - Frames
    - Bits
    - Segments

17. Which layer segments and reassembles data into a data stream?

18. Which layer provides the physical transmission of the data and handles error notification, network topology, and flow control?

19. Which layer manages device addressing, tracks the location of devices on the network, and determines the best way to move data?

20. What is the bit length and expression form of a MAC address?

Lab 1.2: Defining the OSI Layers and Devices

Fill in the blanks with the appropriate layer of the OSI reference model or hub, switch, or router device.

Description	Device or OSI Layer
This device sends and receives information about the Network layer.	
This layer creates a virtual circuit for transmitting between two end stations.	
This layer uses service access points.	
This device uses hardware addresses to filter a network.	
Ethernet is defined at these layers.	
This layer supports flow control and sequencing.	
This device can measure the distance to a remote network.	
Logical addressing is used at this layer.	
Hardware addresses are defined at this layer.	
This device creates one big collision domain and one large broadcast domain.	
This device creates many smaller collision domains, but the network is still one large broadcast domain.	
This device breaks up collision domains and broadcast domains.	

Lab 1.3: Identifying Collision and Broadcast Domains

In Figure 1.24, identify the number of collision domains and broadcast domains in each specified device. Each device is represented by a letter.

1. Hub

2. Bridge

3. Switch

4. Router

FIGURE 1.24   Identifying collision and broadcast domains

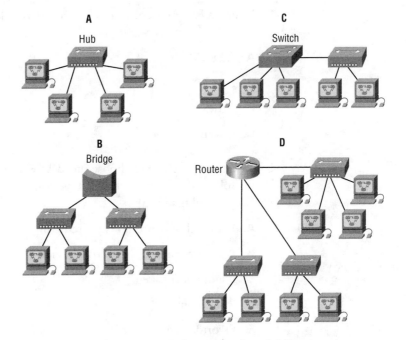

The answers to the Written Labs can be found following the answers to the Review Questions for this chapter.

Review Questions

1. Which of the following ATM Adaptation layers would you choose if you were running LANE?

   A. AAL1

   B. AAL2

   C. AAL3/4

   D. AAL5

2. Which ATM protocol allows Ethernet network traffic to flow through as ATM?

   A. AAL2

   B. AAL3

   C. AAL5

   D. LANE

3. Token Ring networks choose one device to be an active monitor. Of the following choices, which are performed by the active monitor? (Choose all that apply.)

   A. Removal of continuously circulating packets

   B. Promoting additional active monitors

   C. Issuing new tokens

   D. Ring timing

   E. Error detection

4. Which layer of the OSI reference model do bridges work at?

   A. Session

   B. Bridge

   C. Network

   D. Data Link

5. If your customer needs to transfer voice and video, which require high network bandwidth, on what network design area should you focus your efforts?

   A. Network layer media

   B. Network layer protocols

   C. Transport layer

   D. Network layer management

6. What is the Network layer of the OSI reference model responsible for?

   A. Bridging

   B. Regenerating the digital signal

   C. Routing packets through an internetwork

   D. Gateway services

7. Match the datagram type to the layer of the OSI reference model where it is used. (Choose all that apply.)

   A. Application layer PDUs are also known as segments.

   B. Presentation layer PDUs are also known as frames.

   C. Session layer PDUs are also known as bits.

   D. Transport layer PDUs are also known as segments.

   E. Network layer PDUs are also known as packets.

   F. Data Link layer PDUs are also known as frames.

   G. Physical layer PDUs are also known as bits.

8. Which of the following pairs are Presentation layer standards? (Choose three.)

   A. MPEG and MIDI

   B. PICT and JPEG

   C. ASCII and EBCDIC

   D. NFS and SQL

9. Which of the following are Session layer standards?

    A. MPEG and MIDI

    B. NFS and SQL

    C. ASCII and EBCDIC

    D. PICT and JPEG

10. When a Token Ring device needs to transmit data, what must it first do?

    A. Create a token.

    B. Wait for a token.

    C. Wait for the NAUN to respond.

    D. Wait for the active monitor to poll it.

11. Which three of the following are true statements about connection-oriented sessions? (Choose all that apply.)

    A. The segments delivered are acknowledged back to the sender upon their receipt.

    B. Any segments not acknowledged are dropped.

    C. Segments are sequenced back into their proper order upon arrival at their destination.

    D. A manageable data flow is maintained in order to avoid congestion, overloading, and the loss of any data.

12. CPE is an acronym for which of the following?

    A. Central processing engineering

    B. Central processing equipment

    C. Customer processing equipment

    D. Customer premises equipment

13. CSU/DSU is an acronym for which of the following?

   A. Channel service unit/digital service unit

   B. Channel service unit/data service unit

   C. Channel service unit/digital service unit

   D. Can't send in uniform/don't send another unit

14. Which of the following devices blocks broadcasts by default?

   A. Hubs

   B. Repeaters

   C. Switches

   D. Routers

15. Which of the following methods can be used to attach FDDI devices? (Choose all that apply.)

   A. Single attachment stations

   B. Full-duplex stations

   C. Dual attachment stations

   D. Concentrators

   E. Half-duplex stations

16. Match the IEEE 802.3 protocol type to its corresponding physical medium. (Choose all that apply.)

   A. 10Base2 is also known as 50-ohm coax (thinnet).

   B. 10Base5 is also known as 50-ohm coax (thicknet).

   C. 10BaseFL is also known as UTP (unshielded twisted-pair).

   D. 10BaseT is also known as UTP (unshielded twisted-pair).

17. What are the advantages of using fiber rather than copper as a network medium? (Choose all that apply.)

    A. Security

    B. Low cost

    C. 100Mbps

    D. Larger network diameter

    E. Immunity to RFI and EMI

18. What type of media access is used by Ethernet?

    A. Multiplexing

    B. MAC addressing

    C. Polling

    D. Token passing

    E. Contention

19. What type of media access is used by SDLC?

    A. Contention

    B. MAC addressing

    C. Polling

    D. Token passing

    E. Multiplexing

20. Which type of simultaneous transmissions are supported by ISDN networks? (Choose all that apply.)

    A. Voice

    B. Frame Relay

    C. Video

    D. Data

    E. LANE

Answers to Review Questions

1. D. AAL5 is the ATM Adaptation layer used when running Ethernet on ATM or LANE.

2. D. LANE (LAN Emulation) is the protocol used for Ethernet on ATM.

3. A, C, D. The active monitor is responsible for removing loose tokens sent by failed stations and issuing new tokens. The active monitor is also responsible for ring timing.

4. D. Bridges are devices that operate at the Data Link layer. They forward frames between segments based on station MAC addresses.

5. A. Different types of media—coaxial cable, twisted pair, and fiber—support different transfer rates.

6. C. The Network layer performs routing based on logical addressing and uses a best-path route determination for all packets.

7. D, E, F, G. PDUs at the Transport, Network, Data Link, and Physical layers are also known by the type of datagram unique to each layer. Most other layers simply refer to the PDU type as datagrams.

8. A, B, C. Presentation layer standards are responsible for conversion, formatting, and encapsulation.

9. B. The Session layer includes standards used when two stations create a session and exchange data of a common file system.

10. B. Preventing data collisions, Token Ring networks use tokens to ensure that only one station is allowed to transmit while all other stations wait.

11. A, C, D. At the Transport layer, segments are acknowledged and sequenced into their proper order. Data flow is also a function of the Transport layer that is used to avoid congestion and data loss.

12. D. Customer premises equipment (CPE) includes LAN devices, a router, and usually a CSU/DSU.

13. B. A CSU/DSU is included in CPE and is responsible for timing, and channel multiplexing and demultiplexing.

14. D.   Routers work at the Network layer and prevent broadcasts from traveling across the network by creating broadcast domains.

15. A, C, D.   SASs, DASs, and concentrators are FDDI devices used in FDDI networks to allow for single or multiple connection points.

16. A, B, D.   The IEEE 802.3 protocol type defines many physical medium types. 10Base2 designates a 10Mbps baseband cable, with a limit of 200 meters.

17. A, D, E.   Fiber medium is the most expensive medium type, but it provides many advantages over coax or twisted-pair cabling and can support much greater speeds.

18. E.   Contention is another description for CSMA/CD. All stations contend for access to the media, and data collisions often occur.

19. C.   SDLC uses polling to determine which stations need to transmit to help prevent data collisions.

20. A, C, D.   ISDN networks were developed by the phone companies to support simultaneous transmission of voice, video, and data using analog phone lines with digital signaling.

Answers to Written Labs

This section contains the answers for Labs 1.1, 1.2, and 1.3.

Answers to Lab 1.1

1. The Application layer is responsible for finding the network resources broadcast from a server and adding flow control and error control (if the application developer chooses).

2. The Physical layer takes frames from the Data Link layer and encodes the 1s and 0s into a digital signal from transmission on the network medium.

3. The Network layer provides routing through an internetwork and through logical addressing.

4. The Presentation layer makes sure that data is in a readable format for the Application layer.

5. The Session layer sets up, maintains, and terminates sessions between applications.

6. PDUs at the Data Link layer are called frames. As soon as you see "frame" in a question, you know the answer.

7. The Transport layer uses virtual circuits to create a reliable connection between two hosts.

8. The Network layer provides logical addressing, typically IP addressing and routing.

9. The Physical layer is responsible for the electrical and mechanical connections between devices.

10. The Data Link layer is responsible for framing data packets.

11. The Session layer creates sessions between different hosts' applications.

12. The Data Link layer frames packets received from the Network layer.

13. The Transport layer segments user data.

14. The Network layer creates packets out of segments handed down from the Transport layer.

15. The Physical layer is responsible for transporting 1s and 0s in a digital signal.

16. Segments, packets, frames, bits.

17. The Transport layer segments and reassembles data into a data stream.

18. The Data Link layer provides the physical transmission of the data and handles error notification, network topology, and flow control.

19. The Network layer manages device addressing, tracks the location of devices on the network, and determines the best way to move the data.

20. 48 bits (6 bytes) expressed as a hexadecimal number is the bit length and expression form of a MAC address.

Answers to Lab 1.2

Description	Device or OSI Layer
This device sends and receives information about the Network layer.	router
This layer can create a virtual circuit for transmitting between two end stations.	Transport layer
This layer uses service access points.	Data Link layer (LLC sublayer)
This device uses hardware addresses to filter a network.	bridge or switch
Ethernet is defined at these layers.	Data Link and Physical layers
This layer supports flow control and sequencing.	Transport layer
This device can measure the distance to a remote network.	router
Logical addressing is used at this layer.	Network layer
Hardware addresses are defined at this layer.	Data Link layer (MAC sublayer)
This device creates one big collision domain and one large broadcast domain.	hub

Description	Device or OSI Layer
This device creates many smaller collision domains but the network is still one large broadcast domain.	switch or bridge
This device breaks up collision domains and broadcast domains.	router

Answers to Lab 1.3

1. Hub: One collision domain, one broadcast domain

2. Bridge: Two collision domains, one broadcast domain

3. Switch: Four collision domains, one broadcast domain

4. Router: Three collision domains, three broadcast domains

Chapter

2

LAN Segmentation

CCDA EXAM TOPICS COVERED IN THIS CHAPTER:

✓ Given a network design or a set of requirements evaluate a solution to incorporate equipment and technology within a Campus design.

Layer 2 (L2) switching is the process of using the hardware address of devices on a LAN to segment a network. When Cisco discusses switching, they're talking about Layer 2 switching unless they say otherwise. However, Cisco also performs Layer 3 (L3) switching, which really means *routing*, but through a device with more options than a basic router can perform.

Switches truly have changed the way networks are designed and implemented. If a pure switched design is properly implemented, the result is a clean, cost-effective, and resilient internetwork. Routing protocols have processes for stopping network loops from occurring at the Network layer. However, if you have redundant physical links between your switches, routing protocols won't do a thing to stop loops from occurring at the Data Link layer. That's exactly the reason the Spanning-Tree Protocol (STP) was developed—to put a stop to loops in a Layer 2 switched internetwork.

In contrast to the networks of yesterday that were based on collapsed backbones, today's network design is characterized by a flatter architecture—thanks to switches. So now what? How do you break up broadcast domains in a pure switched internetwork? By creating virtual LANs (VLANs), that's how!

This chapter delves into the nitty-gritty of both Layer 2 and Layer 3 switching; it surveys and compares network design before and after switching technologies were introduced. It also discusses the essentials of the Spanning-Tree Protocol and explores how it works within a switched network. The remaining topics in this chapter are VLANs, frame tagging, and Ethernet networking. But first, let's discuss the advantages and disadvantages of using a bridge, router, or LAN switch to segment a network.

Relieving Network Congestion

With a combination of powerful workstations, audio and video to the desktop, and network-intensive applications, 10Mbps Ethernet networks no longer offer enough bandwidth to fulfill the business requirements of the typical large business.

As more and more users are connected to the network, an Ethernet network's performance begins to lag as users fight for more bandwidth. Like too many cars getting onto a freeway at rush hour, this increased utilization forces an increase in network congestion as more users try to access the same network resources. Congestion causes users to scream for more bandwidth. However, simply increasing bandwidth can't always solve the problem. Problems like a slow server CPU or insufficient RAM on the workstations and servers can also be culprits and need to be considered.

One way to solve congestion problems and increase the networking performance of your LAN is to divide single Ethernet segments into multiple network segments. This process is called *network segmentation*, and it maximizes the available bandwidth. Some of the technologies you can use for network segmentation are

Physical segmentation   You can segment the network with bridges and routers, thereby breaking up the collision domains. This minimizes packet collisions by decreasing the number of workstations on the same physical segment.

Network switching technology (microsegmenting)   Like a bridge or router, switches can also provide LAN segmentation capabilities. LAN switches (for example, the Cisco Catalyst 5000) provide dedicated, point-to-point, packet-switched connections between their ports. Since this provides simultaneous switching of packets between the ports in the switch, it increases the amount of bandwidth open to each workstation.

Full-duplex Ethernet devices   *Full-duplex Ethernet* can provide almost twice the bandwidth of traditional Ethernet networks. However, for this to work, both the network interface cards (NICs) and their switch ports must be able to run in full-duplex mode.

Fast Ethernet   Replacing 10Mbps devices with *Fast Ethernet* devices can provide 10 times the amount of bandwidth available from 10BaseT.

It should be no surprise that reducing the number of users per collision domain increases the bandwidth on your network segment. A *collision domain* is the network area within which *data frames* that have collided are propagated. *Repeaters* and *hubs* propagate collisions. *Switches*, *bridges*, and *routers* do not. By keeping the traffic local to the network segment and not propagating collisions, users have more available bandwidth and enjoy noticeably better response time than if they simply had one large network segment in place.

Figure 2.1 shows an Ethernet network with repeaters. This network appears to be one large Ethernet network to all workstations, and basically it *is* one large collision domain. It's a good idea to segment your network with bridges and routers when it grows too large. However, these devices use different technologies that can cause some delay and reduce communication efficiency, which is why it is so important to segment your network correctly.

FIGURE 2.1   Ethernet network with repeaters

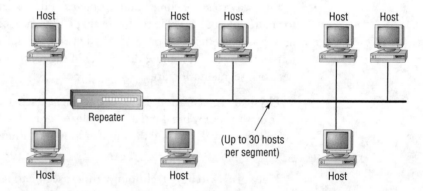

Segmentation with a Bridge

As discussed in Chapter 1, "Introduction to Internetworking," a bridge can segment or break up your network into smaller, more manageable pieces. But if the bridge is incorrectly placed in your network, it can cause more harm than good!

Bridges do their work at the MAC sublayer of the *Data Link layer*. They create separate physical and logical network segments to reduce traffic load. There are solid advantages to bridging: By segmenting a logical network into multiple physical pieces, bridging ensures network reliability, availability, scalability, and manageability.

As Figure 2.2 shows, bridges work by examining the MAC or hardware addresses in each data frame and forwarding the frame to the other physical segments—but only if necessary. These devices dynamically build a forward-ing table of information composed of each *MAC address* and the segment on which that address is located.

FIGURE 2.2 Segmentation with a bridge

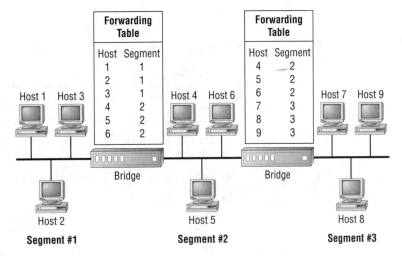

Now for the bad news.... One drawback to using bridges is that if the destination MAC address is unknown to the bridge, the bridge forwards the frame to all segments except the port it received the frame from. Also, a 20–30 percent latency period to process frames can occur. Latency is the time is takes for a frame to get from the source host to the destination host. This delay can increase significantly if the frame cannot be forwarded immediately due to current activity on the destination segment.

Bridges forward broadcast packets and multicast packets to all other segments to which the bridge is attached. Because the addresses from these broadcasts are never seen by the bridge and therefore are not fil-tered, broadcast storms can result. Later in this chapter you will see how bridges run a protocol called Spanning-Tree Protocol to avoid this type of forwarding.

Segmentation with a Router

As you know, routers work at the *Network layer* and are used to route packets to destination networks. Routers, like bridges, use tables to make routing decisions. However, routers keep information only on how to get to remote networks in their tables, not to get to hosts; they use this information to route packets through an internetwork. For example, routers use IP addresses instead of hardware addresses when making routing decisions. The router keeps a routing table for each protocol on the network. A Cisco router keeps one routing table for AppleTalk, a different one for IPX, and still another for IP, as shown in Figure 2.3.

FIGURE 2.3 Routing tables are kept for each Network layer routing protocol.

IP ROUTING TABLE		IP ROUTING TABLE	
Subnet	Interface	Subnet	Interface
172.16.10.0	E0	172.16.30.0	E0
172.16.20.0	S0	172.16.20.0	S0
172.16.30.0	S0	172.16.10.0	S0

IPX ROUTING TABLE		IPX ROUTING TABLE	
Network Number	Interface	Network Number	Interface
117	S0	10	S0
108	E0	108	E0
10	S0	117	S0

AppleTalk ROUTING TABLE		AppleTalk ROUTING TABLE	
Cable Range	Interface	Cable Range	Interface
2–2	E0	1–1	E0
10–10	S0	10–10	S0
1–1	S0	2–2	S0

The advantages of segmentation with routers are:

Manageability   Multiple routing protocols give the network manager who is creating an internetwork a lot of flexibility.

Increased functionality   Cisco routers provide features addressing the issues of flow, error, and congestion control, plus fragmentation, reassembly, and control over packet lifetime.

Multiple active paths   Using the protocol, source service access points (SSAPs), destination service access points (DSAPs), and path metrics, routers can make informed routing decisions, as well as interpret the next layer protocol. Routers can have more than one active link between devices, which is a definite plus.

Broadcast control   Since routers do not forward broadcasts the same way that bridges and switches do, they are able to contain broadcasts to localized *broadcast domains*.

To provide these featured advantages, routers must be more complex and more software-intensive than bridges. Routers provide a lower level of performance than bridges in terms of the number of frames or packets that can be processed per unit. A router must examine more fields in a packet than a bridge, resulting in a 30–40 percent loss of throughput for acknowledgment-oriented protocols and a 20–30 percent loss for sliding-window protocols.

Switching Services

Layer 2 switching is hardware based, which means it uses the MAC address from the host's NIC cards to filter the network. Unlike bridges that use software to create and manage a filter table, switches use application-specific integrated circuits (ASICs) to build and maintain their filter tables. But it's still okay to think of a Layer 2 switch as a multiport bridge because their basic reason for being is the same—to break up collision domains.

Layer 2 switches and bridges are faster than routers because they don't take up time looking at the Network layer header information. Instead, they look at the frame's hardware addresses before deciding to either forward the frame or drop it.

Layer 2 switching provides the following:

- Hardware-based bridging media access control (MAC)

- Wire speed

- Low latency

- Low cost

What makes Layer 2 switching so efficient is that no modification to the data packet takes place. The device only reads the frame encapsulating the packet, which makes the switching process considerably faster and less error-prone than routing processes are.

And if you use Layer 2 switching for both workgroup connectivity and network segmentation (breaking up collision domains), you can create a flatter network design with more network segments than you can with traditional 10BaseT shared networks.

Plus, Layer 2 switching increases bandwidth for each user because, again, each connection (interface) into the switch is its own collision domain. This feature makes it possible for you to connect multiple devices to each interface.

The Limitations of Layer 2 Switching

Since users commonly stick Layer 2 switching into the same category as bridged networks, you might tend to think it has the same hang-ups and issues that bridged networks do. Keep in mind that bridges are good and helpful things if you design the network correctly, keeping their features and limitations in mind. And to design well with bridges, the two most important considerations are

- You absolutely must break up the collision domains correctly.

- The right way to create a functional bridged network is to make sure that its users spend 80 percent of their time on the local segment.

Bridged networks break up collision domains, but remember, that network is still one large broadcast domain. Both Layer 2 switches and bridges shouldn't break up broadcast domains, something that not only limits your network's size and growth potential but also reduces its overall performance. Broadcasts and multicasts, along with the slow convergence time of the Spanning-Tree Protocol, can give you some major grief as your network grows. These are the major reasons why Layer 2 switches and bridges cannot completely replace routers (Layer 3 devices) in the internetwork.

Bridging versus LAN Switching

It's true—Layer 2 switches really are pretty much just bridges that give you many more ports, but there are some important differences you should always keep in mind:

- Bridges are software based, while switches are hardware based because they use an ASIC chip to help make filtering decisions.

- Bridges can only have one spanning-tree instance per bridge, while switches can have many. (I'm going to tell you all about the Spanning-Tree Protocol in a bit.)

- Bridges can only have up to 16 ports—max! A switch can have hundreds.

Three Switch Functions at Layer 2

There are three distinct functions of Layer 2 switching; be sure to remember these—you'll need them for the exam:

- Address learning
- Forward/filter decisions
- Loop avoidance

Address Learning

With address learning, Layer 2 switches and bridges remember the source hardware address of each frame received on an interface, and they enter this information into a MAC database called a *forward/filter table*. When a switch is first powered on, the MAC forward/filter table is empty, as you can see in Figure 2.4.

FIGURE 2.4   Empty forward/filter table on a switch

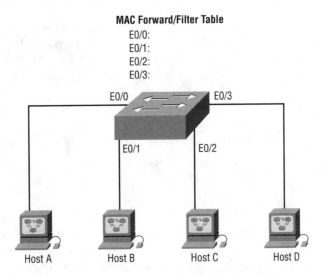

When a device transmits and an interface receives a frame, the switch places the frame's source address in the MAC forward/filter table, allowing it to remember which interface the sending device is located on. The switch then has no choice but to flood the network with this frame because it has no idea where the destination device is actually located.

If a device answers this broadcast and sends a frame back, then the switch takes the source address from that frame and places that MAC address in its database as well, associating this address with the interface that received the frame. Since the switch now has both of the relevant MAC addresses in its filtering table, the two devices can now make a point-to-point connection. The switch doesn't need to broadcast like it did the first time because now the frames can and will only be forwarded between the two devices. This is exactly the thing that makes Layer 2 switches better than hubs. In a hub network, all frames are forwarded out all ports every time— no matter what! Figure 2.5 shows the processes involved in building a MAC database.

FIGURE 2.5 How switches learn hosts' locations

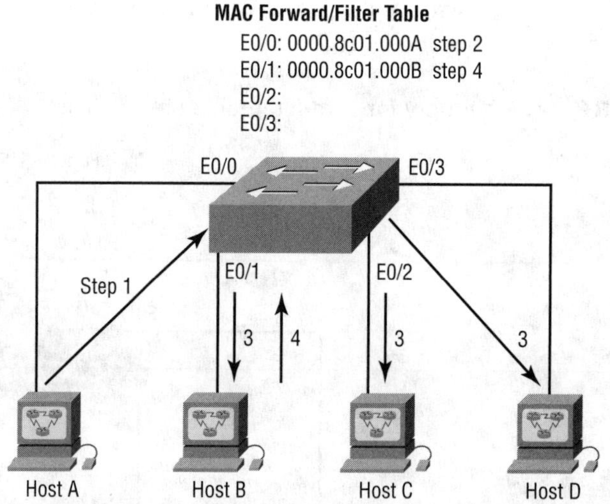

MAC Forward/Filter Table
E0/0: 0000.8c01.000A step 2
E0/1: 0000.8c01.000B step 4
E0/2:
E0/3:

In Figure 2.5, you can see four hosts attached to a switch. When the switch is powered on, it has nothing in its MAC address filter/forward table, just like in Figure 2.4. But when the hosts start communicating, the switch places the source hardware address of each frame in the table along with the port to which the frame's address corresponds.

Let me give you an example of how a forward/filter table is populated:

1. Host A sends a frame to Host B. Host A's MAC address is 0000.8c01 .000A; Host B's MAC address is 0000.8c01.000B.

2. The switch receives the frame on the E0/0 interface and places the source address in the MAC address table.

Switch interface addressing is covered in Appendix B, "Solutions to Case Studies."

3. Since the destination address is not in the MAC database, the frame is forwarded out all interfaces.

4. Host B receives the frame and responds to Host A. The switch receives this frame on interface E0/1 and places the source hardware address in the MAC database.

5. Host A and Host B can now make a point-to-point connection, and only those two devices receive the frames. Hosts C and D do not see the frames, nor are their MAC addresses found in the database because they haven't yet sent a frame to the switch.

If Host A and Host B don't communicate to the switch again within a certain amount of time, the switch flushes their entries from the database to keep it as current as possible.

Forward/Filter Decisions

When a frame is received on an interface, the switch looks at the destination hardware address and finds the exit interface in the MAC database. The frame is only forwarded out the specified destination port.

When a frame arrives at a switch interface, the destination hardware address is compared to the forward/filter MAC database. If the destination hardware address is known and listed in the database, the frame is only sent out the correct exit interface. The switch doesn't transmit the frame out any interface except for the destination interface. This preserves bandwidth on the other network segments and is called *frame filtering*.

If the destination hardware address is not listed in the MAC database, then the frame is broadcast out all active interfaces except the interface on which the frame was received. If a device answers the broadcast, the MAC database is updated with the device's location (interface).

If a host or server sends a broadcast on the LAN, the switch broadcasts the frame out all active ports by default. Remember that the switch only creates smaller collision domains, but it's still one large broadcast domain by default.

Loop Avoidance

If multiple connections between switches are created for redundancy purposes, network loops can occur. The Spanning-Tree Protocol (STP) is used to stop network loops while still permitting redundancy. Redundant links between switches are a good idea because they help prevent complete network failures in the event that one link stops working.

It sounds great, but even though redundant links can be extremely helpful, they often cause more problems than they solve. This is because frames can be broadcast down all redundant links simultaneously, creating network loops as well as other evils. Here's a list of some of the ugliest problems:

- If no loop avoidance schemes are put in place, the switches flood broadcasts endlessly throughout the internetwork. This is sometimes referred to as a *broadcast storm*. (But most of the time it's referred to in ways we're not permitted to repeat in print!) Figure 2.6 illustrates how a broadcast can be propagated throughout the network. Observe how a frame is continually being broadcast through the internetwork's physical network media.

FIGURE 2.6 Broadcast storm

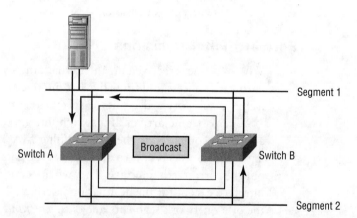

- A device can receive multiple copies of the same frame since that frame can arrive from different segments at the same time. Figure 2.7 demonstrates how a large number of frames can arrive from multiple segments simultaneously. The server in this figure sends a unicast frame to Router C. Since it's a broadcast, Switch A forwards the frame, and Switch B provides the same service—it forwards the broadcast. This is bad because it means that Router C receives that unicast frame twice, causing additional overhead on the network.

- You may have thought of this one: The MAC address filter table is totally confused about the device's location because the switch can receive the frame from more than one link. And what's more, the bewildered switch could get so caught up in constantly updating the MAC filter table with source hardware address locations that it fails to forward a frame! This is called *thrashing* the MAC table.

FIGURE 2.7   Multiple frame copies

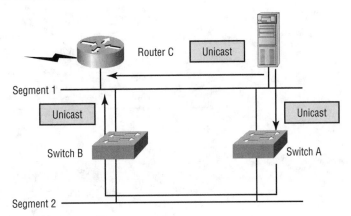

- One of the nastiest things that can happen is multiple loops generating throughout an internetwork. This means that loops can occur within other loops, and if a broadcast storm also occurs, the network won't be able to perform switching—period!

All of these problems spell "hosed" or "pretty much hosed" and are decidedly evil situations that must be avoided, or at least fixed somehow. That's where the Spanning-Tree Protocol comes into the game. It was developed to solve each and every one of the problems I just told you about.

80/20 Rule

The traditional campus network placed users and groups in the same physical location. If a new salesperson was hired, they had to sit in the same physical location as the other sales personnel and be connected to the same physical network segment in order to share network resources. Any deviation from this caused major headaches for the network administrators.

The rule that needed to be followed in this type of network was called the *80/20 rule* because 80 percent of the users' traffic was supposed to remain on the local network segment and only 20 percent or less was supposed to cross the routers or bridges to the other network segments. If more than 20 percent of the traffic crossed the network segmentation devices, performance issues arose. Figure 2.8 illustrates a traditional 80/20 network.

FIGURE 2.8   A traditional 80/20 network

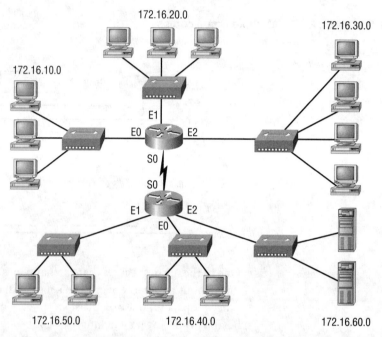

Because network administrators are responsible for network design and implementation, they improved network performance in the 80/20 network by making sure all the network resources for the users were contained within their own network segment. These resources included network servers, printers, shared directories, software programs, and applications.

The 80/20 rule is a foundation for traditional network design, and the campus-wide virtual LAN (VLAN) model relies on it heavily. When 80 percent of the traffic is within a workgroup (VLAN), then 80 percent of the packets flowing from the client to the server are switched locally. The logical workgroup is dispersed in a campus-wide VLAN, but is still organized so that 80 percent of traffic is contained within it. The 20 percent that's left leaves the network or subnet through a router.

The New 20/80 Rule

Many of you have probably seen distributed data storage and retrieval cropping up in new and existing applications. In these instances, traffic patterns are moving in an opposite direction, toward a principle known as the *20/80 rule*. In this scenario, only 20 percent of traffic is local to the workgroup LAN, and 80 percent of the traffic leaves the workgroup.

In a traditional network design (where the 80/20 rule is in force), only a small amount of traffic passes through L3 devices. These devices are typically routers because issues of performance rarely arise. However, the newer enterprise networks use servers located in the enterprise edge or in server farms. With increased traffic from clients to these distant servers, performance now becomes an issue. Devices with high-speed, L3 processing are necessary to handle higher requirements in the building distribution and campus backbone.

With new web-based applications and computing, any PC can be a subscriber or publisher at any time. Also, because businesses are pulling servers from remote locations and creating server farms (sounds like a mainframe, doesn't it?) to centralize network services for security, reduced cost, and administration, the old 80/20 rule is obsolete and could not possibly work in this environment. All traffic must now traverse the campus backbone, which means you now have the 20/80 rule in effect. Figure 2.9 shows the new 20/80 network.

FIGURE 2.9 A 20/80 network

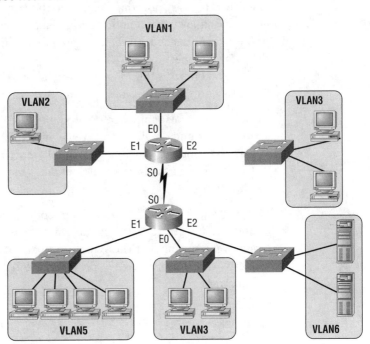

The problem with the 20/80 rule is not the network wiring and topology as much as it is the routers themselves. They must be able to handle an enormous number of packets quickly and efficiently at wire speed. This is probably where you should be talking about how great Cisco routers are and how your networks would be nothing without them. We'll get to that later in this chapter—trust us.

Layer 2 (L2) Multicasting

The concept of forming a multicast group is the basis for IP multicast. This means that any group or collection of receivers can indicate interest in receiving a particular stream of data. The group itself isn't limited by physical or departmental boundaries, and the hosts can be located anywhere on the network as well. Hosts join the group by using the Internet Group Management Protocol (IGMP) in order to receive data going to that group.

Multicast routing protocols such as Protocol Independent Multicast (PIM) guide the delivery of traffic through multicast-enabled routers. The router to the switch port forwards the incoming multicast stream.

One problem is that the default for an L2 switch is to forward all multicast traffic to every port that belongs to the same VLAN on the switch. Talk about a monkey wrench in the works. This activity defeats the very purpose of the switch, which is to send traffic only to the ports that need to receive the data. Bummer!

The good news is that there are several ways Cisco switches can circumvent this little problem. Ones commonly used include:

Cisco Group Management Protocol (CGMP)   A Cisco proprietary solution found on all Cisco LAN switches. The multicast receiver registration (using the IGMP) is accepted by the router and communicated by CGMP to the switch; the switch updates its forwarding table with that information.

IGMP snooping   The switch intercepts multicast receiver registrations and updates the forwarding table with that information. The IGMP snooping means that the switch is aware of L3 because IGMP is a Network layer protocol. Typically, the IGPM packet recognition is hardware assisted.

Quality of Service (QoS)

Have you had any problems with a utility, with an airline, or with a particular retailer lately? Lots of corporations promise quality of service; darn few deliver on what their brand pledges they will provide you. In networking, QoS has to do with the proper handling of traffic. Fortunately, Cisco has a track record of reliability in this area.

Because they don't have knowledge of L3 or higher information, access switches provide QoS based only on the L2 or input port. This allows you to define traffic from a particular host as high-priority traffic on the uplink port. The scheduling feature on the output port of an access switch ensures that traffic from such ports is served first. If input traffic is properly marked, the expected service when traffic passes distribution and core layer switches is then assured.

Better yet, because distribution and core layer switches are typically L3-aware, they can provide QoS on a port basis and also using higher layer parameters, such as port numbers, IP addresses, or QoS bits in the IP packet. These devices are more finely tuned to differences in traffic based on the application and so are able make QoS more exclusive. Though QoS in distribution and core switches must be provided in both directions of flow, policing is usually enabled on the distribution layer devices.

Your goal in QoS for Voice over IP (VoIP) is to provide for packet loss and delay within parameters that do not affect voice quality. One obvious solution is to provide enough bandwidth at all points in the network, but that'll cost you. Or you can apply a QoS mechanism at the stressed-out points in the network. (Counseling usually doesn't work in these situations. Just kidding!)

The end-to-end network delay at 150 milliseconds is not noticeable to the parties speaking, making it a pretty good design choice for QoS in VoIP. If you want guaranteed low delay for voice at campus speeds, you can set up a separate outbound queue for real-time traffic. Since burst-prone data traffic, such as file transfers, uses a different queue, packet loss is not an issue because the separate queue for voice guarantees low delay.

QoS is the princess' foot in the glass slipper where multilayer campus design is concerned. The entrance to the network is the wiring-closet switch (access switch). Packet classification is a multilayer service applied at this switch. A characteristic port number recognizes VoIP traffic flows. An IP type of service (ToS) value indicating "low delay voice" defines VoIP packets. If VoIP packets encounter congestion in the network, the local switch or router applies appropriate congestion management based on the ToS value. And that's a wrap for QoS.

Spanning-Tree Protocol (STP)

Back before it was purchased and renamed Compaq, a company called Digital Equipment Corporation (DEC) created the original version of the *Spanning-Tree Protocol (STP)*. The IEEE later created its own version of STP called 802.1d. All Cisco switches run the IEEE 802.1d version of STP, which isn't compatible with the DEC version.

STP's main task is to stop network loops from occurring on your Layer 2 network (bridges or switches). It vigilantly monitors the network to find all links, making sure that no loops occur by shutting down any redundant ones. The Spanning-Tree Protocol (STP) uses the *spanning-tree algorithm (STA)* to first create a topology database, and then search out and destroy redundant links. With STP running, frames are only forwarded on the premium, STP-picked links.

Before describing the details of how STP works in the network, you need to understand some basic ideas and terms and how they relate within the Layer 2 switched network:

Spanning-Tree Protocol A bridge protocol that uses the STA to find redundant links dynamically and create a spanning-tree topology database. Bridges exchange *Bridge Protocol Data Unit (Bpdu)* messages with other bridges to detect loops and then remove them by shutting down selected bridge interfaces.

Root bridge This is the bridge with the best bridge ID. With STP, the key is for all the switches in the network to elect a root bridge that becomes the focal point in the network. All other decisions in the network—like which port is to be blocked and which port is to be put in forwarding mode—are made from the perspective of this root bridge.

Bridge Protocol Data Unit (Bpdu) All the switches exchange information to use in the selection of the root switch, as well as for subsequent configuration of the network. Each switch compares the parameters in the Bpdu that they send to one neighbor with the one that they receive from another neighbor.

Bridge ID This is how STP keeps track of all the switches in the network. The bridge ID is determined by a combination of the bridge priority (32768 by default on all switches) and the base MAC address. The lowest bridge ID becomes the root bridge in the network.

Non-root bridge All bridges that are not the root bridge. These exchange Bpdu with all bridges and update the STP topology database on all switches, preventing loops and providing a measure of defense against link failures. A non-root bridge designates its root port as the one on which it is receiving Bpdus with the lowest cost to root, breaking ties in favor of the lowest port ID. A non-root bridge forwards the Bpdus received on its root port out its designated ports (defined later) after incrementing the Bpdu cost. A bridge will forward the Bpdu that caused it to become a non-root bridge on all ports (except the incoming port).

Root port Always the link directly connected to the root bridge, or the shortest path to the root bridge. If more than one link connects to the root bridge, then a port cost is determined by checking the bandwidth of each link. The lowest cost port becomes the root port.

Designated port Either a root port or a port that has been determined as having the best cost—it is designated as a forwarding port.

Port cost Determined when multiple links are used between two switches and none are root ports. The cost of a link is determined by the bandwidth of a link.

Non-designated port A port with a lower cost than the designated port that is put in blocking mode.

Forwarding port A port that forwards frames.

Blocked port A port that does not forward frames in order to prevent loops.

When to Worry about Spanning-Tree Protocol

If you have less than six switches in your internetwork, then depending on the amount of users in your network, you typically would just let the STP do its job and not worry about it.

However, if you have dozens of switches and hundreds of users in your network, then it's time to consider how the STP is running. If you do not set the root switch in this larger switched network, your STP may never converge between switches, which could bring your network down.

Setting the timers and root switch are covered in the Sybex *CCNP: Switching Study Guide.*

LAN Switch Types

LAN switch types decide how a frame is handled when it's received on a switch port. Latency—the time it takes for a frame to be sent out an exit port once the switch receives the frame—depends on the chosen switching mode. There are three switching modes:

- Cut-through
- FragmentFree
- Store-and-forward

Cut-Through (Real-Time)

When in cut-through or real-time mode, the switch waits for the destination hardware address to be received before it looks up the destination address in the MAC filter table. With the *cut-through* switching method, the LAN switch copies only the destination address (the first six bytes following the preamble) onto its onboard buffers. That done, it then looks up the hardware destination address in the MAC switching table, determines the outgoing interface, and proceeds to forward the frame toward its destination.

A cut-through switch really helps to reduce latency because it begins to forward the frame as soon as it reads the destination address and determines the outgoing interface. And after it determines the destination port, the subsequent frames are immediately forwarded out through it.

With some switches, you get an extra supercool feature: the flexibility to perform cut-through switching on a per-port basis until a user-defined error threshold is reached. At the point that threshold is attained, the ports automatically change over to store-and-forward mode so they stop forwarding the errors. And, when the error rate on the port falls back below the threshold, the port automatically changes back to cut-through mode.

FragmentFree (Modified Cut-Through)

FragmentFree, or modified cut-through, is the default switching mode for the Catalyst 1900 switch. In this mode, the switch checks the first 64 bytes of a frame before forwarding it for fragmentation, thus guarding against possible collisions. FragmentFree switching is a modified form of cut-through switching, in which the switch waits for the collision window (64 bytes) to pass before forwarding. This is because if a packet has an error, it almost always occurs within the first 64 bytes. It means each frame is checked into the data field to make sure no fragmentation has occurred.

FragmentFree switching mode provides better error checking than the cut-through mode with practically no increase in latency. It's the default switching method for the Catalyst 1900 switches.

Store-and-Forward

Store-and-forward switching is Cisco's primary LAN switching method. When in store-and-forward mode, the LAN switch copies the entire frame onto its onboard buffers and then computes the *cyclic redundancy check (CRC)*. Because it copies the entire frame, latency through the switch varies with frame length.

The frame is discarded if it contains a CRC error, if it's too short (less than 64 bytes including the CRC), or if it's too long (more than 1,518 bytes, including the CRC). If the frame doesn't contain any errors, the LAN switch looks up the destination hardware address in its forwarding or switching table to find the correct outgoing interface. When it does, out goes the frame toward its destination. This is the mode used by the Catalyst 5000 series switches, and you can't modify it.

With store-and-forward switching, the complete data frame is received on the switch's buffer, a CRC is run, and then the switch looks up the destination address in the MAC filter table. Figure 2.10 delimits the different points where the switching mode takes place in the frame.

FIGURE 2.10   Different switching modes within a frame

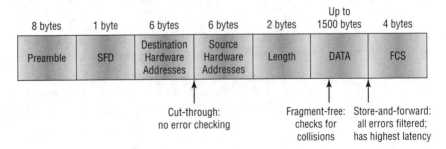

> ### 🌐 Real World Scenario
>
> ## Practical Configuration of Switching Modes
>
> Many of the Cisco switches (the Catalyst 2950 series, for example) can be configured for multiple modes of switching to meet network demands. For instance, you can configure a switch port to use cut-through switching for lower latency and specify a threshold value at which the switch changes to store-and-forward switching if a high rate of errors is detected or what's called a *collision window* passes. (A collision window is the maximum amount of time required to detect an error.) You can also specify the type of traffic that should be processed using cut-through or store-and-forward switching. For example, you can configure unicast traffic to use cut-through switching and broadcast traffic to use only store-and-forward switching. There are typically different time-sensitive considerations for unicast and broadcast traffic. Multicast traffic can also be configured for either type of switching. Depending upon the type of multicast traffic, video, IP/TV, and synchronous learning, there are different considerations for permitted latency.
>
> Configuring the different switching modes on a Cisco switch is relatively easy when using the command line. For example, on the Catalyst 2950 series switches, if you enter `switching-type ?`, two options are available: fragment-free and store-and-forward. You can type `switching-type fragment-free` or `switching-type store-and-forward` to set either switching mode globally on that switch. The third switching-type option, cut-through, does not display since it is the default.

Introduction to Virtual LANs (VLANs)

You've seen *virtual local area networks (VLANs)* mentioned several times in this chapter already. At long last, this section discusses them in detail. As you can see from Figure 2.11, Layer 2 switched networks are typically designed as flat networks. Every broadcast packet transmitted is seen by every device on the network, regardless of whether the device needs to receive that data or not.

FIGURE 2.11   Flat network structure

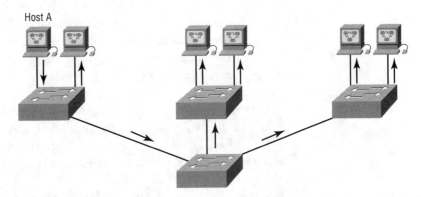

By default, routers allow broadcasts only within the originating network, but switches forward broadcasts to all segments. The reason it's called a *flat network* is because it's one broadcast domain, not because its design is physically flat.

Notice in Figure 2.11 that Host A is sending a broadcast and all ports on all switches are forwarding this broadcast, except for the port that originally received it. Now look at Figure 2.12, which pictures a switched network. It shows Host A sending a frame with Host D as its destination, and as you can see, that frame is only forwarded out the port where Host D is located. This is a huge improvement over the old hub networks, unless having one collision domain by default is what you really want.

FIGURE 2.12   The advantage of a switched network

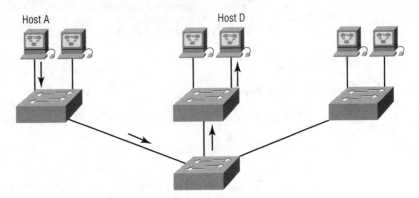

Now you already know that the largest advantage gained by having a Layer 2 switched network is that it creates individual collision domain segments for each device plugged into the switch. This scenario frees you from the Ethernet distance constraints, so now larger networks can be built. But with each new advance, you often encounter new issues—the larger the number of users and devices, the more broadcasts and packets each switch must handle!

And there's another benefit of VLANs—security! In the typical Layer 2 switched internetwork, all users can see all devices by default. And you can't stop devices from broadcasting, nor can you stop users from trying to respond to broadcasts. Your security options are dismally limited to placing passwords on the servers and other devices.

But not if you create VLANs, my friend! Yes, indeed, you can solve many of the problems associated with Layer 2 switching with VLANs—as you'll soon see.

There are several ways that VLANs simplify network management:

- The VLAN can group several broadcast domains into multiple logical subnets.

- Network adds, moves, and changes are achieved by configuring a port into the appropriate VLAN.

- A group of users needing high security can be put into a VLAN so that no users outside of the VLAN can communicate with them.

- As a logical grouping of users by function, VLANs can be considered independent from their physical or geographic locations.

- VLANs can enhance network security.

- VLANs increase the number of broadcast domains while decreasing their size.

Broadcast Control

Broadcasts occur in every protocol, but how often they occur depends upon three factors:

- The type of protocol

- The application(s) running on the internetwork

- How these services are used

Some older applications have been rewritten to reduce their bandwidth needs, but there's a new generation of applications that are incredibly bandwidth-greedy, consuming all they can find. These bandwidth abusers are multimedia applications that use broadcasts and multicasts extensively. And faulty equipment, inadequate segmentation, and poorly designed firewalls only serve to compound the problems that these broadcast-intensive applications create. All of this has truly added a new dimension to network design, while generating new challenges for a network administrator. Making sure the network is properly segmented in order to isolate one segment's problems and keeping those problems from propagating throughout the internetwork is imperative. The most effective way of doing this is through strategic switching and routing.

Since switches have become more cost-effective lately, many companies are replacing their flat hub networks with a pure switched network and VLAN environment. All devices in a VLAN are members of the same broadcast domain and receive all broadcasts. The broadcasts, by default, are filtered from all ports on a switch that are not members of the same VLAN. This is great because it offers all the benefits you gain with a switched design without the serious anguish you would experience if all your users were in the same broadcast domain!

Security

But there's always a catch, so let's get back to those security issues. A flat internetwork's security used to be tackled by connecting hubs and switches together with routers. So it was basically the router's job to maintain security. This arrangement was pretty ineffective for several reasons. First, anyone connecting to the physical network could access the network resources located on that physical LAN. Second, all anyone had to do to observe any and all traffic happening in that network was to simply plug a network analyzer into the hub. And in that same vein, users could join a workgroup by just plugging their workstations into the existing hub. So basically, this was non-security!

This is why VLANs are so cool. By building them and creating multiple broadcast groups, administrators can now have control over each port and user! The days when users could just plug their workstations into any switch port and gain access to network resources are history, because the administrator is now awarded control over each port and whatever resources that port can access.

Also, because VLANs can be created in accordance with the network resources a user requires, switches can be configured to inform a network management station of any unauthorized access to network resources. And if you need inter-VLAN communication, you can implement restrictions on a router to achieve it. You can also place restrictions on hardware addresses, protocols, and applications—now you're talking security!

Flexibility and Scalability

If you're paying attention to what you've read so far, you know that Layer 2 switches only read frames for filtering—they don't look at the Network layer protocol. And by default, switches forward all broadcasts. But if you create and implement VLANs, you're essentially creating smaller broadcast domains at Layer 2.

This means that broadcasts sent out from a node in one VLAN won't be forwarded to ports configured to be in a different VLAN. So by assigning switch ports or users to VLAN groups on a switch or group of connected switches (called a *switch fabric*), you gain the flexibility to add only the users you want into that broadcast domain regardless of their physical location! This setup can also work to block broadcast storms caused by a faulty network interface card (NIC) and prevent an application from propagating the storms throughout the entire internetwork. Those evils can still happen on the VLAN where the problem originated, but the disease is just quarantined to that one ailing VLAN.

Another advantage is that when a VLAN gets too big, you can create more VLANs to keep the broadcasts from consuming too much bandwidth—the fewer users in a VLAN, the fewer users affected by broadcasts. This is well and good, but you absolutely need to keep network services in mind and understand how the users connect to these services when you create your VLAN. It's a good move to try and keep all services—except for the e-mail and Internet access that everyone needs—local to all users whenever possible.

To understand how a VLAN looks to a switch, it's helpful to begin by first looking at a traditional network. Figure 2.13 shows how a network was created by connecting physical LANs using hubs to a router.

In Figure 2.13, you can see that each network was attached with a hub port to the router. (Each segment also had its own logical network number, though this is not obvious from the figure.) Each node attached to a particular physical network had to match that network number in order to be able to communicate on the internetwork. Notice that each department had its own LAN, so if you needed to add new users to Sales, for example, you would just plug them into the Sales LAN, and they would automatically be part of the Sales collision and broadcast domain. This design really worked well for many years.

FIGURE 2.13 Physical LANs connected to a router in a traditional network

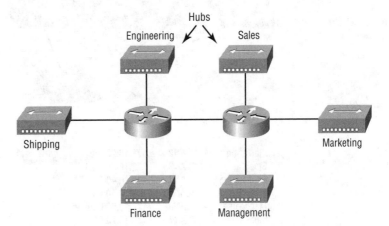

But this design has one major flaw: What happens if the hub for Sales is full and you need to add another user to the Sales LAN? Or, what do you do if there's no more physical space in the location where the Sales team is located for this new employee? Well, let's say there just happens to be plenty of room in the Finance section of the building. That new Sales team member will just have to sit on the same side of the building as the Finance people, and you'll just plug the poor soul into the hub for Finance.

Doing this obviously makes that the new user part of the Finance LAN, which is bad for many reasons. First and foremost, you now have a security issue because this new user is a member of the Finance broadcast domain and can therefore see all the same servers and network services that all of the Finance folks can. Second, for this user to access the Sales network services he or she needs to get the job done, they would need to go through the router to log in to the Sales server—not exactly efficient!

Now let's look at what a switch accomplishes. Figure 2.14 demonstrates how switches remove the physical boundary to solve this problem.

Figure 2.14 shows how six VLANs (numbered 2 through 7) are used to create a broadcast domain for each department. Each switch port is then administratively assigned a VLAN membership, depending on the host and which broadcast domain it must be in.

FIGURE 2.14 Switches removing the physical boundary

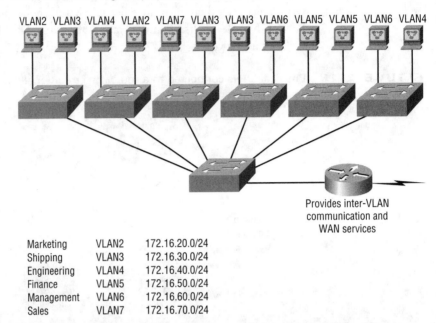

Marketing	VLAN2	172.16.20.0/24	
Shipping	VLAN3	172.16.30.0/24	
Engineering	VLAN4	172.16.40.0/24	
Finance	VLAN5	172.16.50.0/24	
Management	VLAN6	172.16.60.0/24	
Sales	VLAN7	172.16.70.0/24	

So now, if you need to add another user to the Sales VLAN (VLAN 7), you can just assign the port needed to VLAN 7, regardless of where the new Sales team member is physically located—nice! This illustrates one of the sweetest advantages to designing your network with VLANs over the old collapsed backbone design. Now, cleanly and simply, each host that needs to be in the Sales VLAN is merely assigned to VLAN 7.

Notice that the VLAN numbers start with VLAN number 2. The number is irrelevant, but you might be wondering, what happened to VLAN 1? VLAN 1 is an administrative VLAN, and even though it can be used for a workgroup, Cisco recommends that you use this for administrative purposes only. You can't delete or change the name of VLAN 1, and by default, all ports on a switch are members of VLAN 1 until you change them.

Each VLAN is considered a broadcast domain, so it must also have its own subnet number, as illustrated in Figure 2.14. And if you're also using Internetwork Packet Exchange (IPX), then each VLAN must also be assigned its own IPX network number.

Now let's get back to that "because of switches, you don't need routers anymore" misconception. In Figure 2.14, notice that there are seven VLANs or broadcast domains, counting VLAN 1. The nodes within each VLAN can communicate with each other, but not with anything in a different VLAN, because the nodes in any given VLAN "think" that they're actually in a collapsed backbone as in Figure 2.13.

And what handy little tool do you need to enable the hosts in Figure 2.13 to communicate to a node or host on a different network? You guessed it— a router! Those nodes positively need to go through a router—or some other Layer 3 device—just like when they're configured for VLAN communication (as you can see in Figure 2.14). It's the same as if you were trying to connect different physical networks. Communication between VLANs must go through a Layer 3 device, so don't expect routers to disappear any time soon! However, a lot of work can be done with Layer 3 switches, which you'll learn more about in a minute.

VLAN Memberships

VLANs are usually created by an administrator, who then assigns switch ports to each VLAN. These are called *static VLANs*. If the administrator wants to do a little more work up front and assign all the host devices' hardware addresses into a database, the switches can be configured to assign VLANs dynamically whenever a host is plugged into a switch.

Static VLANs

Static VLANs are the usual way of creating VLANs, and they're also the most secure. The switch port that you assign a VLAN association always maintains that association until an administrator manually changes that port assignment.

This type of VLAN configuration is comparatively easy to set up and monitor, and it works well in a network where the movement of users within the network is controlled. And, although it can be helpful to use network management software to configure the ports, it's not mandatory.

In Figure 2.14, each switch port is configured with a VLAN membership by an administrator based on which VLAN the host needed to be a member of; the device's actual physical location doesn't matter. The broadcast domain that the hosts become a member of is an administrative choice. Remember that each host must also have the correct IP address information. For example, each host in VLAN 2 must be configured into the 172.16.20.0/24 network. It's also important to remember that if you plug a host into a switch, you must verify the VLAN membership of that port. If the membership is different than what is needed for that host, then the host will not be able to reach the needed network services, like a workgroup server, for example.

Dynamic VLANs

Dynamic VLANs determine a node's VLAN assignment automatically. Using intelligent management software, you can enable hardware (MAC) addresses, protocols, or even applications to create dynamic VLANs. It's up to you! For example, suppose MAC addresses have been entered into a centralized VLAN management application. If a node is then attached to an unassigned switch port, the VLAN management database can look up the hardware address and assign and configure the switch port to the correct VLAN. This is very cool—it makes management and configuration easier because if a user moves, the switch assigns them to the correct VLAN automatically. But you have to do a lot more work initially setting up the database.

Cisco administrators can use the VLAN Management Policy Server (VMPS) service to set up a database of MAC addresses that can be used for the dynamic addressing of VLANs. A VMPS database maps MAC addresses to VLANs.

Identifying VLANs

As frames are switched throughout the internetwork, switches must be able to keep track of all the different frame types, plus understand what to do with them depending on the hardware address. And remember, frames are handled differently according to the type of link they are traversing. There are two different types of links in a switched environment:

Access links   This type of link is only part of one VLAN and it's referred to as the *native VLAN* of the port. Any device attached to an access link is unaware of a VLAN membership—the device just assumes it's part of a broadcast domain, but it has no understanding of the physical network.

Switches remove any VLAN information from the frame before it's sent to an access link device. Access link devices cannot communicate with devices outside their VLAN unless the packet is routed through a router.

Trunk links   Trunks can carry multiple VLANs and originally got their name from the telephone system trunks that carry multiple telephone conversations.

Trunk links are 100Mbps or 1000Mbps point-to-point links between two switches, between a switch and router, or between a switch and server. They carry the traffic of multiple VLANs—from 1 to 1005 at a time. You can't run them on 10Mbps links.

Trunking allows you to make a single port part of multiple VLANs at the same time. This can be a real advantage. For instance, you can actually set things up to have a server in two broadcast domains simultaneously so that your users won't have to cross a Layer 3 device (router) to log in and access it. Another benefit to trunking is when you're connecting switches. Trunk links can carry some or all VLAN information across the link, but if the links between your switches aren't trunked, only VLAN 1 information is switched across the link by default. This is why all VLANs are configured on a trunked link unless cleared by an administrator by hand.

Figure 2.15 shows how the different links are used in a switched network. Both switches can communicate to all VLANs because of the trunk link between them. And remember, using an access link only allows one VLAN to be used between switches. As you can see, these hosts are using access links to connect to the switch, so that means they're communicating in one VLAN only.

FIGURE 2.15   Access and trunk links in a switched network

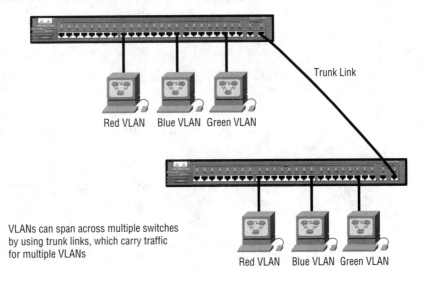

Trunk Link

Red VLAN   Blue VLAN   Green VLAN

VLANs can span across multiple switches
by using trunk links, which carry traffic
for multiple VLANs

Red VLAN   Blue VLAN   Green VLAN

Frame Tagging

You can also create your VLANs to span more than one connected switch. In Figure 2.12, hosts from various VLANs are spread across many switches. This flexible, power-packed capability is probably the main advantage to implementing VLANs!

But this can get kind of complicated—even for a switch—so there needs to be a way for each switch to keep track of all the users and frames as they travel the switch fabric and VLANs. (Remember that a switch fabric is a group of switches sharing the same VLAN information.) This is where *frame tagging* comes in. This frame identification method uniquely assigns a user-defined ID to each frame. Sometimes people refer to it as a *VLAN ID* or *color*.

Here's how it works: Each switch that the frame reaches must first identify the VLAN ID from the frame tag. Then it finds out what to do with the frame by looking at the information in the filter table. If the frame reaches a switch that has another trunked link, the frame is forwarded out the trunk link port.

Once the frame reaches an exit to an access link, the switch removes the VLAN identifier. This is so the destination device can receive the frames without having to understand their VLAN identification.

VLAN Identification Methods

So VLAN identification is what switches use to keep track of all those frames as they're traversing a switch fabric. It's how switches identify which frames belong to which VLANs.

There's more than one trunking method:

IEEE 802.1q Created by the IEEE as a standard method of frame tagging, 802.1q actually inserts a field into the frame to identify the VLAN. If you're trunking between a Cisco switched link and a different brand of switch, you have to use 802.1q for the trunk to work.

The basic purpose of ISL and 802.1q frame-tagging methods is to provide interswitch VLAN communication.

LAN emulation (LANE) LANE is used to communicate multiple VLANs over ATM.

802.10 (FDDI)   Employed for sending VLAN information over FDDI, 802.10 uses a SAID field in the frame header to identify the VLAN. This is also proprietary to Cisco devices.

There's one other trunking method you must know about. It's the Inter-Switch Link (ISL) protocol.

Inter-Switch Link (ISL) Protocol

The Inter-Switch Link (ISL) protocol is proprietary to Cisco switches, and it's used for Fast Ethernet and Gigabit Ethernet links only. ISL routing can be used on a switch port, on router interfaces, and on server interface cards to trunk a server. This is a very good approach if you're creating functional VLANs and you don't want to break the 80/20 rule. A trunked server is part of all VLANs (broadcast domains) simultaneously, so users don't have to cross a Layer 3 device to access it.

ISL is a way of explicitly tagging VLAN information onto an Ethernet frame. This tagging information allows VLANs to be multiplexed over a trunk link through an external encapsulation method, which allows the switch to identify the VLAN membership of a frame over the trunked link.

By running ISL, you can interconnect multiple switches and still maintain VLAN information as traffic travels between switches on trunk links. ISL provides a low-latency, full wire-speed performance, in contrast to Fast Ethernet, which uses either half- or full-duplex mode.

Cisco created the ISL protocol, and so it's proprietary in nature to Cisco devices only. If you need a non-proprietary VLAN protocol, use the 802.1q described in the Sybex *CCNP: Switching Study Guide*.

Anyway, ISL is an external tagging process, which means the original frame isn't altered—it's only encapsulated with a new 26-byte ISL header. It also adds a second four-byte frame check sequence (FCS) field at the end of the frame. Because the frame has been encapsulated by ISL with information, only ISL-aware devices can read it. These frames can be up to a whopping 1,522 bytes long, and devices that receive them may record them as a giant frame because it's over the maximum of 1,518 bytes allowed on an Ethernet segment.

On multi-VLAN (trunk) ports, each frame is tagged as it enters the switch. ISL NICs allow servers to send and receive frames tagged with multiple VLANs so they can traverse multiple VLANs without going through a router. This is good because it reduces latency. ISL makes it easy for users to access servers quickly and efficiently without having to go through a router every time they need to communicate with a resource. This technology can also be used with probes and certain network analyzers, and administrators can use it to include file servers in multiple VLANs simultaneously.

ISL VLAN information is added to a frame only if the frame is forwarded out a port configured as a trunk link. The ISL encapsulation is removed from the frame if the frame is forwarded out an access link. This is an important ISL fact, so make a mental note and don't forget it!

Layer 3 (L3) Switching

Tra-di-tion, Tra-di-tion! Can't you just hear the song from "Fiddler on the Roof"? Well, tradition is the foundation that you build today upon. That unfortunately means changes in the tradition itself. But before changing a tradition, carefully consider all your options. If you tweak that handed-down pumpkin pie recipe too much, you'll hear from Uncle Jack or Cousin Gertrude next Thanksgiving.

LAN switches have been L2 devices from the beginning. Modern L3 switches provide higher OSI-level functionalities and can replace routers in the LAN switched environment. Your choice of pure L2 or L3 switches in the enterprise network is no small matter and requires a complete understanding of your network topology and customer needs.

The simple function of an L3 device is to separate network segments. Traditionally, the L3 device was a router. Today, network designers prefer an L3 switch. These two devices differ in the type of information they process to determine the output interface. L2 switching forwards frames based on Data Link layer information (MAC address), while L3 switching forwards frames based on Network layer information (IP address).

A single- or two-L2 broadcast domain backbone isn't a great solution for large enterprise networks. A better choice for the campus backbone is L3 switches due to scalability and flexibility issues. L3-switched campus backbones are preferred over the L2 backbone for many reasons, including:

- Large scalability potential

- Reduced number of connections between L3 switches. Each L3 distribution switch (router) connects to one L3 campus backbone switch.

This simplifies any-to-any connectivity between distribution and backbone switches.

- Flexible topology with no spanning-tree loops. There is no L2 switching either in the backbone or on the distribution links to the backbone because all the links are routed. Arbitrary topologies are supported because of the routing protocol used in the backbone.

- Better support for network services because of L3 support in the backbone switches.

- Multicast and broadcast control. If you have a Layer 2 backbone, you have to create multiple VLANs to provide any type of broadcast control.

One of the many things to consider for the L3 backbone switches is the performance of L3 switching. L3 switches require more sophisticated devices for high-speed packet routing. L3 switches support routing in the hardware, although the hardware in your network may not support all its features. If a certain feature is not supported in the hardware, it must be performed in software, which may impinge on data transfer. Other issues surround QoS and access list support. Hardware cannot process QoS tables or security tables if they consist of too many entries. These limitations will degrade the L3 switch's performance. And better performance was your goal for using the L3 switch in the first place! If you're experiencing excessive broadcasts on your corporate LANs, the best solution is to add L3 switching where appropriate and create VLANs.

In addition, an L3 switch uses a route processor, where an L2 switch uses an ASIC chip to make forward/filter decisions.

Full-Duplex Ethernet

Full-duplex Ethernet can both transmit and receive simultaneously, but the node requires a dedicated switch port, not a hub, to be able to do so.

Full-duplex Ethernet uses point-to-point connections and is typically referred to as *collision-free* since it doesn't share bandwidth with any other devices. Frames sent by two nodes cannot collide because there are physically separate transmitting and receiving circuits between the nodes.

If you have a full-duplex 10Mbps Ethernet operating bidirectionally on the same switch port, you can theoretically have 20Mbps aggregate throughput.

Full-duplex Ethernet can now be used in 10BaseT, 100BaseT, and 100BaseFL media, but all devices (NICs, for example) must be able to support full-duplex transmission.

Half-Duplex Ethernet Design

Figure 2.16 illustrates the circuitry involved in *half-duplex* Ethernet. When a station is sending to another station, the transmitting circuitry is active at the transmitting station, and the receiving circuitry is active at the receiving station. This uses a single cable similar to a narrow one-way bridge.

FIGURE 2.16 Half-duplex circuitry

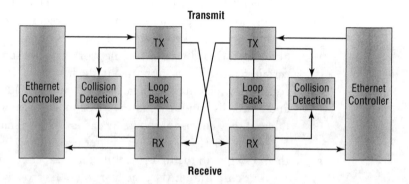

Full-Duplex Ethernet Design

Figure 2.17 illustrates full-duplex circuitry. Full-duplex Ethernet switch technology (FDES) provides a point-to-point connection between the transmitter of the transmitting station and the receiver of the receiving station. Half-duplex, standard Ethernet can usually provide up to 60 percent of the bandwidth available. In contrast, full-duplex Ethernet can provide a full 100 percent because it can transmit and receive simultaneously and because collisions don't occur.

In order to run full-duplex Ethernet, you must have the following:

- Two 10Mbps or 100Mbps paths

- Full-duplex NICs

- Loopback and collision detection disabled

- Software drivers supporting two simultaneous data paths

- Adherence to Ethernet distance standards

- 10BaseT/100BaseT: 100 meters

- 10BaseFL/100BaseFL: 2 kilometers

FIGURE 2.17   Full-duplex circuitry

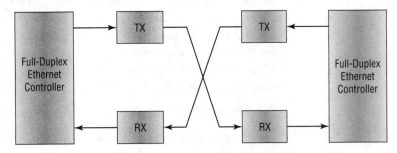

100BaseT Fast Ethernet

In 1995, the IEEE approved the IEEE 802.3u, the 100BaseT Ethernet standard. It defines the Physical and Data Link layers, uses the Carrier Sense Multiple Access with Collision Detection (CSMA/CD) protocol, and is 10 times faster than 10BaseT. Some of the new technology stars are:

100BaseFX   100BaseFX is Ethernet over fiber-optic cable at 100Mbps using 802.3 specs. It uses a two-strand, 50/125-micron or 62.5/125-micron multimode fiber-optic cable.

100BaseT4   100BaseT4 uses 802.3 specs, 100Mbps over Category 3, 4, or 5 cabling with a standard RJ-45 connector.

100BaseTX   100BaseTX is Fast Ethernet over Category 5 cabling. It's compatible with, and adheres to, 802.3 specifications. It can also use two-pair, 100-ohm shielded twisted-pair (STP) cable or Type 1 STP cable.

100BaseX   100BaseX refers to either the 100BaseTX or 100BaseFX media. This standard was approved to ensure compatibility between the Ethernet CSMA/CD and ANSI X3T9.5 standard.

100VG AnyLan 100VG AnyLan is IEEE movement into Fast Ethernet and Token Ring that appears to be going nowhere fast, mostly because it's not compatible with the 802.3 standards and Cisco doesn't support it.

The Advantages of Fast Ethernet

Migrating or upgrading to 100BaseT from 10BaseT can substantially improve network throughput and overall performance. Because 100BaseT uses the same signaling techniques as 10BaseT, a gradual migration to 100BaseT doesn't have to be expensive or time-consuming. Partially converting your LAN is a viable alternative to converting all clients simultaneously. The advantages of 100BaseT over 10BaseT are as follows:

- 100BaseT has 10 times the performance of 10BaseT.

- Existing cabling and network equipment can be used.

- 100BaseT can use 10Mbps and 100Mbps together.

- 100BaseT uses tried-and-true CSMA/CD technology.

- Migration is easy.

And now, the catch: There can be some cost involved in replacing old NICs with new 10/100 cards, and it's possible that rewiring the building or floor might be necessary if the existing equipment is too old and doesn't meet the 100BaseT specifications.

100BaseT Specifications

100BaseT networks use the same time slots that 10BaseT networks do. What is meant by "time slots"? Time slots require a station to transmit all its bits before another station can transmit its packet. For 100BaseT networks to transmit in the same time slots, the distance must be reduced. This means that instead of the 5-4-3 rule that the standard Ethernet uses (5 network segments, 4 repeaters, only 3 segments populated) you can use only two Class II repeaters in a 100BaseT network. The timing in Fast Ethernet is shorter (10 percent of Ethernet). The maximum frame size (time slot) is 1,518 bytes. The physical distance is reduced because both Fast Ethernet and regular Ethernet specifications state that the round-trip time must not exceed 512 bit times. Since Fast Ethernet transmits faster, a signal of 512 bits covers a shorter distance.

100BaseT Repeaters

You can still use repeaters in your network to extend the distance of your shared Ethernet network, or in switches with dedicated segments. Repeaters can actually reduce 100BaseFX maximum distances, because the repeater delays eat up the timing budget. This repeater will, however, extend 100BaseTX distances. The different types of repeaters available are

Class I A translational repeater that can support both 100BaseX and 100BaseT4 signaling. The allowable delay for a Class I repeater is 140 bit times.

Class II A transparent repeater has shorter propagation delay, but supports *either* 100BaseX *or* 100BaseT4, not both at the same time. The allowable delay for a Class II repeater is only 92 bit times.

FastHub 300 A repeater compatible with the IEEE 802.3u standard for Fast Ethernet. The FastHub 300 delivers 10 times the performance of a 10BaseT hub.

Table 2.1 shows the cable type, the connector type, and the maximum distance between end nodes.

TABLE 2.1 Cable Type, Connector Type, and Maximum Distance between End Nodes

Port Type	Cable	Connector Type	Distance
100BaseTX	Category 5	RJ 45	100 meters
100BaseFX	50/125 or 62.5/125	SC/ST/MIC	512 meters. Half-duplex restricted to 512 meters. No restrictions for full-duplex. (Distance restrictions due to signal attenuation still apply.)

Table 2.2 shows the maximum distance between end nodes with repeaters.

TABLE 2.2 Maximum Distance between End Nodes with Repeaters

Standard or Repeater Type	Number of Repeaters	UTP Medium	UTP and Fiber Media (TX/FX)
802.3u	One Class I repeater	200 meters	261 meters
	One Class II repeater	200 meters	308 meters
	Two Class II repeaters	205 meters	216 meters
FastHub 300	One Class II repeater	200 meters	318 meters
	Two Class II repeaters	223 meters	236 meters
FastHub 300, plus one third-party 100BaseT class II repeater	Two Class II repeaters	214 meters	226 meters

Summary

This chapter explained the differences between cut-through, store-and-forward, and FragmentFree switching. Cut-through switching provides for low latency but is prone to forwarding errors. Store-and-forward switching eliminates the errors at Layer 2 but has the highest latency. FragmentFree switching reads the first 64 bytes of the frame and has moderate latency and error detection.

Full- and half-duplex Ethernet have differing requirements. Full-duplex Ethernet requires compatible network cards and switched networks but can provide for more bandwidth. Half-duplex Ethernet was originally designed into many networks and only requires hubs.

Fast Ethernet doubles the bandwidth of Ethernet but requires cabling that meets the 100Base specification. However, Fast Ethernet does have distance limitations due to attenuation.

The Spanning-Tree Protocol (STP) was developed to eliminate loops between bridges and switches. Physical loops are often designed into the network for redundancy, but these loops can cause traffic and broadcast problems during operation. STP uses the spanning-tree algorithm (STA) to locate the loops and eliminate them by calculating a best path to the root bridge or switch.

VLANs allow for logical groupings, simplified changes, broadcast control, and security. Layer 3 routing is required for traffic to move between VLANs, and frame tagging is used to track VLAN traffic between network switches.

Exam Essentials

Remember the advantages of segmenting your LAN with switches. Know that most network congestion problems are related to too many hosts on a particular network segment. Switches provide for the segmentation of hosts and a less congested network design.

Know the reasons to segment your LAN with bridges. Bridges are an earlier form of a switch with fewer ports to segment groups of hosts instead of individual hosts, but they still provide the segmentation for a less congested network design.

Understand the placement of routers in your network design. Routers operate at the Network layer and control network broadcasts. A properly routed network creates a more efficient design and less network traffic at each NIC or device.

Understand the difference between a Layer 2 switch and a Layer 3 switch. The Layer 2 (L2) switch makes forward/filter decisions based on hardware (MAC) address. The Layer 3 (L3) switch uses a route processor if packets are forwarded to another remote network.

Understand the advantages of using a Layer 3 backbone over a Layer 2 backbone. By using a Layer 3 backbone you can reduce the number of connections between switches and scale to a large size all while keeping your broadcasts under control.

Remember the three LAN switch methods and the benefits of each.
The three LAN switch methods are cut-through, store-and-forward, and FragmentFree. Cut-through switching waits for the destination hardware address only before forwarding the frame (low latency). Store-and-forward switching waits for the entire frame. A CRC is run, and then the switch finds the destination port in the MAC filter table and forwards the frame (high latency, fewer errors). FragmentFree switching (also known as modified cut-through) checks the first 64 bytes for fragmentation and then forwards the frame.

Know the differences between half-duplex and full-duplex Ethernet.
When network devices are configured for half-duplex Ethernet, a single line is used to tie the devices together, causing them to share their send and receive times. When devices are configured for full-duplex Ethernet, they can send and receive simultaneously using parallel lines.

Understand the operation and benefits of the Spanning-Tree Protocol.
The Spanning-Tree Protocol (STP) uses the spanning-tree algorithm (STA) to find redundant paths to a root bridge or switch and to eliminate the loops between two or more network segments.

Key Terms

Before you take the exam, be certain you are familiar with the following terms:

20/80 rule	cut-through
80/20 rule	cyclic redundancy check (CRC)
Bridge Protocol Data Unit (Bpdu)	data frames
bridges	Data Link layer
broadcast domains	dynamic VLANs
broadcast storm	Ethernet
collision domain	Fast Ethernet
collision window	flat network

FragmentFree	repeaters
frame filtering	routers
frame tagging	spanning-tree algorithm (STA)
full-duplex	Spanning-Tree Protocol (STP)
half-duplex	static VLANs
hubs	store-and-forward
MAC address	switch fabric
native VLAN	switches
Network layer	thrashing
network segmentation	virtual local area networks (VLANs)

Written Lab

Answer the following questions about switching methods:

1. Which LAN switch method has the highest latency?

2. Which LAN switch method only reads the hardware destination address before forwarding the frame?

3. What is used at Layer 2 to prevent switching loops?

4. Which LAN switch method receives the complete frame before beginning to forward it?

5. Which two LAN switch methods have a constant latency?

6. Which LAN switch method is also known as modified cut-through?

7. What is used to prevent switching loops in a network with redundant switched paths?

8. Which LAN switch method runs a CRC on every frame the switch receives?

The answers to the Written Lab can be found following the answers to the Review Questions for this chapter.

Review Questions

1. What is one advantage of using switches instead of hubs at a customer location?

   A. Each port in a switch creates its own broadcast domain.

   B. Each port in a switch creates its own collision domain.

   C. Each port in a switch creates its own broadcast and collision domains.

   D. It depends on the type of servers.

2. Your customer asks you why they should upgrade to Fast Ethernet. After you tell the customer it is 10 times faster, they ask what are the disadvantages of upgrading. What do you tell them?

   A. Installation difficulty.

   B. Expense.

   C. The physical distance.

   D. There are no disadvantages.

3. You have excessive broadcasts on your customer's LANs. What solutions would benefit the customer? (Choose all that apply.)

   A. Adding more hubs

   B. Adding Layer 3 switching

   C. Creating VLANs

   D. Using more routers

4. Which of the following is a characteristic of a switch, but not of an active hub?

   A. Switches forward packets based on the IPX or IP address in the frame.

   B. Switches forward packets based only on the IP address in the packet.

   C. Switches forward packets based on the IP address in the frame.

   D. Switches forward packets based on the MAC address in the frame.

5. How does the cut-through switching technique work?

   A. The LAN switch copies the entire frame into its on-board buffers and then looks up the destination address in its forwarding (switching) table and determines the outgoing interface.

   B. The switch waits only for the header to be received before it checks the destination address and starts forwarding the packets.

   C. Cut-through switching uses broadcast addresses as source addresses.

   D. Cut-through switching uses a Class II repeater in a collision domain.

6. How do switches use the store-and-forward switching technique?

   A. The switch waits only for the header to be received before it checks the destination address and starts forwarding the packets.

   B. The LAN switch copies the entire frame into its on-board buffers and then looks up the destination address in its forwarding (switching) table and determines the outgoing interface.

   C. The switch uses a Class II repeater in a collision domain.

   D. The switch uses broadcast addresses as source addresses.

7. Which of the following are needed to support full-duplex Ethernet? (Choose all that apply.)

   A. Multiple paths between multiple stations on a link

   B. Full-duplex NICs

   C. Loopback and collision detection disabled

   D. Automatic detection of full-duplex operation by all connected stations

8. Which of the following are not used by full-duplex Ethernet? (Choose all that apply.)

   A. Collision detection

   B. MAC addressing

   C. 10-megabit transmission

   D. Loopback

9. You are creating VLANs at your customer location. The manager comes by to ask why and reminds you of your statement that spending money on switches would solve all their problems. What do you tell her? (Choose all that apply.)

    A. You need to break up the collision domains.

    B. You need to break up the broadcast domains.

    C. VLANs help to extend the time-to-live in the IP header.

    D. Security between departments can be accomplished with VLANs since no traffic leaves a VLAN unless it is first routed.

10. Which of the following are among the advantages of creating VLANs? (Choose all that apply.)

    A. Datagram filtering

    B. Breaking up broadcast domains

    C. Creating networks by function rather than by location

    D. Long time-to-live packet control when using IP

11. Which two of the following statements describe frame tagging?

    A. Frame tagging examines particular info about each frame.

    B. An ID is placed in the header of each frame as it traverses the switch fabric.

    C. A user-assigned ID is added to each frame.

    D. Filter tables are built as part of frame tagging.

12. Which of the following statements describes a full-duplex transmission?

    A. Full-duplex transmission uses a single cable.

    B. Full-duplex transmission uses a point-to-point connection from the transmitter of the transmitting station to the receiver of the receiving station.

    C. Full-duplex transmission involves data transmission in both directions, but only one direction at a time.

    D. Full-duplex transmission involves data transmission in only one direction.

13. If a frame is received at a switch and only the destination hardware address is read before the frame is forwarded, what type of switching method are you using?

   A. Cut-through

   B. Store-and-forward

   C. Store-and-cut

   D. FragmentFree

14. Which two Layer 2 features are used on Cisco switches to optimize multicast?

   A. OSPF Multicast

   B. CGMP

   C. Multicast IP forwarding

   D. IGMP snooping

15. Which of the following statements is true for the store-and-forward switching method?

   A. It is the default switching method for all Cisco switches.

   B. It only reads the destination hardware address before forwarding the frame.

   C. Latency varies depending on frame length.

   D. Latency is constant.

16. What does the spanning-tree algorithm (STA) do?

   A. STA is implemented by STP to prevent loops.

   B. STA forwards packets through a switch.

   C. STA restores lost frames.

   D. STA prevents API duplication in bridged networks.

17. What are three advantages of a Layer 3 backbone over a Layer 2 backbone?

    A. Reducing the number of connections between L3 switches (peering)

    B. Multiple spanning-tree instances

    C. Scalability to a very large size

    D. Multicast and broadcast control on the backbone

18. What is the IEEE specification for the Spanning-Tree Protocol (STP)?

    A. 802.2u

    B. 802.3q

    C. 802.1d

    D. 802.6

19. A Layer 3 switch transmits data outside the source network by using which of the following?

    A. Bridging tables

    B. EIGRP tables

    C. Route processors

    D. RIP

20. Of the three switching types, which one has the highest latency?

    A. Cut-through

    B. FragmentFree

    C. Store-and-forward

    D. Store-and-cut

Answers to Review Questions

1. B.   Individual collision domains per switch port provide for a more efficient network design. Hubs create a flat network design and can be very inefficient since workstations must share the bandwidth.

2. C.   The timing in Fast Ethernet is shorter (10 times faster than 10Mbps Ethernet). The maximum frame size (time slot) is 1,518 bytes. The physical distance is reduced because both Fast Ethernet and regular Ethernet specifications state that the round-trip time must not exceed 512 bit times. Since Fast Ethernet transmits faster, a signal of 512 bits covers a shorter distance.

3. B, C.   By using a combination of Layer 3 switches and VLANs, you can break up broadcast domains and create more bandwidth where needed.

4. D.   A switch forwards packets based on the MAC address of the frame; an active hub only repeats signals.

5. B.   After the first 64 bytes are received and checked for fragments, the frame is forwarded to the destination hardware address.

6. B.   Store-and-forward switching has the highest latency but provides for the most error-free network design.

7. B, C.   Most NICs support full-duplex configuration, which disables loopback and collision detection.

8. A, D.   When an NIC is configured for full-duplex Ethernet, the collision detection and loopback are disabled.

9. B, D.   VLANs are a configuration option available in switches, and they allow further control of network traffic.

10. B, C.   When VLANs are used to control broadcast traffic, the need for routers is reduced. VLANs also serve the purpose of controlling traffic regardless of the physical port connection in the switch fabric.

11. B, C.   Two methods of identifying a frame as it moves throughout the switch fabric are adding a VLAN ID to each frame and adding a user-assigned ID to each frame.

12. B.   Using multiple parallel lines, full-duplex transmission allows for simultaneous transmit and receive paths.

13. A. Cut-through switching is the fastest of the switching types but is more likely to forward fragmented or damaged frames.

14. B, D. One problem is that the default for an L2 switch is to forward all multicast traffic to every port that belongs to the same VLAN on the switch. The commonly used solutions are Cisco Group Management Protocol (CGMP) and IGMP snooping.

15. C. Although store-and-forward has the highest latency of the switching methods, it checks the entire contents of each frame, thus providing for error-free delivery.

16. A. The spanning-tree algorithm calculates the best path from each bridge or switch port to a root bridge or switch and provides for loop-free networks.

17. A, C, D. By using an L3 switching backbone over an L2 backbone you can reduce the number of connections between backbone switches; this process is called peering. Since it is Layer 3, STP is not used. In addition, you can scale to a very large size and provide broadcast control, which is not possible in an L2 backbone without creating multiple VLANs.

18. C. 802.1d is the IEEE specification for STP.

19. C. A Layer 3 switch uses a route processor to determine how a packet is forwarded outside the source network. A Layer 2 switch uses a MAC address table to create forward/filter decisions.

20. C. Store-and-forward is the slowest of the switching methods, but it provides for error detection.

Answers to Written Lab

1. Store-and-forward

2. Cut-through

3. Spanning-Tree Protocol (STP)

4. Store-and-forward

5. Cut-through, FragmentFree

6. FragmentFree

7. Spanning-Tree Protocol (STP)

8. Store-and-forward

Chapter

3

Network Protocols

CCDA EXAM TOPICS COVERED IN THIS CHAPTER:

✓ Given a network design or set of requirements evaluate a solution that meets IP addressing needs.

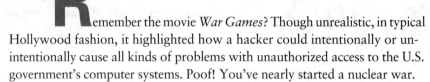

Remember the movie *War Games*? Though unrealistic, in typical Hollywood fashion, it highlighted how a hacker could intentionally or unintentionally cause all kinds of problems with unauthorized access to the U.S. government's computer systems. Poof! You've nearly started a nuclear war.

The *Transmission Control Protocol (TCP)/Internet Protocol (IP)* was created by the Department of Defense (DOD) as a protocol to ensure data integrity and maintain communications in the event of catastrophic war. TCP/IP is the protocol of choice today for many networks including the Internet. When designed and implemented correctly, a TCP/IP network can be a very dependable and resilient one, unlike the system in the *War Games* movie. This chapter will explain everything you need to know about TCP/IP.

This chapter also looks at Internetwork Packet Exchange (IPX), a protocol that is still widely deployed in many internetworks. We will describe the operation of IPX and compare it to the OSI reference model and addressing scheme.

The main topics addressed in this chapter are:

- Describe the TCP/IP *protocol* and describe the difference between connection-oriented and connectionless protocols.

- Identify the methods commonly used to resolve host names to IP addresses and IP addresses to MAC addresses.

- Describe the Novell IPX protocol and the basics of network and client services.

TCP/IP

Remember our discussion in Chapter 1 covering the OSI model? Well, the DOD model, upon which TCP/IP is based, is a condensed version of the OSI model. It comprises four, instead of seven, layers:

- Process/Application

- Host-to-Host

- Internet

- Network Access

Figure 3.1 compares the four-layer DOD model and the seven-layer OSI reference model. As you can see, the two are similar in concept, but each has a different number of layers with different names.

FIGURE 3.1   The DOD model and the OSI model

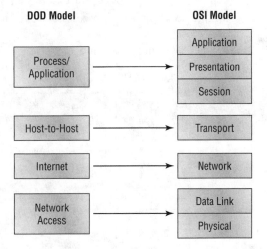

If you were to set the DOD and OSI models side-by-side, here is a snapshot of how their layers would compare. We'll discuss each in more detail as we move through the chapter.

Multiple protocols at the DOD model's Process/Application layer perform the functions described at the OSI model's corresponding top three layers (Session, Presentation, and Application). The Process/Application layer defines protocols for node-to-node application communication and controls user interface specifications.

The Host-to-Host layer parallels the functions of the OSI model's Transport layer, defining protocols for setting up the level of transmission service for applications. It tackles issues like creating reliable end-to-end communication and ensuring the error-free delivery of data. It handles packet sequencing and maintains data integrity.

The Internet layer corresponds to the OSI model's Network layer, designating the protocols relating to the logical transmission of packets over the entire network. It takes care of the addressing of hosts by giving them an IP (Internet

Protocol) address and handles the routing of packets among multiple networks. It also controls the communication flow between two hosts.

At the bottom of the DOD model, the Network Access layer monitors the data exchange between the host and the network. The equivalent of the Data Link and Physical layers of the OSI model, the Network Access layer oversees hardware addressing and defines protocols for the physical transmission of data.

While the DOD and OSI models are alike in design and concept and have similar functions in similar places, *how* those functions occur are different. This difference requires the DOD model to have a very different suite of protocols than those of the OSI model. Figure 3.2 shows the TCP/IP protocol suite and how its protocols relate to the DOD model layers.

FIGURE 3.2 The TCP/IP protocol suite

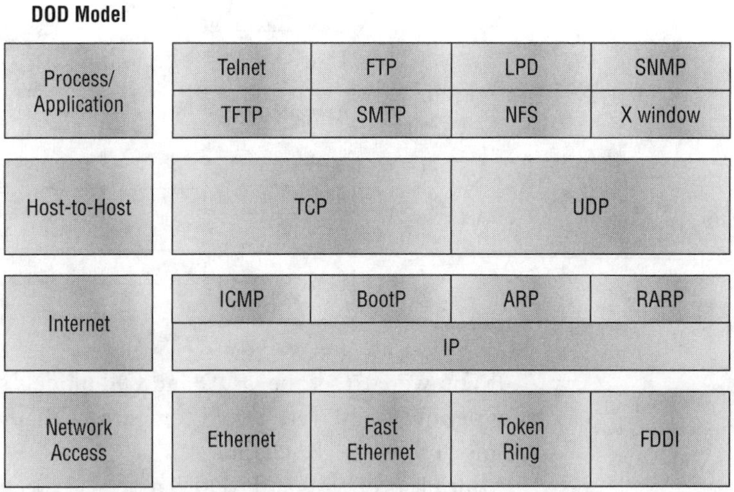

DOD Model

Process/Application	Telnet	FTP	LPD	SNMP
	TFTP	SMTP	NFS	X window
Host-to-Host	TCP		UDP	
Internet	ICMP	BootP	ARP	RARP
	IP			
Network Access	Ethernet	Fast Ethernet	Token Ring	FDDI

Process/Application Layer Protocols

As discussed earlier in this book, one of the design goals of the creators of the Internet was to have applications that could run on different computer platforms, in different places, and yet, somehow, still communicate. A great goal—but difficult to execute because of the sheer number of manufacturers and their designers' and engineers' preferences. In the DOD model, the answer came in the form of Process/Application layer protocols, which address the ability of one application to communicate with another, regardless of hardware platform, operating system, and other features of the two hosts.

Most applications written with TCP/IP protocols can be characterized as *client/server* applications. This means that there are two major parts to the software involved and that they are probably running on at least two different machines.

The server part of this software duo usually runs on the machine where the data actually resides. The server tends to be powerful (or should be), because much of the data processing and storage is done on it. It works like this: The client software sends requests to the server software for it to fulfill. Typical requests might include searches for information, printing, e-mailing, application services, and file transfers.

In addition to communicating with the server, another function of client software is to provide an interface for the user(s) with the information they need. It also permits these users to manipulate the data they've received from the server.

These matters explained, let's move along and investigate the types of protocols that populate the DOD model's Process/Application layer and what they do.

Telnet

The chameleon of protocols, *Telnet*'s specialty is terminal emulation. It allows a user on a remote client machine, called the *Telnet client*, to access the resources of another machine, the *Telnet server*. Telnet achieves this by pulling a fast one on the Telnet server and making the client machine appear as though it were a terminal directly attached to the local network. This projection is actually a *software image*, a virtual terminal that can interact with the chosen remote host. These emulated text-mode terminals can execute refined procedures like displaying menus that allow users to choose options from them and thereby access the applications on the duped server. Users begin a Telnet session by running the Telnet client software and then logging on to the Telnet server.

Telnet's capabilities are limited to running applications or snooping around on the server like a telescope on a submarine. It can't be used for file-sharing functions like downloading information. To actually get the goods, you have to use the next protocol on the list: FTP.

FTP (File Transfer Protocol)

The *File Transfer Protocol (FTP)* is the protocol that actually lets you transfer files; it can facilitate file transfer between any two machines running TCP/IP. But FTP isn't just a protocol—it's also a program. Operating as a protocol, FTP is used by applications. As a program, it is employed by users to perform file tasks by hand. FTP allows access to directories and files and permits certain directory operations, such as relocating into different directories. FTP teams up with Telnet to transparently log you in to the FTP server and then provides for the transfer of files.

When accessing a host through FTP, users must contend with an authentication login secured with passwords and usernames and designed by system administrators to restrict access. You might succeed in gaining access by adopting the username "anonymous," but once in, your access likely will be limited. System administrators rely on their users to choose hard-to-guess passwords to keep out hackers.

Even when being employed by users manually as a program, FTP's functions are limited to listing and manipulating directories, typing file contents, and copying files between hosts. It can't execute remote files as programs.

SMTP (Simple Mail Transfer Protocol)

The *Simple Mail Transfer Protocol (SMTP)*, commonly used to transfer e-mail, employs a spooled (queued) method of mail delivery. Once a message has been sent to a destination, the message is spooled to a device—usually a disk. The server software at the destination posts a vigil, regularly checking this queue for messages. When it detects messages, it delivers them to their destination.

LPD (Line Printer Daemon)

The *Line Printer Daemon (LPD)* protocol is designed for printer sharing. The LPD daemon, along with the LPR (Line Printer) program, allows print jobs to be spooled and sent to the network's printers.

X Window

Designed for client/server operations, *X Window* defines a protocol for the writing of graphical user interface (GUI) based client/server applications. The idea is to allow a program (the client) to run on one computer and display a program (a window server) on another computer.

Host-to-Host Layer Protocols

The Host-to-Host layer's main purpose is to shield the upper layer applications from the complexities of the network and functions like the Transport layer in the OSI model. In fact, the term "Transport layer" is often used interchangeably with Host-to-Host. This layer says to the upper layer, "Just give me your data, with any instructions, and I'll begin the process of getting your information ready for sending." The following sections describe the two main protocols at this layer.

TCP (Transmission Control Protocol)

In elementary school we had "safety monitors" on every floor who watched the hallways for violators during recess and lunch. They had a set of rules and limited authority. For instance, they could send you back to your room to walk the distance again if they caught you running. If your infraction was severe, they reported you to a teacher or even the principal. I tried everything to break the rules without getting caught (kind of like a hacker). Yet they did preserve a kind of order in what could be a chaotic environment.

TCP's role is something like a hall monitor. TCP has been around since networking's early years, when WANs weren't very reliable. It was created to mitigate that problem, so reliability is TCP's strong point. It tests for errors, resends data if necessary, and reports the occurrence of an error to the upper layers if it can't solve the problem itself.

Did you see the same TV documentary I did about the process of moving the famous London Bridge to Havasu City, Nevada? Engineers numbered, disassembled, transported, and reassembled bridge pieces in sequence. Voila! Instant tourist attraction (that I hope doesn't become a Stonehenge that messes up the minds of archeologists in future millennia).

Like the London Bridge move, TCP takes large blocks of information from an application and breaks them down into segments. It numbers and sequences each segment so that the destination's TCP protocol on the receiving end can put the segments back into the order that the application intended. Unlike the bridge process, after these segments have been sent, TCP waits for acknowledgment for each one from the receiving end's TCP, retransmitting the ones that haven't been acknowledged.

Before it starts to send segments down the model, the sender's TCP protocol contacts the destination's TCP protocol in order to establish a connection. What is created is known as a *virtual circuit*. This type of communication is called *connection-oriented*. During this initial handshake, the two TCP layers also agree on the amount of information that's going to be sent before the recipient's TCP sends back an acknowledgment. With everything agreed upon in advance, the path is paved for reliable Application layer communication to take place.

TCP is a full-duplex, connection-oriented, reliable, accurate protocol, and establishing all these terms and conditions, in addition to checking for errors, is no small task. It's very complicated and, not surprisingly, very costly in terms of network overhead. TCP should be used in situations when reliability is of utmost importance.

UDP (User Datagram Protocol)

The *User Datagram Protocol (UDP)* can be used in place of TCP. UDP is the scaled-down economy model, and is considered a *thin protocol*. Like a thin person on a park bench, UDP doesn't take up a lot of room—in this case, on a network. It also doesn't offer all the bells and whistles of TCP, but it does do a fabulous job of transporting information that doesn't require reliable delivery—and it does it using far fewer network resources. (Please note that UDP is covered thoroughly in RFC 768.)

Some situations definitely call for UDP rather than TCP; for instance, when the matter of reliability is already accomplished at the Process/Application layer. Network File System (NFS) handles its own reliability issues, making the use of TCP both impractical and redundant. However, this is decided by the application developer, not by the user who wants to transfer data faster.

UDP receives upper layer blocks of information, instead of streams of data like TCP, and breaks them into segments. Also like TCP, each segment is given a number for reassembly into the intended block at the destination. However, UDP does *not* sequence the segments and does not care in which order the segments arrive at the destination. At least it numbers them. But after that, UDP sends them off and forgets about them. It doesn't follow through, check up on, or even allow for an acknowledgment of safe arrival—complete abandonment. Because of this, it's referred to as an *unreliable protocol*. This does not mean that UDP is ineffective, only that it doesn't handle issues of reliability.

There are more things UDP doesn't do. It doesn't create a virtual circuit, and it doesn't contact the destination before delivering information to it. It is therefore also considered a *connectionless* protocol.

Key Concepts of Host-to-Host Protocols

Table 3.1 highlights some of the key concepts that you should keep in mind regarding these two protocols.

TABLE 3.1 Key Concepts in Comparing TCP and UDP

TCP	UDP
Virtual circuit	Unsequenced
Sequenced	Unreliable
Acknowledgments	Connectionless
Reliable	Low overhead

Connection-Oriented and Connectionless Network Services

This chapter has covered both connection-oriented and connectionless network services in the Transport layer (OSI model) and in the Host-to-Host layer (DOD model). A telephone analogy might help you understand how TCP works. Most of you know that before you speak with someone on a phone, you must first establish a connection with that other person—wherever they might be. This is like a virtual circuit with the TCP protocol. If you were giving someone important information during your conversation, you might ask, "Did you get that?" A query like that is similar to a TCP acknowledgment. From time to time, for various reasons, people also ask, "Are you still there?" They end their conversations with a "goodbye" of some kind, putting closure on the phone call. These types of functions are also done by TCP.

Using UDP, however, is more like sending a postcard. To do that, you don't need to contact the other party first. You simply write your message, address it, and mail it. This is analogous to UDP's connectionless orientation. Since the message on the postcard is probably not urgent, you don't need an acknowledgment of its receipt. Similarly, UDP does not involve acknowledgments.

Internet Layer Protocols

There are two main reasons for the Internet layer's existence: routing and providing a single network interface to the upper layers. None of the upper layer protocols, and none of those on the lower layer, have any functions relating to routing. The complex and important task of routing is the job of the Internet layer. IP (Internet Protocol) essentially *is* the Internet layer. The other protocols found here merely exist to support it. IP contains the "Big Picture" (city map) and could be said to "see all," in that it is aware of all the interconnected networks (roadways). It can do this because all the machines on the network have a software (logical) address called an *IP address*, which is described more thoroughly later in this chapter.

IP looks at each packet's IP address. Then, using a routing table, it decides where a packet is to be sent next, choosing the best path. The Network Access layer protocols at the bottom of the DOD model don't possess IP's enlightened scope of the entire network; they deal only with physical links.

The second reason for the Internet layer is to provide a single network interface to the upper layer protocols. Without this layer, application programmers would need to write "hooks" into every one of their applications for each different Network Access protocol. This would not only be tedious, it would lead to different versions of each application—one for Ethernet, another one for Token Ring, and so on. To prevent this, IP provides one single network interface for the upper layer protocols. That accomplished, it's then the job of IP and the various Network Access protocols to get along and work together.

All network roads don't lead to Rome—they lead to IP. And all the other protocols at this layer, as well as all those at the upper layers, use it. Never forget that. All paths through the DOD model go through IP. The following sections describe the protocols at the Internet layer.

IP (Internet Protocol)

Identifying devices on networks requires answering these two questions:

- Which network is it on?

- What is its ID on that network?

The first answer is the *software*, or *logical address* (the correct street). The second answer is the *hardware address* (the correct mailbox). All hosts on a network have a logical ID called an IP address. This is the software, or logical, address and it contains valuable encoded information that greatly simplifies the complex task of routing. (Please note that IP is discussed in RFC 791.)

IP receives segments from the Host-to-Host layer and fragments them into datagrams (packets). IP also reassembles datagrams back into segments on the receiving side. Each datagram is assigned the IP address of the sender and the IP address of the recipient. Each machine that receives a datagram makes routing decisions based upon the datagram's destination IP address.

ARP (Address Resolution Protocol)

When IP has a datagram to send, it has already been informed by upper layer protocols of the destination's IP address. However, IP must also inform a Network Access protocol, such as Ethernet or Token Ring, of the destination's hardware address. If IP doesn't know the hardware address, it uses the *Address Resolution Protocol (ARP)* to find this information. As IP's detective, ARP interrogates the network by sending out a broadcast asking the machine with the specified IP address to reply with its hardware address. In other words, ARP translates the software (IP) address into a hardware address— for example, the destination machine's Ethernet board address—and from it, deduces its whereabouts.

This hardware address is technically referred to as the *media access control (MAC) address* or physical address. ARP is talked about in detail in the section "IP Address Resolution" later in this chapter.

RARP (Reverse Address Resolution Protocol)

When an IP machine happens to be a diskless machine (like a printer), it has no way of initially knowing its IP address, but it does know its MAC address. The *Reverse Address Resolution Protocol (RARP)* discovers the identity of these machines by sending out a packet that includes its MAC address and a request to be informed of what IP address is assigned to that MAC address. A designated machine, called a *RARP server*, responds with the answer, and the identity crisis is over. RARP uses the information it *does* know about the machine's MAC address to learn its IP address and complete the machine's ID portrait.

Network Access Layer Protocols

Programmers for the DOD model didn't define protocols for the Network Access layer; instead, their focus began at the Internet layer. In fact, this is exactly the quality that makes this model easy to implement on almost any hardware platform. This versatility is also one of the reasons the Internet protocol suite is so popular. Every protocol listed here relates to the physical transmission of data. The following are the Network Access layer's main duties:

- Receiving an IP datagram and framing it into a stream of bits—1s and 0s—for physical transmission. (The information at this layer is called a *frame*.) An example of a protocol that works at this level is CSMA/CD (Carrier Sense, Multiple Access with Collision Detection). Again, the protocol's name indicates its purpose. It checks the cable to see if there's already another PC transmitting (Carrier Sense), allows all computers to share the same bandwidth (Multiple Access), and detects and retransmits collisions (Collision Detection). Essentially, it's the highway patrol of the Network Access layer.

- Specifying the MAC address. Even though the Internet layer determines the destination MAC address, it's the Network Access protocols that actually place the MAC address into the MAC frame.

- Ensuring that the stream of bits making up the frame has been accurately received by calculating a CRC (cyclic redundancy checksum).

- Specifying the access methods to the physical network, such as contention-based for Ethernet (first come, first served), token passing (wait for token before transmitting) for Token Ring and FDDI, and polling (wait to be asked) for IBM mainframes.

- Specifying the physical media, connectors, electrical signaling, and timing rules.

Physical and Logical Addressing

It's important to understand the difference between physical and logical addressing. The names appear to say the same thing, but they don't. The following discussion will help you differentiate between them.

Data Link layer addressing, or physical (hardware) addressing, describes a unique address that is burned into each network interface card (NIC) by the manufacturer. Think of the hardware address like the address to your house. It must be different from the other addresses or your mail just isn't going to get to you. The hardware address is a 48-bit address expressed as 6 bytes, as shown in Figure 3.3. The first 3 bytes, known as the *vendor code*, are given to the manufacturer by the IEEE. The IEEE administers this Organizational Unique Identifier (OUI) so there aren't any duplicate hardware addresses floating around. The second 3 bytes are made up by the manufacturer and are generally part of the serial number of the card.

FIGURE 3.3 MAC addresses

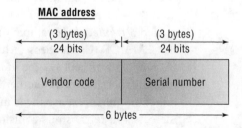

Logical addressing, sometimes referred to as *virtual addressing*, is used at the Network layer and is hierarchical in scheme, unlike physical addresses, which use a flat addressing scheme. The logical address defines more than the house on a street. The logical address can define the country, state, zip code, city, street, street address, and even the name. Examples of protocols that use logical addresses are IP and IPX.

Some of the technologies used to implement the Network Access layer are

- LAN-oriented protocols
  - Ethernet (thick coaxial cable, thin coaxial cable, twisted-pair cable)
  - Fast Ethernet
  - Token Ring
- WAN-oriented protocols
  - Point-to-Point Protocol (PPP)
  - X.25
  - Frame Relay

IP Address Resolution

The process of address resolution involves asking a question and receiving an answer. In the case of IP address resolution, the question posed might be, "Which device is the owner of IP address 172.16.8.8?" The resolution, or answer, to that question would include the MAC address of the NIC, as encoded by the manufacturer. In essence, IP address resolution is the linking of an IP (or software address) to a hardware (or MAC) address.

Regardless of where the ultimate destination is located, ARP always uses a local broadcast to determine where data should be sent. If the destination happens to be on a remote network, the local default gateway's hardware address will be used to hop over to it. Once the mystery address has been resolved, it's recorded in a table called the *ARP cache*. If additional messages are sent to the same destination, the ARP cache will be checked first to prevent unnecessary network traffic generated by a broadcast.

You might also remember the discussion of RARP. Like inductive vs. deductive reasoning, RARP is the inverse operation of ARP; RARP is used to get an IP address from a MAC address. Serial Line Address Resolution Protocol (SLARP) can be used on serial links to resolve network addresses.

Local Resolution

Each subnet of the network can be thought of as an island that contains a city—say, Maui. So long as you never have to leave that island, you've remained local—or as is the case with computers, on the local network.

The process of resolving the IP address of a machine existing on the local network is shown in Figure 3.4 and described following the figure. While reading through these steps, notice how ARP works in a way that minimizes network overhead.

FIGURE 3.4 Resolving a local IP address

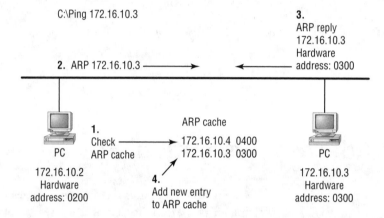

1. The destination machine's IP address is checked to see if it is on the local network. If so, the host system then checks its ARP cache for the machine's hardware address.

2. Provided that the ARP address didn't find 172.16.10.3 in the host system's ARP cache, ARP attempts to enter it by sending a message requesting the IP address's owner to send back its hardware address. Because the hardware address is still unknown, the ARP message is sent out as a broadcast that's read by each and every system on the local network. Like a self-addressed envelope that's sent inscribed with all the information necessary to get it back to its sender, both the IP address and the hardware address of the requesting system are included in the broadcast message.

3. The reply message is sent directly to the hardware address of the requesting system. Only the owner of the requested IP address responds. All other systems disregard the request.

4. Upon receiving the reply, the requesting machine appends the address into its ARP cache. Now you can begin to establish communication.

The ARP Cache

The ARP cache is a table used to store both IP addresses and their corresponding MAC addresses. Each time communication is initiated with another machine, it checks its ARP cache for a matching entry. If it doesn't find one, an ARP request is broadcast, the address is resolved, and the resulting information is then entered into its ARP cache. The address is now handy for the next time communication with that device is necessary, much like an entry in your home address book would be. Additionally, the ARP cache maintains the hardware broadcast address (ffffffffffff) for the local subnet as a permanent entry. Though it doesn't appear when the cache is viewed, this entry exists for the purpose of allowing a host to accept ARP broadcasts.

The ARP system is kind of like jail. Like all ARP entries (IP addresses have both a hardware address and a time stamp), every jail inmate has a number and exit date. In both cases, depending on the entry/inmate's behavior, the time spent "inside" will vary. Though lifetimes aren't definite for inmates, both ARP entries and inmates have them, along with maximum time periods for their duration. Old ARP entries are released early when the ARP cache becomes full, just as older inmates may be released early depending on the jail's capacity. Occasionally, a judge assigns the death penalty or consecutive lifetime sentences to an individual inmate—like making a manual entry into the ARP table. The only time these special inmates are released is when they die (deleted from the ARP cache); a pardon is given, allowing the inmate to begin a new life (restarting the computer); or if the system discovers it has the wrong person (a broadcast notifying ARP of a new, corrected hardware address).

Remote Resolution

When it comes to computer operations, communications are usually much simpler if they involve devices within the local network. But there are exceptions to the rule, and they typically involve a remote location. Complex internetworks with subnets have bridges or routers set up between them that connect them together. These devices are filters that sort data according to its destination—they don't allow all data to cross indiscriminately.

To distinguish which data gets to pass through, routers look at the IP address destination located in the packet's header, whereas bridges look at a frame's header for the destination hardware address. Going back to the subnet island of Maui, let's say you find it necessary to contact someone or something that doesn't reside there, but lives on another island—Molokai. Since those who populate Molokai aren't Maui locals, by attempting to make contact with them, you are attempting remote communication. Let's pretend that to reach them, you must cross a drawbridge. Unless you arrive at the drawbridge with a specific remote Molokai address, the bridge operator will keep the bridge drawn, and you won't be allowed to cross.

Figure 3.5 and the steps immediately following it illustrate the process of resolving the IP address of a machine located on a remote network. These steps are repeated at every router the data encounters en route to its final destination.

FIGURE 3.5 Resolving a remote IP address

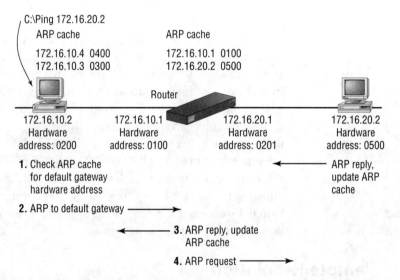

1. The destination IP address is checked to see if it is on the local network. Once determined otherwise, the system checks its local routing table for a path to the remote network. If a path is found, the ARP cache is checked for the hardware address of the default gateway specified in the routing path.

2. When an entry for the default gateway is not found, an ARP request is generated to determine the hardware address of the default gateway or router. Since the only thing that is known about the destination is that it is on a remote network, the router is used as the medium to reach the remote destination.

3. The router replies with its hardware address to the requesting host. The source host then uses Internet Control Message Protocol (ICMP) to issue an echo request back to the router but addressed to the destination host. The router then delivers the echo request to the remote network, which eventually reaches the destination host. The router then repeats step 1 (check if it's local or remote), and then takes action accordingly. Generally, unless a routing path is found at the server, steps 1 through 3 are repeated until the client machine is on a local network. Note that the router can use either a broadcast or its cache in determining the hardware address of the destination host.

4. The destination host also responds to the ARP request with an ARP reply. Since the requesting system is on a remote network, that reply is sent to the router. (It responds to a ping request with an ICMP echo reply sent to the source host.) As with previous resolutions, if the router (default gateway) is not in the ARP cache, a local IP address resolution scenario takes place to determine the router's address.

 Real World Scenario

How MAC and IP Addresses Change and Remain the Same

Think of the MAC address as the physical envelope and the IP address as the written text on the envelope. The MAC address or envelope changes hands or mailboxes many times from a source to a destination while the logical addressing or written text on the envelope remains the same except when the network is configured for NAT (Network Address Translation). The source MAC address is never the same when it reaches the destination (mail carrier or mailbox changes) if routing is involved, but the source and destination IP addresses (written text upon the envelope) remain the same. MAC addresses are 48 bits or 6 bytes in length, for example, 00-A0-C9-EE-1E-55. You can see that the MAC address is expressed as a hexadecimal number for display purposes.

Finding other network MAC addresses from your system is a simple process of displaying the ARP cache. For instance, when you type **arp -a** at the command line, a table appears that includes the columns Internet Address, Physical Address, and Type. The Internet Address column has the IP address (Layer 3 address) that corresponds to the physical address

> (MAC address, Layer 2) for any other systems your system has recently net-worked with. The Type column usually indicates "dynamic," which means the entry was added as a result of recent networking. You can also add static entries to the ARP cache that will speed up the process of Layer 3-to-Layer 2 resolution and that don't expire after a few minutes.

Novell IPX

Novell *IPX (Internetwork Packet Exchange)* has been in use since its release in the early 1980s. It's similar to XNS (Xerox Network Systems), developed by Xerox at its Palo Alto Research Center in the 1960s; IPX even shares a likeness with TCP/IP. IPX is really a family of protocols that coexist and interact to empower sound network communications.

Novell IPX Protocol Suite

IPX doesn't map directly to the OSI model, but its protocols still function in layers. When designing IPX, engineers were more concerned with perfor-mance than with strict compliance to existing standards or models. Even so, comparisons can be made.

Figure 3.6 illustrates the IPX protocols, layers, and functions relative to those of the OSI model.

FIGURE 3.6 IPX protocol suite and the OSI model

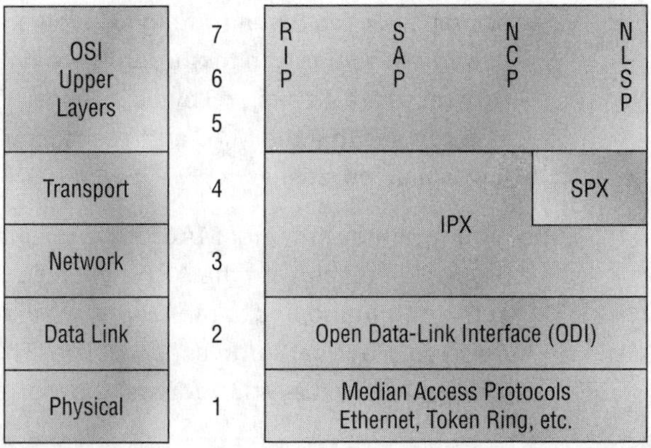

IPX

IPX performs functions at Layers 3 and 4 of the OSI model. It controls the assignment of IPX addresses (software addresses) on individual nodes, governs packet delivery across internetworks, and makes routing decisions based on information provided by the routing protocols, RIP or NLSP. IPX is a connectionless protocol (similar to TCP/IP's UDP), so it doesn't require any acknowledgment that packets were received from the destination node. To communicate with the upper layer protocols, IPX uses *sockets*. These are similar to TCP/IP ports in that they are used to address multiple, independent applications running on the same machine.

SPX

SPX (Sequence Packet Exchange) adds connection-oriented communications to the otherwise connectionless IPX. Through it, upper layer protocols can ensure data delivery between source and destination nodes. SPX works by creating virtual circuits or connections between machines, with each connection having a specific connection ID included in the SPX header.

RIP

RIP (Routing Information Protocol) is a distance-vector routing protocol used to discover IPX routes through internetworks. It employs ticks (1/18 of a second) and hop count (number of routers between nodes) as metrics for determining preferred routes.

SAP

SAP (Service Advertising Protocol) is used to advertise and request services. Servers use SAP to advertise the services they offer, and clients use it to locate network services.

NLSP

NLSP (NetWare Link Services Protocol) is an advanced link-state routing protocol developed by Novell. It is intended to replace both RIP and SAP.

NCP

NCP (NetWare Core Protocol) provides clients with access to server resources; functions such as file access, printing, synchronization, and security are all handled by NCP.

What does the presence of routing protocols, connection and connectionless transport protocols, and application protocols indicate to you? All of those factors add up to the fact that IPX is capable of supporting large internetworks running many applications. Understanding how Novell uses these protocols clears the way for you to include third-party devices (such as Cisco routers) into an IPX network.

Client/Server Communication

Novell NetWare follows a strict client/server model (there's no overlap): a NetWare node is either a client or a server, and that is that. You won't find *peer* machines that both provide and consume network resources here. Clients can be workstations running MacOS, DOS, Windows, OS/2, UNIX, or VMS. Servers generally run Novell NetWare. NetWare servers provide the following services to clients:

- file

- print

- message

- application

- database

As you would think, NetWare clients depend on servers to locate all network resources. Every NetWare server builds a SAP table composed of all the network resources that it's aware of. (We'll explain how they do this a bit later in this chapter.) When clients require access to a certain resource, they issue an IPX broadcast called a *GNS (Get Nearest Server)* request so they can locate a NetWare server that provides the particular resource the client needs. In turn, the servers receiving the GNS check their SAP tables to locate a NetWare server that matches the specific request, then respond to the client with another GNS response. The GNS response points the client to a specific server to contact for the resource it requested. If none of the servers hearing the client's GNS request have the requested service or know of a server that does in their SAP tables, they simply don't respond, leaving the requesting client without the ability to access the requested resource.

Why do you care? Because Cisco routers build SAP tables, too, and they can respond to client GNS requests just as if they were NetWare servers. This doesn't mean they *offer* the services that NetWare servers do, just that their responses are identical when it comes to locating services. The

GNS response to a client can come from a local NetWare server or from a Cisco router, and generally, if there are local NetWare servers present, they should respond to the client's request. But if there are no local NetWare servers, the local Cisco router that connects the client's segment to the IPX internetwork can respond to the client's GNS request. This saves the client from having to wait for remote NetWare servers to respond. A second advantage of this arrangement is that precious WAN bandwidth isn't occupied with GNS conversations between clients on a segment with no local NetWare server and remote NetWare servers, as shown in Figure 3.7.

FIGURE 3.7 Remote IPX clients on a serverless network

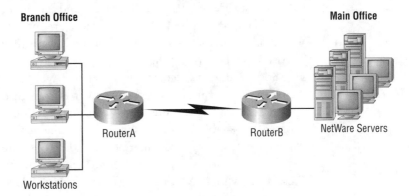

In this figure you see client workstations at the remote office site: they require access to server resources at the main office. In this situation, RouterA answers client GNS requests from its SAP table rather than forwarding the request across the WAN to the main office servers. The clients never realize or care that there isn't a NetWare server present on their LAN.

This communication insulates the client from the task of locating and tracking available network resources—it places that burden on the server instead. The client simply broadcasts a GNS and waits for a response. From the client's perspective, all network resources respond as though they were local, regardless of their physical location in the internetwork.

Server-Server Communication

Communications between two NetWare servers are a bit more complicated than client/server communications. As mentioned earlier, servers are responsible for maintaining tables of all available network resources, regardless of whether those resources are local to the server. Plus, keep in mind that each server must be able to locate *any* resource on the internetwork.

Servers exchange two types of information using two separate protocols: SAP and RIP. As their names suggest, SAP communicates service information, and RIP communicates routing information.

NetWare servers use SAP to advertise the services they offer by sending out a SAP broadcast every 60 seconds. The broadcast includes all services that the server has learned about from other servers—not just the ones they furnish. All servers receiving the SAP broadcast incorporate the information into their own SAP tables; they then rebroadcast it in their own SAP updates. Because SAP information is shared among all servers, all servers eventually become aware of all available services and are thereby equipped to respond to client GNS requests. As new services are introduced, they're added to SAP tables on local servers, then rebroadcast until every server knows they exist and where to get them.

So how does a Cisco router fit in here? Well, as far as SAP is concerned, that router acts just like another NetWare server. By default, a SAP broadcast won't cross a Cisco router. A Cisco router catalogs all SAPs heard on any of its IPX-enabled interfaces in its SAP table; it then broadcasts the whole table from each of those interfaces at 60-second intervals just as NetWare servers do, unless you change the settings. This is an important point, especially with WAN links. The router isolates SAP broadcasts to individual segments and passes along only the summarized information to each segment.

RIP information is exchanged between servers much the same way that SAP information is. Servers build routing tables that contain entries for the networks they're directly connected to; then they broadcast this information on to all IPX-enabled interfaces. Other servers on those segments receive those updates and broadcast their RIP tables on their IPX interfaces. Just as SAP information travels from server to server until all servers are enlightened, RIP information is proliferated until all servers and routers know of the internetwork's routes. RIP information is also broadcast at 60-second intervals, as is SAP information.

IPX Addressing

After you've struggled through IP addressing, IPX addressing should seem like a day at the beach. The IPX addressing scheme has several features that make it much easier to understand and administer than the TCP/IP scheme.

IPX addresses use 80 bits (10 bytes) of data. As with TCP/IP addresses, IPX addresses are hierarchical and divided into a network and a node portion.

The first four bytes always represent the *network address*, and the last six bytes always represent the node address. There's none of that Class A, Class B, or Class C TCP/IP stuff in IPX addressing—the network and node portions of the address are always the same length. So after subnet masking, this is sweet indeed!

As with IP network addresses, the network portion of the address is assigned by administrators and must be unique on the entire IPX internetwork. Node addresses are automatically assigned to every node. When an IPX node powers up, it gets the network address from a router and then attaches that to the front of the MAC (hardware) address that comes from the NIC installed in the node. A NetWare server can also give the network address to a node, but a NetWare server can also be called a router.

This offers several notable advantages over TCP/IP addressing. Since client addressing is dynamic (automatic), you don't have to run Dynamic Host Configuration Protocol (DHCP) or manually configure each individual workstation with an IPX address. Also, since the hardware address (Layer 2) is included as part of the software address (Layer 3), there's no need for a TCP/IP ARP equivalent in IPX.

As with TCP/IP addresses, IPX addresses can be written in several formats. Most often, they're written in hexadecimal, such as 00007C80.0000.8609.33E9. The first 8 hexadecimal digits (00007C80) represent the network portion of the address; the remaining 12 hexadecimal digits (0000.8609.33E9) represent the node portion and are the MAC address of the workstation. When referring to the IPX network, it's a common IPX custom to drop leading 0s. This done, the preceding network address would be referred to as *IPX network 7C80*. The node portion is commonly divided into three sections of four hexadecimal digits divided by periods, as in this example.

Summary

Since TCP/IP is likely to be around for a while, you need to be familiar with its layers, processes, and functions. TCP/IP is a popular network protocol choice. The Process/Application layer includes many protocols that interface with the users' programs. The Host-to-Host layer is responsible for connection-oriented or connectionless communication. The Internet layer includes IP and its error reporting protocol ICMP and the resolution protocols ARP and RARP.

Connection-oriented TCP/IP applications rely on TCP and the guarantee of delivery, whereas connectionless applications use UDP and are often described as best-effort delivery. Internet layer protocols of the TCP/IP suite are responsible for logical addressing, address assignment, and logical-to-physical address resolution. Physical addresses are assigned by the NIC manufacturer and map to a logical address at the Internet layer.

The Novell protocol suite includes upper layer protocols responsible for routing and network services. At the Transport layer, you'll find SPX, which is equivalent in function to TCP and IPX at the Network layer and is used for logical addressing, much like IP.

IPX addressing is used by all IPX-network-assigned devices but includes the logical and physical address, eliminating the need for further resolution.

Exam Essentials

Remember the DOD Model and its layers.   The TCP/IP DOD model defines four layers: the Process/Application layer, the Host-to-Host layer, the Internet layer, and the Network Access layer.

Understand the function and purpose of the Process/Application layer protocols.   Telnet is used for remote terminal emulation, FTP allows file transfer, SMTP is used to move mail, LPD is used for sharing printers, and X Window allows for GUI applications on client/server networks.

Understand the function and purpose of the Host-to-Host layer protocols. TCP is a connection-oriented, guaranteed, transport protocol, and it requires virtual circuits from end-to-end for data delivery. UDP is a connectionless, non-guaranteed, transport protocol and does not require end-to-end circuits for data delivery.

Understand the function and purpose of Internet layer protocols.   IP provides for the logical addressing and is used by hosts and routers to locate networks and clients. ARP is used to resolve an IP address to a MAC address or to resolve logical-to-physical addressing of network devices. RARP is used by diskless workstations to map their MAC addresses to their IP addresses as assigned by the RARP server for a given session.

Understand the function and purpose of the Network layer.   MAC addresses are used by each and every device connected to the network and are defined by a vendor code and serial number. Frames are converted to bits, media access methods are chosen, and electrical signaling is used to place data on the wire at the Network layer.

Remember the Novell IPX Protocol suite and its protocols and functions.
IPX is a connectionless, non-guaranteed delivery protocol for logical
device addressing. SPX is a connection-oriented, guaranteed delivery
protocol using virtual circuits. RIP is a distance-vector routing protocol
using ticks and hops as a metric. SAP is used to advertise and request
services by servers and clients. NLSP is an advanced link-state routing
protocol. NCP provides clients with access to network servers' services
such as file and print.

Key Terms

Before you take the exam, be certain you are familiar with the following terms:

Address Resolution Protocol (ARP)

NLSP (NetWare Link Services Protocol)

ARP cache

RARP server

connectionless

Reverse Address Resolution Protocol (RARP)

connection-oriented

RIP (Routing Information Protocol)

File Transfer Protocol (FTP)

SAP (Service Advertising Protocol)

GNS (Get Nearest Server)

Simple Mail Transfer Protocol (SMTP)

hardware address

sockets

Internet Protocol (IP)

SPX (Sequence Packet Exchange)

IP address

Telnet

IPX (Internetwork Packet Exchange)

Transmission Control Protocol (TCP)

Line Printer Daemon (LPD)

User Datagram Protocol (UDP)

logical address

virtual circuits

NCP (NetWare Core Protocol)

X Window

Review Questions

1. Which protocol works at the Internet layer and is responsible for making routing decisions?

   A. TCP

   B. UDP

   C. IP

   D. ARP

2. Which of the following can be used to transport files between hosts?

   A. Telnet

   B. FTP

   C. SMTP

   D. ARP

3. Which protocol can be used to transport mail messages across an internetwork?

   A. Telnet

   B. FTP

   C. SMTP

   D. ARP

4. Which protocol provides remote virtual terminal access?

   A. Telnet

   B. FTP

   C. SMTP

   D. ARP

5. Which of the following statements is true?

   A. TCP is connection-oriented; UDP uses acknowledgments only.

   B. Both TCP and UDP are connection-oriented, but only TCP uses windowing.

   C. TCP is connection-oriented, but UDP is connectionless.

   D. TCP and UDP both have sequencing, but UDP is connectionless.

6. What does the acronym ARP stand for?

   A. ARP Resolution Protocol

   B. Address Restitution Protocol

   C. Address Resolution Phase

   D. Address Resolution Protocol

7. Which of the following protocols is used to get an IP address from a known MAC address?

   A. ARP

   B. RARP

   C. IP

   D. TCP

   E. UDP

8. Which two of the following protocols are used at the Transport layer?

   A. ARP

   B. RARP

   C. IP

   D. TCP

   E. UDP

9. Which of the following is a connectionless protocol at the Transport layer?

   A. ARP

   B. RARP

   C. IP

   D. TCP

   E. UDP

10. Which of the following protocols provides connection-oriented transport to upper layer protocols?

    A. RIP

    B. NLSP

    C. SPX

    D. NCP

11. In TCP/IP, which of the following functions are performed by IP at the Internet layer of the DOD model? (Choose all that apply.)

    A. Connection-oriented delivery of data

    B. Routing

    C. Routing through an internetwork

    D. Providing single network interface to upper layers

    E. Setup and establishment of full-duplex communication channel

12. Which of the following can respond to a client GNS request? (Choose all that apply.)

    A. Local NetWare server

    B. Remote NetWare server

    C. Local client

    D. Cisco router

13. Of the following TCP/IP protocols, which is most like IPX?

   A. A connectionless protocol like UDP

   B. A connection-oriented protocol like TCP

   C. An address resolution protocol like ARP

   D. A file transfer protocol like FTP

14. How often do servers exchange SAP information unless set otherwise?

   A. Every 15 seconds

   B. Every 30 seconds

   C. Every 60 seconds

   D. Every 120 seconds

15. Given the IPX address 00007C81.00A0.2494.E939, which of the following is the associated IPX network address and which is the node address?

   A. Network address: 00a0, node address: 2494 E939

   B. Network address: 00007C81, node address: 00a0.2494.e939

   C. Network address: 00A0.2494, node address: E939

   D. Network address: 7C81 00a0, node address: 2494.e939

16. Of the following TCP/IP protocols, which is most like SPX? Clue: SPX is at Layer 4 of the OSI model.

   A. A connectionless protocol like UDP

   B. A connection-oriented protocol like TCP

   C. An address resolution protocol like ARP

   D. A file transfer protocol like FTP

17. Which of the following protocols are at Layer 3 of the OSI Model? (Choose all that apply.)

A. IPX

B. SPX

C. IP

D. TCP

E. UDP

18. How many bytes are in an IPX address?

A. 4

B. 8

C. 10

D. 20

19. Which two of the following methods are used to resolve network addresses to MAC addresses?

A. Hello Protocol (HP)

B. Router Query Protocol (RQP)

C. Serial Line Address Resolution Protocol (SLARP)

D. Dynamic Address Resolution (DAR)

E. Address Resolution Protocol (ARP)

20. Which of the following statements is true regarding IPX addresses assigned to a node?

A. A NetWare administrator defines the node address when installing the software.

B. NetWare nodes receive their address from a DHCP server.

C. NetWare nodes request a node address at bootup.

D. NetWare nodes use the hardware MAC address.

Answers to Review Questions

1. C. Routers use IP and logical addressing to determine packet routing.

2. B. FTP is used to both send and receive data between hosts on the network.

3. C. SMTP is used to send or transport mail messages between hosts of a network.

4. A. Telnet allows for remote access and terminal emulation between hosts.

5. C. TCP uses virtual circuits to send sequenced, acknowledged, reliable data between hosts. UDP sends data unsequenced, unacknowledged, unreliable, but with low overhead.

6. D. Address Resolution Protocol is the correct term.

7. B. RARP is the protocol used by diskless workstations to determine their IP address given their MAC address.

8. D, E. TCP and UDP are the protocols used at the Transport layer in the TCP/IP protocol suite. The Host-to-Host layer functions like the Transport layer in the OSI model. In fact, the term "Transport layer" is often used interchangeably with Host-to-Host.

9. E. UDP is the connectionless Transport layer protocol while TCP is the connection-oriented Transport layer protocol. The Host-to-Host layer functions like the Transport layer in the OSI model. In fact, the term "Transport layer" is often used interchangeably with Host-to-Host.

10. C. SPX is the protocol used by the IPX/SPX protocol suite for connection-oriented data delivery at the Transport layer. The Host-to-Host layer functions like the Transport layer in the OSI model. In fact, the term "Transport layer" is often used interchangeably with Host-to-Host.

11. B, C. IP is used for the logical addressing of network devices and destination of network routes by routers.

12. A, D. NetWare servers always respond to local GNS broadcast requests by clients, and Cisco routers can be configured to respond to clients where NetWare servers do not exist on their local networks.

13. A.   IPX is a protocol designed very much like UDP and is connectionless.

14. C.   Every 60 seconds, servers exchange their SAP table entries to build a comprehensive list of network services.

15. B.   The first 32 bits represent the assignable IPX network address, and the final 48 bits represent the node address, also known as the MAC address.

16. B.   TCP is most like SPX and uses connection-oriented, sequenced, acknowledged, reliable, virtual circuits for data delivery.

17. A, C.   Both IPX and IP are responsible for logical addressing at Layer 3 of the OSI model and are used by hosts, routers, and routing protocols to determine host and network addressing.

18. C.   10 bytes (80 bits) is the length of an IPX address using the 32-bit network address and the 48-bit node address.

19. C, E.   SLARP is rare in today's networks but was designed to resolve network addresses to MAC addresses and operates much like ARP.

20. D.   An IPX address includes the node's MAC addresses and eliminates the need for logical-to-physical address resolution used in IP networks.

Pre-Design Procedures

CCDA EXAM TOPICS COVERED IN THIS CHAPTER:

- ✓ Gather and evaluate information regarding an organization's existing social requirements.
- ✓ Gather and evaluate information regarding a network owner's current data network and future needs.
- ✓ Gather and evaluate information regarding a network owner's current voice network and future needs.
- ✓ Identify possible opportunities for network improvement.
- ✓ Validate gathered information.
- ✓ Document relevant findings.
- ✓ Develop an implementation plan.

Now that we've covered some of the basics of internetworking, you are ready to begin the design process. Let's begin by introducing Cisco's Small- to Medium-Sized Business Framework, a framework that can be used to categorize and solve typical customer issues. Before getting started in the actual design process, there are two preliminary steps you need to complete. The first step is a thorough inventory of the customer's current network. This step is almost always necessary and would only be skipped if there were no existing network. The second step is to evaluate the customer's needs and expectations in detail. These two steps provide the equivalent of a location (where the customer's network is currently), a direction, and a final location (customer's needs and expectations). Once this information is established, the actual design process can begin. This chapter explains how to gather this information; Chapters 5 through 11 describe the design process.

The main topics addressed in this chapter are as follows:

- Identify all the data you should gather to characterize the customer's existing network.

- Document the customer's current applications, protocols, *network topology*, and number of users.

- Document the customer's business issues that are relevant to a network design project.

- Assess the health of the customer's existing network and make conclusions about the network's ability to support growth.

- Determine the customer's requirements for new applications, protocols, number of users, peak usage hours, security, and network management.

- Diagram the flow of information for new applications.

- Isolate the customer's criteria for accepting the performance of a network.

- List some tools that will help you characterize new network traffic.

Cisco's Small- to Medium-Sized Business Solutions Framework

Cisco has recognized the changing needs of business and has been quick to respond to those needs with technology. If you were to go back in time 10 years, the *LAN* was a very different entity. Today there are technologies in the corporate LAN such as Fast Ethernet, switching, TCP/IP, voice, video, ATM, Layer 3 switching, and others. Cisco has assembled many independent technologies for switched internetworks into a scalable architecture called *CiscoFusion*. This allows network designers to use various features of Cisco's IOS to solve a variety of problems.

Chapters 1 through 3 defined the differences between Layer 2 and Layer 3 of the OSI model. They talked about how *Ethernet* works and how to segment Ethernet (Layer 2) LANs. Those chapters also discussed IP and IPX (Layer 3) and their responsibilities. We will continue to build on these concepts throughout this book. The real question that arises is that with so many tools available, how does a network designer identify which technology is right to solve a particular problem? Cisco has responded to this need by creating the Small- to Medium-Sized Business Solutions Framework. This framework categorizes most customer problems into one of three categories:

- Media problems

- Protocol problems

- Transport problems

and proposes solutions to each of these.

This framework is typically represented as a triangle, as seen in Figure 4.1.

As mentioned, Cisco has categorized most customer design problems into one of these three categories. However, they did not stop there. Cisco created specific *solutions* for each category as well! This makes the Small- to Medium-Sized Business Solutions Framework a real tool that you can use throughout the design process. Let's take a quick look at the problems that would appear in each category and at Cisco's solutions for that category.

FIGURE 4.1 Cisco's Small- to Medium-Sized Business Solutions Framework

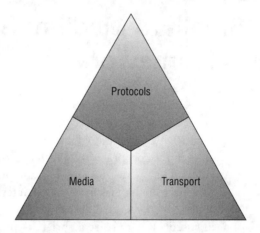

Media Problems

Media problems are defined as problems relating to contention for use of the *media* itself. They are identified by high rates of utilization. For example, a *Token Ring* network at 80 percent utilization is experiencing a media problem. With Ethernet, you can monitor collision rate in addition to utilization to determine if media problems exist. We will discuss acceptable rates of utilization later in this chapter; this information will assist you in identifying media problems. When media problems are identified, the recommended solution is to use LAN switching (separate *collision domains*).

Protocol Problems

Protocol problems result when protocols designed for workgroup environments are used in significantly larger environments. Consider AppleTalk, for example. AppleTalk handles many tasks such as address assignment, name resolution, and broadcast-domain assignment automatically. However, to do all of this, AppleTalk generates considerable broadcast traffic. Or consider IPX, which was discussed in Chapter 3, "Network Protocols." How did servers advertise their services? Their routes? How did workstations locate those services and routes? That's right, they used *broadcasts*! Now, this is not a bad thing until you try to hook hundreds or even thousands of IPX nodes together on a single switched LAN. Isolating protocol problems involves counting the number of broadcasts per second or the number of workstations per broadcast domain. When protocol problems are identified, the recommended solution is to use routing (separate *broadcast domains*).

Transport Problems

Transport problems result when extreme demands are placed on the network. For example, many IS departments are being required to implement either video-conferencing solutions or video-streaming solutions or both! These types of applications require large amounts of bandwidth and have very little tolerance for delay, retransmissions, error rates, or anything other than perfect, prompt data delivery. Issues such as delay, available bandwidth, and application errors identify these problems. Using Fast Ethernet switching and, where appropriate, ATM, solves transport problems.

PDIOO Methodology

In this section, I'm going to introduce you to what's known as the *PDIOO methodology*. PDIOO is an acronym that stands for planning, design, implementation, operation, and optimization. It reflects the various phases of a typical network's life cycle—you'll come across each phase in the regular operation of all networks. Though each phase is important, network design is a vital phase of PDIOO methodology.

There's an innate, contingent connection between network design and each of the other PDIOO phases because design essentials are found in each phase and each phase is critical to consider when making network design decisions.

The following is a description of each individual yet correlated PDIOO life cycle phase, plus there's one more phase (retirement) that I'll cover in this section as well.

Planning   The network requirements are what you need to pinpoint in the planning phase. Important considerations for this phase include determining exactly where you plan to install the network, its objectives, and the types of services it will provide and to whom, etc. Once you've established these specifications, you've clarified your fundamental network requirements.

Design The set of network requirements identified in the planning phase is the basis of what you'll use to design the network. It's also important to consider any information obtained though discussions with managers and administrators as well as any data gained through the analysis and audits of the existing network if you're upgrading. With a solid network design model in hand, you're ready to move on to the implementation phase.

Implementation With an approved design—and any additional equipment the design requires—the next step is to implement the new network. This is where you'll get to test the design and see if it's valid or if you'll need to tweak it a bit to get it there.

Operation The operation phase is where the true viability of the network design is tested. Any weaknesses discovered are addressed here, and the network's actual performance levels that are monitored during day-to-day operations supply the information you need to move into the optimization phase.

Optimization This phase hinges upon solid, practical network management that's objectively directed toward detecting and working out any glitches before they evolve into serious problems. The optimization phase is highly significant because if issues can't be troubleshot effectively or if the network's performance breaks down over time, redesigning the network is probably necessary. Major changes in service requirements due to growth, restructuring, etc., can also make redesigning the network essential. This last scenario is where having a clear, accurate picture about throughput, responsiveness, and the types and frequency of resources accessed provides an invaluable tool with which to create a new and viable network design.

Retirement Although not technically part of the PDIOO process, the retirement of the network—or parts of the network—is a natural progression in the life cycle of a network. As new technology develops and needs evolve, all or part of the network often becomes obsolete. The outdated equipment is then either retired or repositioned somewhere else in the network where the demands on it won't overwhelm its limited capacity.

The Current Network

With the discussion of Cisco's framework behind us, let's look at the customer's existing network. Like it or not, most networks are not new networks but are updates of existing networks. Very few companies can afford to say, "Scrap everything." They must carry some pieces of their existing network forward. Therefore, it is critical to first understand how the customer's network is currently performing. Gaining an understanding of the customer's current network gives you a starting point, a point of reference. This understanding is required later when discussing the customer's needs. For example, when the customer tells you, "I want my new LAN to be faster and more secure," you cannot understand exactly what he means unless you understand just how fast and secure his *current* LAN is. The customer gave you relative statements in saying "more secure" and "faster;" you must understand the customer's current network in order to understand these statements.

You begin categorizing the customer's current network by gathering data about it. This information is divided into two categories: administrative data and technical data. Administrative data is generally gathered from company management and includes information such as the company's business goals, corporate structure, geographic locations, current and future staffing, and policies and politics that will affect the design of a new network. This information paints a picture of the corporate environment and helps identify business constraints (business issues, not technical issues, that will affect the final network design). Technical data is taken from the customer's current network and can usually be gathered from the IS department or using network analysis tools (discussed in Chapter 11, "Network Management"). Technical data includes protocols in use, collision rates, broadcast rates, packet flows, segment utilization, and other network-related issues.

Administrative Data

Administrative data helps you to understand the workings of the company whose network you will be designing. Administrative data allows you to identify *business constraints* that may arise throughout the design and implementation processes. Business constraints are defined as any nontechnical item that will affect your final design. There are many types of administrative data you may wish to gather. The following list contains questions you might want to answer as you gather administrative data:

- Who will be your technical contact(s) within the company?

- Who will be involved in the design process, and how involved will they be?

- Who will approve your design?

- Is the company's climate one of acceptance to change, or is there resistance to your changes?

- Has someone else tried and failed in this project?

- How does the company's IS department feel about your involvement (assuming you are external to the company)?

- Who reports to whom? Who can override decisions made by your contacts?

- What are the company's growth expectations? Will they be expanding significantly? Do they want to expand?

- How is their industry performing, and how are they competing in their industry?

- Where (geographically) are the users located?

- What are their staffing levels like?

- Once the new network is in place, who will run it? Does the company have internal personnel who are capable, or will they need training? Will they need to increase staffing to support the new network?

Gathering this data may present challenges, especially if there is any resistance in some parts of the company to the project. You will probably have to work with several different departments such as personnel, technology, management, and even Human Resources, to gather all of this information. However, gathering the administrative data is an important step that will pay significant dividends in your final design. At most, it will allow you to gain insight into the company's vision and design a network that helps them attain their goals. At least, it will prevent you from stepping on the wrong toes as you complete your design process.

Technical Data

As the name implies, technical data has more to do with technology than administrative data. It helps you to better understand how the customer's network is operating, and as explained earlier, this will help you understand the customer's expectations. Technical data to be gathered on the customer's network includes the following:

- Analyze the current network for media problems. Media problems are caused by too many devices sharing a *network segment* (collision domain). Symptoms include high latency and difficulty in accessing services.

- Analyze the *protocols* being used in the current network. Are they appropriate to the scale of the network? Some protocols are fine for small networks, but as the network grows and becomes increasingly more complicated and segmented, these protocols do not scale well.

- Take inventory of which networked applications are currently being used and what applications the customer plans on implementing or migrating to in the future.

- Examine the information flows within the company. What paths do information flows such as e-mail, database access, etc., use to cross the internetwork?

- Find out where shared data is located and who accesses it.

- Measure network traffic between segments. Is there data accessed from outside the network such as Internet resources?

As you can see, technical data focuses on Layer 3 technologies (IP, IPX, DDP, and routing) and on Layer 2 technologies (switching). The data gathered here will be categorized using Cisco's Small- to Medium-Sized Business Solutions Framework, and from that point, problems will be identified and solved.

There are many tools available to help you gather this data. These tools include *protocol analyzers*, network management stations, and others. These tools are explained in detail in Chapter 11.

Now that we have discussed administrative and technical data and the differences between the two, let's look at a road map that you can use to evaluate the state of the customer's current network.

Design Methodology

Having a consistent, systematic approach for designing a network from the ground up or for modifying an existing network is essential to creating a viable network that truly meets the needs of those it's going to service. You simply must have a concise methodology—an established set of steps to refer to for preventing wasted energy and time spent reinventing the wheel. A solid plan is a very good tool to have, but it's also very important to be flexible. With that in mind, here are some basic precepts to follow that will help you avoid common pitfalls and problems and instill confidence in your work to those depending on the integrity of your design:

- Make sure all design steps are fully addressed.

- Make sure your network design is consistent to facilitate its implementation, maintenance, and optimization.

- Make sure your plan is concise and clear so that both managers and clients are able to understand that you've carefully thought out the network design structure to meet their needs.

- You must provide a realistic and solid framework to facilitate the design process for any and all involved.

With those concepts in mind, read through the following design methodology steps. Some of them relate directly to the design phase itself. Others relate indirectly, being relevant to one or more of the other PDIOO phases:

1. Know and understand the client's exact requirements.

2. Map the client's existing network.

3. Determine the viable network solutions or topology design.

4. Plan the actual implementation.

5. Create the model network.

6. Write it all down.

7. Implement and verify the actual design.

8. Look, listen, and learn.

Let's look at each of these steps in great detail.

Know and understand the client's exact requirements.   This step is accomplished by mining all pertinent information from your client accurately and thoroughly; you do this during the PDIOO planning phase.

Map the client's existing network.   You only need to follow this step if your job is to redesign and/or upgrade a network that already exists. If that's the case, network audits and network analysis are your best tools. Network auditing consists of testing and examining the existing network's integrity, performance, and quite likely, its scalability as well. Network analysis deals with analyzing network behavior—the levels of traffic, congestion factors, etc.—and is ascertained during the PDIOO optimization phase.

Determine the viable network solutions or topology design.   This is where you create the real-world model of the actual, working network that you intend to eventually implement. Decisions herein center upon specifying and determining the network infrastructure—the hardware and software, routing protocols, intelligent network services, QoS, physical topology, etc. Also highly relevant to this step are determining factors like network solutions such as Voice over IP (VoIP) and content networking. The information required to make these decisions accurately is acquired during the first two design methodology steps.

Plan the actual implementation.   This is the time to prepare proper implementation procedures and delimit and clarify the design's real cost assessment. Preparing this documentation in advance serves to facilitate and illuminate what the implementation will require in order for it to be actualized.

Create the model network.   You really could skip this step, but it can be very useful for both you and your client. Having a prototypical model of the final product you're proposing can prove highly useful in verifying why your design should actually be implemented. If you opt to create the model network, you should present it at the dawn of the PDIOO implementation phase.

Write it all down.   Document the design. Yes—document that design! If you need help with this step, look over the section on implementing design methodology covered in Chapter 5.

Implement and verify the actual design.   This is where you build the actual network you've designed and you test that design in a real-world environment in order to verify if it does in fact work as you planned it would.

Look, listen, and learn. You've built the design—does it fly? Here is where you get to see if the network you've designed and built really works. And if it doesn't really work, at least you get a chance to monitor it, discover why, and fix it before anyone notices! Even good designs need tweaking sometimes, and this is the step where you monitor the network's operation and check it for errors and potential issues. You troubleshoot and modify according to any probable or potential error you've discovered, hoping to avoid redesigning the entire network. But if your testing is proving so dismal that you'll need to actually redesign the network, here's where you'll find that out—after the network is built and operational. Hopefully, this won't be you, and in the worst case, you'll just need to tweak things a bit!

Portraying the Current Network

Cisco recommends 12 items that should be inventoried in the customer's current network. These 12 items will, in most cases, generate most or all of the administrative and technical data. The items to gather are

1. Existing applications

2. Existing network protocols

3. Network topology and addressing

4. Potential bottlenecks in the current network

5. Business constraints

6. Existing network availability

7. Existing network performance

8. Existing network reliability

9. Existing network utilization

10. Status of existing routers

11. Existing network management system(s)

12. Overall health of existing network

Let's look at each of these items in more detail.

Existing applications The objective here is to itemize major applications in use by the customer. Understanding which applications are used where will allow you to map packet flow and better understand the customer's expectations. For example, a customer LAN used to exchange large CAD drawings may require more bandwidth than a customer LAN used exclusively to exchange spreadsheets, even though both are file transfer operations.

Existing network protocols   This list will give you a complete picture of protocols in use by your customer. This information will be invaluable in later design steps, as you plan for items such as routing protocols and network addressing. It is important to list each and every network protocol currently in use by the customer, including routing, routed, and bridged protocols.

Network topology and addressing   You will want to construct a document called a *high-level topology* of the customer's current network. This is a map that includes all major network segments, routers, *bridges*, *switches*, servers, and other devices. It does not have to be too detailed; the idea is to get the big picture of the overall network. This item can usually be obtained from the customer.

Consider Figure 4.2. Notice that the map presents the overall internetwork rather than focusing on details such as the type of hubs, the type of hardware used for the workstations and servers, *WAN* protocols, etc. Even the number of servers and workstations is approximated! This map will be used along with the customer's requirements to create a new high-level topology map of the customer's proposed network. Don't worry, we'll practice these maps and give examples of each later in this chapter when we do our case studies.

Once you have the high-level topology of the customer's current network, you can add addressing information. The idea is to identify anything that you might need later when designing the new network's addressing scheme.

Potential bottlenecks in the current network   When identifying bottlenecks, just measuring bandwidth utilization is not sufficient. It is important to understand the profile of traffic on each network segment. Whenever possible, use a protocol analyzer to identify local and non-local traffic on segments. This will help you identify three types of traffic:

- Traffic where both source and destination are local

- Traffic where either source or destination is local

- Traffic where neither source nor destination is local

FIGURE 4.2 High-level topology map

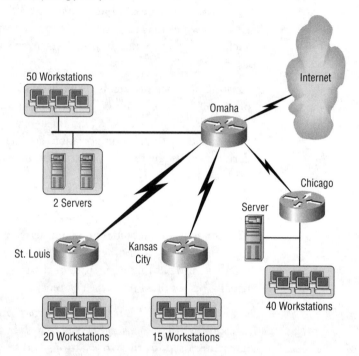

Understanding what type of traffic exists on a network will help you later in your design.

Business constraints This is the point where you review the administrative data you have gathered. As mentioned, any network design in the real world involves many nontechnical administrative and political factors. As part of your evaluation of the customer's current network, it is essential that you understand any of these factors that have influenced the current network design. Otherwise, a well-intentioned improvement on your part might result in unfortunate consequences. Gather any nontechnical data that will be relevant to your design. Make sure to get a full understanding of the company's policies regarding technology. These would include naming standards, addressing standards, routing protocols, etc.

Existing network availability In order to understand the condition of the current network, gather statistics on network *down time* and the *mean time between failure (MTBF)*. The MTBF is the average time between network outages, so the higher the number, the better. You may wish to document costs associated with down time, if available.

Existing network performance   Network performance is a measure of *latency* between two network devices. When latency is high, deeper analysis is required to ascertain the cause of the latency. Remember the customer who wanted the "faster" network? By measuring existing network performance, you can discover what the customer means by "faster." Select several critical hosts and servers and measure response times using a protocol analyzer.

Existing network reliability   Network reliability is different than network availability. While network availability measures *up time*, network reliability measures error rates when the network is "up." Even when networks are working, there are still transmission errors that occur. By measuring network reliability, you can discover potential problems with the existing network. This can be accomplished by using a tool such as a protocol analyzer or a network-monitoring or management tool to monitor each network segment. You may want to consider the following properties for a given segment over a 24-hour period:

- Number of frames
- Traffic (in MB) transmitted
- Number of CRC (cyclic redundancy checksum) errors
- Number of runts/giants (Ethernet)
- Number of collisions (Ethernet)
- Number of broadcast frames and *multicast* frames.

Existing network utilization   You need to use a protocol analyzer to gather information on network utilization. You will want to collect data on total network utilization and gather a breakdown of information about each individual protocol on the segment.

Status of existing routers   You may want to check out the overall health of the *routers* currently running on the network. Check for items such as media errors and CPU utilization and take note of memory utilization. This information will augment the data already collected on the media segments and will give you the additional insight about how well your routers are doing under the current load. This information will be important later in the design process as you consider routing protocols and routing equipment.

Existing network management system(s) Make a list of all network management tools being used and which platform they run on. Be sure to include version information and document items such as method of gathering data, devices managed, and reporting capabilities. Gather samples of any reports, maps, or output from the *network management system.* As with other issues, understanding the customer's current system will help you better understand their expectations for their new network management system.

Overall health of existing network Once you have gathered all of the relevant information you need about the current network, you should be able to compose a fairly accurate picture of the health of the current network. Cisco has made some specific recommendations for potential warning signs. They include

- Ethernet segments should not exceed 40 percent network utilization.

- Token Ring segments should not exceed 70 percent network utilization.

- WAN links should not exceed 70 percent network utilization.

- Response time should be less than 1/10 of a second (100 milliseconds).

- Broadcasts/multicasts should not be more than 20 percent of overall traffic.

- On Ethernet, there should be no more than one CRC error per one million bytes of data on any network segment.

- No Cisco router CPU utilization should exceed 75 percent.

Evaluation of Needs and Expectations

Now that you have established just where the customer is with their current network, you need to establish where the customer wants to go. There are several items that you need to establish with your customer, including

- Business constraints

- Security requirements
- Manageability requirements
- Application requirements
- Performance requirements

This section will discuss each of these in a bit more detail. Once this data is gathered, you will most likely want to record it in a document that specifies exactly what the customer's requirements are.

Business Constraints

Are you getting the idea that business constraints are a big part of the network design? Business constraints include items such as timelines, staffing, training, budgets, and project approval. For example, it is important to establish what, if any, down time on the existing network is permissible when new equipment is installed and configured. In many environments, you may have to leave existing services installed and running while the new networking equipment goes in. It is important to establish these expectations up front, because they will significantly affect design. For example, if down time is not tolerable, you may have to order a router with additional interfaces that will only be used a short time to interconnect the old and new networks. All of these types of items can affect the design, although they are not purely technical in nature. It is important to establish these constraints up front with the customer.

Security Requirements

Security is something that everyone wants. Internet connections are always a worry (Who doesn't have a hacker story?), and internal threats are always present. Chapter 13, "Designing Networks for Integrated Security and Voice Transport," discusses methods of designing secure topologies. However, it is important to establish customer expectations with respect to security before beginning the design process. Unfortunately, security is not free. It typically requires additional equipment purchases as well as upgrading some equipment to handle security roles. Almost every customer will want Fort Knox security—this is the time to establish what type of security they can realistically both pay for and live with.

Real World Scenario

Increasing Security on Your Networks

As previously mentioned, security typically requires additional equipment purchases, including firewalls, authentication, intrusion detection, and public key infrastructure systems. However, before any actual network design work is started, security equipment and design must be considered.

Management must define the business security requirements and support the use of the aforementioned security equipment and design. All too often, management wants data, networks, and devices secured but at the same time, they do not want to be inconvenienced nor do they want users to be inconvenienced by a new design. Security equipment and design can only protect your networks if the policies and procedures of security are clearly defined and followed; management must be organized and decisive in the planning process. Security policies and procedures need to include a definition for router access lists, firewall rules, allowable authentication methods, intrusion detection, reaction, and data encryption. Without definitive policies and procedures in place and being followed, your networks could become the targets of both inside and outside security attacks.

When writing security policies and procedures, there are a few main areas that must addressed. These areas include

- Know your enemy
- Costs and risk factors
- Controlling your secrets
- Human factors
- Known weaknesses
- Business environment
- Physical security
- Trust

Lateral thinking and a willingness to explore any and all changes made to your networks and their effects on security require that you take a proactive approach and that you practice security in everything you and your users execute on the network.

Some suggested guidelines for writing your own security policies and procedures can be found in ISO 17799 and in *Information Security Policies Roles and Responsibilities Made Easy, Version 1* by Charles Cresson Wood.

Manageability Requirements

Some customers will only require the ability to produce pretty graphics for PowerPoint slides of their network management systems. Others will want to capture and evaluate any byte crossing any segment and know every gatherable statistic on their network devices. As with security, increased functionality implies increased cost. Use the customer's existing network management tools (which you categorized earlier) as a starting point for expectations and then discuss how the customer would like to increase the manageability of the network. Make sure to establish specific checkpoints, like "measure network utilization on all WAN links," rather than nonspecific items, such as "manage network better."

Application Requirements

Applications will have the greatest influence on data flow. Even though the CCDA exam does not focus on installing networked applications, you must understand which applications your customer will run across their network. After all, if there were no applications, the network traffic would consist of routing updates and little more. Understanding where key servers are to be placed, expected traffic levels, and protocol support is crucial to the design process. You would not want to get to the end of the design process and have your customer tell you, "By the way, we are placing our e-mail server with 10,000 accounts at site A," which you have connected to the corporate network with a DDR BRI!

Performance Requirements

In the end, what do you need? Do you really need T3 performance on the WAN? Don't neglect issues such as scalability here. The idea is not to decide an absolute minimum but to evaluate what acceptable levels of performance (measured in response time, bandwidth utilization, etc.) really are, and how to ensure that those levels can be preserved through both network growth (more nodes) and increased utilization (more packets).

Summary

PDIOO is an acronym that stands for planning, design, implementation, operation, and optimization. You learned the various steps of PDIOO in this chapter and how each phase is important to the network design.

In this chapter you also learned how to gather both administrative and technical data for a customer's current network, and you were introduced to a process for examining the customer's network to gather pertinent information. This process includes collecting information about applications being used, protocols in the network, current network design, and potential bottlenecks. In this process you need to consider the statistics for network outages, performance, reliability, and utilization. You should also include status of the major routers and network management tools. Also discussed were tools and methods that could be used to gather this data and then store and analyze it.

Next, we discussed analysis of the customer's expectations with regard to the new network. We pointed out that finding a balance between cost and functionality is often a factor and discussed setting realistic expectations. We also looked at the following five topics for establishing expectations: business constraints, security, manageability, application requirements, and performance requirements.

Exam Essentials

Understand Cisco's Small- to Medium-Sized Business Solutions Framework. Cisco's solutions framework categorizes most problems into one of three areas. Media problems are identified as high rates of utilization and can be addressed with separate collision domains. Protocol problems can be attributed to broadcasts and can be addressed with separate broadcast domains. Transport problems can be similar to small freeways, and the need for larger amounts of bandwidth is justified.

Understand how to gather information about the current network. In order to determine the proper network setup, you must first consider the existing network. Administrative data helps you understand the workings of the company, and the potential business constraints are nontechnical items that will affect your final network design. Technical data helps you understand the customer's expectations and can be gathered with protocol analyzers and network management stations.

Know how to map the current network. Mapping existing applications, network protocols, network topologies, addressing maps, and current bottlenecks will help you understand the customer's needs and give you a complete picture. It will also help you understand current and future design challenges and current bottlenecks that will help you identify the three network traffic types, the source and destination, and local and non-local segment traffic.

Understand business constraints and network availability, performance, reliability, and utilization. Business constraints include the nontechnical administrative data and political factors. Network availability, performance, reliability, and utilization will help you to identify network down time, latency, up time with possible errors, and percent of network usage.

Be able to use existing routers and network management systems to gather information for a successful network design. The overall health, CPU, and memory utilization of existing network routers will be important information later in the design process for the consideration of network protocols and routing equipment. Existing network management systems and the data they provide will help you understand the customer's current system and the customer's expectations.

Know the overall health of the customer's network. You need to be able to determine the limitations of the existing network. Ethernet segments should not exceed 40 percent utilization or exhibit more than one CRC error per one million bytes of data on any network segment. Token Ring segments and WAN links should not exceed 70 percent utilization. Network response time should be less than 1/10 of a second (100 milliseconds). Broadcasts/multicasts should not be more than 20 percent of the overall network traffic. No router CPU utilization should exceed 75 percent.

Know how to evaluate the needs and expectations of the customer. Business constraints can be a major factor in a successful network design. Buy-in from the customer's staff, users, and management is crucial for any designer. Security, manageability, application, and performance requirements most often will require a give-and-take process between the customer and the network designer. A network design and the customer's expectations will need to meet on middle ground.

Key Terms

Before you take the exam, be certain you are familiar with the following terms:

bridges	network management system
broadcast domains	network segment
broadcasts	network topology
CiscoFusion	PDIOO methodology
collision domains	protocol analyzers
down time	protocols
Ethernet	routers
high-level topology	switches
LAN	Token Ring
latency	transport
mean time between failure (MTBF)	up time
media	WAN
multicast	

Case Studies

This section will introduce three case studies that we will use throughout the remainder of this book. We will refer back to these case studies in future chapters as we introduce new technologies to discuss how the new technologies would affect these three scenarios.

Have-A-Seat

Have-A-Seat's world headquarters is located in Atlanta, with office and warehouse space in Los Angeles, Seattle, Miami, and Boston. In addition, they have two European offices in London and Barcelona. They have manufacturing facilities in Brazil, the Philippines, and Quebec. Have-A-Seat has noticed increasing competition in the area of high-end furniture and has decided to make a significant investment in technology to remain competitive in the marketplace. Dave Jones is the Project Manager for this expansion.

Currently in Atlanta, Have-A-Seat has an IBM mainframe with 90 terminals on a Token Ring network. The mainframe is used for all of Have-A-Seat's inventory, production scheduling, shipping information, accounting, and payroll. Additionally, there are 30 PCs in Atlanta used for standard office-suite applications, and a pair of Windows NT servers used for file and print services. These PCs are primarily used by management, and they have terminal emulation software loaded so that they can also access the mainframe. Finally, there is a remote-access device housing eight modems used for dial-in access to the mainframe by the sites in the field.

The six field offices and warehouses each have 10 terminals that access the mainframe in Atlanta using a shared dial-up connection. These field offices also each have a small Ethernet LAN with 15 PCs and a Windows NT server that is used for local file and print services. These PCs do not currently have any method of accessing mainframe resources.

Finally, the three production facilities each have 20 terminals that access the mainframe in Atlanta just as the terminals at the office and warehouse facilities do, using a shared dial-up connection. They do not have any LAN or PCs currently in use.

Have-A-Seat's plan is to replace all of the terminals with PCs. They have already contracted with another company to install a web server on their mainframe and develop web-based applications to replace all of their current applications in accessing their data store. Therefore, the WAN migration must happen at the same time that the web server conversion takes place. Dave has scheduled a one-week outage approximately four months from now for this event to take place.

The network will need to be configured to support TCP/IP, and browser software will need to be installed on all PCs. Additionally, Dave will install Microsoft Exchange on one of his servers in Atlanta to host e-mail services for the entire company.

Dave has concerns about security on the LAN in Atlanta and wants to install switches and deploy VLANs to help ensure security. He will not be migrating the mainframe away from the Token Ring network, but he will migrate all PCs and servers to Ethernet. Therefore, he needs a solution that will support both Ethernet and Token Ring in Atlanta.

Dave is sure that he will need dedicated point-to-point connections between all of his sites and Atlanta. He also wants to have some backup connection available between the three production facilities and Atlanta should their primary link fail. Dave has considered installing an Internet connection in Atlanta, but has concerns about both security on Have-A-Seat's internal network and inappropriate use by Have-A-Seat's employees. He would like to go ahead and install the connection, but he needs a design that will meet all of his needs.

Finally, Dave needs LAN solutions for the six remote offices and three production facilities. The Ethernet in the remote offices will need to be upgraded, and network equipment will need to be identified and purchased. Dave is curious about the benefits of installing Ethernet switches on such small LANs.

Exercises

1. What applications is the customer running?

2. Draw a high-level topology map of the customer's current network.

3. Draw a high-level topology map of the customer's proposed network.

MPS Construction

Mike Smith is CIO of MPS Construction. MPS is headquartered in Denver, with branches in Salt Lake City, Kansas City, Omaha, and Boise. They have been growing rapidly, and they intend to open branches in two or three more cities next year. In anticipation of their upcoming growth, Mike has budgeted to implement a WAN that will scale with MPS's plans.

The Denver office houses 40 PCs used by administrative personnel. There are also 50 laptop computers in Denver that are used on both current job sites and when bidding new jobs. Payroll and benefits for the entire company are handled in Denver, and Mike has recently installed a new accounting package on a DEC Alpha running Windows NT there. Mike has another Windows NT server running on Intel hardware used for file and print services. When Mike installed the NT servers, he was able to upgrade the network to Category 5 cable through the Denver office, and he has installed 10BaseT hubs for the PCs and servers.

The field offices each have 10 PCs used by local office personnel, plus 40 laptops for use by employees on job sites and when bidding new jobs. The PCs are connected with Category 3 cable and 10BaseT hubs. Currently, the remote sites have a single PC configured to dial in to Denver using ISDN to access the accounting server and file server. Printing is all handled locally.

Mike's concerns fall into two categories. The first has to do with designing his WAN. He has considered replacing the ISDN with Frame Relay so that connectivity will be continuous. However, he is not sure that he wants to pay for a 24×7 WAN at remote sites when there are only five workstations. He needs a solution for his WAN that will allow connectivity from all remote workstations into the Denver headquarters, yet is cost-effective. He would also like to be able to send and receive Internet e-mail to communicate with vendors, but he does not want any traffic other than e-mail to or from the Internet.

Second, Mike needs to provide a dial-in solution for the laptops. He needs to allow every laptop in each city to be able to access the network resources remotely. Most of the employees carrying laptops rarely if ever visit the branch offices; they work exclusively on job sites. However, they still need to access company server resources. Most job sites have analog phone lines available nearby, and for those that do not, MPS will pay for wireless telephone access. Mike has requested your help in designing the access servers to be used at each location.

Exercises

1. Draw a high-level topology map of the customer's current network.

2. Draw a high-level topology map of the customer's proposed network.

Willow Creek School District

Scott Baker is Director of Technology for the Willow Creek School District. Willow Creek has been installing computers for years at their district office as well as at their two high schools, three junior high schools, and seven elementary schools. They have just received a grant to upgrade their entire school district's network. They want to install a WAN that connects all of the schools to the district office and provides Internet access to all schools in the district. They have contacted you to help them design their new network.

Currently, at the district office they have a Token Ring network installed using Category 5 cabling. There are 30 PCs connected to the Token Ring network, along with one Novell server and one AS400. The Novell server is used for local file and print services, as well as for local e-mail. The AS400 stores all student attendance and grade information for the entire district.

Right now, five of the PCs have PC Anywhere installed, and the schools access the AS400 by dialing in to one of these five PCs and then entering their data. All PCs have standard office applications installed and e-mail clients and software to access the AS400.

Both high schools use 10BaseT hubs and are currently wired with Category 5 cabling. Each school has 140 PCs and 110 Apple Macintosh computers. The PCs are used by the administration and by the business departments; the Macintoshes are used throughout the rest of the school. Two PCs at each high school are configured with PC Anywhere and a modem to dial in to the district office and enter data into the AS400. Additionally, each school has two Novell servers used for file and print services. Finally, each high school recently installed a Cisco 2511 router. Each router has a T1 Frame Relay connection to the Internet through a local ISP, and eight modems are attached to the router that are used by faculty and staff for dial-in access to the school's network and for Internet access.

The junior high schools each have 60 PCs and 60 Macintosh computers. They recently rewired each building, replacing coax used for 10Base2 with Category 5 cabling and 10BaseT hubs. The PCs are used by administration and faculty; the Macintoshes are used by faculty and students. One PC at each school is running PC Anywhere and has an attached modem for dialing into the district office and entering data into the AS400. Finally, each junior high school has a Novell server that is used for local file and print services.

The elementary schools each have one PC and 30 Macintosh computers. The PC is running PC Anywhere and has an attached modem to dial into the district office and enter data into the AS400. The elementary schools each had Category 5 cabling installed throughout the building at the same time that the junior high schools were upgraded. However, there are no hubs or other networking equipment installed yet, and the machines operate as stand-alone computers. Administration, faculty, and students use the Macintosh computers.

Scott would like to install a Frame Relay network with permanent virtual circuits (PVCs) connecting each of the schools to the district office. Additionally, he would like to move the T1s to the Internet from the high schools to the district office. Then, each school would have Internet access via the district office using these two T1s. He anticipates that in addition to TCP/IP, he will need IPX and AppleTalk connectivity between all sites for the sharing of resources. He has already purchased access to several online educational resources, and he anticipates that Internet utilization will increase significantly as educators begin to use these resources.

Scott would like to remove the Token Ring network at the district office and install Ethernet. He would like your advice on upgrading the schools to either Fast Ethernet or switched Ethernet, especially in the high schools, where the district intends to add multimedia development to the curriculum next year. He intends to keep the Novell servers in place, but he would like to add an additional server at the district office and allow the seven elementary schools (who do not have local servers) to access the common server at the district office for e-mail and file storage. He intends to purchase Novell's GroupWise product and enable the web-based access, allowing both PC and Macintosh users to access e-mail using their web browsers.

Scott also is purchasing a new software package to replace the AS400. The new package runs on Windows NT and uses HTTP for all communications. However, until the new Ethernet network is in place, the new server is installed, and the data is migrated, he must keep the AS400 running and accessible from all of the schools. He is willing to keep a small Token Ring network running at the district office until this is done.

Exercises

1. What protocols is the customer running?

2. Create a detailed network design drawing of Willow Creek's district office's proposed network.

Review Questions

1. Which of the following are categories included in Cisco's Small- to Medium-Sized Business Solutions Framework? (Choose all that apply.)

   A. Media

   B. Subnetting

   C. Routing

   D. Protocol

   E. Contention

   F. Transport

2. Which of the following identifies customer protocol problems?

   A. Broadcasts

   B. Contention

   C. Collisions

   D. Latency

   E. High utilization

3. Which of the following is a solution for customer media problems?

   A. Implementing routing to reduce broadcast domains

   B. Implementing switching to reduce collision domains

   C. Implementing encryption to protect user data

   D. Implementing Fast Ethernet switching or ATM

4. Suppose that MPS Construction decides to upgrade all of their PCs and laptops to Windows 2000. How many client licenses will they need to purchase?

   A. 80

   B. 210

   C. 290

   D. 330

5. Suppose that the Willow Creek School District decides to upgrade the version of Microsoft Office on each of their Macintoshes. How many client licenses will they need to purchase?

   A. 440

   B. 610

   C. 860

   D. 920

6. Which of the following represents an application currently running on PCs at Have-A-Seat?

   A. PC Anywhere

   B. Office-suite applications

   C. Web Server

   D. CAD

7. How many users at Have-A-Seat have been using terminal emulation software?

   A. 30

   B. 90

   C. 210

   D. 400

8. Which protocols are currently running on Willow Creek's network?

   A. IP only

   B. IP and IPX

   C. IP and AppleTalk

   D. IP, IPX, and AppleTalk

9. Consider the following figure. Which of the following does this graphic represent?

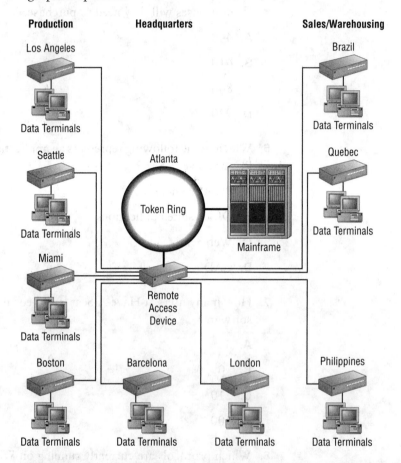

A. A high-level topology of Have-A-Seat's current network

B. A high-level topology of Have-A-Seat's proposed network

C. A detailed network design drawing of Have-A-Seat's current network

D. A detailed network design drawing of Have-A-Seat's proposed network

10. Consider the following figure. Which of the following does this graphic represent?

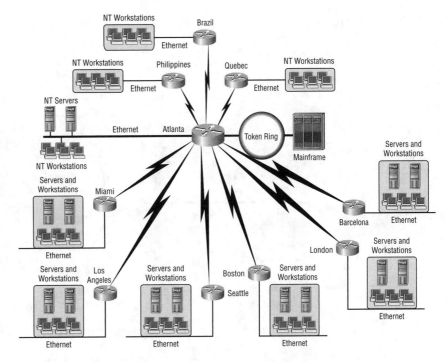

A. A high-level topology of Have-A-Seat's current network

B. A high-level topology of Have-A-Seat's proposed network

C. A detailed network design drawing of Have-A-Seat's current network

D. A detailed network design drawing of Have-A-Seat's proposed network

11. Consider the following figure. Which of the following does this graphic represent?

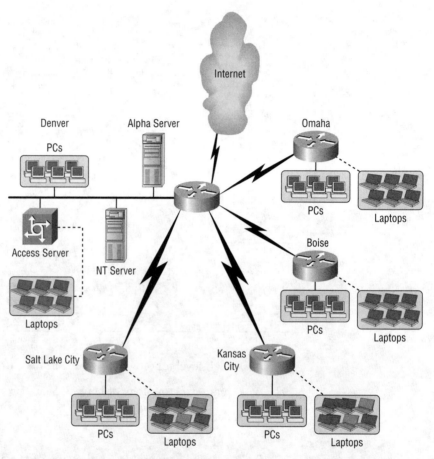

A. A high-level topology of MPS Construction's current network

B. A high-level topology of MPS Construction's proposed network

C. A detailed network design drawing of MPS Construction's current network

D. A detailed network design drawing of MPS Construction's proposed network

12. Consider the following figure. Which of the following does this graphic represent?

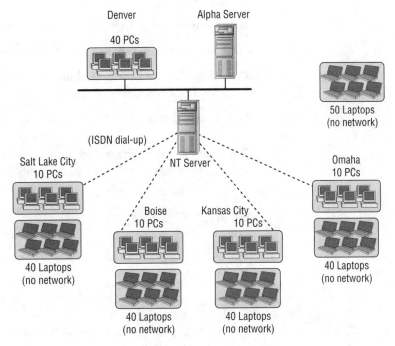

A. A high-level topology of MPS Construction's current network

B. A high-level topology of MPS Construction's proposed network

C. A detailed network design drawing of MPS Construction's current network

D. A detailed network design drawing of MPS Construction's proposed network

13. Suppose you are given the task of diagramming packet flow for Have-A-Seat's new web-based database access. Which of the following would be your first step in completing this diagram?

A. Specify which web server software Have-A-Seat will be installing.

B. Specify which web browser software Have-A-Seat will be installing.

C. Locate all workstations that will access the new web server.

D. Identify a network-addressing scheme.

14. Which of the following needs to be better understood before Have-A-Seat's network utilization can be anticipated for their new network?

    A. The overhead of running a web server on the mainframe

    B. The percentage of broadcasts on Have-A-Seat's segments

    C. The anticipated traffic volume for common operations on Have-A-Seat's new web server

    D. The timeline for installing the new network hardware

15. Which of the following network utilization percentages would indicate saturation on an Ethernet segment? (Choose all that apply.)

    A. 31%

    B. 43%

    C. 75%

    D. 91%

    E. 100%

16. Which of the following network utilization percentages would indicate saturation on a Token Ring segment? (Choose all that apply.)

    A. 31%

    B. 43%

    C. 75%

    D. 91%

    E. 100%

17. Which of the following network utilization percentages would indicate saturation on a WAN segment? (Choose all that apply.)

    A. 31%

    B. 43%

    C. 75%

    D. 91%

    E. 100%

18. Broadcasts should not exceed what percentage of overall traffic?

    A. 1%

    B. 5%

    C. 10%

    D. 20%

19. At what level of CPU utilization would you consider a Cisco router at capacity?

    A. 25%

    B. 50%

    C. 75%

    D. 100%

20. Which of the following identifies a schedule constraint for Have-A-Seat's implementation?

    A. Have-A-Seat's replacement of terminals with PCs

    B. Have-A-Seat's implementation of TCP/IP

    C. Dave's concerns about security on the Atlanta LAN

    D. Have-A-Seat's web server migration

Answers to Review Questions

1. A, D, F.   Media problems are related to utilization, protocol problems are usually caused by excessive broadcasts, and transport problems can be caused by bandwidth limitations.

2. A.   Protocol problems defined in Cisco's Small- to Medium-Sized Business Solutions Framework are usually related to excessive broadcasts.

3. B.   According to Cisco's Small- to Medium-Sized Business Solutions Framework, media problems can be solved by reducing the size of collision domains.

4. C.   In the MPS Construction case study there are a total of 290 PCs, all of which require an operating system license to install Windows 2000.

5. B.   In the Willow Creek School District case study there are a total of 610 Macintoshes, all of which require a license to upgrade Microsoft Office.

6. B.   In the Have-A-Seat case study there are 30 PCs in the Atlanta office that use standard office-suite applications.

7. A.   In the Have-A-Seat case study there are a total of 30 users who have been using terminal emulation software.

8. D.   In the Willow Creek School District case study, the protocols IP, IPX, and AppleTalk are present on the network.

9. A.   The graphic is a typical representation of a high-level topology; this graphic represents Have-A-Seat's current network.

10. B.   The graphic is a typical representation of a high-level topology; this graphic represents Have-A-Seat's proposed network.

11. B.   The graphic is a typical representation of a high-level topology; this graphic represents MPS Construction's proposed network.

12. A.   The graphic is a typical representation of a high-level topology; this graphic represents MPS Construction's current network.

13. C.   Analyzing and predicting packet flow requires knowledge of the clients and the server.

14. C.   In the Have-A-Seat case study, web-based applications will replace their current applications for accessing their data store, so the anticipated traffic volume needs to be assessed.

15. B, C, D, E.   Cisco defines an Ethernet segment utilized at 40 percent or greater to be saturated.

16. C, D, E.   Cisco defines a Token Ring segment utilized at 70 percent or greater to be saturated.

17. C, D, E.   Cisco defines a WAN segment utilized at 70 percent or greater to be saturated.

18. D.   Cisco states that broadcast traffic should be less than 20 percent of all network traffic.

19. C.   Cisco defines a router CPU utilization of 75 percent or greater to be at capacity.

20. D.   In the Have-A-Seat case study, another company has been contracted to install a web server and develop web-based applications. This could cause schedule conflicts or delays when scheduling the WAN migration.

Chapter

5

Designing Modular Network Topologies

CCDA EXAM TOPICS COVERED IN THIS CHAPTER:

✓ Design solutions to meet network owner needs applying the Enterprise Composite Network Model.

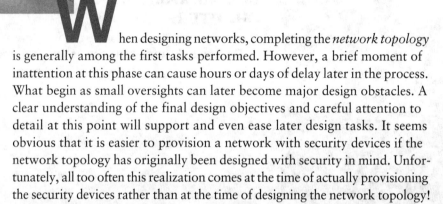

When designing networks, completing the *network topology* is generally among the first tasks performed. However, a brief moment of inattention at this phase can cause hours or days of delay later in the process. What begin as small oversights can later become major design obstacles. A clear understanding of the final design objectives and careful attention to detail at this point will support and even ease later design tasks. It seems obvious that it is easier to provision a network with security devices if the network topology has originally been designed with security in mind. Unfortunately, all too often this realization comes at the time of actually provisioning the security devices rather than at the time of designing the network topology!

This chapter will discuss network topology designs that help you optimize these network features, including scalability, efficiency, and dependability. Given this, we will discuss designing a network structure that meets customer requirements for performance, security, capacity, and scalability, given a specified topology and internetworking constraints. I'll cover the elements of a hierarchical network as specified by the ISO. And, finally, this chapter will cover the advantages, disadvantages, scalability issues, and applicability of standard internetwork topologies.

Hierarchical Topologies

Most of us learned hierarchy early in life. Anyone with older siblings learned what it was like to be at the bottom of a hierarchy! Regardless of where you were first exposed to hierarchy, most of us experience it in many aspects of our lives. Hierarchy helps you to understand where things belong, how things fit together, and what functions go where. It brings order and understandability to otherwise complex models. If you want a pay raise, hierarchy dictates that you ask your boss, not your subordinate. That is the person whose role it is to grant (or deny) your request.

Hierarchy has many of the same benefits in network design that it does in other areas. When used properly in network design, it makes networks more predictable. It helps you to define and expect at which levels of hierarchy you should perform certain functions. You would ask your boss for a raise because of his position in the business hierarchy; you would not ask your subordinate. Likewise, you use tools like access lists at certain levels in hierarchical networks and avoid them at other levels. Let's face it, large networks can be extremely complicated, with multiple *protocols*, detailed configurations, diverse technologies, etc. Hierarchy helps you to summarize a complex collection of details into an understandable model. Then, as specific configurations are needed, the model dictates the appropriate manner in which those configurations should be applied.

Benefits of Hierarchical Topologies

Hierarchy can be applied to network topology in many ways, and Cisco has long encouraged using *hierarchical* design when designing the network topology. The benefits of hierarchy to network topology include improvements to

- *Scalability*
- *Manageability*
- *Performance*
- *Cost*

Let's look at each of these in a bit more depth.

Scalability

Hierarchical networks are easier to scale than other models. Hierarchical networks are actually composed of many individual modules, each with a specific position within the hierarchy. Because their design is modular, expansion can often be as simple as adding new modules into the overall internetwork.

Consider the network shown in Figure 5.1. This example has one main office, two regional offices, and four sales offices. Notice that the configuration is hierarchical.

FIGURE 5.1 A basic hierarchical network

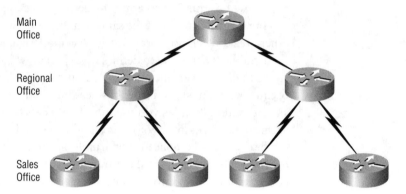

Now suppose that this company grows to the network shown in Figure 5.2. Here, a regional office and four sales offices have been added. Notice that the size of the network has nearly doubled without significantly changing the network topology! Since hierarchies are modular by nature, additional modules (*routers*) were added into the existing hierarchy in a predictable way. It is not necessary to reconfigure the entire network for every expansion, and growth can be dealt with in a controlled and efficient, rather than painful, manner.

FIGURE 5.2 An expanded hierarchical network

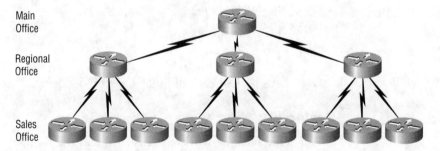

Manageability

Anyone familiar with legacy *Ethernet* will recognize what great fun it is to troubleshoot 10Base2. If the network is down, where do you begin (assuming you lack sophisticated diagnostic tools)? 10BaseT may have required more cable to install, but the cost was almost always justified because it is so much easier to troubleshoot a star-type network than a bus-type network. Hierarchical networks offer similar advantages in troubleshooting. It is much simpler to isolate problems within a hierarchy than in other models such as meshed networks. Consider the example in Figure 5.2. When the *WAN* links fail, it is easy to isolate where the break is with just a few pings. Congestion issues are also easier to isolate and remedy in hierarchical networks than with other designs.

Performance

Performance alone may well justify hierarchical network design. Networks that use hierarchical design can take advantage of advanced routing features such as *route summarization*. This means smaller routing tables and faster convergence in large networks. Meshed networks require larger routing tables and converge slower due to the greater number of possible paths.

Cost

In the end, overall cost is often the driving force. Due to the properties discussed in this section, hierarchical networks generally require fewer administrator hours to maintain and can make more efficient use of hardware and other resources. Hardware needs can be anticipated more readily than in non-hierarchical networks. WAN bandwidth can be more accurately purchased and shared between layers of hierarchy.

Three-Layer Hierarchical Model

Cisco defines three layers of hierarchy, each with specific functionality:

- Core
- Distribution
- Access

Each layer has specific responsibilities. Remember, however, that the three layers are logical and not necessarily physical. The concept of three layers does not have to mean three separate devices. Consider the OSI model, another logical hierarchy. The seven layers describe functions but not necessarily protocols, right? Sometimes a protocol maps to more than one layer of the OSI model, and sometimes multiple protocols communicate within a single layer. In the same way, when you build physical implementations of hierarchical networks, you may have many devices in a single layer, or you might have a single device performing functions at two layers. The definition of the layers is logical, not physical.

Before examining these layers and their functions, consider a common hierarchical design as illustrated in Figure 5.3. The phrase "keep local traffic local" has almost become a cliché in the networking world. However, the underlying concept has merit. Hierarchical design lends itself perfectly to fulfilling this concept. Now, let's take a closer look at each of the layers.

FIGURE 5.3 Hierarchical network design

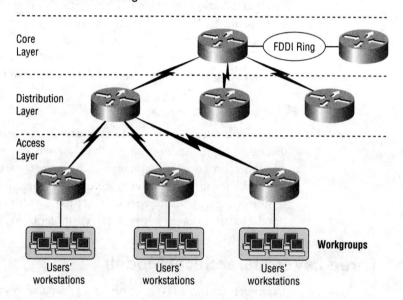

Core Layer

The *core layer* is literally the core of the network. At the top of the hierarchy, it is responsible for transporting large amounts of traffic both reliably and quickly. If there is a failure in the core layer, *every single* user can be affected. Therefore, *fault tolerance* is an issue. The core is likely to see large volumes of traffic. Speed and *latency* are driving concerns here. Given the function of the core, you can now consider some design specifics. Let's start with some things that you know you *don't* want to do at the core:

- Don't do anything to slow down traffic. This includes using access lists, routing VLANs, packet filtering, any type of packet manipulation, etc.

- Don't support workgroup access.

- Avoid expanding the core when the internetwork grows (i.e., adding routers). If performance becomes an issue in the core layer, give preference to upgrades over expansion.

There are a few tasks that you want to make sure to get done as you design the core. They include

- Design the core layer for high reliability. This means redundancy and fault tolerance should both be included.

- Design with speed in mind. The core should have very little latency; it should be fast and efficient.

- Select routing protocols with lower convergence times. Fast and redundant data link connectivity is no help if your routing tables are shot!

A common question network designers face today is the question of whether to use Layer 2 (bridging) or Layer 3 (routing) in the core. Each of these solutions offers some advantages and disadvantages. Layer 2 is generally faster and more scalable but offers less control over load balancing, broadcast control, and router peering. As with many design decisions, it depends on the situation which technology is more appropriate in the core.

Distribution Layer

The *distribution layer* is where much of the action is. Whereas in the core the emphasis is speed, at the distribution layer the emphasis is control. This is the place to implement policies for the network. Here, you can exercise considerable flexibility in defining network operation. There are several tasks that generally should be done at the distribution layer:

- Implementing tools such as access lists, packet filtering, QoS, and queuing

- Implementing security and network policies, including address translation and firewalls

- Redistribution between routing protocols, including static routing

- Route summarization and route filtering

- Load balancing

- Routing between VLANs, and other workgroup support functions

- Providing redundant connections for access devices

Avoid implementing functions at the distribution layer that exclusively belong to one of the other layers.

Access Layer

The *access layer* controls user and workgroup access to internetwork resources. Some of the functions to be included at this layer are

- Continued (from the distribution layer) access control and policies

- Creation of separate *collision domains* (*segmentation*)

- Workgroup connectivity into the distribution layer

Technologies such as DDR (dial-on-demand routing) and Ethernet switching are frequently seen in the access layer. Static routing (instead of dynamic routing protocols) is seen here as well. There are some functions to avoid at the access layer. Take a look at Figure 5.4.

FIGURE 5.4 Access layer additions

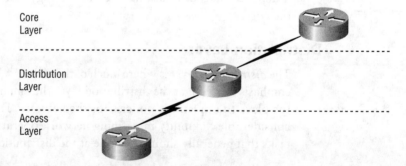

New routers should not be added below the access layer. To do so would expand the diameter of the network, which breaks the predictability of the topology. Should you need to add new routers to support additional workgroups, they should communicate through the distribution layer and thus be *peers* (instead of subordinates) to the other access layer routers.

As already noted, having three separate levels does not have to imply three separate routers. There could be fewer routers, or there could be more routers. Remember, this is a *layered* approach. In this book's case studies, you will consider several scenarios where the functionality of several layers is collapsed inside a single internetworking device.

The three-layer model should be adequate for most small- to medium-sized networks. Only the largest networks might require additional layers.

The Enterprise Composite Network Model

We have just finished discussing hierarchical network design using the core, distribution, and access layers. The principles are sound, and they work. Now let's discuss how to apply them and how they can work in the real world. We'll do this through a discussion of modularity. How do you eat an elephant? One bite at a time, right? Well, how do you build large, scalable networks? You got it—one module at a time.

One challenge you face when using the core, distribution, and access model is that it is not always clear which layer is where in an end-to-end network view. Suppose, for example, that an enterprise has several large campus sites, many small WAN-connected branches, and several external connections to Internet service providers, telecommunications carriers, etc. How and where is the distribution layer?

You'd probably answer by saying that there are several distribution layers, and you'd be correct. In the campus LAN, you may have access devices (Catalyst 3524s, for example), and a distribution layer switch (Catalyst 6500s) that aggregates the access devices. In the WAN, you may have distribution routers (7200s) that aggregate remote branch WAN connections for connectivity back to a central site. How about the Internet connection and DMZ; is there a distribution layer there?

The answer to the preceding question involves analyzing the enterprise in separate modules and applying the three-layer hierarchical design to each module. The campus LAN as a module has access, distribution, and core layers. As a module, the campus LAN can be replicated from campus to campus while still maintaining hierarchy. The WAN module has a similar hierarchy and can also be replicated as the number of WAN-connected sites increases. You don't discard the three-layer design; you realize that modern networks can be extremely complex so you break the network down into modules and apply the hierarchy to the modules. Cisco calls this model the *Enterprise Composite Network Model*.

The Enterprise Composite Network Model defines three functional areas or high-level modules. These modules have clearly defined boundaries, and hierarchy (core-distribution-access) is still applied within the modules. We will be discussing the internals of each module shortly. These three functional areas are as follows:

- Enterprise Campus
- Enterprise Edge
- Service Provider Edge

These three functional areas are not necessarily equal in size. They are intended to define the functional areas of the enterprise network within which hierarchical principles can be applied. Remember, these modules are simply pieces of the overall enterprise network. Let's take a look at each of these functional areas in more detail.

Enterprise Campus Modules

The *Enterprise Campus* functional area contains four major modules. It applies to a single campus and can easily be replicated campus to campus. The four modules of the Enterprise Campus functional area are as follows:

Campus Infrastructure module   The Campus Infrastructure module describes the infrastructure within a building. It is divided into three sub-modules, which correspond to the three-layer hierarchy. The Building Access sub-module represents the access layer, the Building Distribution sub-module represents the distribution layer, and the Campus Backbone sub-module represents the core. Each building has a separate access layer and distribution layer sub-module, all interconnected by the Campus Backbone sub-module. The Campus Infrastructure module handles communications between the other modules of the Enterprise Campus functional area.

Network Management module   The Network Management module represents the network management function in the campus environment. It includes functions such as IDS management, syslogging, SNMP management, network monitoring, and out-of-band management (OBM).

Server Farm module   The Server Farm module contains critical servers and connects them to the Campus Infrastructure Campus Backbone in a highly available way. These servers include all vital functions such as DNS, DHCP, file and print, e-mail, application, etc.

Edge Distribution module   The Edge Distribution module provides distribution layer functions between the Enterprise Campus functional area and the Enterprise Edge functional area (discussed next). The need for a distribution layer between the Campus Backbone and Enterprise Edge modules allows for campus control mechanisms such as access control and security, as well as high-availability and high-capacity communications.

Enterprise Edge Modules

The *Enterprise Edge* functional area also includes four modules. Each of these modules is connected to the Edge Distribution module of the Enterprise Campus functional area. This bridges the gap between the campus site and WAN connectivity. Realize that not every enterprise includes every module. The four modules are as follows:

E-Commerce module   The E-Commerce module contains servers and applications largely intended for external consumption in for-profit activities. Web servers, application and database servers, firewalls, IDS, Layer 4 switches, and content engines all live here.

Internet Connectivity module   The Internet Connectivity module differs from the E-Commerce module in that devices here are supportive of the enterprise not necessarily directly as commerce services. Items such as SMTP mail servers, DNS and public FTP servers, web servers, and firewalls are included in this module.

Remote Access and VPN module   As the name implies, the Remote Access and VPN module includes remote access services, as well as VPN access devices.

WAN module   The WAN module includes the traditional enterprise WAN. Connections from remote offices, external vendors, and SOHO connections are aggregated on a distribution layer device, then handed off through the Edge Distribution module of the Enterprise Campus functional area to the campus backbone.

Service Provider Edge Modules

The *Service Provider Edge* functional area includes three modules. These functions are not generally implemented by the enterprise itself; instead, they are purchased services. Nevertheless, they do involve network connectivity. The three modules are as follows:

Internet Service Provider module   As the name implies, each ISP is a separate module. They are attached to the Enterprise Edge Internet Connectivity, Remote Access and VPN, and E-Commerce modules. Multiple ISPs can provide higher availability.

PSTN module   The PSTN module represents the dial-up components of the enterprise network. ISDN, POTS, and cellular technologies are all included in this module. DDR WAN backup links may also be included.

Frame Relay/ATM module   The Frame Relay/ATM module includes all WAN technologies used within the enterprise. Contrary to its name, this module includes more than just Frame Relay and ATM; it also includes SONET, DSL, wireless, leased lines, and any other permanent WAN connections.

Fault-Tolerant Topologies

Some networks are more important than others. Of course, *all* networks are important, right? However, in some situations network availability (or the lack thereof) can be much more costly. When designing networks, there are many features that when used can significantly increase fault tolerance and decrease the possibility of network outages. Perhaps you have worked with servers that included disk mirroring, RAID, or even redundant servers. That is one form of protection. This section will discuss techniques that ensure that first, hosts can find a path to the internetwork, and second, once they find a path, the path actually works!

Redundant LAN Configurations

It does little good to install routers at the access level if the workstations cannot find and use them. This leads you to investigate how different workstations find routers that lead to the internetwork, and how you can help those workstations find redundant paths out of the *LAN*.

For instance, most network administrators have configured a default router (or default gateway) on a host when setting up TCP/IP. This, along with IP address, subnet mask, and perhaps DNS server, is standard when configuring any TCP/IP device.

Consider the network illustrated in Figure 5.5. Workstation A and Workstation B are assigned the default gateway of 172.16.10.1. ServerA, which has two NICs, also gets a default gateway of 172.16.10.1. Workstation C, however, must be assigned a default gateway of 172.16.20.1, which is the first (and only, in this diagram) router that it sees. It cannot contact the router at 172.16.10.1 directly because they are on separate data link networks! Once the administrator has this all mapped out, he can configure all of the devices with TCP/IP information.

FIGURE 5.5 A sample internetwork

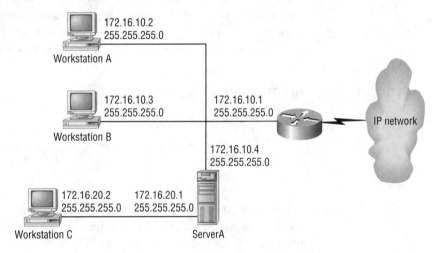

Some implementations of TCP/IP will allow for multiple default gateways, while others provide for the workstation to listen to routing updates to learn of routers. Any of these methods will provide the client with redundant paths out should the primary router fail, and redundancy should be considered when available. Unfortunately, the most common method of default router configuration is to statically assign the default router at the client. This means that should the router fail, there are two options: fix the router or reconfigure the workstation. Hardly fault tolerant! There are two Cisco solutions to this problem: HSRP and proxy ARP support.

HSRP

HSRP stands for Hot Standby Router Protocol. HSRP can allow IP devices to keep working through their default router even when that router fails. It does this by creating what Cisco calls a *phantom* router on the network. This phantom router does not exist physically, but it has a MAC address and an IP address. Workstations are configured to use the phantom router's IP address as a default gateway. The phantom address is actually passed among the physical routers participating in HSRP. If the physical router hosting the phantom router's MAC and IP addresses fails, another physical router will automatically answer to the phantom's MAC and IP address and accept the traffic. The workstations need never be aware that the hardware they are talking to has changed, and the MAC and IP addresses they have been using continue to function as if nothing has ever happened!

Figure 5.6 is a diagram of the network from the workstation's view. It is a logical, not physical, diagram. The workstation believes that there is a single router connecting it to the larger internetwork. It is configured with the IP address of this router for use as a default gateway.

FIGURE 5.6 An HSRP example—logical

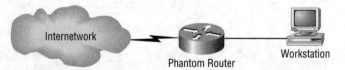

However, the actual hardware looks a bit different, as shown in Figure 5.7. There are actually two routers, only one of which is currently answering to the phantom router's MAC and IP addresses. The two routers in Figure 5.7 must communicate to ensure that the phantom router's IP and MAC addresses are always available. After configuration, one of the two routers is chosen to be *active* and the other to be *standby*. The active router will proceed to answer requests for the phantom router's IP and MAC addresses. It will also communicate with the standby router using "hello" messages. If for some reason the standby router is unable to communicate using hellos with the active router, it assumes that the active router has failed, and it begins to answer requests addressed to the phantom router's IP and MAC addresses. The end result is that the workstation ends up with redundant IP paths out, even though it is statically configured to look for a single path out.

FIGURE 5.7   An HSRP example—physical

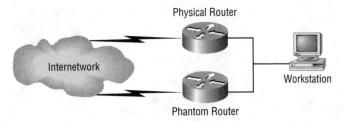

Proxy ARP

Some IP stacks can be configured to take advantage of *proxy ARP*. You may recall that under normal circumstances, workstations will only ARP for IP addresses that are on their local network. However, when using proxy ARP, these workstations will send out ARP requests for *every* IP device that they want to communicate with, regardless of whether it is on their local network or not. Any router hearing this request, and able to reach the desired IP address, can respond to the ARP with its own MAC address. From the workstation's view, it looks like the whole world is one big LAN. The routers take care of the details of reaching remote segments. Proxy ARP is now enabled by default in all Cisco routers.

The end result is that workstations can dynamically locate redundant paths out of the LAN. By sending out the ARP request (which is a broadcast), a response can come from any router able to reach the required destination. Thus if one router fails, the workstation can immediately begin to communicate with the internetwork through any other available routers. You can easily see proxy ARP in action by just setting your Windows machine's default gateway to be the same as your own IP address and watching it go!

Redundant WAN Connections

As you have just seen, there are several techniques to provide redundancy in the links between clients and servers on the LAN. Now let's consider ways to provide redundancy inside the WAN.

Consider the network illustrated in Figure 5.8. This is a *full mesh* network, where every node has a direct link to every other node. For fault tolerance, this is great! However, it is far from efficient and does not scale well. Also, it has departed from the hierarchical topology. However, there is a solution that will preserve hierarchy while providing redundancy in the WAN: a partial mesh topology.

FIGURE 5.8 A full mesh network

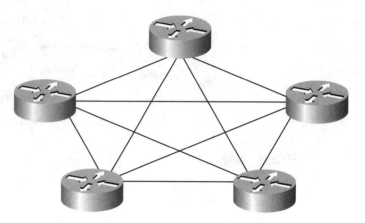

Partial Mesh Topology

A *partial mesh* has been implemented in the network shown in Figure 5.9. Notice that the hierarchy has been preserved, yet each node has a redundant link to the layer above it. This design provides all the advantages of hierarchical design, is scalable, and can take advantage of load balancing.

FIGURE 5.9 A redundant hierarchical network

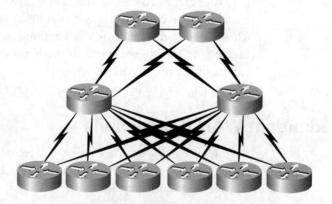

There are several ways to add the additional WAN connections. They could be added in identical pairs—that is, you could install two T1 lines rather than one. This provides the ultimate in redundancy. If one T1 fails, there is another one waiting to go. However, from a cost perspective this can be similar to buying two new cars just in case one gets a flat tire. True, you will probably never have to walk to work, but that security will certainly cost you.

An alternative to having identical connections to the next layer is to have links that are not the same, that is, perhaps a T1 and a 56K backup line. Should the primary line fail, internetwork connectivity can be preserved, although generally at a reduced level. Once again, cost will most likely determine the capacity of the backup line.

Cisco has a solution that is a special case of this second example, that is, where the two connections are not the same. In this case, the second, or backup, line is not even running until the primary line fails! You will learn about this solution next.

DDR Backup

Not all redundant links have to be dedicated lines. In many cases, an ISDN BRI is used to back up a dedicated leased line. This can be a great advantage, because you will probably not want to bring the ISDN up unless the primary line fails (or becomes overloaded). Cisco's *DDR (dial-on-demand routing)* allows this configuration. The ISDN line can be configured to come up only when the primary line either fails or is under heavy load. Of course, should the primary line fail and you have to depend on your backup, you will likely not have the same bandwidth available that you normally do. However, you will probably be paying significantly less than you would to have a pair of dedicated lines.

DDR configuration is covered in greater detail in the *CCNP/CCIP: BSCI Study Guide,* also by Sybex.

Performance: Load Balancing

Redundant links are not cheap to operate, but in some situations they are called for. If you are going to pay for redundant links, you would likely want to use both lines when they are both available, and that brings us to *load balancing*.

With most IP routing protocols, load balancing is automatic. Dynamic routing protocols are supposed to find the redundant paths, and dynamic IP routing protocols will use both available paths. However, this is not always a good thing.

Difficulties can arise when the multiple paths out do not have the same bandwidth or cost. Suppose that you have a T1 and a 56Kbps line (for backup) connecting your access layer router into distribution layer routers, as shown in Figure 5.10.

FIGURE 5.10 Pinhole congestion

T-1

56K   Access Router

Some routing protocols (for example, those that use hop count) could see these two paths and load balance across them just fine until the 56K is full. At that point, the load is equally balanced. However, these protocols are not smart enough to realize that over 90 percent of the total bandwidth is going unused on the T1! Once any link is operating at capacity, these routing protocols are not capable of sending additional traffic across links still not at capacity, because they do not understand capacity as a metric. This problem is called *pinhole congestion* and is avoided by using advanced routing protocols such as Enhanced IGRP.

Summary

Network topology design can make the rest of the design process either significantly easier or more difficult. Cisco recommends using a hierarchical network design, which offers many benefits, including predictability, scalability, efficiency, cost control, and security.

Furthermore, Cisco recommends that small- to medium-sized businesses use a three-layered approach to hierarchy consisting of these layers: core, distribution, and access. Each layer has clearly defined functions, and once the network is established, it can scale significantly before it needs to be re-engineered. The core layer at the top of the hierarchy is for transporting large amounts of traffic reliably and quickly. Fault tolerance should be designed within the core layer, and high speed and low latency should be the driving concerns. The distribution layer should be designed for network traffic policies; control mechanisms such as access lists, packet filters, address translation, and redistribution; DDR; static routing; and firewall rules. The access layer at the bottom of the hierarchy is where users connect and should be where collision domains are defined.

In practice, you can break the real-world enterprise down into simpler modules using the Enterprise Composite Network Model. It segments the network into three functional areas, each of which contains multiple modules. Those functional areas are Enterprise Campus, Enterprise Edge, and Service Provider Edge. This is not a replacement for hierarchical design; rather, it is a systematic and scalable way to implement the hierarchical design principles.

Topologies that enhance network fault tolerance are often required. IP features such as HSRP and proxy ARP can improve fault tolerance in the workstation-to-router communication. Redundant WAN links can provide additional fault tolerance and can be used inside of hierarchical designs. Technologies such as DDR provide for backup links. When redundant links are used, design consideration should be given to load balancing. Issues such as pinhole congestion should be identified and avoided.

Exam Essentials

Remember the benefits of hierarchical network topology design. Hierarchical networks are easier to scale, they permit easier manageability, they offer better performance, and they minimize support and troubleshooting costs.

Understand the layers and design use of the Cisco three-layer hierarchical model. The core layer is responsible for high-speed, low-latency traffic flow and should not include traffic-management design controls. The distribution layer is where traffic control occurs in the hierarchical model and should include traffic-management designs. The access layer at the bottom of the model controls user and workgroup access to the internetwork and can include access control and network policies much like the distribution layer.

Remember the three functional areas of the Enterprise Composite Network Model. The three functional areas of the Enterprise Composite Network Model are Enterprise Campus, Enterprise Edge, and Service Provider Edge. Each functional area is made up of several modules.

Remember the fault-tolerant topology design redundancies. HSRP allows devices to keep working through their default router, even when that router fails, by using a phantom router to switch between redundant routers. Proxy ARP–configured routers provide redundancy to workstations since the workstation doesn't need a hard-coded default gateway and routers can be replaced and located again. DDR allows a redundant link to provide backup in case the primary link fails or is under heavy load.

Key Terms

Before you take the exam, be certain you are familiar with the following terms:

access layer	manageability
collision domains	network topology
core layer	partial mesh
cost	peers
DDR (dial-on-demand routing)	performance
distribution layer	phantom
Enterprise Campus	pinhole congestion
Enterprise Composite Network Model	protocols
Enterprise Edge	proxy ARP
Ethernet	route summarization
fault tolerance	routers
full mesh	scalability
hierarchical	segmentation
HSRP	Service Provider Edge
LAN	switches
latency	WAN
load balancing	

Case Studies

Let's take a look at how hierarchy and security apply to the three case study companies.

Have-A-Seat

1. Dave had requested a method of providing a backup should the WAN link between production facilities and the Atlanta headquarters fail. Describe your recommendations on solving this problem using DDR and dedicated links.

MPS Construction

1. Draw a diagram of how you would implement MPS's Internet connection and discuss how you would provide the limitations that Mike has requested. Be sure to specify which modules of the Enterprise Composite Network Model are being represented.

2. Mike has mentioned that his network must scale to accommodate new sites as they are added. Describe how a modular design will allow Mike to achieve this objective.

Willow Creek School District

1. Draw a diagram of Willow Creek's network and identify the three layers of hierarchy present.

2. Scott mentioned that he will maintain two T1s to the Internet. Discuss any concerns regarding load balancing and redundancy over these two lines.

Review Questions

1. Which of the following are advantages of hierarchical design? (Choose all that apply.)

   A. Fault tolerance

   B. Scalability

   C. Ease of manageability

   D. Predictability

   E. All of the above

2. Which of the following are layers in Cisco's three-layer hierarchical design? (Choose all that apply.)

   A. Backbone

   B. Core

   C. End node

   D. Access

   E. Distribution

3. Which of the following should be included at the core layer? (Choose all that apply.)

   A. Packet filtering

   B. Firewalls

   C. Fast throughput

   D. Fault tolerance

   E. Additional devices

4. How many layers of hierarchy should you add below the access layer?

   A. None

   B. One

   C. Two

   D. Three

   E. Four

5. Which of the following are permitted at the distribution layer? (Choose all that apply.)

   A. Packet filtering

   B. Access lists

   C. Queuing

   D. Redundant WAN connections

   E. Firewalls

6. Which of the following are generally associated with the core layer of the network? (Choose all that apply.)

   A. Security

   B. High capacity

   C. Fault tolerance

   D. Packet filtering

7. Which of the following are modules in the Enterprise Campus functional area of the Enterprise Composite Network Model? (Choose all that apply.)

   A. Enterprise Edge

   B. Server Farm

   C. Network Management

   D. All of the above

8. Which of the following methods will allow IP workstations to dynamically locate routers? (Choose all that apply.)

   A. HSRP

   B. Workstation listening to routing protocols

   C. Router location request

   D. Proxy ARP

   E. RTMP

9. You need to add a new site to your hierarchical network. Which of the following are possible places to connect the new site into your existing network?

   A. Access layer

   B. Distribution layer

   C. Core layer

   D. The corporate office

10. When designing fault-tolerant network topologies, which of the following can DDR accomplish? (Choose all that apply.)

    A. Back up a primary link in case of failure.

    B. Promote a router from the access layer to the distribution layer.

    C. Populate Enhanced IGRP tables with routing information.

    D. Back up a primary link in case of heavy network load.

    E. Back up a primary link in case of routing problems.

11. Select the topology in which it is easiest to troubleshoot connectivity issues.

    A. Bus

    B. Ring

    C. Hierarchical

    D. Mesh

12. Which three of the following are functional areas of the Enterprise Composite Network Model?

    A. Enterprise Campus

    B. Core

    C. Distribution

    D. Enterprise Edge

    E. Service Provider Edge

13. You have a T1 link from an access layer router to a distribution layer router and a BRI DDR connection to another distribution layer router. The DDR is configured to run in case of failure. Which of the following do you have?

    A. Proxy ARP

    B. Fault tolerance

    C. Load balancing

    D. HSRP

    E. None of the above

14. Which of the following are advantages of Layer 3 switching over Layer 2 switching in the core of a network? (Choose all that apply.)

    A. Broadcast control

    B. Spanning tree

    C. Latency

    D. Load balancing

    E. Router peering

15. You have two routers that will be participating in HSRP. How many IP and MAC addresses will the workstations use for their default router?

    A. None, they communicate with the phantom router.

    B. One

    C. Two

    D. Three

16. What is the problem caused during IP load balancing by routing protocols that use hop count as a metric?

    A. Pinhole congestion

    B. Failure

    C. Convergence delay

    D. You can't load balance IP.

17. You have a T1 link from an access layer router to a distribution layer router and a BRI DDR connection to another access layer router. The DDR is configured to run in case of failure. Which of the following do you have?

    A. Proxy ARP

    B. Pinhole congestion

    C. Load balancing

    D. HSRP

    E. None of the above

18. How can redundant links be added into a hierarchical design without breaking the hierarchy?

    A. Full mesh

    B. Partial mesh

    C. Creating a ring

    D. Redundant links can't be added into a hierarchical design without breaking the hierarchy.

19. Your customer has a hierarchical network design. Redundancy and reliability are most important at which layer?

    A. Backbone

    B. Distribution

    C. Access

    D. Core

20. In general, at which layer of Cisco's hierarchical model are functions such as packet filtering, route summarization, and routing protocol redistribution performed?

    A. Access

    B. Distribution

    C. Core

    D. Enterprise Campus

Answers to Review Questions

1. E.   All of the answers are advantages of hierarchical design and provide many benefits when managing and troubleshooting networks.

2. B, D, E.   Cisco's three-layer hierarchical model is made up of the core, distribution, and access layers. These three layers are not always clearly defined within each and every network design, but they serve as a guideline.

3. C, D.   The core layer is responsible for high-speed traffic flow and redundancy.

4. A.   The access layer where users connect is the bottom layer and should not have any other layers below it.

5. A, B, C, D, E.   All of these traffic-management technologies are usually implemented at the distribution layer, but they can extend into the access layer.

6. B, C.   The core layer is concerned with capacity and fault tolerance. Packet filtering and security are generally implemented at the distribution layer.

7. B, C.   The four modules of the Enterprise Campus functional area are Campus Infrastructure, Network Management, Server Farm, and Edge Distribution. Enterprise Edge is a separate functional area, not a module of the Enterprise Campus functional area.

8. B, D.   Proxy ARP is used by IP workstations, while IPX and AppleTalk workstations listen for routing protocol updates, or they request them from the network.

9. B.   You should avoid changing the diameter and consistency of the core layer, and the access layer is for "local site" client access.

10. A, D, E.   Floating routes and OSPF demand circuits allow DDR to bring up a second link in the event of routing problems.

11. C.   One of the main design purposes of hierarchical networks is troubleshooting. The other purpose is network management.

12. A, D, E.   The three functional areas of the Enterprise Composite Network model are Enterprise Campus, Enterprise Edge, and Service Provider Edge.

13. B.   From a single access layer router, multiple distribution layer connections provide for fault tolerance.

14. A, D, E.   Layer 3 switching aids in broadcast control, load balancing, and router peering.

15. B.   The advantage of HSRP is that the clients never need to change their default router configuration, even when a router failure occurs. They are always configured to use the phantom router IP and MAC addresses.

16. A.   RIP and IGRP use hop count as a metric and cannot detect links of different speeds. Consequently, they can't detect when redundant links are unequally used.

17. E.   You have broken the hierarchical model by connecting two access layer routers.

18. B.   A full mesh addition would break the hierarchy and create a flat network design.

19. D.   The core layer affects all other layers in the hierarchical network design, so redundancy and reliability are crucial at this layer.

20. B.   Packet filtering, route summarization, and redistribution are generally handled at the distribution layer.

Chapter 6

Enterprise WAN Design

CCDA EXAM TOPICS COVERED IN THIS CHAPTER:

✓ Given a network design or a set of requirements evaluate a solution to incorporate equipment and technology within a Campus design.

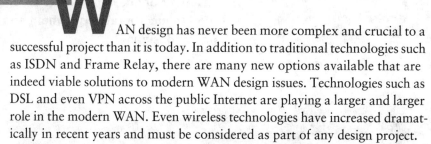

WAN design has never been more complex and crucial to a successful project than it is today. In addition to traditional technologies such as ISDN and Frame Relay, there are many new options available that are indeed viable solutions to modern WAN design issues. Technologies such as DSL and even VPN across the public Internet are playing a larger and larger role in the modern WAN. Even wireless technologies have increased dramatically in recent years and must be considered as part of any design project.

This chapter introduces WAN design. We will organize the many technologies into categories, discussing the pros and cons of each. We will discuss WAN design methodologies and the steps to take in starting the WAN design. We will look at several specific WAN technologies, both tried-and-true as well as several new options. Finally, we will discuss specific WAN technologies and their particulars.

This chapter addresses the following topics:

- Wide area networking options

- Planning and design methodologies

- Cisco hardware and implementation issues

- WAN technologies in detail

WAN Options

When wide area networks (WANs) are required, there are three broad categories the network designer has to choose from:

- Private networks

- Leased networks

- Public networks

Private networks are relatively rare. They are networks where the WAN customer actually owns the WAN infrastructure. This includes cabling, fiber, switching equipment, etc. Leased networks are the most common; they are wide area services purchased from a service provider. Public networks generally involve attaching sites to the public Internet and allowing them to communicate across the public space.

Cisco supports each of these different types of WANs, providing ample flexibility and many options for meeting internetworking business requirements. Let's consider each of these WAN types.

Private Networks

As mentioned, private networks are relatively rare due to their cost and lack of flexibility. Few enterprises have the capacity to install truly private networks. Do you really want to know what it would cost to run fiber from Denver to Chicago? A cost-effective example of a private network is a large university (or other) campus where the distances are relatively short. In this case, the cost of installing the fiber or copper to connect separate buildings is relatively small compared to the cost of paying an external service provider to connect buildings only a few hundred yards apart. Another example of a private network might include wireless technologies. Your humble author has installed more than one microwave system capable of covering significant distances.

While the up-front costs of private networks can be considerable, there are advantages. Once installed, operating costs are relatively low compared to other offerings, and maintenance and management are simplified in that no external entity is involved.

Leased Networks

There are many technologies for Layer 2 and Layer 3 that are available in the marketplace when a leased WAN network is required. However, they can be consolidated into several large categories. This section discusses three of these categories:

- Dedicated leased lines
- Circuit-switched networks
- Packet-switched networks

Most of the available technologies fit into one of these three categories.

Dedicated Leased Lines

Point-to-point serial links are dedicated links that provide full-time connectivity. They connect into a CSU/DSU (channel service unit/data service unit), which then plugs into the demarc provided by the telephone company.

Figure 6.1 shows how point-to-point connections can be made between remote offices and the corporate office.

FIGURE 6.1   Point-to-point connections between branches and the corporate office

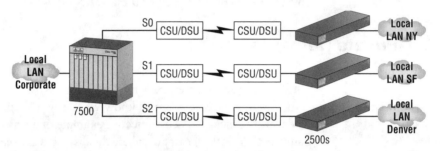

If the established business requirements dictate that constant connection and steady data flow must prevail, a dedicated point-to-point connection can be an optimal solution. But even so, this approach does have a disadvantage associated with it: Point-to-point connections require that you pay tariffs for them even when the connection is in an idle state with no data being transmitted. Essentially, you pay for the entire pipe whether you use it or not.

Dedicated lines are always the preferred choice when they are available and cost-effective. However, in many situations dedicated lines tend to be significantly more expensive than other alternatives.

Circuit-Switched Networks

The fundamental advantage of circuit-switched networks is cost savings. When you hear "circuit-switched," think "phone call." This type of WAN connection literally makes a "call" when data needs to be transferred and then "hangs up" when finished. Since you only pay for the time you use and not for the time you do not use, this solution can be more cost-effective than the dedicated leased lines discussed earlier.

Any user with an asynchronous modem can make connections to an internetwork using the PSTN (Public Switched Telephone Network), and there are many common situations requiring this type of access. Users who are traveling can dial in to gather e-mails or update a database, while others may want to dial in from home to finish projects, send and retrieve e-mails, and even print documents to be available for them when they arrive at work the next day.

ISDN is another common circuit-switched network. ISDN interfaces can be activated when needed and then allowed to disconnect when they're no longer required. One common use of ISDN is as a backup when another network fails. Since it is circuit-switched, it can be a very cost-effective backup, assuming your primary connection is reasonably stable!

Packet-Switched Networks

Packet-switched networks (PSNs) are essentially shared networks. In this case, it is almost like you are getting a dedicated leased line and then "selling off" the bandwidth you don't use. You do this by sharing the infrastructure with other customers of the service provider.

Packet-switched services are usually run over a publicly maintained network such as the PSTN, but if necessary, a large organization can build a PSN. PSN data delivery can take place within frames, packets, or cells, and occurs transparently to end users.

PSNs can be either private or public networks. Switching devices forward packets using an internal addressing scheme, which can be entirely different from what's used on the LAN. This is because a switch that's located at the WAN provider's office typically checks the address field of the packets only and then carries out the forwarding based on the static routes configured by an administrator.

Frame Relay is a common packet-switched technology used in networks today. It allows your organization the ability to pay for a certain amount of bandwidth (CIR), and then use more bandwidth if it's available (bursting). For many longer distance situations, Frame Relay can be significantly less expensive than dedicated leased lines. In addition, it can be indistinguishable as far as application traffic is concerned, depending on the application, of course.

Public Networks

Most of you are aware that the most commonly used public network is the Internet. In many cases, it is significantly cheaper to connect two geographically dispersed sites to a local ISP than to invest in any of the WAN technologies discussed thus far in this chapter. These sites can then use the public Internet to carry their data back and forth. The advantages of the Internet include reduced cost, but of course, this comes at a price. There are no guarantees for delivery across the Internet; connectivity is strictly a best-effort affair.

Common technologies used when connecting to the Internet include DSL and cable modems. Virtual private network (VPN) technology is commonly used to protect data crossing the public network.

Planning and Designing WANs

With the overview of WAN technologies out of the way, let's take a deeper look at the actual planning and design process. First, we'll look at the methodology used in design: PDIOO (planning, design, implementation, operation, and optimization). After that, we will discuss the important criteria you need to consider when completing the design.

PDIOO

PDIOO stands for planning, design, implementation, operation, and optimization. This methodology for designing the Enterprise Edge WAN can be broken down into three main steps:

1. Analyze the customer requirements.

2. Characterize the existing network.

3. Design the topology.

Let's spend a few moments on each of these steps.

Analyze the Customer Requirements

There are many things to learn about the customer's network before proceeding further with the design. Application traffic and flows must be discovered and mapped. You must anticipate new applications, network growth, and the relocation of existing application traffic. Do any of the new applications have specific network requirements (VoIP, for example)? Is growth projected? Where? Answers to these questions will help prevent networks from becoming obsolete before they are implemented.

Characterize the Existing Network

This step includes an inventory of current network assets, as well as a characterization of the current network's ability to expand to meet new network requirements. Do the network devices have the memory, processing power, and other capabilities to handle the new requirements? Can my current routers handle IPSec *and* QoS? Can some of them? How have current Layer 2 technologies been working? Can you leave some of these pieces in place? Answers to these questions help the designer to understand the starting point of the implementation.

Design the Topology

Once the preceding steps have been completed, the next step is to create the network topology. This should consider existing resources, but should also include the new requirements such as backup or redundant connections, bandwidth issues, and software and QoS requirements.

WAN Design Criteria

WAN designs should minimize the cost of bandwidth and optimize bandwidth efficiency. For example, you want to minimize the cost of bandwidth and optimize bandwidth efficiency between the corporate office and the remote offices.

As a company grows, it's imperative that its internetwork grow with it. The network's administrator must understand the various user-group differences regarding their specialized needs for the melange of LAN and WAN resources and find a way to meet—or better yet exceed—these requirements while planning for growth as well. The following important factors must be considered when defining and researching business requirements for the purposes of internetwork design or refinement:

Availability Because networks are so heavily relied upon—they're ideally up and running 24 hours a day, 365 days a year—failures and down time must be minimized. It's also vital that when a failure does occur, it's easy to isolate so that the time needed to troubleshoot the problem is reduced.

Bandwidth Accurately determining the actual and eventual bandwidth requirements with information gathered from both users and management is crucial. It can be advantageous to contract with a service provider to establish connectivity between remote sites. Bandwidth considerations are also an important element for the next consideration—cost.

Cost In a perfect world, you could install nothing but Cisco switches that provide switched 100Mbps to each desktop with gigabit speeds between data closets and remote offices. However, since the world's not perfect and often budget constraints simply won't allow for doing that, Cisco offers an abundance of switches and routers tailored to many wallet sizes. This is one major reason why it's so important to accurately assess your actual needs. A budget must be carefully delimited when designing an internetwork.

Ease of management   The ramifications associated with creating any network connections, such as the degree of difficulty, must be understood and regarded carefully. Factors associated with configuration *management* include analyses of both the initial configuration and the ongoing configuration tasks related to running and maintaining the entire internetwork. Traffic management issues—the ability to adjust to different traffic rates, especially in bursty networks—also apply here.

Types of application traffic   Application traffic can be typically composed of small to very large packets, and the internetwork design must reflect and regard the typical traffic type to meet business requirements.

Routing protocols   The characteristics of these protocols can cause some ugly problems and steal a lot of precious bandwidth in networks where they're either not understood or not configured properly.

Implementation Issues

Connectivity between LANs and WANs implies routing. Any WAN design must consider the "off ramp" to the LAN, and that is the router. Here, you look at the routing process inside a router. This process comes into play each time information goes from LAN to WAN and back again. Finally, you look at the switching process inside the router. Cisco devices offer several types of switching paths, and understanding this technology is required to correctly design WAN access devices.

The Routing Process

Routers are Layer 3 devices that are used to forward incoming packets to their destination by using logical addressing. IP addresses are logical addresses. Routers share information about these logical addresses with each other, and this information is stored in route tables. The router uses the route table to map the path through the router to the destination IP address.

Two processes must be present for routing to work properly. First is *path determination*, which means that the router knows a route that leads to the desired destination address. The second is actually moving the packet from the inbound interface to the proper outbound interface.

For example, suppose a packet is forwarded to Router B via the routing process. Router B tells Router A that it knows a route to the destination address. Once Router B has the packet, it finds the outgoing port associated to the destination address of 172.16.1.10. Once the route is found, the router moves the packet to the outgoing interface Serial 1. After the packet reaches interface Serial 1, it is routed toward the destination of 172.16.1.10.

This is the basic routing process. For routes to be shared among adjacent routers, a routing protocol must be used. Routing *protocols* are used for routers to be able to calculate, learn, and advertise route table information.

Metrics are associated with each route that is present in the route table. Metrics are calculated by the routing protocol to define the cost of getting to the destination address. Some algorithms use hop count (the number of routers between it and the destination address), whereas others use a vector of values.

Once a metric is assigned to a route, a router advertises this information to all adjacent routers. Thus, each router maintains a topology and map of how to get to connected networks. By connected, we do not mean directly connected, but simply that there exists some type of network connection between the destination address and the router.

Switching Modes of Routers

The *switching path*—the logical path that a packet follows when it's switched through a router—takes place at Layer 3 of the OSI model. There are many types of switching, and it is important not to confuse them. This section successfully explains methods used by routers to move a packet from an incoming interface to the correct outgoing interface. By using switching paths, extra lookups in route tables are eliminated, and processing overhead is reduced.

The router's physical design and its interfaces allow for a variety of switching processes on the router. This frees up the processor to focus on other tasks instead of looking up the source and destination information for every packet that enters the router.

We have already discussed router architecture, so let's focus directly on the details of each switching type. The most processor-intensive method (*process switching*) is discussed first; the discussion ends with the most efficient method of switching (Cisco Express Forwarding).

Process Switching

As a packet arrives on an interface to be forwarded, it eventually is copied to the router's process buffer, and the router performs a lookup on the Layer 3 address. (*Eventually* means that there are a few steps before the packet is copied to the route processor buffer.) Using the route table, an exit interface is associated with the destination address. The processor encapsulates and forwards the packet with the added new information to the exit interface while the router initializes the fast switching cache. Subsequent packets that require process switching and are bound for the same destination address follow the same path as the first packet.

Overhead ensues because the processor is occupied with Layer 3 lookups—determining which interface the packet should exit from and calculating the cyclical redundancy checksum (CRC) for the packets. If every packet required all of that to be routed, the processor could get really bogged down. The answer is to use fast switching whenever and wherever possible.

Fast Switching

Fast switching is an enhancement from process switching. The first packet of a new session is copied to the interface processor buffer. The packet is then copied to the bus and sent to the switch processor. A check is made against other switching caches (for example, silicon or autonomous) for an existing entry. Fast switching is then used because no entries exist within the more efficient caches. The packet header is copied and sent to the route processor, where the fast switching cache resides. Assuming that an entry exists in the cache, the packet is encapsulated for fast switching and sent back to the switch processor. Finally, the packet is copied to the buffer on the outgoing interface processor. From there, it is sent out the interface.

Fast switching is on by default for lower end routers like the 4000/2500 series. Sometimes, it's necessary to turn fast switching off when troubleshooting network problems. Because packets don't move across the route processor after the first packet is process-switched, you can't see them with packet-level tracing. It's also helpful to turn off fast switching if the interface card's memory is limited or consumed, or to alleviate congestion when low-speed interfaces become flooded with information from high-speed interfaces.

Autonomous Switching

Autonomous switching works by comparing packets against the autonomous switching cache. You probably recognize a pattern by now. When a packet arrives on the interface processor, it checks the switching cache closest to it. So far, all of these caches reside on other processor boards. The same is true of autonomous switching. The silicon switching cache is checked first; then the autonomous cache is checked. The packet is encapsulated for autonomous switching and sent back to the interface processor. Notice that this time, the packet header was not sent to the route processor.

Autonomous switching is available only on AGS+ and Cisco 7000 series routers that have high-speed controller interface cards.

Silicon Switching

Silicon switching is available only on the Cisco 7000 with an SSP (Silicon Switch Processor). Silicon-switched packets are compared to the silicon switching cache on the SSE (silicon switching engine). The SSP is a dedicated switch processor that offloads the switching process from the route processor, which provides a fast switching solution. However, packets must still traverse the backplane of the router to get to the SSP and then back to the exit interface.

Optimum Switching

Optimum switching follows the same procedure as the other switching algorithms. When a new packet enters the interface, it is compared to the optimum switching cache, rewritten, and sent to the chosen exit interface. Other packets associated with the same session then follow the same path. All processing is carried out on the interface processor, including the CRC. Optimum switching is faster than both fast switching and NetFlow switching, unless you have implemented several access lists.

Optimum switching replaces fast switching on the high-end routers. As with fast switching, optimum switching also needs to be turned off to view packets while troubleshooting a network problem.

Distributed Switching

Distributed switching happens on the VIP (Versatile Interface Processor) cards (which have a switching processor onboard), so it's very efficient. All required processing is done right on the VIP processor, which maintains a copy of the router's routing cache. With this arrangement, even the first packet doesn't need to be sent to the route processor to initialize the switching path, as it does with the other switching algorithms. Router efficiency increases as more VIP cards are added.

NetFlow Switching

NetFlow switching is really more of an administrative tool than a performance-enhancement tool. It collects detailed data for use with circuit accounting and application-utilization information. Due to all the additional data that NetFlow collects (and may export), expect an increase in router overhead—possibly as much as a five percent increase in CPU utilization.

NetFlow switching can be configured on most interface types and can be used in a switched environment. ATM, LAN, and VLAN technologies all support NetFlow switching; the Cisco 7200 and 7500 series routers provide its implementation.

NetFlow switching does much more than just switching—it also gathers statistical data, including protocol, port, and user information. All of this is stored in the NetFlow switching cache according to the individual flow that's defined by the packet information (destination address, source address, protocol, source and destination port, and the incoming interface). The data can be sent to a network management station to be stored and processed there.

The NetFlow switching process is very efficient. An incoming packet is processed by the fast or optimum switching process, and then all path and packet information is copied to the NetFlow cache. The remaining packets that belong to the flow are compared to the NetFlow cache and forwarded accordingly.

The first packet that's copied to the NetFlow cache contains all security and routing information, and if an access list is applied to an interface, the first packet is matched against it. If it matches the access list criteria, the cache is flagged so that the remaining packets in the flow can be switched without being compared to the list. (This is very effective when a large amount of access list processing is required.)

Do you remember reading that distributed switching on VIP cards is really efficient because it lessens the load to the Route/Switch Protocol (RSP)? Well, NetFlow switching can also be configured on VIP interfaces.

NetFlow gives you amenities such as the security flag in the cache that allows subsequent packets of an established flow to avoid access list processing. It's comparable to optimum and distributed switching and is much better if access lists (especially long ones) are placed in the switching path. However, the detailed information NetFlow gathers and exports does load down the system, so plan carefully before implementing NetFlow switching on a router.

Cisco Express Forwarding

Cisco Express Forwarding (CEF) is a switching function designed for high-end backbone routers. It functions on Layer 3 of the OSI model, and its biggest asset is the capability to remain stable in a large network. However, it's also more efficient than both the fast and optimum default switching paths.

CEF is wonderfully stable in large environments because it doesn't rely on cached information. Instead of using a CEF cache, it refers to two alternate resources. The *Forwarding Information Base (FIB)* consists of information duplicated from the IP route table. Every time the routing information changes, the changes are propagated to the FIB. Thus, instead of comparing old cache information, a packet looks to the FIB for its forwarding information. CEF stores the Layer 2 MAC addresses of connected routers (or next hop) in the *adjacency table*.

Even though CEF features advanced capabilities, you should consider several restrictions before implementing CEF on a router. According to the document "Cisco Express Forwarding," available from the Cisco web page CCO `http://www.cisco.com/warp/public/cc/pd/iosw/iore/tech/cef_wp.htm`, system requirements are quite high. The processor should have at least 128MB of RAM, and the line cards should have 32MB each. CEF takes the place of VIP distributed switching and fast switching on VIP interfaces. The following features aren't supported by CEF:

- ATM Data Exchange Interface (DXI)

- Token Ring

- Multi-point PPP

- Access lists on the Gigabit Switch Router (GSR)

- Policy routing

- Network Address Translation (NAT)

- Switched Multimegabit Data Service (SMDS)

Nevertheless, CEF does many things—even load balancing is possible through FIB. If there are multiple paths to the same destination, the IP route table knows about them all. This information is also copied to the FIB, which CEF consults for its switching decisions.

Load balancing can be configured in two different modes. The first mode is load balancing based on the destination (called *per-destination load balancing*); the second mode is based on the packet (called *per-packet load balancing*). Per-destination load balancing is on by default and must be turned off to enable per-packet load balancing.

Accounting may also be configured for CEF, which furnishes you with detailed statistics about CEF traffic. Two specifications can be made when collecting CEF statistics:

- Collect information on traffic that's forwarded to a specific destination.

- Collect statistics for traffic that's forwarded through a specific destination.

CEF was designed for large networks. If reliable and redundant switching paths are necessary, CEF is the way to go. However, keep in mind that its hardware requirements are significant, and it lacks support for many Cisco IOS features.

WAN Design

When either redesigning an existing network or building a new network from scratch, you have to include WAN technologies in your design, that is, unless you only have one building to configure, of course. Understanding the different WAN technologies and protocols is critical in your design process.

Since 1997, when the 802.11 wireless specifications were released, WAN technologies have changed dramatically. Before wireless networking, your only option was to either put in copper or fiber cable between buildings or lease copper or fiber connections from a provider. Although wireless is an important part of WAN and LAN design, the current CCDA objectives do not cover wireless technologies, so this section discusses the current options that you can lease from a provider. Let's move on to discuss the feasible WAN protocols that you can use in your design.

WAN Protocols

It is important to understand as many protocols supported by Cisco as possible. As you understand the different WAN protocols, you make better design decisions. This section discusses the following Cisco-supported WAN protocols:

- SDLC

- HDLC

- ISDN

- PPP

- Frame Relay

- DSL

SDLC

SDLC (Synchronous Data Link Control) was developed by IBM during the mid-1970s for use in SNA (Systems Network Architecture) environments. Subsequent to the implementation of SDLC by IBM, SDLC formed the foundation for numerous similar protocols, including HDLC and LAPB.

Bit-synchronous protocols owe their success to their expanded efficiency, flexibility, and in some cases, greater speed, with SDLC in the lead as the chief SNA Data Link layer protocol for WAN links. Versatile SDLC supports many link types and topologies, such as

- Point-to-point and multi-point links

- Bounded and unbounded media

- Half-duplex and full-duplex transmission facilities

- Circuit and packet-switched networks

SDLC also supports two network node types:

Primary stations Primary stations control the operation of other stations; poll secondaries in a predetermined order; and set up, tear down, and manage links.

Secondary stations Secondary stations are controlled by a primary station. If a secondary station is polled, it can transmit outgoing data. An SDLC secondary station can send information only to the primary station, and even then only after the primary station grants permission.

HDLC

The *HDLC (High-Level Data Link Control)* protocol is a popular ISO-standard, bit-oriented, Data Link layer protocol that specifies an encapsulation method for data on synchronous serial data links.

HDLC's development began when the ISO modified SDLC and came up with HDLC. Thereafter, the ITU-T (International Telecommunication Union Telecommunication Standardization Sector) tweaked HDLC a bit more and released Link Access Procedure (LAP), and then LAPB (Link Access Procedure, Balanced). After that, the IEEE (Institute of Electrical and Electronic Engineers) went to work on HDLC, and the result was the IEEE 802.2 specification.

HDLC is the default encapsulation used by Cisco routers over synchronous serial links. Cisco's HDLC is proprietary—it won't communicate with any other vendor's HDLC implementation. But don't give Cisco grief for it—everyone's HDLC implementation is proprietary. When we discussed our routers in Chapter 5, "Designing Modular Network Topologies," we were using HDLC encapsulation on all of our serial links.

Transfer Modes

HDLC supports the following transfer modes:

Normal response mode (NRM)   NRM is implemented with SDLC. Under NRM, a secondary can't communicate with a primary until the primary asks it to.

Asynchronous response mode (ARM)   ARM allows secondaries to communicate with a primary without permission from it.

Asynchronous balanced mode (ABM)   ABM introduced the combined node—one that can act as either a primary station or as a secondary station. All ABM communication takes place between a number of combined nodes, and combined stations can originate transmissions without permission.

LAPB   Integrated into the X.25 protocol stack, LAPB shares the same frame format, frame types, and field functions as both SDLC and HDLC. It's confined to the ABM transfer mode, and with it, you can establish circuits with either DTE (data terminal equipment) or DCE (data communications equipment). Devices that initiate communication are deemed primaries, and those that respond are deemed secondaries.

ISDN

ISDN (Integrated Services Digital Network) is a digital service designed to run over existing telephone networks—the ability to deliver a true digital service across your existing local loop is very cool indeed. ISDN can support both data and voice—a telecommuter's dream. ISDN applications require bandwidth, because typical ISDN applications and implementations include high-speed image applications (such as Group IV facsimile), high-speed file transfer, video conferencing, and multiple links into homes of telecommuters.

ISDN is actually a set of communication protocols proposed by telephone companies that allows them to carry data and voice. It gives you a group of digital services that simultaneously convey data, text, voice, music, graphics, and video to end users, and it was designed to achieve this over the telephone systems already in place. ISDN is referenced by a suite of ITU-T standards encompassing the OSI model's Physical, Data Link, and Network layers.

ISDN Terminals

Devices connecting to the ISDN network are known as terminals, and there are two types:

TE1 Terminal equipment type 1 refers to those terminals that understand ISDN standards.

TE2 Terminal equipment type 2 refers to those terminals that predate ISDN standards. To use a TE2, you have to use a terminal adapter (TA).

ISDN Reference Points

ISDN has four reference points that define logical interfaces:

R reference point The R reference point defines the reference point between non-ISDN equipment (TE2) and a TA.

S reference point The S reference point defines the reference point between user terminals and an NT2.

T reference point The T reference point defines the reference point between NT1 and NT2 devices.

U reference point The U reference point defines the reference point between NT1 devices and line-termination equipment in a carrier network. (This is only in North America where the NT1 function isn't provided by the carrier network.)

ISDN Protocols

ISDN protocols are defined by the ITU, and there are several series of protocols dealing with diverse issues:

- Protocols beginning with the letter *E* deal with using ISDN on the existing telephone network.
- Protocols beginning with the letter *I* deal with concepts, terminology, and services.
- Protocols beginning with the letter *Q* cover switching and signaling.

ISDN Switch Types

AT&T and Nortel are responsible for the majority of the ISDN switches in place today, but additional companies also make them. In Table 6.1, under "Keyword," you'll find the right keyword to use along with the isdn switch-type command to configure a router for the variety of switches to which it's going to connect. If you don't know which switch your provider is using at their central office, simply call them to find out.

TABLE 6.1 ISDN Switch Types

Switch Type	Keyword
AT&T basic rate switch	Basic-5ess
Nortel DMS-100 basic rate switch	Basic-dms100
National ISDN-1 switch	Basic-ni1
AT&T 4ESS (ISDN PRI only)	Primary-4ess
AT&T 5ESS (ISDN PRI only)	Primary-5ess
Nortel DMS-100 (ISDN PRI only)	Primary-dms100

Basic Rate Interface

ISDN BRI (Basic Rate Interface) service provides two B channels and one D channel. The BRI B channel service operates at 64Kbps and carries data. The BRI D channel service operates at 16Kbps and usually carries control and signaling information. The D channel signaling protocol spans the OSI reference model's Physical, Data Link, and Network layers. BRI also provides framing control for a total bit rate of up to 144Kbps.

When configuring ISDN BRI, you'll need to obtain SPIDs (service profile identifiers), and you should have one SPID for each B channel—two for BRI. You can think of SPIDs as the telephone number of each B channel. The ISDN device gives the SPID to the ISDN switch, which then allows the device to access the network for BRI or PRI service. Without a SPID, many ISDN switches don't allow an ISDN device to place a call on the network. Not all configurations require unique SPIDs, however. Some are autosensed. Ask your service provider to be sure.

Real World Scenario

The Many Uses of ISDN BRI

ISDN BRI was developed and released by many telephone companies in the early 1980s as a solution to digital signaling over an existing pair of copper wires supporting simultaneous voice, video, and data. In North America, the NT1 is provided by the subscriber and is usually built into a TE1 device such as a router or modem card and connects to the U reference point or loop, back to the central office.

ISDN BRI is often used in SOHO (small office, home office) networks as a primary connection for voice, video, and data traffic. It is also used as a backup connection for larger networks that use Frame Relay as their primary connection. ISDN in a SOHO network affords users with proper equipment the benefit of sharing a single line for voice and data. Cisco routers are available with local POTS (plain old telephone service) connections for voice traffic using standard telephones. ISDN-capable telephones are an option when connecting directly to ISDN but are generally more expensive. In most cases, one of the ISDN data channels must disconnect to allow a voice call, but that leaves the other channel available and connected for data. Proper planning and configuration is crucial when defining the use of the POTS connections at the router since users need to decide if voice calls will override data and issue the proper Cisco IOS commands into running `config`.

ISDN BRI as a backup to Frame Relay requires more hardware and configuration. In some cases, a Cisco router can be equipped with interfaces for Frame Relay and ISDN, or two routers can be used and configured for backup using floating static routes and DDR. For more information, see the article "Configuring ISDN Backup for WAN Links Using Floating Static Routes" at the URL `http://www.cisco.com/warp/public/125/fr_isdn_backup.html`.

Primary Rate Interface

The ISDN Primary Rate Interface (PRI) service delivers 23 B channels and one 64Kbps D channel in North America and Japan, for a total bit rate of up to 1.544Mbps.

In Europe, Australia, and other parts of the world, ISDN provides 30 B channels and one 64Kbps D channel, for a total bit rate of up to 2.048Mbps.

Dial-on-Demand Routing (DDR)

DDR is a common use of ISDN. With it, the administrator can define "interesting" traffic on the router and initiate WAN links based on that traffic. Access lists define interesting traffic, so there's a great deal of flexibility given to the administrator. For instance, an expensive ISDN connection to the Internet can be initiated to retrieve e-mail, but not for a WWW request. DDR is an effective tool in situations where WAN access is charged in some time interval, and it's best to use it in situations where WAN access is infrequent.

DDR provides the missing software ingredient for creating a fully functional backup system. Versatile DDR can be used over several different types of connections and is supported in Cisco IOS version 9 and later. It supports the networking protocols IP, IPX, AppleTalk, and others. DDR's flexibility reaches even further. It can be used over several different types of interfaces—synchronous and asynchronous serial interfaces, as well as ISDN.

PPP

PPP (Point-to-Point Protocol) is a data-link protocol that can be used over either asynchronous (dial-up) or synchronous (ISDN) media and that uses LCP (Link Control Protocol) to build and maintain data-link connections.

The basic purpose of PPP is to transport Layer 3 packets across point-to-point links. Figure 6.2 shows the protocol stack compared to the OSI Reference model.

FIGURE 6.2 Point-to-point protocol stack

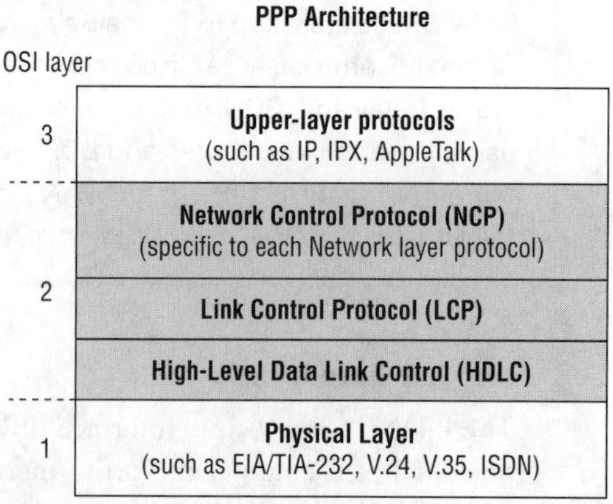

PPP contains four main components:

EIA/TIA-232-C EIA/TIA-232-C is the Physical layer international standard for serial communication.

HDLC   HDLC is a method for encapsulating datagrams over serial links.

LCP   LCP provides a method of establishing, configuring, maintaining, and terminating the point-to-point connection.

NCP   NCP (Network Control Protocol) is used for establishing and configuring different Network layer protocols. PPP is designed to allow the simultaneous use of multiple Network layer protocols. Two examples of protocols here are IPCP (IP Control Protocol) and IPXCP (Internetwork Packet Exchange Control Protocol).

Another new PPP feature is the support for multiple protocols. SLIP supported only IP, but through NCP, PPP supports IP, IPX, AppleTalk, DECnet, OSI/CLNS, and transparent bridging. NCP is actually a family of protocols—one for each Layer 3 protocol supported by PPP. PPP specifies an authentication mechanism, while CHAP and PAP are typically used. It is extensible so other companies (like Microsoft) can implement their own security.

Multilink PPP

By using ISDN with PPP encapsulation, Cisco routers can support multiple connections over the same physical interface. This allows Cisco routers to use dial-up connections to establish more than one connection at a time to an access server. Why would you want a router to be able to do that? Because if it can, you're granted twice the bandwidth of a single dial-up line. The capacity to increase bandwidth between point-to-point dial-up connections by grouping interfaces, then splitting and recalculating packets to run over that group of interfaces, is called *multilink*.

Before you can run multilink, you must define the interesting packets using the `dialer-list` global command. This command directs the router to search for specific network protocols for making and keeping a link active. You can apply a dialer list to an interface using the subcommand `dialer-group`.

Frame Relay

Recently, the high-performance WAN encapsulation method known as Frame Relay has become one of the most popular technologies in use. It operates at the Physical and Data Link layers of the OSI reference model and was originally designed for use across ISDN interfaces. But today, Frame Relay is used over a variety of other network interfaces.

Cisco Frame Relay supports the following protocols:

- IP
- DECnet
- AppleTalk
- Xerox Network Service (XNS)
- Novell IPX
- Connectionless Network Service (CLNS)
- International Organization for Standards (ISO)
- Banyan VINES
- Transparent bridging

Frame Relay provides a communications interface between DTE and DCE devices. DTE consists of terminals, PCs, routers, and bridges—customer-owned end node and internetworking devices. DCE consists of carrier-owned internetworking devices.

Popular opinion maintains that Frame Relay is more efficient and faster than X.25 because it assumes error checking will be done through higher layer protocols and application services.

Frame Relay provides connection-oriented, Data Link layer communication via virtual circuits just as X.25 does. These virtual circuits are logical connections created between two DTEs across a packet-switched network, which is identified by a *DLCI (data-link connection identifier)*. (We'll get to DLCIs in a bit.) Also, like X.25, Frame Relay uses both PVCs (permanent virtual circuits) and SVCs (switched virtual circuits), although most Frame Relay networks use PVCs.

Frame Relay with Cisco Routers

When configuring Frame Relay on Cisco routers, you need to specify it as an encapsulation on serial interfaces. There are only two encapsulation types: Cisco and IETF (Internet Engineering Task Force). The following router output shows the two different encapsulation methods when choosing Frame Relay on your Cisco router:

```
RouterA(config)#int s0
RouterA(config-if)#encapsulation frame-relay ?
 ietf Use RFC1490 encapsulation
 <cr>
```

The default encapsulation is Cisco unless you manually type in **IETF**, and Cisco is the type used when connecting two Cisco devices. You opt for the IETF encapsulation if you need to connect a Cisco device to a non-Cisco device with Frame Relay. So before choosing an encapsulation type, check with your ISP and find out which one they use. (If they don't know, hook up with a different ISP!)

DLCIs (Data Link Connection Identifiers)

Frame Relay PVCs are identified by DLCIs. A Frame Relay service provider such as the telephone company typically assigns DLCI values, which are used by Frame Relay to distinguish between different virtual circuits on the network. Since many virtual circuits can be terminated on one multi-point Frame Relay interface, many DLCIs are often affiliated with it.

For the IP devices at each end of a virtual circuit to communicate, their IP addresses need to be mapped to DLCIs. This mapping can function as a multi-point device—one that can identify to the Frame Relay network the appropriate destination virtual circuit for each packet that is sent over the single physical interface. The mappings can be done dynamically through IARP (Inverse ARP) or manually through the Frame Relay map command.

Frame Relay uses DLCIs the same way that X.25 uses X.121 addresses, and every DLCI number can be given either global or local meaning everywhere within the Frame Relay network. However, the customary implementation is to give each DLCI local meaning. What does this mean? It means that DLCI numbers do not necessarily need to be unique. Two DLCI numbers can be the same on different sides of a link, because Frame Relay maps a local DLCI number to a virtual circuit on each interface of the switch.

Configuring a DLCI number to be applied to an interface is as follows:

```
RouterA(config-if)#frame-relay interface-dlci ?
 <16-1007> Define a DLCI as part of the current⏎
   subinterface
RouterA(config-if)#frame-relay interface-dlci 16
```

LMI (Local Management Interface)

The *LMI (Local Management Interface)* was developed in 1990 by Cisco Systems, StrataCom, Northern Telecom, and Digital Equipment Corporation, and became known as the Gang-of-Four LMI or Cisco LMI. This gang took the basic Frame Relay protocol from the CCIT and added extensions onto the protocol features that allow internetworking devices to communicate easily with a Frame Relay network.

The LMI global-addressing extension gives Frame Relay DLCI values global rather than local significance. DLCI values become DTE addresses that are unique in the Frame Relay WAN. The global-addressing extension adds functionality and manageability to Frame Relay internetworks. Individual network interfaces and the end nodes attached to them, for example, can be identified by using standard address-resolution and discovery techniques. In addition, the entire Frame Relay network appears to be a typical LAN to routers on its periphery.

The LMI is a signaling standard between a CPE device and a frame switch. The LMI is responsible for managing and maintaining status between these devices. LMI messages provide information about the following:

Keepalives Keepalives verify that data is flowing.

Multicasting Multicasting provides a local DLCI PVC.

Multicast addressing Multicast addressing provides global significance.

The status of virtual circuits The status of virtual circuits provides DLCI status.

 Beginning with IOS version 11.2, the LMI type is autosensed. This enables the interface to determine the LMI type supported by the switch.

If you're not going to use the autosense feature, you'll need to check with your Frame Relay provider to find out which LMI type to use instead. The default type is Cisco, but you may need to change to ANSI or Q.933A. The three different LMI types are depicted in the following router output:

```
RouterA(config-if)#frame-relay lmi-type ?
 cisco
 ansi
 q933a
```

As seen in the output, all three standard LMI signaling formats are supported:

Cisco Cisco is the LMI type defined by the Gang of Four. This is the default LMI type.

ANSI Annex D defined by ANSI standard T1.617

ITU-T (q933a) Annex A defined by Q.933

Subinterfaces

You can have multiple virtual circuits on a single serial interface and yet treat each as a separate interface. These are known as *subinterfaces*. Think of a subinterface as a hardware interface defined by the IOS software.

One advantage gained through using subinterfaces is the ability to assign different Network layer characteristics to each subinterface and virtual circuit, such as IP routing on one virtual circuit and IPX on another.

Partial Mesh Networks

You can use subinterfaces to mitigate *partial mesh* Frame Relay networks and split-horizon protocols. For example, say you are running the IP protocol on a LAN network. If they're on the same physical network, Router A can talk to Router B, and Router B can talk to Router C—you can usually assume that Router A can talk to Router C. Though this is true with a LAN, it's not true with a Frame Relay network, unless Router A has a virtual circuit to Router C.

In Figure 6.3, Network 1 is configured with five locations. To be able to make this network function, you would have to create a meshed network as shown in Network 2. However, even though Network 2's example works, it's an expensive solution—configuring subinterfaces as shown in the Network 3 solution is much more cost-effective.

FIGURE 6.3   Partial meshed network examples

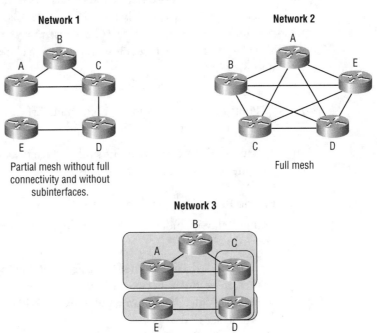

Network 1

Partial mesh without full
connectivity and without
subinterfaces.

Network 2

Full mesh

Network 3

Partial mesh with full connectivity
using subinterfaces

In Network 3, configuring subinterfaces actually works to subdivide the Frame Relay network into smaller subnetworks—each with its own network number. So locations A, B, and C connect to a fully meshed network, while locations C and D and locations D and E are connected via point-to-point connections. Locations C and D connect to two subinterfaces and forward packets.

Defining Subinterfaces

You define subinterfaces with the int s0. subinterface number command as follows:

```
RouterA(config)#int s0
RouterA(config)#encapsulation frame-relay
RouterA(config)#int s0.?
 <0-4294967295> Serial interface number
RouterA(config)#int s0.16 ?
 multipoint    Treat as a multipoint link
 point-to-point Treat as a point-to-point link
```

You can define an almost limitless number of subinterfaces on a given physical interface. However, you can only define as many subinterfaces as the router will support. Each subinterface takes an IDB (interface description block); on a 2500, you only have 255 total IDBs. In the preceding example, we chose to use subinterface 16, because that represents the DLCI number assigned to that interface. However, you can choose any number between 0 and 4,292,967,295.

There are two types of subinterfaces:

Point-to-point   A point-to-point subinterface is used when a single virtual circuit connects one router to another.

Multi-point   A multi-point subinterface is used when the router is the center of a star of virtual circuits.

Frame Relay Congestion Control

Frame Relay includes many "control" parameters for traffic congestion control.

DE (Discard Eligible)   When a Frame Relay router detects congestion on the Frame Relay network, it will turn the DE bit on in a Frame Relay packet header. The Frame Relay switch will discard the packets with the DE bit set first.

FECN (Forward Explicit Congestion Notification)   When the Frame Relay network recognizes congestion in the cloud, the switch will set the

FECN bit in a Frame Relay packet to tell the destination that the path just traversed is congested.

BECN (Backward Explicit Congestion Notification) When the switch detects congestion in the Frame Relay network, it will set the BECN bit in a Frame Relay packet and send it to the source router, telling it to slow down the rate at which it is transmitting packets.

CIR (Committed Information Rate)

Frame Relay providers allow customers to buy a lower amount of bandwidth than what they really might need. This is called the *committed information rate (CIR)*. What this means is that the customer can buy bandwidth of, for example, 256k, but it is possible to burst up to T1 speeds. The CIR specifies that as long as the data input by a device to the Frame Relay network is below or equal to the CIR, then the network will continue to forward data for the PVC. However, if data rates do exceed the CIR, it is not guaranteed.

It is sometimes possible to also purchase a *Bc (committed burst)*, that allows customers to exceed their CIR for a specified amount of time. In this situation, the DE bit will always be set.

Choose a CIR based on realistic, anticipated traffic rates. Some Frame Relay providers allow you to purchase a CIR of zero. You can use a zero CIR to save money if retransmission of packets is acceptable.

DSL (Digital Subscriber Line)

DSL is a technology that allows ordinary PSTN copper to be used for high-speed data communications. In essence, it is a new way of using existing infrastructure. Given the amount of installed copper, it is no wonder that DSL has become such a popular option.

Most readers of this book will be familiar with DSL as an Internet-connectivity technology. As mentioned earlier, when using public networks to connect diverse sites, DSL—in conjunction with VPN technology—may well prove to be a cost-effective and viable solution. However, this is not the only flavor of DSL available. There are several types of DSL that may be appropriate in different situations:

ADSL (asymmetric DSL) ADSL, as the word asymmetric implies, has differing upload and download capacities. From the end-site perspective, there is a maximum upload capability of 2Mbps and a maximum download capability of 8Mbps. Varieties of ADSL vary depending on service providers, and symmetric configurations up to 640kbps are possible. ADSL also allows a PSTN voice line to be shared with the DSL line.

SDSL (symmetric DSL) SDSL is symmetric; that is, upload and download speed are matched. The maximum transmission rate is 1.54Mbps. SDSL does not allow sharing with a PSTN voice line.

IDSL (ISDN DSL) IDSL is similar to ISDN, except it is always on and it is not circuit-switched like ISDN. Maximum transmission rate is 144kbps.

HDSL (high bit-rate DSL) HDSL provides symmetric communications with maximum transmission rates up to 1.54Mbps. There are two revisions available: HDSL and HDSL-2. HDSL allows for any transmission rate up to 1.54Mbps and runs across two pairs of wires. It is not compatible with a PSTN line. HDSL-2 runs only at 1.54Mbps, but requires only one pair of wires and is compatible with ADSL.

Summary

This chapter introduced the several types of WAN technologies and categorized them into three main types: private, leased, and public. WAN design was introduced, and the steps of the PDIOO methodology were discussed. Finally, a look at the technologies of route selection and switching inside the router were presented.

Several specific WAN technologies were described in this chapter. SDLC was used by IBM mainframes and ported for use by networking vendors in the form of HDLC, which is the default encapsulation on Cisco router serial interfaces. ISDN is an alternative to slow analog lines and is a popular backup connection type for today's high-speed Frame Relay networks. PPP is implemented on many of today's networks to provide Data Link layer transport for Network layer protocols. Frame Relay has become a very popular WAN connection type along with the routing hardware. Frame Relay supports many different Network layer protocols and is readily available from local carriers and router manufacturers. There are many design considerations with Frame Relay, including DLCI, LMI, subinterface needs, and meshed network designs. The best solution for most designs is a partial mesh topology with subinterfaces creating full connectivity between all networks. Finally, DSL is increasingly popular as an Internet-connectivity tool and as a technology that can use existing copper originally installed for the PSTN.

Exam Essentials

Remember the common switching modes used in network designs. Process switching is a preferred mode in most designs. Using the route table, process switching forwards all subsequent packets out the same interface as the first. Fast switching is on by default on the lower end routers such as the 2500 and 4000 series and is an enhancement when processor and interface limitations are present. Autonomous, silicon, optimum, distributed, and NetFlow switching modes are used primarily in higher end Cisco routers and are designed to move large amounts of network packets efficiently.

Be familiar with the different WAN design solutions. Designing for availability, bandwidth, cost, management, and application and routing protocol needs requires familiarity with available WAN solutions. WAN bandwidths come in all speeds, from 56K analog modems to T3 and beyond. Dial-up capability, leased lines and packet-switched services are solutions to specific design needs.

Remember the different WAN protocols and their intended use. SDLC was developed and used by IBM in their mainframe network designs. HDLC is a derivative of SDLC and is the default WAN protocol on Cisco routers. ISDN is a popular, moderate-speed, or backup solution to Frame Relay, which offers high speed and availability.

Understand the many configuration needs of Frame Relay. DLCIs, LMIs, and subinterfaces are all configuration needs of Frame Relay. DLCIs are assigned by the provider and are only locally significant to a connection's configuration. LMIs can now be autosensed by Cisco's IOS version 11.2 and greater, but Cisco is the default LMI type. Subinterfaces offer a design solution to address configuration needs when working with partial mesh networks.

Key Terms

Before you take the exam, be certain you are familiar with the following terms:

adjacency table	management
autonomous switching	NetFlow switching
bandwidth	optimum switching
Bc (committed burst)	path determination
Cisco Express Forwarding (CEF)	per-destination load balancing
committed information rate (CIR)	per-packet load balancing
cost	PPP (Point-to-Point Protocol)
DDR (dial-on-demand routing)	process switching
DLCI (data-link connection identifier)	protocols
DSL (digital subscriber line)	routers
fast switching	SDLC (Synchronous Data Link Control)
Frame Relay	silicon switching
HDLC (High-Level Data Link Control)	subinterfaces
ISDN (Integrated Services Digital Network)	switching path
LAN	WAN
LMI (Local Management Interface)	

Case Studies

Now that you have learned about WAN design and technologies, let's see how these issues apply to the three case studies in this book.

Have-A-Seat

There are no case study exercises for Have-A-Seat in this chapter.

MPS Construction

1. Mike had questions about his WAN technology. He was not sure he wanted to pay for 24×7 WAN connections. What alternatives could you recommend?

2. Mike needs a remote access solution. What would you recommend for him?

Willow Creek School District

1. Scott has expressed an interest in installing a Frame Relay network for the Willow Creek School District. What recommendations might you have for him? How would you connect the PVCs? What hardware would you place in the district office?

Review Questions

1. Which of the following protocols support PPP? (Choose all that apply.)

   A. HDLC

   B. LCP

   C. SDLC

   D. NCP

   E. LAPB

2. Which of the following contains Frame Relay flow control information?

   A. DLCI

   B. IARP

   C. LMI

   D. BECN

3. Which of the following is a method used by Frame Relay for addressing PVCs to IP addresses?

   A. IARP

   B. MIL

   C. SLARP

   D. DLCI

4. What is a TE2 device used for in an ISDN connection?

   A. Connecting an NT2 device to a U reference point

   B. Connecting an S/T interface to a U reference point

   C. Connecting a non-ISDN terminal to ISDN through a TA

   D. Connecting to ISDN through a four-wire, twisted-pair digital link

5. Which of the following statements are true regarding DLCIs? (Choose all that apply.)

   A. DLCIs are not necessarily unique.

   B. DLCIs are not necessary with PVCs.

   C. DLCIs initiate a Frame Relay communication exchange.

   D. DLCIs are logical identifiers for Frame Relay virtual circuits.

6. In the Have-A-Seat case study, they currently have ISDN lines. Which of the following tasks would best demonstrate that the ISDN lines are adequate?

   A. Set up a lab and simulate a 64Kbps leased line connected to the Internet for browsing.

   B. Perform a simple demonstration of a web browser's performance on an ISDN line to an Internet site.

   C. Implement the network with the existing 9600bps lines and let Have-A-Seat see that the performance is lacking.

   D. Perform a simple demonstration of a web browser's performance on the internetwork on a 33Kbps connection.

7. Suppose that you want to create a full mesh network. Which of the following will be the most cost-effective WAN type?

   A. PPP

   B. DDR

   C. SONET

   D. Frame Relay

8. Which of the following are valid LMI features? (Choose all that apply.)

   A. Multicasting

   B. Global addressing

   C. Route determination

   D. Connectionless routing

   E. Dynamic host addressing

   F. Virtual circuit status messaging

9. What is one of the first things you should do when determining if you should upgrade your network to a switched network?

    A. Pull fiber to all the floors.

    B. Determine the characteristics of the network traffic.

    C. Configure your VLANs.

    D. Change the TTL on your PCs to 1.

10. Which of the following statements are true about CIR (committed information rate)? (Choose all that apply.)

    A. Choose a CIR based on realistic, anticipated traffic rates.

    B. The CIR must match the DLCI of the PVC.

    C. You can use a zero CIR to save money if retransmission of packets is acceptable.

    D. The LMI keeps track of the CIR and provides the route information to the PVC.

11. How many LMI types are supported?

    A. Two

    B. Three

    C. Four

    D. Five

12. Which of the following statements are true about LMI? (Choose all that apply.)

    A. LMIs map DLCI numbers to virtual circuits.

    B. LMIs map X.121 addresses to virtual circuits.

    C. LMIs report the status of virtual circuits.

    D. LMI messages provide information about the current DLCI values.

13. Which of the following is a disadvantage of having point-to-point connections?

   A. A point-to-point connection requires that tariffs be paid even when the connection is in an idle state and no data are being transmitted.

   B. A point-to-point connection requires users to dial the connection manually when data need to be transmitted.

   C. A point-to-point connection requires interesting traffic to be defined on the router with access lists when data need to be transmitted.

   D. A point-to-point connection requires a lease through an ISP using a point-to-point routing protocol.

14. What is the solution for using partial mesh Frame Relay networks with split-horizon protocols?

   A. DLCI addressing

   B. X.121 addresses

   C. Secondary Ethernet interfaces

   D. Subinterfaces

15. Which of the following are the types of LMI methods used by Cisco routers? (Choose all that apply.)

   A. Cisco

   B. ANSI

   C. IETF

   D. q933a

16. Which of the following DSL types generally uses asymmetric transmission?

   A. ADSL

   B. SDSL

   C. IDSL

   D. HDSL

17. Which of the following DSL types can share a line with a PSTN line? (Choose all that apply.)

    A. ADSL

    B. SDSL

    C. IDSL

    D. HDSL

18. Which of the following DSL types is similar to ISDN?

    A. ADSL

    B. SDSL

    C. IDSL

    D. HDSL

19. Which type of network is Frame Relay?

    A. Private network

    B. Leased line

    C. Packet-switched network

    D. Circuit-switched network

20. Which network type generally has the highest up-front costs?

    A. Private network

    B. Leased line

    C. Packet-switched network

    D. Public network

Answers to Review Questions

1. A, B, D.   PPP is a vendor-neutral protocol. PPP supports many vendor-specific protocols.

2. D.   BECN contains Frame Relay backward explicit control notification information, which requests that the source router slow down its transmission rate.

3. A.   Inverse ARP provides dynamic mapping of DLCI to IP addresses.

4. C.   A TE2 device is for connecting non-ISDN equipment directly to the ISDN line.

5. A, D.   DLCIs are only locally significant and are used to identify the user ends of a Frame Relay circuit.

6. B.   Testing a user's application on the customer's existing network can help to demonstrate performance issues.

7. D.   Frame Relay supports subinterfaces, allowing you to create full mesh design with less than a full mesh connection topology.

8. A, B, F.   Multicasting, global addressing, and virtual circuit status messaging are supported by LMIs because of their globally significant addressing.

9. B.   Characteristics, better known as baselines, allow you to measure network traffic for planning and design purposes.

10. A, C.   To meet the cost and performance goals of your network design, you should purchase a CIR that meets your needs.

11. B.   Three LMI types were created by the Gang of Four: Cisco, ANSI, and q933a, but the Cisco LMI type is the default for Cisco routers.

12. C, D.   LMIs include Frame Relay virtual circuit status messages and DLCI values.

13. A.   Point-to-point connections can be a more expensive option than dial-in, dial-on-demand, or packet-switched connections.

14. D.   Implementing subinterfaces is the correct solution for use in Frame Relay networks supporting split-horizon routing protocols.

15. A, B, D.   Cisco, ANSI, and q933a are the three LMI methods supported by Cisco routers.

16. A.   As the name implies, asymmetric DSL (ADSL) uses asymmetric transmission.

17. A, D.   ADSL can share a line with a PSTN line, as can HDSL-2.

18. C.   IDSL is similar to ISDN, the main difference being that IDSL is not circuit-switched.

19. C.   Frame Relay is a packet-switched network. While it could be a private network, Frame Relay is generally purchased from a service provider.

20. A.   A private network implies that the infrastructure is owned by the enterprise using the network and thus has higher up-front costs than leased or public network types.

Network Addressing and Naming

THE CCDA TOPICS COVERED IN THIS CHAPTER INCLUDE:

✓ Given a network design or set of requirements evaluate a solution that meets IP addressing needs.

Network addressing is an area that certainly deserves attention at the design phase. Many routing protocols and IOS features can take advantage of a well-designed addressing scheme. Conversely, a poorly designed addressing scheme can result in larger route tables that can adversely affect performance. Aside from these issues, a planned approach to network addressing makes networks more predictable and easier to manage. Those who will administer the network you design will appreciate your attention to a well-thought-out addressing scheme on a daily basis.

Let's begin by looking at VLSM and VLSM design considerations. We'll then move on to route summarization, also known as route aggregation or supernetting. We will look at classless interdomain routing (CIDR), private addressing, and NAT, and the benefits they offer. Once we've covered these aspects of internetwork addressing, we'll turn our attention to network (host) addressing design.

Extending IP Addresses

In the past, when the Network Information Center (NIC) assigned a network number to an organization, it assigned either the first octet (a Class A network), the first two octets (a Class B network), or the first three octets (a Class C network). The organization could take this one network number and further subdivide it into smaller networks through a process called *subnetting*.

To illustrate, let's say that your organization has been assigned the Class B network 172.16.0.0. You have several different network segments, each of which needs a unique network number. So you decide to subnet your network. You use a *subnet mask* of 255.255.255.0. The subnet mask determines which portion of your IP address belongs to the network portion and which part belongs to the host portion. If you write your subnet mask out in binary, as illustrated in Table 7.1, the 1s correspond to the network portion of the address, and the 0s correspond to the node portion of the address.

TABLE 7.1 IP Address Example

Decimal	172	16	0	0
Binary	10101100	00010000	00000000	00000000
Decimal	255	255	255	0
Binary	11111111	11111111	11111111	00000000

So in your case, instead of having one network (172.16.0.0) with 65,534 available hosts numbers, you have 254 networks (172.16.1.0–172.16.254.0) with 254 available host numbers in each subnet.

You can calculate the number of hosts available on a subnet by using the formula $2n - 2$ = number of available host IPs, where n is the number of hosts bits (in your example, 8). The minus 2 (–2) represents all host bits on and all hosts bits off, which are reserved for the subnet address and the broadcast address and cannot be used for addressing of hosts.

Similarly, the number of networks (or subnets) can be calculated with nearly the same formula: $2n - 2$ = number of available networks, where n is the number of subnet bits (in your example, 8). So with subnetting, you have balanced your need for available network and host numbers. However, there may be instances where you need fewer host numbers on a particular subnet and more host numbers on another. The –2 represents all subnet bits on and all subnet bits off.

Let's extend this example to include a serial link between two routers, as shown in Figure 7.1.

FIGURE 7.1 IP address example

Network 172.16.10.0/24

172.16.10.1

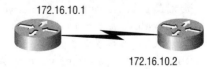

172.16.10.2

Because these are routers and not switches, each interface belongs to a different network. However, the serial interfaces need to share the same network to talk. How many IP numbers do you really need on the network interconnecting the two routers? You only need two IP numbers, one for each serial interface, as shown in Figure 7.1. Unfortunately, you have an 8-bit subnet mask (i.e., 255.255.255.0), so you're wasting 252 of the 254 available numbers on the subnet.

One possible solution to this dilemma is to use *variable-length subnet masks (VLSMs)*.

Variable-Length Subnet Masks (VLSMs)

IP version 4 addresses are composed of a network portion and a host portion that can be thought of like a two-part zip code with its five-digit prefix and four-digit suffix. The prefix directs the post office to a general destination—the city and state—and the suffix resolves to a street address or a P.O. box. An IP address, with its network and node portions, works much the same way, as you can see in Figure 7.2.

FIGURE 7.2 The makeup of an IP version 4 address

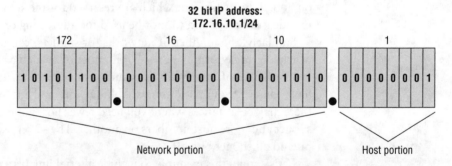

The network portion works just like the five-digit prefix of a zip code, and the node or host portion is the unique identifier, similar to the four-digit suffix of a zip code. An IP version 4 address consists of 32 bits broken down into four 8-bit segments known as *octets*. As shown in Figure 7.2, the first three octets define the network portion, and the last octet defines the host. We'll discuss how the network and host portions may be changed by providing certain information later in this chapter.

For a router to route data, it obviously needs to know where to send it. Routers don't maintain information for every unique address in their tables because doing so would make their tables so huge that they would require enormous amounts of memory and processing time. It's much more practical and efficient for them to maintain a table that contains only the network information. If a unique host or address isn't directly connected to a router, it looks in its table to find the appropriate path on which to send the data for them to reach their particular destination. So a router doesn't need to know a specific host's address; its only concern is to accurately identify the network on which it's located.

The specification of the host and network portions within an IP address establishes an inherent hierarchy consisting of different network lengths being advertised throughout a network or over the Internet. Using a hierarchy when implementing IP addressing provides two main benefits:

- Since IP addresses can be broken down into smaller subnets to accommodate addressing requirements, address space is conserved.

- Route information can be summarized, greatly reducing the size of route tables and the need for the router to know a route to every network.

Figure 7.3 shows what is meant by varying network portion length.

FIGURE 7.3   Hierarchical IP address structure

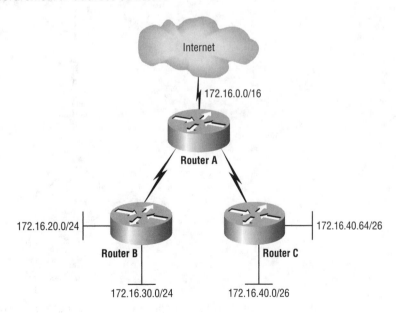

Longer network prefixes reside near the bottom of the network tree. The network length is depicted by a /24 or /26 suffixed to an IP address, which specifies the number of bits (beginning from the left) that define the network portion. The first 24 binary bits are equal to the first three octets in the dotted decimal format of an IP address.

As you move up through the network diagram, you can see that the network prefix gets smaller—decreasing from /24 and /26 down to /16. This hierarchy enables routers to determine where to send data when the packet's destination isn't directly connected to the local router. A good example of this can be seen in Figure 7.4, which portrays three different WANs connected to the Internet.

FIGURE 7.4 Hierarchical routing decisions

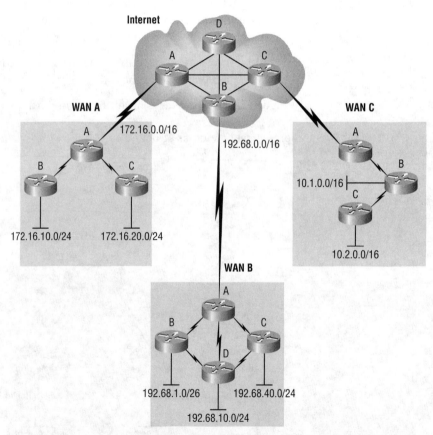

Each WAN has a specific network that it advertises to the Internet, but it doesn't reveal every host that resides within the network. It advertises information to the Internet only in the most general manner possible.

WAN A advertises the network 172.16.0.0/16 (equivalent to advertising the 172.16.0.0 network as a Class B IP address). Many different host addresses exist within WAN A that fall within the IP address range specified by the /16 subnet. However, to preserve the hierarchy, only a general address is advertised.

So if a host that's on WAN C wants to reach a host on WAN B (192.68.10.2), it sends the packet to the default gateway router. At this point, the router is interested only in the network portion of the IP address in the packet's header. After determining which network the packet is destined for, the router forwards the packet to the next hop. In this example, the packet is forwarded to Router A within WAN C and then to Internet Router C. Then Internet Router C learns about network 192.68.0.0/16 from Internet Router B. So as you can see, no information has been advertised about where 192.68.10.0 is located. Since WAN B advertised general information (that it knows about all 192.68.0.0/16 addresses), it doesn't need to advertise that it has routes to 192.68.10.0/24, 192.68.1.0/26, and 192.68.40.0/24.

All of this can be made clear by working back down the hierarchical tree. Once the packet is forwarded to the border router in WAN B, that device is the one that needs to know the more specific information. At the border router's level, each subnet is advertised. Therefore, a proper routing decision can be made, and the packet reaches its correct destination on network 192.68.10.0.

How is the length of the network prefix determined? To answer that, let's review IP version 4 addressing. In the beginning (see RFC 760), IP version 4 addresses weren't assigned classes. Instead, the network portion of the address was assigned to the first octet. This allowed for only 254 IP networks. To resolve this dilemma, RFC 791 was defined and written. This RFC converted a previously *classless* IP address structure into specific classes—five to be exact. The three most common ones are Classes A, B, and C, and prefix lengths were defined as 8 bits, 16 bits, and 24 bits, corresponding to Classes A, B, and C respectively. The first three bits in the first octet were used to determine the IP address class.

Table 7.2 shows how classes were defined by RFC 791.

TABLE 7.2 RFC 791 IP Class Assignments

Address Class	Bit Specification
A	0
B	10
C	110

These bit specifications not only defined the IP class, but they also predefined the shortest subnet mask for the address.

The assigned masks are depicted in Table 7.3, wherein the prefix for each class varies from 8 bits to 24 bits. You can see a prefix of 8 bits, with the first bit set to 0 (2^7), which allows for 126 Class A networks. The Class B prefix of 16 bits, with the first bit set to 1 and the second bit set to 0 (2^{14}), allows for 16,384 Class B networks. Finally, the Class C prefix of 24 bits, with three bits being used for class definition (2^{21}), allows for 2,097,152 Class C networks. So as you can see, the available network numbers, using the *classfull* scheme, are finite. Although 2,097,152 networks seems like a very large number of networks, when you look at it within a global frame of reference, you can see that they can eventually run out.

TABLE 7.3   Classfull IP Subnet Mask Assignments

Address Class	Subnet Mask
A	255.0.0.0
B	255.255.0.0
C	255.255.255.0

To deal with (and work around) these inherent limits, new methods of subnetting needed to be developed and implemented—the *variable-length subnet mask (VLSM)* is one of those methods. Because the VLSM provides much greater flexibility when deploying IP version 4 addresses, it's much more efficient than just using standard classfull subnets. Instead of being forced to use predefined masks, a network designer can be more specific with regard to the number of hosts that can be assigned to a given network segment.

We have discussed the importance of an addressing hierarchy and the information routers need to route data, as well as the differences between classic IP subnets and the VLSM approach. Now we'll move on to discuss in detail the important design considerations when planning a network.

VLSM Design Considerations

If you look at the 32-bit IP address again—understanding that the address is divided into the network and host (node) portions—using VLSM, you can create the division between the two at any point desired. To understand what is meant by dividing the network and host portions, refer to Figure 7.5.

FIGURE 7.5   VLSM subnet adjustment

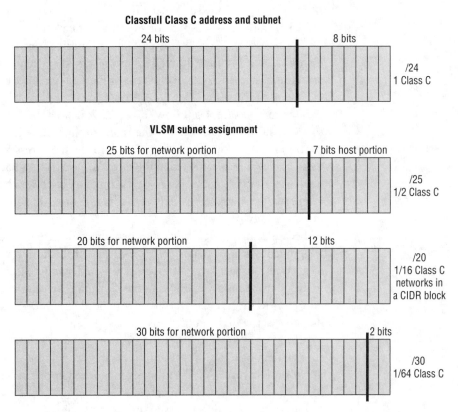

Figure 7.5 depicts a generic 32-bit IP address. The dark line signifies the division between the network and host portions of the address. As discussed previously, in classfull IP subnets, the division could take place only after 8, 16, and 24 bits. It was those divisions that created the subnet masks shown in Table 7.3.

However, by using VLSM, the division can be slid to the left or right to adjust the subnet mask. Why is this important? Because as the division between network and host identifying bits is moved, the number of hosts on the defined network changes respectively.

For reference, take the classfull Class C address. A Class C address contains 254 host nodes—254 because 0 and 255 are reserved for network and broadcast addresses. As depicted in Figure 7.5, when the mask is between the 24th and 25th bit, it is a Class C address with 254 hosts. On the second example in Figure 7.5—the first example of a VLSM-manipulated IP address—you can see that the division lies between the 25th and 26th bits. This allows seven bits for host identification and is the equivalent of one-half of a Class C address. The numerical definition would be 0 to 127, and because 0 and 127 are reserved for network and broadcast addresses, one-half of the remaining Class C addresses gives you 126 host addresses.

Two more examples follow in Figure 7.5, with the VLSMs' equivalency to a Class C address shown at the right. In the third example, the network portion is 20 bits long, leaving 12 bits for host addresses. So referencing these numbers, you can see that the range is from 0 to 4,095. If you subtract 2, you're left with 4,094 possible hosts for this network. The fourth example is a network that reserves only two bits for host addresses, permitting two hosts per network.

Because greater flexibility can be achieved through VLSM IP address assignment within a network, it's an efficient method to choose if you need to accommodate a large number of hosts. This increase in availability is made possible simply by moving the division between the network and host addresses to the left. Conversely, if you need more networks, all you have to do is move the division to the right.

VLSM goes much further than just increasing subnet mask tractability for the network. Traditionally, only one subnet could be assigned to a network. However, VLSM allows for more than one subnet to be assigned to a network—but there's a catch.

Discontinuous IP addresses should be avoided. To implement VLSM properly, the networks you're working with should be physically connected to the same router. Why is this important? Take a core router, for example. Core routers usually have many connections from other routers and switches—even from other LAN segments linked into them. For a picture of this architecture, look at Figure 7.6.

Figure 7.6 shows a core router with several connections. Instead of using a separate Class C address for each link, VLSM can be implemented to more efficiently utilize a classfull Class B network.

FIGURE 7.6   VLSM implementation example

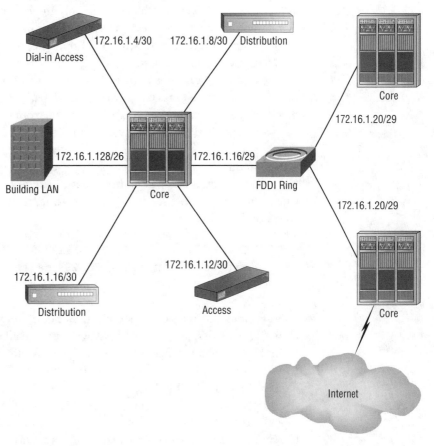

The Class B network has been broken down into six different networks, with each one providing only for the number of hosts necessary. When connecting two routers, only two IP host addresses are needed, and setting the subnet mask to /30 (or 255.255.255.252) defines two host IP addresses for the network. The network numbers in Figure 7.6 designate that the links connecting the core router to either a distribution or an access router use a subnet of /30. This specifies one address for the core router interface and one IP address for the opposite end of the link.

Look at the network diagram again—do you see subnets /26 and /29? Subnet /26 is used to connect to a switch, and using the /26 mask allocates 64 IP addresses to the switch's segment. However, remember that two of those addresses are reserved, so in reality, 62 machines (including the switch and router) can possibly be configured on this segment. The last mask of /29 allows for even fewer hosts. There are only three routers connected to the FDDI ring, and six host addresses can be used within the 172.16.1.20 network. If more routers were added to the FDDI ring, the subnet mask could be modified to allow for more hosts.

The beauty of VLSM is that it allows you to take a Class B address and break it down into a Class C equivalent *CIDR (classless interdomain routing)* block (172.16.1.0) and then create six subnets from that. Why is this useful? Because not only does it conserve IP addresses, it also creates a hierarchy within the core router. This gives the router different networks for each active interface and allows it to just route instead of relying on the ARP table. Can you imagine wasting an entire Class B network on one router? If the Class B network were used without subnetting, the network would be flat, with no hierarchy.

We've used three different masks—/26, /29, and /30—and it's recommended that you don't use more than two or three different masks for each network.

So far it looks pretty easy, doesn't it? But don't forget, a great number of networks were designed when VLSM wasn't yet available, and routing protocols like RIP and IGRP don't carry subnet mask information along with the IP address. So networks designed and implemented before routing protocols like Enhanced IGRP (EIGRP), OSPF, and RIP2 were available could have IP addresses allocated in a way that just doesn't facilitate grouping them into blocks for VLSM implementation. With cases like these, you would have to renumber IP addresses—a rather deplorable task that many network administrators don't want anything to do with—to implement VLSM.

However, VLSM can greatly enhance potential IP address allocation and simultaneously create a hierarchical architecture within the network. So if renumbering the network is necessary to implement VLSM, it's well worth it in the long run. If you do, you'll be able to utilize IP address space more efficiently, plus (believe it or not) network management will be much easier. For instance, just imagine how much easier it is to write access lists on a router that uses a block of addresses instead of separate networks.

VLSM Structure

As the name suggests, VLSMs can have different subnet masks for different subnets. So, if you have a serial point-to-point link between two routers, you could have a subnet mask of 255.255.255.252. If you do the math and look at your subnet in binary, you see that you have only two host bits, as shown in Table 7.4.

TABLE 7.4 A VLSM Example

Decimal	255	255	255	252
Binary	11111111	11111111	11111111	11111100

Therefore, this subnet mask will give you only two host IPs ($2^2 - 2 = 2$), which is exactly what you need for your serial link. Now, remember that to get this working on an internetwork, you need a classless routing protocol like EIGRP, OSPF, or even RIPv2.

 Real World Scenario

Should You Really Use a /30 on Your Internetwork?

Probably. What a great solution this mask is if you have many WAN point-to-point links. There are a few issues you need to keep in mind:

- You must be running a routing protocol that supports VLSM. OSPF, RIPv2, and EIGRP are the typical routing protocols used in these types of networks.

- It is possible that your CSU/DSU needs an IP address. Yes, it's true. Some ISPs have been putting IP addresses on their CSU/DSUs to help mange them. If this is true with your network, then a /30 network won't work. You'd have to use a /29. Just keep this in mind and ask your ISP before you configure your network.

As an example, take a look at Figure 7.7, which shows a router with 14 interfaces, all using the same subnet mask.

Notice that you have 14 subnets, each with 14 hosts on each interface. The only option is to use the 255.255.255.240 mask, because this gives you 14 subnets. However, you get only 14 hosts on each LAN and WAN because of the bits reserved for subnetting. The WAN links, though, are point-to-point and use only two IP addresses. Each WAN link is assigned 14 host IDs, which can be inefficient. Now take a look at Figure 7.8.

FIGURE 7.7 Fourteen subnets with no VLSM applied

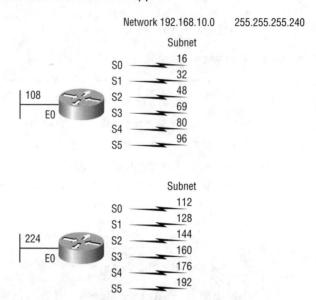

Network 192.168.10.0   255.255.255.240

Subnet
S0 —— 16
S1 —— 32
S2 —— 48
108   S3 —— 69
E0   S4 —— 80
S5 —— 96

Subnet
S0 —— 112
S1 —— 128
S2 —— 144
224   S3 —— 160
E0   S4 —— 176
S5 —— 192

FIGURE 7.8 Fourteen subnets with VLSM applied

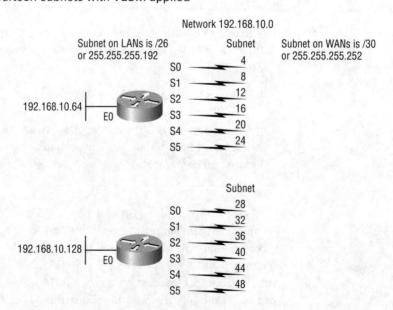

Network 192.168.10.0

Subnet on LANs is /26   Subnet   Subnet on WANs is /30
or 255.255.255.192   or 255.255.255.252

S0 —— 4
S1 —— 8
S2 —— 12
192.168.10.64   S3 —— 16
E0   S4 —— 20
S5 —— 24

Subnet
S0 —— 28
S1 —— 32
S2 —— 36
192.168.10.128   S3 —— 40
E0   S4 —— 44
S5 —— 48

Because you can use different size masks on each interface, you now get 2 hosts per WAN interface and 64 hosts per LAN interface! What a difference.

Not only can you get more hosts on a LAN, you still have room to add more WANs and LANs on the same network. Very efficient.

To create VLSMs quickly and efficiently, you need to understand how block sizes and charts work together to create the VLSM masks. Table 7.5 shows you the block sizes used when creating VLSMs with Class C networks. For example, if you need 25 hosts, you'll need a block size of 32. If you need 11 hosts, you'll use a block size of 16. Memorize the block sizes in this table.

TABLE 7.5   Block Sizes

Prefix	Mask	Hosts	Block Size
/26	192	62	64
/27	224	30	32
/28	240	14	16
/29	248	6	8
/30	252	2	4

The next thing to do is to create a VLSM table. Figure 7.9 shows you the three steps used in creating a VLSM table.

FIGURE 7.9   The three steps in creating a VLSM table

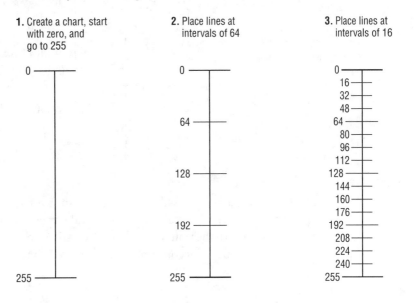

You can be even more thorough and create a fourth and fifth step, which build the table in groups of 8 and 4, which is necessary for your WAN links.

Let's take your block size and VLSM table and create a VLSM using a Class C network address for the network in Figure 7.10. Then fill out the VLSM table as shown in Figure 7.11.

FIGURE 7.10   VLSM network example one

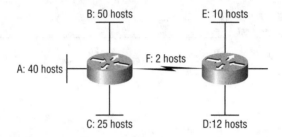

FIGURE 7.11   VLSM table example one

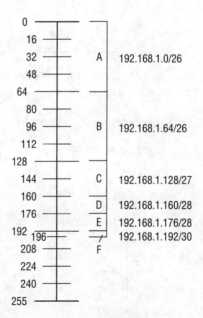

Notice that you used the network address of 192.168.1.0 and added the prefix of each block size used. Now, take those addresses and masks and apply them to the router interfaces. You still have plenty of room for growth. You could never accomplish this with one subnet mask.

Let's do another one together. Figure 7.12 shows a network with six interfaces, each needing a different number of hosts.

FIGURE 7.12 VLSM network example two

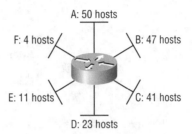

First, create your VLSM table and use your block size chart to fill in the table with the subnets you need. Figure 7.13 shows a possible solution.

FIGURE 7.13 VLSM table example two

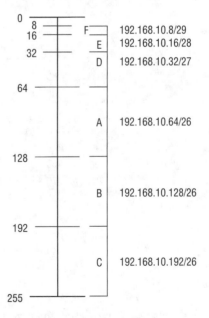

Notice that you used almost the entire range of address space. Not too much room for network growth in this example.

Let's do another example. Figure 7.14 shows a network with four routers and eight networks, four of which are WANs. Create a VLSM network using the VLSM chart.

FIGURE 7.14 VLSM network example three

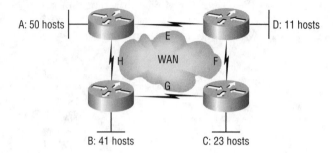

Figure 7.15 shows a possible solution. You still have room for growth in this one.

FIGURE 7.15 VLSM table example three

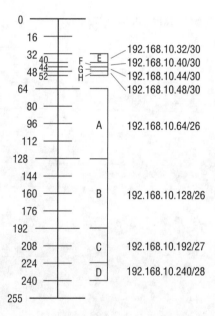

Let's do one more, just to make sure you have this down pat. Figure 7.16 shows the network on which you want to run a VLSM network. Create a VLSM table and reserve your block sizes.

Notice that you have three routers and seven networks. Okay, get to work. Figure 7.17 shows a possible solution for network example four. You have plenty of room for growth.

FIGURE 7.16 VLSM network example four

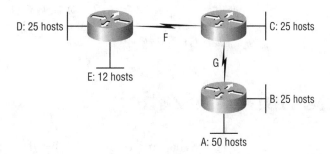

FIGURE 7.17 VLSM table example four

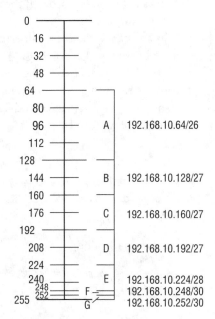

Now that you have seen how valuable VLSMs can be in preserving those precious IP addresses, be aware that there is a catch. Specifically, if you use a classfull routing protocol (a protocol that advertises routes at the Class A, Class B, and Class C boundaries) such as RIPv1 or IGRP, then VLSMs are not going to work.

RIPv1 and IGRP routing protocols do not have a field for subnet information. Therefore, the subnet information gets dropped. This means that if a router running RIP has a subnet mask of a certain value, it assumes that *all* interfaces within the classfull address space have the same subnet mask. Classless routing protocols, however, do support the advertisement of subnet information. So you can use VLSM with routing protocols such as RIPv2, EIGRP, or OSPF.

Route Summarization

In the chapter introduction, I briefly mentioned the concept of *route summarization*. So what is it, and why do you need it? On very large networks, there may be hundreds or even thousands of individual networks and sub-networks being advertised. All these routes can be very taxing on a router's memory and processor.

In many cases, the router doesn't even need specific routes to each and every subnet (e.g., 172.16.1.0/24). It would be just as happy if it knew how to get to the major network (e.g., 172.16.0.0/16) and let another router take it from there. A router's ability to take a group of subnetworks and summarize them as one network (i.e., one advertisement) is called *route summarization*, as shown in Figure 7.18.

 In some of the literature, you may find route summarization referred to as *route aggregation* or *supernetting*.

FIGURE 7.18 Route summarization

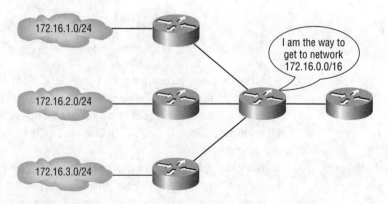

Besides reducing the number of routing entries that a router must keep track of, route summarization can also help protect an external router from making multiple changes to its routing table due to instability within a particular subnet. For example, let's say that you were working on a router that connected to 172.16.2.0/24. As you were working on the router, you rebooted it several times. If you were not summarizing your routes, an external router would see each time that 172.16.2.0/24 went away and came back. Each time, it would have to modify its own routing table. However, if your external router were receiving only a summary route (i.e., 172.16.0.0/16), then it wouldn't have to be concerned with your work on one particular subnet.

Summarization is the process of combining networks to save routing table entries. For example, it is typically more efficient to advertise 172.16.0.0 instead of 254 subnets starting with 172.16.1.0 going to 172.16.254.0. Supernetting can save a lot of room in a routing table!

You can use supernetting in a variety of networks (typically those that are large), using all types of routers and routing protocols. This section shows you how to create a supernet and then how to apply it to Cisco routers running both EIGRP and OSPF, the routing protocols usually used in larger networks.

To create a summarized entry, you gather the networks you want to combine and then write them out in binary. Let's combine the following in an effort to save routing table entries:

- 10.1.0.0 through 10.7.0.0

- 172.16.16.0 through 172.16.31.0

- 192.168.32.0 through 172.16.63.0

First, notice that the networks can easily be summarized because they are contiguous. An example of a range of networks that would be a poor choice for summarization is 172.16.10.0, 172.16.14.0, and 172.16.44.0. A non-contiguous range of networks makes for an inefficient summarization entry.

Supernetting 10.1.0.0 through 10.7.0.0

First, put everything into binary and then follow the bits, starting on the left and stopping when the bits do not line up. Notice where you stopped using boldface in the following:

```
10.1.0.0     00001010.00000001.00000000.00000000
10.2.0.0     00001010.00000010.00000000.00000000
```

```
10.3.0.0    00001010.00000011.00000000.00000000
10.4.0.0    00001010.00000100.00000000.00000000
10.5.0.0    00001010.00000101.00000000.00000000
10.6.0.0    00001010.00000110.00000000.00000000
10.7.0.0    00001010.00000111.00000000.00000000
```

Now, create a network number using only the boldface bits. Do not count the bits that are not in boldface. The second octet has no bits on (1s in the boldface section), so you get this:

```
10.0.0.0
```

To come up with the mask, now count all the boldface bits as 1s. Because 8 bits in the first octet and 5 bits in the second are boldface, you get this:

```
255.248.0.0
```

Supernetting 172.16.16.0 through 172.16.31.0

Let's put the network addresses into binary and use boldface for the bits starting on the left and moving to the right until they stop lining up:

```
172.16.16.0  10101100.0001000.00010000.00000000
172.16.17.0  10101100.0001000.00010001.00000000
172.16.18.0  10101100.0001000.00010010.00000000
172.16.19.0  10101100.0001000.00010011.00000000
172.16.20.0  10101100.0001000.00010100.00000000
172.16.21.0  10101100.0001000.00010101.00000000
172.16.22.0  10101100.0001000.00010110.00000000
172.16.23.0  10101100.0001000.00010111.00000000
172.16.24.0  10101100.0001000.00011000.00000000
172.16.25.0  10101100.0001000.00011001.00000000
172.16.26.0  10101100.0001000.00011010.00000000
172.16.27.0  10101100.0001000.00011011.00000000
172.16.28.0  10101100.0001000.00011100.00000000
172.16.29.0  10101100.0001000.00011101.00000000
172.16.30.0  10101100.0001000.00011110.00000000
172.16.31.0  10101100.0001000.00011111.00000000
```

Count only the boldface bits and only the bits that are on (1s) to get the following network address:

```
172.16.16.0
```

Now, create the mask by counting all the bits that are in boldface up to the point where they stop lining up. You have 9 bits in the first octet, 8 bits in the second octet, and 4 bits in the third octet. That is a /20 or this:

255.255.240.0

Try this shortcut. Take the first number and the very last number and put them into binary:

172.16.16.0 **10101100.0001000.0001**0000.00000000
172.16.31.0 **10101100.0001000.0001**1111.00000000

Can you see that you actually came up with the same bit numbers lining up? This is a lot easier than writing out possibly dozens of addresses.

Supernetting 192.168.32.0 through 192.168.63.0

In this example, you'll see how to summarize 192.168.32.0 through 192.168.63.0. By using only the first network number and the last, you'll save a lot of time and come up with the same network address and subnet mask:

- First number: 192.168.32.0 = **11000000.10101000.001**00000.00000000

- Last number: 192.168.63.0 = **11000000.10101000.001**11111.00000000

- Network address: 192.168.32.0

- Subnet mask: 255.255.224.0

Design Considerations for Route Summarization

Keep the following information in mind when designing your network summarization points:

- Only classless routing protocols support route summarization. Examples of classless routing protocols include RIPv2, EIGRP, and OSPF. Therefore, if you are working in a RIPv1 or IGRP environment, route summarization is not going to work for you.

- Route summarization is most effective when the addresses have been organized in a hierarchy (i.e., hierarchical addressing). When we speak of addresses being hierarchical, we mean that the IP subnets at the bottom of the tree (i.e., the ones with the longest subnet masks) are subsets of the subnets at the top of the tree (i.e., the ones with the shortest subnet masks). Figure 7.19 will be used to illustrate hierarchical versus non-hierarchical addressing.

FIGURE 7.19 Discontiguous networking example

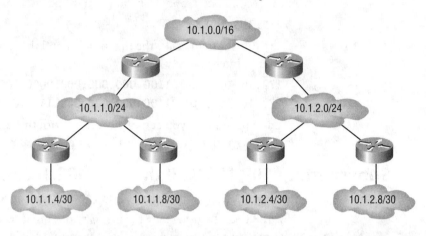

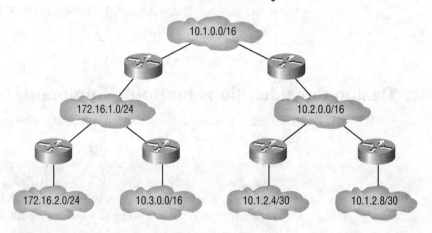

🌐 **Real World Scenario**

When Should You Summarize?

Great question. The answer is, of course, whenever you can. However, this is not an easy answer unless you are building your network from scratch and not trying to fix an already-been-installed-and-screwed-up mess.

Typically, your network will not have been configured in a hierarchical manner, so summarizing network boundaries will be difficult. Also, remember that EIGRP, IGRP, and RIP like to auto-summarize, so be careful how you create your discontiguous networks.

If you have buildings with multiple routes and they are created in a hierarchical and contiguous manner, then you are the lucky one and can perform summary boundaries between buildings. It's a great feeling when you get this working.

In the VLSM section of this chapter, you learned how route summarization in discontiguous networks could cause some hosts to become unreachable. If both Router A and Router B are sending out advertisements to the WAN cloud advertising that they are the path to network 172.16.0.0/16, then devices in the WAN cloud do not know which advertisement to believe.

Remember that you can avoid this situation by proper address planning ahead of time. However, you may find yourself in a situation in which you are dealing with a legacy installation and you need to overcome this issue of discontiguous networks.

One solution is to turn off route summarization on the routers. To keep routing protocols such as RIPv2 and EIGRP from automatically summarizing routes, you can explicitly disable route summarization in the Cisco IOS. The following are examples of IOS configurations in which you are disabling automatic route summarization. As you may remember, OSPF does not automatically summarize.

To turn off auto-summarization for RIP version 2 routed networks, use the following router configuration:

```
router rip
 version 2
 network 10.0.0.0
 network 172.16.0.0
 no auto-summary
```

To turn off auto-summarization for EIGRP routed networks, use the following router configuration:

```
router eigrp 100
 network 10.0.0.0
 network 172.16.0.0
 no auto-summary
```

Another way to allow discontiguous networks to be interconnected over a serial link is to use Cisco's IOS feature called *IP unnumbered*. We'll explain this a bit later in the chapter.

Applying Supernets to Cisco Routers

You can use either EIGRP or OSPF, among others, to advertise a supernet, but EIGRP and OSPF are the most popular. IGRP and RIP (Routing Information Protocol), along with EIGRP, automatically summarize on classfull boundaries. If you have noncontiguous networks—a classfull network separated by another classfull network—you'll need to turn off auto-summarization. Here's how to do that:

```
RouterA(config)#router eigrp 1
RouterA(config-router)#no auto-summary
```

It's not really difficult, but if you don't type that in, your EIGRP routing process will not work. If you have a contiguous network and it is not separated by a discontiguous design, then EIGRP will auto-summarize and you're done.

However, if you want to manually configure a summary router using EIGRP, you use an interface command:

```
RouterA(config)#int e0
RouterA(config-int)#ip summary-address eigrp 1
192.168.32.0 255.255.224.0
```

The EIGRP routing process now advertises networks 192.168.32.0 through 192.168.63.0 as available through interface Ethernet 0.

To configure a summary route advertised by OSPF, you use a routing process command:

```
RouterA(config)#router ospf 1
RouterA(config-router)#area 1 range 172.16.0.0
255.255.240.0
```

The OSPF routing process finds the interfaces assigned to this address range and advertises the summary route out those interfaces for area 1.

Classless Interdomain Routing (CIDR)

Classless interdomain routing (CIDR) is an industry standard for displaying the number of subnet bits used with the IP address of a host or a network. If, for example, you have a 172.16.10.1 address with a 255.255.255.0 mask, instead of writing the IP address and subnet mask separately, you can combine them. For example, 172.16.10.1/24 means that the subnet mask has 24 out of 32 bits on.

The following list shows all the possible CIDRs:

```
255.0.0.0=/8
255.128.0.0=/9
255.192.0.0=/10
255.224.0.0=/11
255.240.0.0=/12
255.248.0.0=/13
255.252.0.0=/14
255.254.0.0=/15
255.255.0.0=/16
255.255.128.0=/17
255.255.192.0=/18
255.255.224.0=/19
255.255.240.0=/20
255.255.248.0=/21
255.255.252.0=/22
255.255.254.0=/23
255.255.255.0=/24
255.255.255.128=/25
255.255.255.192=/26
255.255.255.244=/27
255.255.255.240=/28
255.255.255.248=/29
255.255.255.252=/30
```

Notice that the CIDR list starts at a minimum of /8 and can't go higher than /30. This is because you must leave two hosts at a minimum.

Cisco and CIDR

Cisco has not always followed the CIDR standard. Take a look at the way a Cisco 2500 series router asks you to put the subnet mask in the configuration when using the Setup mode:

```
Configuring interface Ethernet0:
  Is this interface in use? [yes]:return
```

```
Configure IP on this interface? [yes]:return
  IP address for this interface: 1.1.1.1
  Number of bits in subnet field [0]: 8
  Class A network is 1.0.0.0, 8 subnet bits; mask is /16
```

Notice that the router asks for the number of bits used only for subnetting, which does not include the default mask. This is nothing short of idiotic. Cisco used this subnetting method on the CCNA 1.0 exam. When dealing with these types of questions, remember that your answers involve the number of bits used for creating subnets, not the number of bits in the subnet mask. The industry standard is that you count all bits used in the subnet mask and then display that number as a CIDR—for example, /25 is 25 bits.

The newer Cisco routers, however, run a Setup script that no longer asks you to enter the number of bits used only for subnetting. Here is an example of a new 1700 series router in Setup mode:

```
Configure IP on this interface? [no]: y
  IP address for this interface:1.1.1.1
  Subnet mask for this interface [255.0.0.0]:255.255.0.0
  Class A network is 1.0.0.0, 16 subnet bits; mask is /16
```

Notice that the Setup mode asks you to enter the subnet mask address. It then displays the mask in CIDR format. Much better.

Configuring Subnet Mask Display Formats

When configuring IP addresses in a Cisco router, you cannot enter the number of bits used in a subnet mask in a router—for example, 172.16.10.1/24. It would be nice to be able to do that. You must type out the mask: 172.16.10.1 255.255.255.0.

By default, the router displays a CIDR output for the number of bits used in the mask. If you want the router to display the full mask, use the terminal ip netmask-format command as follows:

```
Router#sh int f0
FastEthernet0 is up, line protocol is up
  Hardware is PQUICC_FEC, address is 0050.547d.1787↵
    (bia 0050.547d.1787)
  Internet address is 172.16.10.20/24
Router#terminal ip netmask-format ?
  bit-count    Display netmask as number of significant↵
               bits
```

```
decimal      Display netmask in dotted decimal
hexadecimal  Display netmask in hexadecimal
Router#terminal ip netmask-format decimal
Router#sh int f0
FastEthernet0 is up, line protocol is up
  Hardware is PQUICC_FEC, address is 0050.547d.1787↵
    (bia 0050.547d.1787)
  Internet address is 172.16.10.20 255.255.255.0
```

As an example, to view your mask information in hexadecimal, use the following command:

```
Router#term ip netmask-format hex
Router#sh int f0
FastEthernet0 is up, line protocol is up
  Hardware is PQUICC_FEC, address is 0050.547d.1787↵
    (bia 0050.547d.1787)
  Internet address is 172.16.10.20 0xFFFFFF00
```

Private IP Addresses

Another aspect of TCP/IP routing has to do with private networks. You can use private IP addresses within a network if the network doesn't need to be reached by outside machines. IANA (Internet Assigned Numbers Authority) allocates three blocks of IP addresses for private network use, as shown in Table 7.6.

TABLE 7.6   IANA-Assigned Private Networks

Network	Mask	Block
10.0.0.0	255.0.0.0	1 Class A network
172.16.0.0	255.240.0.0	16 Class B networks
198.168.0.0	255.255.0.0	256 Class C networks

Corporate networks that don't connect to the global Internet can use these addresses. However, if you use these addresses within a network that also contains a globally unique IP address, you must filter the addresses with access lists to avoid advertising them to the Internet. Many companies use private IP address space, and it's imperative that these routes not be announced to the Internet. Although ISPs do not allow private networks to be advertised by their routers, it's good practice to make sure that your enterprise or campus routers do not advertise private networks to the ISP.

So if a host machine is assigned a private IP address, it can't communicate via TCP/IP to the outside world because private network advertisements aren't included in Internet routing tables—unless you provide the privately addressed host with a proxy server that has a globally unique address or uses a Network Address Translation (NAT) service. All the client's requests for information then have the source IP address of the proxy machine and can communicate through it.

You should implement *private addressing* schemes using the same plan you used with global IP addressing schemes—assign contiguous addresses to defined regions so that you can apply summarization. Use VLSM for subnetting to more efficiently utilize allocated networks. Finally, don't forget to run routing protocols that support classless routing.

Always consider the future of the network when you implement private addresses. Some day, some of those machines on what is currently a private network will likely need access to the Internet. Once a network moves from not needing global connectivity to needing globally unique IP addresses, you'll have to readdress.

Using private addresses really helps to conserve your allotment of IP addresses. Because every computer on the network probably doesn't need to access the outside world directly, it's wise to make good use of those private addresses and save the unique ones for machines that require global connectivity.

IP Unnumbered

When you use the `ip unnumbered` command, a serial interface is not on a separate network, as all router interfaces tend to be. Instead, the serial port "borrows" an IP address from another interface. In the following router configuration example, interface Serial 0 is using a borrowed IP address from interface Ethernet 0:

```
interface serial 0
no ip address
ip unnumbered ethernet 0
```

Therefore, by using the `ip unnumbered` command, you ensure that the apparently discontiguous subnets, shown in Figure 7.20, are actually supported. Understand that both sides of the network must be the same address class. In other words, you can't borrow an IP address on one side from a 10.0.0.0 network and then from 172.16.0.0 on the other side of the point-to-point link.

FIGURE 7.20 An `ip unnumbered` example

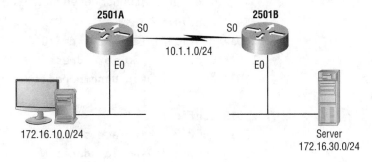

There are a few things to be aware of before using IP unnumbered interfaces. For example, IP unnumbered is not supported on X.25 or SMDS networks (yeah, so what?). Also, since the serial interface has no IP number, you cannot ping the interface to see if it is up, although you can determine the interface status with SNMP. In addition, IP security options are not supported on an IP unnumbered interface.

Figure 7.20 shows an example of using the `ip unnumbered` command on two Cisco routers running a point-to-point T1.

The two routers, 2501A and 2501B, are connected point-to-point, and each has an Ethernet LAN connection.

2501A has the following configuration:

```
2501A#sh run
[output cut]
interface Ethernet0
ip address 172.16.10.1 255.255.255.0
interface serial0
ip address 10.1.1.1 255.255.255.0
```

2501B has the following configuration:

```
2501A#sh run
[output cut]
interface Ethernet0
ip address 172.16.30.1 255.255.255.0
interface serial0
ip address 10.1.1.2 255.255.255.0
```

You can configure ip unnumbered on the serial interfaces as follows:

```
2501A#config t
2501A(config)#interface serial0
2501A(config-if)#no ip address
2501A(config-if)#ip unnumbered ethernet0

2501B#config t
2501B(config)#interface serial0
2501B(config-if)#no ip address
2501B(config-if)#ip unnumbered ethernet0
```

The two routers can now communicate over the serial link without an IP address. You cannot ping the serial interfaces, but by using the show interface command, you can verify that the ip unnumbered command is being used:

```
2501A#sh int serial0
Serial0 is up, line protocol is up
Interface is unnumbered. Using address of Ethernet0
   (172.16.10.1)
```

The New /31 Subnet

Another way that Cisco is helping you save subnets is by using the /31 mask.

/31, are you crazy? That means the mask is 255.255.255.254!

I've been saying throughout this entire chapter that you must have at a minimum two bits for host bits, and this leaves only one bit. Todd, what are you thinking? Well, throughout this chapter, I meant to say that you must have two bits for hosts "most of the time!"

Cisco has announced a new point-to-point subnet mask called the /31 that is used for the same reason that the ip unnumbered command is used: to save address space. The /31 mask can only be used on non-broadcast links like a point-to-point serial link because there is no broadcast address! However, you can put it on a LAN interface; it just won't work for a corporate environment. The /31 mask is meant for point-to-point serial links or point-to-point LAN connections between buildings, for example.

First, you must have a special IOS. Here's the one that I found that worked on my 2600 routers:

```
2600#sh flash
System flash directory:
File  Length    Name/status
  1   6973004   c2600-bin-mz.122-13.T1.bin
[6973068 bytes used, 891252 available, 7864320 total]
8192K bytes of processor board System flash (Read/Write)
```

Once you have an IOS that supports the /31 network mask, then you can configure your point-to-point links as follows:

```
2600#config t
Enter configuration commands, one per line.  End with↵
   CNTL/Z.
2600(config)#int f0/0
2600(config-if)#ip address 10.1.1.0 255.255.255.254
% Warning: use /31 mask on non point-to-point interface↵
   cautiously
2600(config-if)#int f0/1
2600(config-if)#ip address 192.168.10.2 255.255.255.254
% Warning: use /31 mask on non point-to-point interface↵
   cautiously
2600(config-if)#int s0/0
2600(config-if)#ip address 172.16.100.4 255.255.255.254
2600(config-if)#^Z
2600#
```

The preceding example created three point-to-point subnets on two FastEthernet LAN connections and one serial connection. Notice the warning received when using the /31 on a LAN interface. Unless that is a point-to-point link, it just really isn't going to work.

In addition, the preceding example used three subnets: 0, 2, and 4. The class of address doesn't matter, but one of each class of IP address was created just for fun. The valid hosts are 0 and 1, 2 and 3, and 4 and 5.

In the following output, the subnets are shown as 0, 2, and 4, but understand that these subnet numbers are valid host addresses also:

```
2600#sh ip route
[output cut]
     10.0.0.0/31 is subnetted, 1 subnets
C       10.1.1.0 is directly connected, FastEthernet0/0
     192.168.10.0/31 is subnetted, 1 subnets
C       192.168.10.2 is directly connected,↵
        FastEthernet0/1
     172.16.0.0/31 is subnetted, 1 subnets
C       172.16.100.4 is directly connected, Serial0/0
2600#
```

Notice in the router's output that there is no broadcast address for each subnet, only two host addresses.

IP Helper-Address

The ip helper-address command is a static command that is configured on a router interface to direct broadcasts to desired destinations within your internetwork. Configuring the ip helper-address command is simple and straightforward. You just have to be aware of which interface the broadcasts are being received on and where you want to forward these broadcasts to.

For example, in Figure 7.21, the 2501A router Ethernet0 interface receives a *Dynamic Host Configuration Protocol (DHCP)* client request from HostA, which is a broadcast looking for a DHCP server.

FIGURE 7.21   An ip helper-address single server example

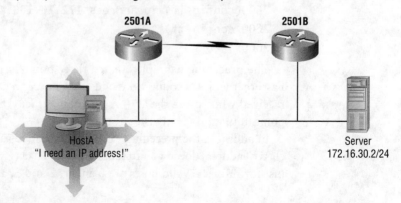

The 2501A router needs to be configured as follows:

2501A#**config t**
2501A(config)#**interface ethernet0**
2501A(config-if)#**ip helper-address 172.16.30.2**

The 2501A router now receives the DHCP client broadcast and forwards this broadcast to the DHCP server, which then provides a DHCP address to the client.

If you have more than one DHCP server for redundancy purposes, as shown in Figure 7.22, you can configure a subnet broadcast address instead of a single server address.

FIGURE 7.22   An ip helper-address multiple server example

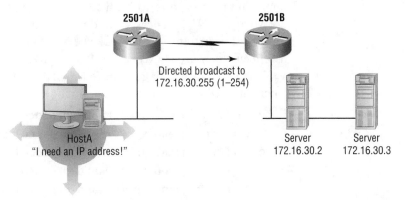

The 2501A router would be configured as follows:

2501A#**config t**
2501A(config)#**interface ethernet0**
2501A(config-if)#**ip helper-address 172.16.30.255**

The 2501 router now takes a DHCP client broadcast and sends this to any DHCP server on the 172.16.30.0 network.

Remember that when you enable the ip helper-address command, you are forwarding more than just DHCP requests. Let's discuss all the ports that are being forwarded.

Forwarded Ports

When you enable the ip helper-address command on an interface, you are not just forwarding broadcasts from DHCP clients. The ip-helper command forwards all these UDP protocols:

- TFTP 69

- DNS 53

- Time 37

- NetBIOS name server 137

- NetBIOS Datagram service 138

- BootP server 67

- BootP client 68

- TACACS 49

This can cause your network to forward broadcasts you do not want forwarded, or it can cause a security problem, or both. Typically, it is important to stop ports 137 and 138 from being forwarded because these are Microsoft NT broadcasts that do not need to be forwarded. However, if you just need to forward DHCP client broadcasts, you can stop all ports from being forwarded except BootP server 67.

To stop the forwarding of unneeded UDP broadcasts, use the following commands from global configuration mode:

```
router(config)#no ip forward-protocol udp 69
router(config)#no ip forward-protocol udp 53
router(config)#no ip forward-protocol udp 37
router(config)#no ip forward-protocol udp 137
router(config)#no ip forward-protocol udp 138
router(config)#no ip forward-protocol udp 68
router(config)#no ip forward-protocol udp 49
```

This configuration now allows only a broadcast for a BootP server, port 67, to be forwarded.

Network Address Translation (NAT)

NAT's basic function is to map *private IP version 4 addresses* to the globally unique IP addresses used to communicate with other Internet hosts. It's available in version 11.2 in the *s* feature set, and you enable it on a border router—one that's located between an enterprise and Internet router.

You can use *NAT* on an entirely private IP network or on one inhabited by a mix of registered and private addresses. There's a very extensive list of possible NAT-oriented scenarios, but overall, NAT is used to provide connectivity between globally and privately addressed hosts. For connectivity between the two types of hosts to be established—for it to happen at all—a source address modification of the privately addressed host must occur. NAT provides this translation.

Let's walk through the NAT process. To help visualize what happens with NAT, refer to Figure 7.23.

FIGURE 7.23   Network address translation

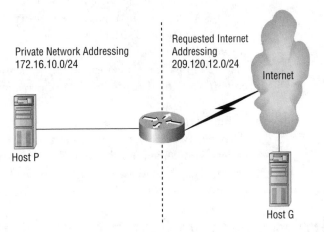

Host P wants to connect with Host G, but since private networks aren't advertised to the Internet, Host G won't be able to respond to Host P—there's no route back to its private address.

This problem is solved by using NAT. Realize that the border router is the only device that understands both the private and public addressing schemes. What NAT does is allow the border router to receive the request from Host P and then forward it on to Host G using the border router's address in the public address space as the return address. Host G then responds to the router, which then forwards the response on to Host P. This allows hundreds or thousands of private addresses to be represented and to communicate with the open Internet using a single registered address.

Here are a few factors to keep in mind when deciding whether to use NAT:

- The cost of purchasing registered IP addresses

- The number of nodes currently configured with private addresses

- The importance of logging, traceability, and security

- Transport delay

- Application sensitivity

As always, the cost of implementation needs to be considered. Even obtaining registered addresses for use with NAT has an associated cost, which you have to pay (unless the provider allocates them without additional cost). Since procuring registered addresses has a dollar factor whether you're going to use NAT or not, it might be possible to just re-address the current network and bypass NAT altogether. When is this a good idea? It's probably easier to just renumber if there aren't a lot of private nodes on the network. Also, when NAT is used end to end, the identity of machines is lost. So if an existing policy mandates strict management information, NAT may not work for you. Because the router must process every packet, there will be delay incurred in packet transport. Some applications simply rely on the end-to-end information that NAT just can't provide. If you have those applications running on your network, implementing NAT could break them.

But all things considered, there are still several advantages to using NAT. If your network is huge, with a multitude of private addresses, it's much easier to implement NAT rather than to re-address. Since NAT allows only specific networks to use the registered IP addresses, it gives you some degree of control over who's able to reach Internet hosts and who isn't.

Address Design Considerations

Once the design for network addressing is done, there is still a bit of work to do. Just as careful network addressing can make internetworks friendlier and more efficient, careful host addressing can also improve the operation of networks. Let's begin with what might be considered the most important addresses on the network: the router and server addresses.

Router Addresses

There are several methods of determining router addresses. Perhaps the most basic method is to choose a particular address or range and use it consistently. On IP version 4 networks, $x.x.x.1$ or $x.x.x.254$ are commonly used as router addresses. For networks with multiple routers, a range of addresses can be reserved. Consistency in addressing facilitates the configuration of the default router or gateway on devices that do not learn them dynamically.

Can you imagine trying to administer even 10 networks where the default router address is some seemingly random number between 1 and 254? How about 100? Standards really pay off here.

When addressing serial connections, standards can be introduced. This may seem unnecessary at first. After all, serial connections such as Frame Relay typically have only two addresses within the network space. However, standards such as specifying that the interface closest to the Internet, or closest to Area 0 or some other designation, always gets the lowest address can allow you to accurately predict the address on the other end of the circuit.

For example, suppose that you have to address the two serial interfaces connecting the Access layer and Distribution layer routers in Figure 7.24. Suppose that you have network 172.16.50.16/30 to address the serial link. The addresses that you have are as follows:

- 172.16.50.16—Network address

- 172.16.50.17—Host address

- 172.16.50.18—Host address

- 172.16.50.19—Broadcast address

Suppose also that you've specified that the lower address is always closer to the core. You would then use the 172.16.50.17 address on the Distribution layer router and use 172.16.50.18 on the Access layer router according to the standard. Now, consider an administrator who understands the standard and who is logged on to the Access layer router. When typing a show-running command, the administrator sees the 172.16.50.18 address on the serial interface. The administrator immediately knows the upstream address and can ping or telnet to it to troubleshoot routing or connectivity problems.

FIGURE 7.24   Serial interface addressing example

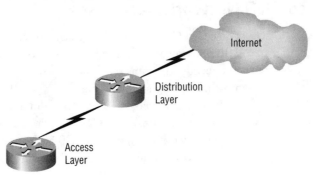

Server Addresses

Just as reserving a range of addresses for router addresses can facilitate network operation, so can reserving a range of addresses for server addresses. Consider reserving a block that can be summarized in a single statement with an access list mask, similar to what was done with route aggregation. For example, the following ranges can be summarized in a single line:

- $x.x.x.1$ through $x.x.x.3$

- $x.x.x.1$ through $x.x.x.7$

- $x.x.x.1$ through $x.x.x.15$

This allows you to specify a policy for all of your servers in a single line in an access list rather than having to enter multiple lines to specify each server as a single host. For example, if you want to allow any TCP traffic to servers at addresses 172.16.50.2, 172.16.50.9, 172.16.50.77, and 172.16.50.166, use the following access list:

```
access-list 101 permit tcp any host 172.16.50.2
access-list 101 permit tcp any host 172.16.50.9
access-list 101 permit tcp any host 172.16.50.77
access-list 101 permit tcp any host 172.16.50.166
```

Notice that four lines are required. Also, any servers that are added in the future will require that you edit the access list. Now, if you have specified all servers to be the 172.16.50.1 through 172.16.50.7 range, you could have used the following line:

```
Access-list 102 permit tcp any 172.16.50.1 0.0.0.7
```

Any additional servers in the range are automatically allowed TCP access by this single line.

Cisco CNS Network Registrar

The *Cisco CNS Network Registrar* offers the ability to synchronize names with dynamically assigned IP addresses. Typically, dynamic DHCP is difficult because the same machine does not always get the same IP address. Since most names are statically mapped to an IP address, when a workstation's IP address changed, its DNS name did as well.

However, with Cisco CNS Network Registrar, you can have the workstation receive a dynamic DHCP address, but the DNS server makes sure that the workstation name remains constant. This ensures that hosts on the

Internet attempting to contact your workstation will be able to do it consistently, as long as they reference your workstation by name.

The Cisco CNS Network Registrar includes

- Domain Name Server Manager tool

- DHCP server

- TFTP server

- NTP server

- Syslog server

IP Version 6 Addresses

With the growth of the Internet since the early 1990s, the IETF, IANA, IAB, and many networking vendors have realized the need for an expanded IP address space. RFC 2373 defines IP version 6 addressing architecture. *IP version 6 addresses* are 128 bits in length and are globally unique. Understanding the format of an IP version 6 address is key to addressing and designing for tomorrow's networks. The following examples show IP version 6 addresses expressed in hexadecimal (preferred) and an example of address abbreviation when fields contain zeros. The first 80 bits define the network and subnet, and the final 48 bits represent the node on the network:

```
FEDC:BA98:7654:3210:FEDC:BA98:7654:3210
```

```
1080:0:0:0:8:800:200C:417A
```

It's not necessary to write the leading zeros in an individual field, but there must be at least one number in every field. It is common for addresses to contain long strings of zero bits. In order to make writing addresses that contain zero bits easier, a special syntax is available to compress the zeros.

The use of "::" indicates multiple groups of 16 bits of zeros. The "::" can only appear once in an address. The "::" can also be used to compress the leading and/or trailing zeros in an address.

For example, the following addresses

```
1080:0:0:0:8:800:200C:417A    a unicast address
FF01:0:0:0:0:0:0:101          a multicast address
0:0:0:0:0:0:0:1               the loopback address
0:0:0:0:0:0:0:0               the unspecified addresses
```

may be represented as

```
1080::8:800:200C:417A        a unicast address
FF01::101                    a multicast address
::1                          the loopback address
::                           the unspecified addresses
```

In IP version 6, the first few bits of the address determine the type of address, much like the classes of addresses available with IP version 4. The following shows the IP version 6 address assignments:

```
010-service provider allocated unicast addresses↵
    (4000::00 through 5FFF:FFFF:FFFF:FFFF:FFFF:FFFF↵
    :FFFF:FFFF)
100-geographically assigned unicast addresses (8000::0↵
    through 9FFF: FFFF:FFFF:FFFF:FFFF:FFFF:FFFF:FFFF)
1111 1110 10-link local addresses (FEC0::0 through FEBF:↵
    FFFF:FFFF:FFFF:FFFF:FFFF:FFFF:FFFF)
1111 1110 11-site local addreses (FEC0::0 through FEFF:↵
    FFFF:FFFF:FFFF:FFFF:FFFF:FFFF:FFFF)
1111 1111-multicast addresses (FF00::0 through all F's)
```

There are no broadcast addresses defined; the all-hosts multicast is used instead. There are many other differences present in IP version 6—everything from packet formats to how a host determines its address. Several books cover IP version 6 in greater detail, and you should consult them to learn more.

IP Version 6 Migration

IP version 6 supports encapsulation into the IP version 4 address space when support for both is needed during migration.

There are three major transition strategies available, which can also be used in combination:

Dual-stack (IPv4 and IPv6 coexist in the router and network) The requirements for the dual-stack migration strategy are that both IPv4 and IPv6 stacks be enabled on the router and client, and at least two computers and their user applications can talk to both protocol versions. Some of the operating systems that currently support the dual-stack method are FreeBSD, Linux, Sun Solaris, and Windows 2000/XP. Routers and clients running dual-stack can fall back to IPv4 to communicate with only

IPv4 routers and clients. To determine which IP protocol they can use, clients can query the DNS server. If DNS returns an IPv6 address for the destination, then the client can use IPv6 to communicate. Interestingly enough, the DNS server does not have to support dual-stack but only IPv6 host record types.

Automatic tunneling (encapsulation of IPv6 packets into IPv4 packets) The automatic tunneling migration approach relies on the IPv4 addresses. When an IPv6 datagram reaches the boundary of the IPv4 network, the router encapsulates it in an IPv4 datagram. As an IPv4 datagram, the new message must have an IPv4 destination address. To derive that address, the router extracts the IPv4 address embedded in the IPv6 packet's destination. The whole process requires no special configuration on any system.

Header translation (allows IPv6-only devices to talk to IPv4 devices) With the header translation method, IPv6 messages travel nearly all the way to the destination, but since the destination does not understand IPv6, it cannot complete the journey. To deliver the client a message, a configured router accepts the IPv6 datagram and converts it to an IPv4 format. When the client responds to the message or datagram, the configured router performs the reverse translation back to IPv6.

Table 7.7 lists the typical IPv4-to-IPv6 migration steps.

TABLE 7.7   IPv4-to-IPv6 Migration Steps

Step	Migration Method
1.	Upgrade DNS servers to handle IPv6 addresses.
2.	Introduce dual-stack systems that support both IPv4 and IPv6.
3.	Add IPv6 addresses to the DNS server.
4.	Rely on tunneling to connect IPv6 networks separated by IPv4 networks.
5.	Remove support for IPv4 from the clients.
6.	Rely on header translation to reach the remaining IPv4-only clients

Real World Scenario

How to Obtain and Test IP Version 6 in Your Network

Connecting your test network to the 6bone network offered by many ISPs requires a 6to4 tunnel to support existing IP version 4 networks. Each Cisco router in your test network needs to support dual-stack protocol, which is included with IOS release 12.2. Once you have configured the border router connected to the ISP, you then need to request IP version 6 addresses. For more information, see the following URL: http://www.cisco.com/en/US/tech/tk648/tk364/technologies_design_guide09186a00800d6a19.shtml.

To obtain and test IP version 6 on a private network without connecting to the 6bone network, identify two Windows 2000 or greater or Linux Red Hat 7.2 or greater workstations, a hub or a switch, and a Cisco router running IOS 12.2 or greater. Connect the workstations to the hubs or switches and connect the hubs or switches to the LAN ports of the Cisco router.

Windows 2000 workstations can be configured to use IP version 6 by downloading the stack software from http://research.microsoft.com/msripv6. You can enable IP version 6 in Windows XP by typing **ipv6 install** at the command line. For Red Hat 7.2, add following line in the file /etc/sysconfig/network: NETWORKING_IPV6="yes". For more information on IP version 6 with Linux, visit http://www.bieringer.de/linux/IPv6/IPv6-HOWTO/IPv6-HOWTO-1.html.

For the Cisco router configuration, in global configuration mode, type **ipv6 unicast-routing**. Then configure the network number and IP address on each interface by entering **ipv6 *address* ipv6-prefix/*prefix-length*** and **ipv6 *address* ipv6-address/*prefix-length* | *local-length***. For more information on configuring IP version 6 on Cisco routers, visit http://www.cisco.com/univercd/cc/td/doc/product/software/ios122/122newft/122t/122t2/ipv6/ftipv6c.htm.

Don't forget to manually assign IP version 6 addresses to your workstations.

IPX Considerations

You may recall that IPX addressing uses an 80-bit address that consists of a 32-bit network address and a 48-bit host address. The host address is taken from the MAC address of the device, thus removing the need for an ARP-equivalent function in IPX. Also, most host addressing is dynamic, meaning that you will never need to configure *IPX addresses* on workstations. However, you will need to have the correct IPX network address to configure the router. This can be obtained either from the local administrator or by typing **config** at the console of the NetWare server.

In many situations, the IPX addressing is already set on individual LANs. Your function is one of gathering existing IPX address information (along with frame type) and ensuring that unique IPX network addresses have been used across the internetwork. It is not uncommon to have many networks configured with common IPX addresses, such as the following:

- 00000001, etc.

- BA5EBA11

- 11111111, etc.

Since host addressing is dynamic, conflicts are easily resolved by reconfiguring NetWare servers with the new addresses. Workstations automatically reconfigure their addresses to conform to the new network address.

If you are able to specify the IPX addressing scheme, and the network includes IP addresses, one trick is to convert the IP network address to hexadecimal and use that for the IPX network address. For example, IP network 172.16.10.0 can be represented as IPX network AC100A00. This is obtained by converting 172 to hexadecimal (AC), then 16 to hexadecimal (10), and so on. This technique allows you to create a single addressing scheme that can be used across both protocols and ensures against duplicate IPX network addresses.

Network Naming Standards

Network naming is one area that is typically overlooked in the design process. However, as with so many other aspects of network design, a well-designed naming scheme greatly simplifies the long-term administration of networks.

Network naming actually plays an important role in overall network administration. Consider DNS names on the Internet for a moment. Suppose that you are attached to an ISP in Colorado and find a website you really like. You can immediately contact your friend in California and forward him the name (URL) of the site. By using the same name, you are both able to access the same site no matter how or from where you access the Internet. Now, suppose that the web server you were looking at moves from its original location to a new location across the country. Suppose that part of this move involves a new IP address. By manipulating the name, you and your friend will likely never even know that the server has moved! Since you are accessing the name, but the webmaster controls the mapping of that name to an IP address, he can change the IP address of the server at will without affecting your ability to find his pages!

When assigning names to devices, generally the more information you can include, the better. For example, server names like *MAIL2* or *DataBase5* are better than *server* or *BigGuy*. Names should be meaningful. Routers can also be named, and as with servers and other hosts, it is better to give them names that describe their function or location.

Summary

This chapter discussed the design of both network addressing and naming. We began by covering route summarization, an important technique that allows you to keep route tables from growing out of control. VLSM allows for discontiguous subnets when using classless routing protocols.

We then discussed private addressing and NAT and how they can be used to stretch out registered addresses. NAT helps conserve IP version 4 addresses and minimizes the cost of public IP purchases. NAT also adds an element of security by hiding real addresses, but that can be a limitation to some applications.

We looked at server and router addressing and discussed some scenarios where planned addresses for these devices can simplify both default router configuration and access list protection.

We looked at DHCP, along with some IPX issues in addressing. DHCP allows for centralized management of IP addresses and can be used across routers by configuring IP helper addresses. IPX addresses are 80 bits in length and include the 48-bit MAC address and up to a 32-bit network address.

Finally, this chapter offered a few suggestions for network naming and looked at the Cisco CNS Network Registrar's ability to dynamically map network names to IP addresses. Descriptive device names are more useful for a network design and troubleshooting.

Exam Essentials

Understand the design benefits and uses of VLSM.   VLSM allows for summarized routes, which reduce route table sizes. Hierarchical design is possible with VLSM, which supports discontiguous subnets and streamlined, simplified access lists, making for a more efficient, easier to troubleshoot network.

Know the benefits and advantages of private IP addresses.   Private IP addressing includes the Class A network 10.0.0.0/8, the Class B network 172.16.0.0/12, and the Class C network 192.168.0.0/16. With IP version 4 address depletion, private IP addresses allow the network designer the flexibility to number all networks and hosts. Private IP addressing also minimizes the cost, public exposure, and security of your networks.

Remember the design advantages of NAT.   NAT is a design solution to a depleted IP version 4 address space, which minimizes the cost of public IP addresses and adds the security of private addresses.

Understand the configuration requirements of DHCP and client addressing.   DHCP provides IP addresses to clients and allows for centralized management with changes. Using the `ip helper-address` command to configure IP helper addresses on a Cisco router, the network designer can provide DHCP addressing to all clients regardless of the network topology.

Know the parts of an IP version 6 address and assignments.   IP version 6 addresses are 128 bits in length and written in hexadecimal for display purposes. The first 80 bits define the network and subnet, and the final 48 bits represent the node on the network. The address 0:0:0:0:0:0:0:1 is the node's loopback address, and FEDC:BA98:7654:3210:FEDC:BA98:7654:3210 is an example of an address with a network portion of FEDC:BA98:7654:3210:FEDC and a node address of BA98:7654:3210.

Identify the importance of network naming standards.   Network naming standards allow the network designer to use a hierarchical naming convention that allows for correct identification and aids network troubleshooters. Descriptive and meaningful names minimize the learning curve and maintenance for users and administrators.

Key Terms

Before you take the exam, be certain you are familiar with the following terms:

Cisco CNS Network Registrar	Network Address Translation (NAT)
classfull	private addressing
classless	private IP version 4 addresses
classless interdomain routing (CIDR)	route summarization
Dynamic Host Configuration Protocol (DHCP)	subnet mask
IP unnumbered	subnetting
IP version 4 addresses	variable-length subnet masks (VLSMs)
IP version 6 addresses	WAN
IPX addresses	

Case Studies

Complete the following exercises for the three case study companies. You may wish to refer back to Chapter 4, "Pre-Design Procedures," to review the complete overview of each company. Once you have completed these exercises, you may compare your solutions to ours in the back of the book. Realize that even though your answers may differ from ours, that does not necessarily mean that one is right and the other is wrong.

Have-A-Seat

1. Would you recommend the use of private addressing for Have-A-Seat's network? How about NAT? Why or why not?

2. Using your high-level topology map from Chapter 4, design an IP addressing scheme for Have-A-Seat.

3. Would you recommend the use of route summarization by Have-A-Seat? Why or why not?

4. Dave has decided that he wants to run DHCP from Atlanta for all workstations on his network. He will use static addresses on all servers and network devices. Draw a high-level topology map of DHCP traffic flow and describe any special implementation details.

MPS Construction

In speaking with Mike, you find that he is willing to use TCP/IP as his exclusive communications protocol. You agree to help him with this transition.

1. Would you recommend the use of private addressing for MPS construction? How about NAT? Why or why not?

Willow Creek School District

There are no exercises for the Willow Creek School District in this chapter.

Review Questions

1. Which of the following best describes route summarization?

   A. Using only one subnet so that the network is flattened out

   B. Grouping multiple networks and advertising them as one larger network

   C. Using supernets on all access-level equipment

   D. Advertising only one of many networks for the entire enterprise or campus

2. When can/should route summarization be used? (Choose all that apply.)

   A. Always

   B. When route tables become too large

   C. When a campus or enterprise router owns several contiguous subnets that share equal high-order bit patterns

   D. When routing protocols are capable of handling prefix length and subnet mask information

   E. When the router IOS is capable of IP classless routing (meaning that the network prefix may be any length, including 32 bits long)

3. How should the following networks be summarized?

   172.16.12.0/24
   172.16.13.0/24
   172.16.14.0/24

   A. 172.16.0.0/16

   B. 172.16.14.0/24

   C. 172.16.12.0/22

   D. 172.16.14.0/22

4. Which of the following commands allows a Cisco router to forward DHCP requests to the appropriate server?

   A. `ip dhcp server`

   B. `ip helper-address`

   C. `ip helper address`

   D. `helper-address`

5. Which of the following best describes private addressing?

   A. Network blocks set aside by IANA for networks that aren't connected to the global Internet

   B. Network blocks that IANA doesn't allow for commercial use

   C. Network blocks used by private industry

   D. A block of three Class B addresses allocated by IANA for anyone to use

6. Which network is not part of IANA-allocated private address blocks?

   A. 172.31.0.0

   B. 10.0.0.0

   C. 198.162.0.0

   D. 192.168.0.0

7. What does NAT mean, and what is it used for?

   A. Network Anonymous Transport: Used to transfer data from privately addressed hosts to the global Internet.

   B. Network Address Translation: Used to renumber a privately addressed network.

   C. Network Address Translation: Used to convert a private IP address into a registered IP address.

   D. Network Address Translation: Uses one address and then proxies connections from a private network to the global Internet.

8. When can NAT be used? (Choose all that apply.)

    A. When application sensitivity isn't an issue (delay)

    B. When end-to-end traceability isn't needed

    C. After the private address blocks have been fully utilized

    D. When a network uses only private addresses

    E. When a network has both private and registered addresses

9. Which of the following best describes DHCP?

    A. An NIC used to configure IP addresses

    B. A method of aggregating route information

    C. A dynamic addressing scheme used by IP and IPX

    D. A protocol used to configure IP hosts

10. Which of the following best allows a host to be configured using a DHCP server in separate broadcast domains?

    A. It cannot be done.

    B. Configure an IP helper address to forward requests to the DHCP server.

    C. Configure the DHCP server to monitor broadcasts on the remote segment.

    D. Enable bridging on all routers to create a single large broadcast domain.

11. What is the maximum number of DHCP servers that can service a single broadcast domain with dynamic addresses?

    A. None

    B. One

    C. Two

    D. Three

    E. No limit

12. Which of the following is a valid IP version 6 node address?

   A. 1080:::::::8:800:200C:417A

   B. 1080:0:::0::8:800:200C:417A

   C. 1080:0:0:0:8:800:200C:417A

   D. FF01::101

13. What feature is no longer supported with IP version 6 addresses?

   A. Loopback addresses

   B. Broadcast addresses

   C. Multicast addresses

   D. Unicast addresses

14. Which of the following are valid IPX network addresses? (Choose all that apply.)

   A. 172.16.0.0

   B. 3

   C. abcde111

   D. 1.001a.3858.1c35

15. Network names should be which of the following? (Choose all that apply.)

   A. Secure and secret

   B. Consistent

   C. Meaningful

   D. Colorful

16. Which of the following utilities allows you to retain consistent DNS names when using dynamic DHCP address assignment?

   A. Bind

   B. Cisco CNS Network Registrar

   C. IOS

   D. NAT

17. When moving a server from one network to another, which of the following steps best retains the existing mappings to that server?

    A. Change the network address and change the name of the server.

    B. Change the network address and don't change the name of the server.

    C. Don't change the network address and change the name of the server.

    D. Don't change the network address and don't change the name of the server.

18. In the Have-A-Seat case study, which tool would be used to synchronize names with dynamically assigned IP addresses?

    A. Netsys

    B. CiscoWorks

    C. Cisco CNS Network Registrar

    D. CiscoHub/Ring manager

19. In the Have-A-Seat case study, what would be the best recommendation for the end-user computers?

    A. Have each IP address assigned administratively.

    B. Let the users assign their own IP addresses.

    C. Use the Cisco CNS Network Registrar.

    D. Use NAT.

20. In the Willow Creek School District, Scott decides he wants to control all IP address assignment centrally. Which of the following will achieve this for him?

    A. NAT

    B. Private addressing

    C. VLSM

    D. DHCP

Answers to Review Questions

1. B.   Route summarization allows for hierarchical network design and addressing.

2. B, C, D.   Route summarization prevents large routing tables, minimizes subnet advertisements, and requires a classless routing protocol.

3. C.   The answer 172.16.12.0/22 allows for a summarization of network 172.16.12.0 through 172.16.14.0 with a 24-bit mask.

4. B.   To better manage and centralize network servers, IP helper addresses can be configured on Cisco routers using the `ip helper-address` command.

5. A.   Private IP addresses are not unique to a single network or organization connected to the Internet.

6. C.   The IANA-allocated private address blocks are 10.0.0.0/8, 172.16.0.0/12, and 192.168.0.0/16.

7. C.   NAT converts private inside addresses to public outside addresses.

8. A, B, D, E.   NAT is typically used with private address blocks.

9. D.   DHCP is used to dynamically assign and centrally manage IP host addresses.

10. B.   Cisco routers support the `ip helper-address` command, allowing centralized DHCP servers.

11. E.   So long as the servers do not overlap in the addresses that they assign out, there is no limit to the number of servers per broadcast domain.

12. C.   IP version 6 allows for the abbreviation of zeroed fields, but only once per address can "::" be used. FF01::101 is an IP version 6 multicast address.

13. B.   IP version 6 addresses no longer support broadcast addresses. The all-hosts multicast is used instead.

14. B, C.   IPX network addresses are a maximum of 24 bits and are displayed in hexadecimal for ease of use.

15. B, C.   Consistent and meaningful network naming practices by the network designer will minimize the learning curve for the network's users and administrators.

16. B.   The Cisco CNS Network Registrar assigns IP addresses to individual hosts based on their DNS name.

17. B.   Of course, you need to map the existing name to the new address in DNS.

18. C.   The Cisco CNS Network Registrar assigns IP addresses to individual hosts based on their DNS name.

19. C.   The Cisco CNS Network Registrar assigns IP addresses to individual hosts for dynamic, centralized management.

20. D.   DHCP assigns IP addresses to individual hosts dynamically and allows for centralized management.

Chapter

8

Routing Protocols

CCDA TOPICS COVERED IN THIS CHAPTER:

✓ Given a network design or a set of requirements evaluate
  a solution that meets routing protocol needs.

Who doesn't like their car to run at its optimum? When the motor is tuned and purring like a cat, life is good. But when the engine sounds as if it's coughing up hairballs, doesn't turn over in the morning, or worse yet, stalls in the middle of an intersection, we all get pretty cranky.

You're probably thinking, where is he going with this and how does it relate to routing protocols? Well, routing protocols compose the information (engine) for getting messages back and forth across networks. Knowing these processes is like knowing your car's engine: it will help you troubleshoot any problems that occur and obtain peak performance from your systems.

Routing protocols are responsible for the exchange of IP address information on enterprise, intranet, and Internet networks. The information shared by routers enables two separate end systems to find a path from one to another, thus establishing communication. As discussed in Chapter 5, "Designing Network Topologies," IP addressing schemes establish a hierarchy that makes path information both distinct and efficient. Routers receive route information via a given interface and then advertise that information out their other physical interfaces. The routing process occurs on Layer 3 of the OSI model.

This chapter will discuss each of the following routing protocols:

- RIP (Routing Information Protocol)

- IGRP (Internal Gateway Routing Protocol)

- EIGRP (Enhanced Internal Gateway Routing Protocol)

Each routing protocol is distinct in the way it functions. However, most routing protocols are one of two major types: *link-state* or *distance-vector*. We'll discuss each type's features and differences at the beginning of this chapter, because understanding how each protocol functions is a very important part of being able to troubleshoot a routing problem. Once you understand how a protocol calculates a route, you can fine-tune the protocol with configuration changes to make it perform at peak efficiency.

OSPF, IS-IS, and NLSP are covered in Chapter 9, "Link-State and Bridging Protocols."

Cisco routers implement several different protocols—some are Cisco proprietary, and others are open standard. The proprietary protocols discussed in this chapter are IGRP and Enhanced IGRP.

Okay, let's get started learning how that engine is supposed to hum.

Routing Protocols

First, let's clarify what is meant by the terms "routed protocols" and "routing protocols," because they are quite different. *Routed protocols* are used between hosts to carry user traffic. Examples of routed protocols include such protocols as IP or IPX. Both IP and IPX can provide enough information in the network header of packets to enable a router to deliver user traffic. Routed protocols specify the type of fields and how they're used within a packet. Packets in routed protocols can be forwarded from source to destination over multiple hops in a network of routers.

The only job that *routing protocols* have is to maintain route tables that are used by routers to make routing decisions. Examples of routing protocols are

- Routing Information Protocol (RIP)

- Open Shortest Path First (OSPF)

- Novell's Link-State Protocol–NetWare Link Services Protocol (*NLSP*)

- Intermediate System–to–Intermediate System (IS-IS)

- Cisco proprietary protocols Interior Gateway Routing Protocol (IGRP) and Enhanced Interior Gateway Routing Protocol (EIGRP)

These protocols provide a way of sharing route information with other routers for the purposes of updating and maintaining tables. These protocols don't send end-user data from network to network—routing protocols only pass routing information between routers.

Routers can support multiple independent routing protocols and can update and maintain route tables for all routed protocols simultaneously. This allows you to create many networks over the same network media.

Routers can do this because routed and routing protocols are focused—they pay no attention to each other's protocols. This is called *ships-in-the-night routing*. Think of ships in a harbor, busy loading or unloading their freight. They pretty much ignore each other except to avoid colliding.

Most network communication occurs within small logical groups. Routing systems often mimic this behavior by designating logical groups of nodes as domains, autonomous systems, or areas.

A routing domain or *autonomous system (AS)* is a portion of an internetwork under common administrative authority. An AS consists of routers that share information using the same routing protocol. With certain protocols you can subdivide an AS into routing areas.

Scalability Features of Routing Protocols

Think of a network as the main drag in your town where the housing subdivisions empty onto. This main drag's ability to handle more cars becomes an issue only with the addition of more housing. And it seems as though the most desirable areas to live in are just like networks: they're always growing.

As networks grow, the extent to which a routing protocol will scale becomes a very critical issue. Network growth imposes a great number of changes to the network environment—the number of hops between end systems, the number of routes in the route table, the different ways a route is learned, and route convergence are all seriously affected by network growth.

Some people enjoy change and excitement in life; others like stability. This is not to judge one type over another, but stability in a network environment is the ultimate goal of every network administrator. (Sorry to all you thrillseekers out there. You'll have to get your kicks elsewhere.) The one place you don't want instability is in your routing processes.

To maintain a stable routing environment, it's absolutely crucial to use a scalable protocol. When the results of network growth are manifest, whether your network's routers will be able to meet those challenges is up to the routing protocol. For instance, if you use a protocol that's limited by the number of hops it can traverse, how many routes it can store in its table, or even by the inability to communicate with other protocols, these limitations will likely slow or halt the growth of your network.

That last area—a protocol's interoperability—becomes important when the need to connect multi-vendor networks arises. Not every network is constructed solely of Cisco equipment, so it's necessary to have a protocol that will allow different vendor types to share routing information.

All of these issues are general scalability considerations. Let's discuss each protocol type separately with respect to these considerations. Each protocol type has pros and cons (along with scalability issues), and the following sections will analyze all of these factors, helping you choose the best protocols for your specific situation.

Scalability Limitations of Distance-Vector Protocols

In small networks (fewer than 100 routers) where the environment is much more forgiving of routing updates and calculations, distance-vector protocols perform pretty well. However, you'll run into several problems when attempting to scale a distance-vector protocol to a larger network—convergence times, router overhead (CPU utilization), and bandwidth utilization all become factors that hinder scalability.

A network's convergence time is determined by the ability of the protocol to propagate changes within the network topology. Distance-vector protocols don't use formal neighbor relationships between routers. A router using distance-vector algorithms becomes aware of a topology change in two ways:

- If a router fails to receive a routing update from a directly connected router

- When a router receives an update from a neighbor notifying it of a topology change somewhere in the network

Routing updates are sent out on a default, or specified, time interval, so when a topology change occurs, it could take up to 90 seconds before a neighboring router realizes what's happened. When the router finally recognizes the change, it recalculates its route table and sends the whole table out to all its neighbors.

Not only can this cause significant network convergence delay, it also devours bandwidth—just think about 100 routers all sending out their entire route tables and imagine the impact on your bandwidth! It's not exactly a sweet scenario, and the larger the network, the worse it gets, because a greater percentage of bandwidth is needed for routing updates.

As the size of the route table increases, so does CPU utilization, because it takes more processing power to calculate the effects of topology changes and then converge using the new information. Also, as more routes populate a route table, it becomes increasingly complex to determine the best path and next hop for a given destination. The following list provides a summary of scalability limitations inherent in distance-vector algorithms:

- Network convergence delay

- Increased CPU utilization

- Increased bandwidth utilization

Scalability Limitations of Link-State Protocols

Link-state routing protocols overcome the scalability issues faced by distance-vector protocols, because the algorithm uses a different procedure for route calculation and advertisement, which enables them to scale along with the growth of the network. This makes them "one-size-fits-all" protocols; they'll work well in large or small environments. But not all their features are necessary in small networks.

Addressing distance-vector protocols' problems with network convergence, link-state protocols maintain a formal neighbor relationship with directly connected routers that allows for faster route convergence. They establish peering by exchanging Hello packets during a session, which cements the neighbor relationship between two directly connected routers. This relationship expedites network convergence, because neighbors are immediately notified of topology changes. Hello packets are sent at short intervals (typically every 10 seconds), and if an interface fails to receive Hello packets from a neighbor within a predetermined hold time, the neighbor is considered down, and the router will then flood the update out all physical interfaces. This is done before the new route table is calculated, so it saves time. Neighbors receive the update, copy it, flood it out their interfaces, and then calculate the new route table. This procedure is followed until the topology change has been propagated throughout the network.

It's noteworthy that the router sends an update concerning only the *new* information—not the entire route table. So the update is a lot smaller, which saves both bandwidth and CPU utilization. Plus, if there aren't any network changes, updates are sent out only at specified, or default, intervals, which differ among specific routing protocols and can range from 30 minutes to 2 hours.

These are key differences that permit link-state protocols to function well in large networks—they don't really have any limitations when it comes to scaling, other than the fact that they're a bit more complex to configure than distance-vector routing protocols.

Interior Routing Protocols

Interior routing is implemented at Layer 3 of the OSI Model. An interior router can use a routing protocol and a specific routing algorithm to accomplish routing.

Some examples of interior routing protocols are as follows:

RIP   RIP is the distance-vector routing protocol used by IP and IPX.

RTMP   RTMP (Routing Table Maintenance Protocol) is similar to RIP, but is used by AppleTalk.

IGRP   IGRP is Cisco's proprietary distance-vector routing protocol.

OSPF   *OSPF* is an IP link-state routing protocol.

Enhanced IGRP   EIGRP is Cisco's balanced distance-vector routing protocol.

IS-IS   IS-IS is a link-state routing protocol similar to OSPF.

As mentioned earlier, most routing protocols can be classified into two basic categories: distance-vector and link-state.

Distance-vector   A distance-vector protocol understands the direction and distance to any network connection on the internetwork. A distance-vector protocol listens to secondhand information to get its updates.

Link-state (shortest path first)   A link-state protocol understands the entire network better than a distance-vector protocol and never listens to secondhand information. Hence, it can make more accurate and informed routing decisions.

Let's take a bit deeper look at the differences between these two types of routing protocols.

Distance-Vector Routing

What happens when a link drops or a connection gets broken? All routers must inform the other routers to update their route tables. But sometimes you hear people complain about routing protocols slowing their network's performance. This can be because of convergence time—not the ubiquitous broadcast problem people love to gripe about regarding distance-vector protocols.

So what is *convergence time*? It's the time it takes for all the routers to update their tables when a reconfiguration or an outage occurs, or when a link drops—basically, whenever a change occurs. No data is passed during this time, and a slowdown is imminent. Once convergence is completed, all routers within the internetwork are operating with the same knowledge, and the internetwork is said to have converged. If convergence didn't happen, routers would possess outdated tables and make routing decisions based on potentially invalid information.

Distance-vector routing protocols update every 10 to 90 seconds. When they do this, it causes all routers to pass their entire route tables to all other known routers. Table 8.1 lists several distance-vector routing protocols and their *update intervals*.

TABLE 8.1 Distance-Vector Update Intervals

Routing Protocol	Update Interval (default)
IP RIP	30 seconds
IPX RIP	60 seconds
RTMP	10 seconds
IGRP	90 seconds

Let's say you have three routers, A, B, and C, as shown in Figure 8.1. Router A has direct connections to Networks 1 and 2. Router B has direct connections to Networks 2 and 3. Router C has direct connections to Networks 3 and 4.

FIGURE 8.1 Distance-vector operation with three routers.

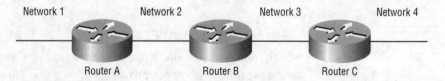

When distance-vector routers start up or get powered on, they get to know their neighbors; that is, they learn the metrics (hops) to the other routers on each of their interfaces. As the distance-vector network-discovery updates continue (every 30 seconds for IP RIP), routers discover the best path to destination networks. The paths are calculated by and based on the number of hops the routers are from each neighbor. In Figure 8.1, Router C knows

Router B is connected to Network 1 by a metric of one. That means it must be a metric of two for Router C to get to Network 1. Router C will never be aware of the whole internetwork—it only knows secondhand what is "gossiped to it."

Remember convergence? Whenever the network topology changes for any reason, route table updates must occur by each router sending out its entire route table in the form of a broadcast to all the other routers. When a router receives the tables, it compares them to its own table. If it discovers a new network, or what it considers a faster way to get to one, it updates its table accordingly with that information.

Hop Count

What's the best way to a network? The original distance-vector routing algorithm maintains that "the fewer hops, the better," and uses only hop counts when making its routing decisions. Take a look at Figure 8.2.

FIGURE 8.2   Distance-vector network decisions

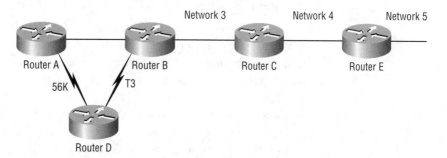

Router A is getting to Router D through a 56KB WAN link. Router A can also reach Router D via Router B, which can get to Router D through a T3. Which is faster? According to distance-vector routing, the fastest route would be through the 56KB pipe. Imagine sending 500MB files to a server plugged into a hub going to Router D. It would take all day (and night)! So why in the world would it choose that path? Because distance-vector routing uses only metrics (hops) to base its routing decisions on, and in its opinion, one hop is better than two. The solution, of course, is to lie to Router A that the metric to Router D via the 56KB circuit is really three. This can be done manually and will cause Router A to determine that two hops are better than three.

Routing Loops

A problem with distance-vector routing is *routing loops*. These can occur because every router is not updated at close to the same time. Let's say that the interface to Network 5 in Figure 8.2 fails. All routers know about Network 5 from Router E. Router A, in its tables, has a path to Network 5 through Routers B, C, and E. When Network 5 fails, Router E tells Router C. This causes Router C to stop routing to Network 5 through Router E. But Routers A, B, and D don't know about Network 5 yet, so they keep sending out update information. Router C will eventually send out its update and cause Router B to stop routing to Network 5, but Router A and Router D are still not updated. To Router A and Router D, it appears that Network 5 is still available through Router B with a metric of three.

So Router A will send out its regular 30-second "Hello, I'm still here—these are the links I know about" message, which includes reachability for Network 5. Routers B and D then receive the wonderful news that Network 5 can be reached from Router A. So Routers B and D send the information that Network 5 is available. Any packet destined for Network 5 will go to Router A to Router B and then back to Router A. This is a routing loop—what do you do to stop it?

Counting to Infinity

The routing loop problem just described is called *counting to infinity*, and it's caused by gossip and wrong information being communicated and propagated throughout the internetwork. Without some form of intervention, each time a packet passes though a router, the hop count increases indefinitely.

One way of solving this problem is to define a maximum hop count. Suppose that a distance-vector routing protocol permits a hop count of up to 15, so anything that requires 16 hops is deemed unreachable. In other words, after a loop of 15 hops, Network 5 will be considered down. This means that counting to infinity, also known as *exceeding TTL*, will keep packets from going around the loop forever. Though a good solution, it won't remove the routing loop itself. Packets will still be attracted into the loop, but instead of traveling on it unchecked, they just whirl around for 16 bounces and then die.

Split Horizon

Another solution to the routing loop problem is called *split horizon*. It reduces incorrect routing information and routing overhead in a distance-vector network by enforcing the rule that information cannot be sent back in the direction from which that information was received. It would have prevented Router A from sending the updated information it received from Router B back to Router B.

Route Poisoning

Another way to avoid problems caused by inconsistent updates is called *route poisoning*. When Network 5 goes down, Router E initiates route poisoning by entering a table entry for Network 5 as 16 or unreachable (sometimes referred to as *infinite*). By poisoning its route to Network 5, Router E is not susceptible to incorrect updates about the route to Network 5. Router E will keep this information in its tables until Network 5 comes up again, at which point it will trigger an update to notify its neighbors of the event.

Route poisoning and triggered updates will speed up convergence time, because neighboring routers don't have to wait 30 seconds (an eternity in computer land) before advertising the poisoned route.

Hold-Downs

And then there are *hold-downs*. Hold-downs work with triggered updates to prevent regular update messages from reinstating a route that's gone down. Hold-downs help prevent routes from changing too rapidly by allowing time either for the downed route to come back or for the network to stabilize somewhat before changing to the next best route. Hold-downs also tell routers to restrict, for a specific time period, any changes that might affect recently removed routes. This prevents inoperative routers from being prematurely restored to other routers' tables.

Hold-downs use triggered updates, which reset the hold-down (HD) timer, to let the neighbor routers know of a change in the network. There are three instances when triggered updates will reset the hold-down timer:

- The HD timer expires.

- The router receives a processing task proportional to the number of links in the internetwork.

- Another update is received indicating the network status has changed.

Link-State Routing

The link-state routing algorithm maintains a more complex table of topology information. Routers using the link-state concept are privileged to a complete understanding and view of all the links of distant routers, plus how they interconnect. The link-state routing process uses link-state packets (LSPs) or Hello packets to inform other routers of distant links. In addition, it uses topological databases, the shortest path first (SPF) algorithm, and of course, a route table.

Network discovery in link-state routing occurs quite differently than it does with distance-vector routing. First, routers exchange Hello packets (LSPs) with one another, giving them a bird's-eye view of the entire network. In this initial phase, each router communicates only its directly connected links. Second, all routers compile all of the LSPs received from the internetwork and build a topological database. After that, the SPF computes how each network can be reached, finding both the shortest and most efficient paths to each participating link-state network. Each router then creates a tree structure with itself representing the root.

The results are formed into a route table, complete with a listing of the best paths—again, the best paths are not simply the shortest but the most efficient. Once these tasks are completed, the routers can use the table for switching packet traffic.

Our senses can help us determine whether we enjoyed a particular restaurant. Our eyes and ears evaluate the ambiance. Our senses of smell, sight, and taste test the food itself. And we may tangibly examine the linens, utensils, or furnishings. This is a link-state approach.

Unlike distance-vector routing, which is similar to a one-sense evaluation, link-state routing understands that in order for a packet to get from Router A to Router D most efficiently, the shortest path is via the T3—not through the painfully slow 56KB line. It knows this because it doesn't simply base its path choice decisions on hop count; it also analyzes characteristics like available bandwidth and the amount of load on links to conclude what is truly the best path to a destination.

Convergence

Link-state routers also handle convergence in a completely different manner than distance-vector does. When the topology changes, the router or routers that first become aware of the event either send information to all other routers participating with the link-state algorithm, or they send the news to a specific router that's designated to consult for table updates.

A router participating in a link-state network must take the following steps in order to converge:

1. Remember its neighbor's name, when it's up/down, and the cost of the path to that router.

2. Create an LSP that lists its neighbor's name and relative costs.

3. Send the newly created LSP to all other routers participating in the link-state network.

4. Receive LSPs from other routers and update its own database.

5. Build a complete map of the internetwork's topology from all the LSPs received, and then compute the best route to each network destination.

Whenever a router receives an LSP, the router recalculates the best paths and updates the route tables accordingly.

Power, Memory, and Bandwidth Needed

Some issues that must be considered when using link-state routing are processing power, memory usage, and bandwidth requirements.

To run the link-state algorithm, routers must have more power and memory available than what they require to run distance-vector routing. A Cisco router is designed specifically for this purpose.

In link-state routing, routers keep track of all their neighbors and all the networks they can reach. All that information—including various databases, the topology tree, and the route table—must be stored in memory!

Dijkstra's algorithm states that a processing task proportional to the number of links in the internetwork multiplied by the number of routers in the network will compute the shortest path. What he means is that you need real processing power, ample memory, and a lot of bandwidth. In other words, you'll make a trip over the Rockies much easier with a V-8, 300-horsepower engine than with 150-horsepower in a four-banger.

Why is the bandwidth requirement so important? Because when a link-state router comes online, it floods the internetwork with LSPs or Hello packets and reduces the bandwidth available for actual data. You remember data, right? That stuff you're trying to get from point A to B.

The good news is that, unlike distance-vector routers, after this initial network deluge, link-state routers update their neighbors only every two hours on the average—unless a new router comes online or a link drops. And this two-hour period can be changed to be compatible with your bandwidth requirements. Let's say you have 56KB links to different continents. Would you use RIP (a distance-vector protocol) that updates every 30 seconds, or OSPF (a link-state protocol) that can be configured to update every 12 hours?

Another great thing about link-state routing is that with it, routers can be configured to use a designated router (DR) as the target to consult for all changes. All other routers on the same segment as the DR can contact this router directly for any pertinent network events instead of using the LSP broadcasts to communicate information.

You might be wondering what happens if the routers don't get an LSP packet? Or what happens if the link is slow and the network topology changes twice before some of the routers even receive the first LSP? Well, link-state routers can implement LSP time stamps, plus they can also use sequence numbers and aging schemes to avoid the spread of inaccurate LSP information. These features would be necessary only in large internetworks.

Comparing Distance-Vector Routing to Link-State Routing

So, as you can see, there are quite a few major differences between distance-vector and link-state routing algorithms. Let's take a moment to go over a few:

- Distance-vector routing gets all its topological data from secondhand information or network gossip, whereas link-state routing obtains a complete and accurate view of the internetwork by compiling LSPs.

- Distance-vector routing determines the best path by counting hops—by metrics. Link-state routing uses bandwidth analysis, plus other pertinent information (better metrics) to calculate the most efficient path.

- Distance-vector routing updates topology changes in 30-second intervals, adjustable in most cases, which can result in a slow convergence time. Link-state routing can be triggered by topology changes, resulting in faster convergence times as LSPs are passed to other routers, sent to a multicast group of routers, or sent to a specific router.

All things considered, when it comes to routing protocols, there isn't any one solution for all networks. Routing choices shouldn't be based solely on speed or cost, because multi-vendor support or standards may well outweigh these factors. Considerations such as network simplicity, the need to set up and manage quickly and easily, or the ability to handle multiprotocols without complex configurations can be pivotal in making proper decisions for your network.

If you're still unclear on the best approach, how about a compromise? Utilizing the strengths of both, or *hybrid routing*, can be a great solution.

Balanced Hybrid Routing

Balanced hybrid, or balanced routing, combines and uses the best of both distance-vector and link-state algorithms.

Although the hybrid approach does employ distance vectors with more accurate metric counts than those used by distance-vector routing alone to determine the path to an internetwork, it can converge quickly, thanks to the use of link-state triggers. Additionally, hybrid routing uses a more efficient link-state protocol that helps mitigate the problem of high bandwidth, processor power, and memory needs.

Some examples of hybrid protocols are OSI's *IS-IS (Intermediate System–to–Intermediate System)* and Cisco's EIGRP (Enhanced Interior Gateway Routing Protocol).

Now that we have discussed the differences in routing protocols in general, let's take a look at some specific routing protocols and how they operate.

RIP (IP Routing Information Protocol)

R*IP* (and IGRP) always summarizes routing information by major network numbers. This is called *classfull routing*. *Classless routing* and *prefix routing* protocols allow contiguous blocks of hosts, subnets, or networks to be represented by a single route. RIP is a classfull routing protocol and does not support prefix routing.

RIP is a distance-vector routing protocol that practices classfull routing, which is used to discover the cost of a given route in terms of hops and store that information in the route table.

The router can then consult the table in selecting the least costly, most efficient route to a destination. It gathers information by watching for route table broadcasts by other routers and updating its own route table in the event that a change occurs.

RIP is specified in RFC 1058 and updated with RFC 1723. Some of the differences defined in RFC 1723 are added security features. RIP messages are now allowed to carry more information in their updates.

RIP Route Tables

At a minimum, RIP route tables provide the following information:

- IP destination address
- A metric (numbered from 1 to 15) indicative of the total cost, in hops, of a particular route to a destination
- The IP address of the next router that a datagram would reach on the path to its destination
- A marker signaling recent changes to a route
- Timers, which are used to regulate performance
- Flags, which indicate whether the information about the route has recently changed
- Hold-downs used to prevent regular update messages from reinstating a route that's no longer functional

- Split horizon used to prevent routing loops

- A *poison reverse* update used to prevent larger routing loops

RIP sends out routing updates at regular intervals and whenever a network topology change occurs.

When a router that's running RIP receives new information indicating a better route to a destination, the new information replaces the older entry in its table. For example, if a router loses a link, it will recalculate the routes in its own tables and then send the revised information out to all its neighbors. Each router will receive this information, update its table accordingly, and then send the information out to all its neighbors.

Neighbors are routers with interfaces to a common network.

All of this sounds pretty cool, but there are a few drawbacks. For one thing, when a topology change takes place, it results in slow convergence. In a large network, this can very well lead to the counting to infinity problem, plus the routing loops that were mentioned earlier.

All things considered, you can see that RIP can be quite useful for routing within small- to moderate-sized internetworks. But, its small hop count limit and single metric don't really allow much flexibility in complex environments.

 Real World Scenario

Another Use for RIP

There's another use for RIP that's not usually published in textbooks or by Cisco. Many of my clients are small businesses, and they use ISDN dial-on-demand for connecting to their ISP. I have found a use for RIP in these scenarios because of its default updates (30 seconds). These types of installations don't normally require a routing protocol, because they are what's commonly referred to as a *stub network*; there are no other networks or routers present.

Normally I only configure a static (default) route to the ISP, but since ISDN is dial-on-demand, the link will time out after normal business hours and external connection requests by users to the internal e-mail server will fail. ISPs don't normally listen to RIP updates from their client's networks, so enabling RIP and allowing the default updates to propagate through the connection to the ISP keeps the link up.

Cisco's recommendation for an ISP-facing router would be to disable RIP updates towards the ISP by using the `passive-interface` command. Since I configure the router to advertise updates out the ISP-facing router, I have had to consider the security ramifications. RIP can be configured to advertise any network you wish with the network *network-number* command.

My solution is to configure a bogus network number and rely on NAT, the firewall, and security policies to secure the client's network. The link remains up, and RIP serves another use.

IGRP (Interior Gateway Routing Protocol)

*I*GRP is a Cisco proprietary routing protocol that uses a distance-vector algorithm because it uses a vector (a one-dimensional array) of information to calculate the best path. This vector consists of four elements:

- Bandwidth
- Delay
- Load
- Reliability

MTU (maximum transfer unit) information is included in the final route information, but it's used as part of the vector of metrics. Each of these elements will be described in detail later. Remember that only bandwidth and delay are used to create a link metric. Load, reliability, MTU, and hop count can be configured through configuration, but that is not typical.

IGRP is intended to replace RIP and create a stable, quickly converging protocol that would scale with increased network growth. As mentioned earlier, it's preferable to implement a link-state protocol in large networks because of the overhead and delay that results from using a distance-vector protocol.

IGRP Features

IGRP has several features included in its algorithm. Table 8.2 lists these features and a brief description of each. These features were added to make IGRP more stable, and a few were created to deal with routing updates and make network convergence happen faster.

TABLE 8.2 IGRP Features

Feature	Description
Configurable metrics	Metrics involved in the algorithm responsible for calculating route information may be configured by the user.
Flash update	Updates are sent out prior to the default time setting. This occurs when the metrics for a route change.
Poison reverse updates	Implemented to prevent routing loops. These updates place a route in *hold-down.*
Unequal-cost load balancing	Allows packets to be shared/distributed across multiple paths.

IGRP Timers

To control performance, IGRP includes timers with default settings for each of the following:

Update timers   Update timers specify how frequently routing update messages should be sent. The default is 90 seconds.

Invalid timers   Invalid timers specify how long a router should wait before declaring a route invalid because it didn't receive a specific update about it. The default is three times the update period.

Hold-down timers   Hold-down timers specify the hold-down period. The default is three times the update timer period, plus 10 seconds.

Flush timers   Flush timers indicate how much time should pass before a route should be flushed from the route table. The default is seven times the routing update period. After both the invalid timer and flush timer expire, IGRP will then flush the invalid route from the table.

IGRP Routes

IGRP is a classfull protocol, which means it doesn't include any subnet information about the network with route information. Three types of routes are recognized by IGRP:

Interior routes   Interior routes are networks directly connected to a router interface.

System routes   System routes are advertised by other IGRP neighbors within the same AS (autonomous system). The AS number identifies the IGRP session, because it's possible for a router to have multiple IGRP sessions.

Exterior routes   Exterior routes are learned via IGRP from a different AS number, which provide information used by the router to set the *gateway of last resort*. The gateway of last resort is the path a packet will take if a specific route isn't found on the router.

To really understand how IGRP routes, it's important to understand the difference between these route types, which are illustrated in Figure 8.3.

FIGURE 8.3   Route types recognized by IGRP

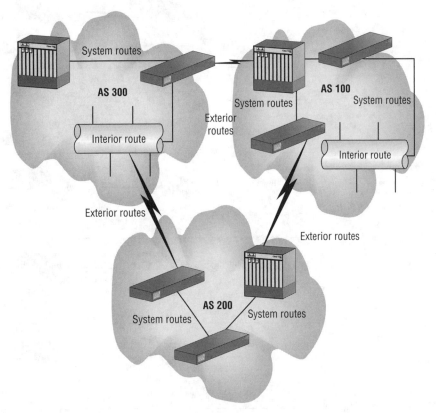

The discussion of the scalability of distance-vector protocols told you that they don't establish a formal neighbor relationship with directly connected routers and that routing updates are sent at designated intervals. IGRP's interval is 90 seconds, which means that every 90 seconds IGRP will broadcast its entire route table to all directly connected IGRP neighbors.

Figure 8.4 portrays how IGRP routing updates work. It depicts three routers, all within the same AS. On the left-hand side of the figure, the relative times (in seconds) for each of the routers are listed. Notice that they're not the actual clock times. The first line shows Routers A and C sending their route tables to Router B. Router B timestamps the routing updates from both routers and will expect to receive updates from them every 90 seconds thereafter. At the next time increment (30 seconds later), Router B broadcasts its route table to both Routers A and C, which they in turn timestamp. They will also expect to receive an update from Router B every 90 seconds based on that time stamp.

FIGURE 8.4 IGRP route update process

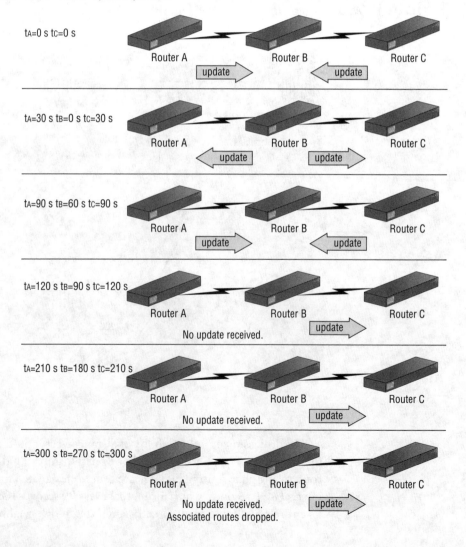

Once the timers for Routers A and C reach 90 seconds, they broadcast their route tables to Router B. Router B then resets its receive timer and expects to receive route updates within 90 seconds. Router B's transmit timer continues to count to 90 seconds and broadcasts the route table when that period elapses. Notice that Router C received an update, but Router A didn't. Because of that, Router C resets its receive timer, but Router A's timer continues to count.

Another 90 seconds elapse, so Router B sends out another update. Again, only Router C receives it. Router A's clock is now at 180 seconds because it hasn't yet received an update.

Finally, an additional 90 seconds passes when Router B broadcasts the route table, and again Router C receives the broadcast and resets its receive timer. However, for the third time, Router A doesn't receive the update, so the algorithm flags the next-hop Router B as unreachable and assigns it a higher metric. After Router A recalculates a new table, it will send out flash updates to all other routers connected to Router A, notifying them that Router B is unreachable.

The total time that passed between the first update received from Router B and the point that Router A flagged Router B as unreachable was 270 seconds. Three consecutive failures to receive an update from a directly connected router are required for IGRP to consider a neighbor unreachable and assign it a new metric. After seven failures, any routes associated with Router B will be removed from the table and no longer advertised.

More than one route can be associated with a next-hop router, so once it's been determined that a next-hop router is down, a router will remove all associated routes from its route table.

Preventing Routing Loops

Two methods are used to prevent routing loops with IGRP:

- Split horizon

- Poison reverse updates

With split horizon, route information learned from a given interface isn't sent back out the same interface. Using Figure 8.5 as a reference, we'll explain split horizon updates.

Router D advertises network 10.2.1.0/24 to Routers A and B. After Router B receives the update and recalculates its own route table, a broadcast update is sent. However, specific route information learned from Router D isn't advertised back to Router D.

Poison reverse updates use a function within IGRP called hold-down, which stops the router from being confused about multiple routes to a given network. If a router has a bunch of routers connected to it, it's possible for it to receive duplicate route advertisements. Figure 8.5 shows a router that's meshed with three other routers. Router A learns of network 10.2.1.0/24 from Routers C and D. If the Ethernet segment connected to Router D fails, Router D will advertise the change to Routers A and B. So Router A will receive information from Router D that network 10.2.1.0/24 is unreachable—a fact that increases its metrics. Router B must recalculate the route table before it can update Router C. At this point, Router A has a higher metric for the 10.2.1.0/24 network. Due to the change in the metric, the router will place the route in hold-down so that updates regarding the network are ignored unless they're received from the router that advertised the increased metric. During hold-down, the network is advertised to other routers with the increased metric.

FIGURE 8.5 Split horizon

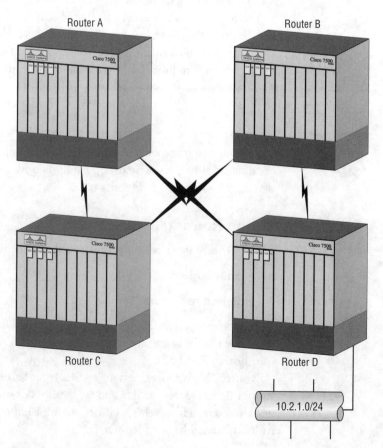

For a detailed explanation of IGRP configuration, see *CCNP: Building Scalable Cisco Internetworks*, also by Sybex.

EIGRP (Enhanced IGRP)

*E*nhanced IGRP (EIGRP) was created to resolve some of the problems with IGRP. One problem is that the entire route table is sent when changes are made in the network; another problem is the lack of formal neighbor relationships with connected routers. EIGRP is a hybrid of both link-state and distance-vector routing algorithms, which brings the best of both worlds together.

EIGRP allows for equal-cost load balancing, incremental routing updates, and formal neighbor relationships, overcoming the limitations of IGRP. This enhanced version uses the same distance-vector information as IGRP, yet with a different algorithm. EIGRP uses DUAL (diffusing update algorithm) for metric calculation.

EIGRP Features and Operation

Table 8.3 lists EIGRP's specific features. Each feature is described in detail in this section. The features offered by EIGRP make it a stable and scalable protocol. Just as IGRP is a Cisco proprietary protocol, so is EIGRP.

TABLE 8.3 EIGRP Features

Feature	Description
Route tagging	Distinguishes routes learned via different EIGRP sessions.
Formal neighbor relationships	Uses the Hello protocol to establish peering.
Incremental routing updates	Only changes are advertised instead of the entire route table.
Classless routing	EIGRP supports subnet and VLSM information.

TABLE 8.3 EIGRP Features *(continued)*

Feature	Description
Configurable metrics	Metric information can be set through configuration commands.
Equal-cost load balancing	Allows traffic to be sent equally across multiple connections.

To aid in the calculation of the best route and load sharing, EIGRP utilizes several databases of information:

Route database   The route database is where the best routes are stored.

Topology database   The topology database is where all route information resides.

Neighbor table   The neighbor table is used to house information concerning other EIGRP neighbors.

Each of these databases exists for IP-EIGRP, IPX-EIGRP, and AppleTalk-EIGRP. Therefore, it is possible for EIGRP to have nine active databases when all three protocols are configured on the router.

Route Tagging

EIGRP functions within defined autonomous systems on a router. It is possible for multiple sessions of EIGRP to run on a single router. Each session is distinguished by the AS number assigned to it. Routers that have EIGRP sessions running under the same AS number speak to each other and share routing information among the other routers in the same AS.

Routes learned via other routers within the AS are considered internal EIGRP routes. It is also possible for one AS session to learn routes from a different EIGRP AS session through redistribution (redistribution will be explained later in Chapter 9). When this occurs, the routes are tagged as being learned from an external EIGRP session. Each type of route is assigned its own administrative distance value.

Neighbor Relationships

The manner in which EIGRP establishes and maintains neighbor relationships is derived through its link-state properties. EIGRP uses the Hello protocol (just as OSPF does) to establish and maintain peering relationships with directly connected routers; these relationships are known as *adjacencies*. Hello packets are sent between EIGRP routers to determine the state of the connection between them. Once the neighbor relation is established via the Hello protocol, the routers can exchange route information.

Each router establishes a neighbor table in which it stores important information regarding the neighbors that are directly connected. This information consists of the neighbor's IP address, hold time interval, smooth round trip timer (SRTT), and queue information. This information is used to help determine when the link state changes.

When two routers initialize communication, their entire route tables are shared. Thereafter, only changes to the route table are propagated. These changes are shared with all directly connected EIGRP-speaking routers. Each of these steps can be summarized as follows:

1. Hello packets are multicast out all of the router's interfaces.

2. Replies to the Hello packets include all routes in the neighbor router's topology database, including the metrics. Routes that are learned from the originating router are not included in the reply.

3. The originating router acknowledges the update to each neighbor via an Ack packet.

4. The topology database is then updated with the newly received information.

5. Once the topology database has been updated, the originating router then advertises its entire table to all the new neighbors.

6. Neighbor routers acknowledge the receipt of the route information from the originating router by sending back an Ack packet.

These steps are used in the initialization of EIGRP neighbors, and they change somewhat when only updates are sent to existing neighbors.

Route Calculation and Updates

Because EIGRP uses distance-vector and link-state information when calculating routes using the DUAL algorithm, convergence is much faster than with IGRP. The trick behind the convergence speed is that EIGRP calculates new routes only when a change in the network directly affects the routes contained in its route table. To make that a little clearer, look at Figure 8.6. In this figure, three routers are meshed, and each has an Ethernet segment connected as well.

FIGURE 8.6 Route updates vs. calculation

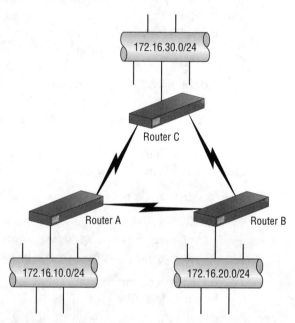

It is important to understand the difference between accepting a routing update and calculating a new route. Some people find these concepts easy to confuse. If a change occurs to a network that is directly connected to a router, all of the relevant information is used to *calculate* a new metric and route entry for it. After the router has calculated the new route, it is advertised to the neighbors.

Using Figure 8.6 as an example, assume that Ethernet 0 on Router C is very congested due to high traffic volumes. Router C then uses the distance and link information to calculate a new metric for network 172.16.30.0. With the new metric in place, the change is propagated to Routers A and B. To understand completely, you need to recognize that the other routers don't do any calculation—they just receive the update. Routers A and B don't need to calculate a new route for network 172.16.30.0 because they learn it from Router C. In other words, not every router has to do the math!

On the other hand, if the link between Router A and Router C becomes congested, both routers would have to calculate a new route metric. The change is then advertised to Router B by both Routers A and C.

Now that you understand the difference between a route update and a route calculation, let's summarize the steps that a router takes to calculate, learn, and propagate route update information.

Calculation and Selection of Routes

The topology database stores all routes and metrics known via adjacent routers. Six routes can be stored for each destination network. From these six routes, the router must select a primary and backup route—the primary route will be added to the route table. While the best route is being chosen for a destination, the route is considered to be in an active state. After the route has been chosen, the route status changes to passive.

Through the use of existing metric information such as bandwidth and delay from both the local and adjacent routers, a composite metric is calculated. The local router adds its cost to the cost advertised by the adjacent router. Cost is another word for metric. By looking at Figure 8.7, you can learn how cost is used to select the successor (best route) and the feasible successor (backup route).

FIGURE 8.7 Best-route selection

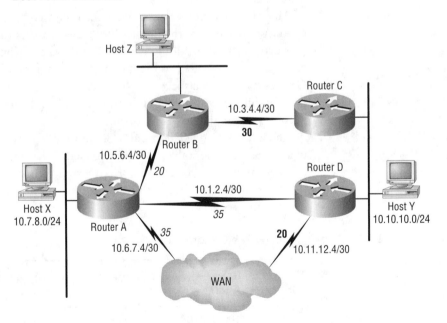

Let's use Router A as an example. Router A has three different routes that tell it how to get to Host Y. You can see that each link has been assigned a cost. The numbers in bold represent *advertised distances*, and the numbers in italics represent *feasible distances*. Advertised distances are costs that routers advertise to neighbors.

In this example, Routers C and D and the WAN all have advertised costs that they send to Router A. In turn, Router A has a feasible distance for every router to which it is connected. The feasible distance is the cost assigned to the link that connects adjacent routers.

The feasible and advertised costs are added together to provide a total cost to reach a specific network. Let's calculate the lowest cost for Host X to get to Host Y. You will use the path from Host X ≻ Router A ≻ Router B ≻ Router C ≻ Host Y for your first path calculation. To calculate the total cost, add 20 (Router A ≻ Router B) to 30 (Router B ≻ Router C), for a final value of 50.

The next path calculated is from Host X ≻ Router A ≻ Router D ≻ Host Y. In this case, there is no advertised cost, so the final value consists of only the feasible cost—35. The final path is calculated in the same manner to give you the result of 55.

Since the lowest cost was 35, the route to 10.10.10.0/24 learned via Router D will be chosen as the successor or primary route. The other two routes remain in the topology table as feasible successors and are used if the successor to Host Y fails.

All of this resembles how a successor is chosen for a king or queen. The one closest by blood (the one with the least cost) is the chosen successor (the primary route). All the rest stand in line, position dependent on how closely they are related to the monarch. In England, for instance, Prince Charles is the chosen successor to Queen Elizabeth. His two sons are next in line (feasible successors). His two brothers follow behind his sons, if the sons become unavailable for any reason.

The information listed in Table 8.4 closely represents what is contained in an actual topology table, though not exactly. The Status field shows whether a new route is being calculated or if a primary route has been selected. In the preceding example, the route is in passive state because it has already selected the primary route.

TABLE 8.4 Topology Table Information

Status	Route—Adjacent Router's Address (Metrics)	Number of Successors	Feasible Distance
P	10.10.10.0/24 via 10.1.2.6 (3611648/3609600) via 10.5.6.6 (4121600/3609600) via 10.6.7.6 (5031234/3609600)	1 (Router C)	3611648

The route with the best metric (lower is better) is chosen as the primary route. The backup route is chosen by selecting the route with the second lowest metric. Primary routes are moved to the route table after selection. It is possible to have more than one primary route.

EIGRP uses the same vector information as IGRP: bandwidth, delay, reliability, load, and MTU. Bandwidth and delay are the two metrics used by default; the others can be configured manually. If you configure reliability, load, and MTU, it can cause the topology table to be calculated more often.

Updates and Changes

EIGRP also has link-state properties. One of these properties is that it propagates only changes in the route table instead of sending an entire new route table to its neighbors. When changes occur in the network, a regular distance-vector protocol will send the entire route table to neighbors. By avoiding sending the entire route table, less bandwidth is consumed. Neighboring routers don't have to re-initialize the entire route table, causing convergence issues; they just have to insert the new route changes. This is one of the big enhancements over IGRP.

Updates can follow two paths. If a route update contains a better metric or a new route, the routers simply exchange the information. If the update contains information that a network is unavailable or the metric is worse than before, an alternate path must be found. The flowchart in Figure 8.8 describes the steps that must be taken to choose a new route.

The router first searches the topology database for feasible successors. If no feasible successors are found, a multicast request is sent to all adjacent routers. Each router will then respond to the query. Depending on how the router answers, different paths will be taken. After the intermediate steps are taken, two final actions can occur. If route information is eventually found, the route is added to the route table, and an update is sent. If the responses from the adjacent routers do not contain any route information, the route is removed from the topology and route tables. After the route table has been updated, the new information is sent to all adjacent routers via a multicast.

For a detailed explanation of EIGRP configuration, see *CCNP: Building Scalable Cisco Internetworks*, also by Sybex.

FIGURE 8.8 Handling route changes

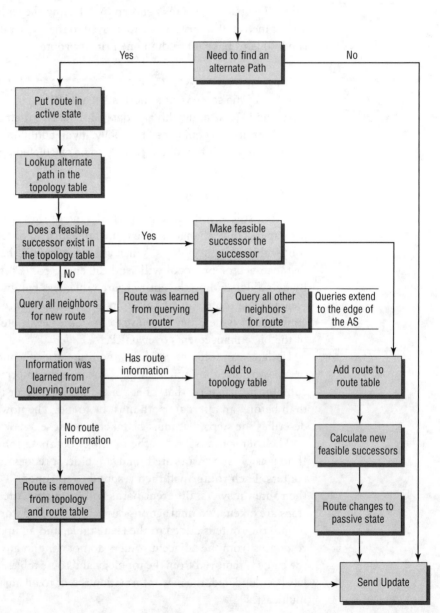

Configuring EIGRP

EIGRP supports several different protocols. Each protocol has specific commands that are used to enable EIGRP. EIGRP can be configured for IP, IPX, and AppleTalk. This subsection will describe in detail how EIGRP is implemented for each of these protocols.

IP

An autonomous system must be defined for each EIGRP session on a router. To start an EIGRP session on a router, use the following command:

```
router eigrp autonomous-system-number
```

After the session has been started, networks that belong to that session need to be added. The networks should be directly connected.

The command to enter the networks must be entered within the EIGRP session configuration. The command and an example are as follows:

```
network network-number
```

where *network-number* is the IP address of a network connected to the router.

```
Router_B#conf t
Enter configuration commands, one per line.  End with↵
   CNTL/Z.
Router_B(config)#router eigrp 200
Router_B(config-router)#network 172.16.0.0
Router_B(config-router)#network 10.0.0.0
Router_B(config-router)#^Z
Router_B#
```

EIGRP assumes that serial connections use T1 speeds. However, it is possible to have slower links, such as 56Kbps or other values, connected to a serial interface. As you have learned previously, bandwidth is one of the two default metrics used to calculate a route's metric. If the bandwidth is slower than T1 speeds, EIGRP will still assign a metric value equivalent to that of a T1. To avoid this confusion, the bandwidth assigned to that interface should be changed. To do this, issue the following command within the Interface Configuration mode:

```
bandwidth bandwidth
```

where *bandwidth* is an integer value between 1 and 10,000,000 that defines the kilobits of bandwidth.

You can stop routing updates from exiting the router via specified interfaces by flagging them as a passive interface from within the EIGRP session using the following command:

```
passive-interface interface-type interface-number
```

where *interface-type* defines the type of interface and *interface-number* defines the number of the interface.

If all that you want to do is allow only certain networks to be advertised, use the distribute-list command. This command was discussed in Chapter 3, "Network Protocols," but let's review it here. This command is issued within the EIGRP session and has the following syntax:

```
distribute-list access-list-number [in | out]⏎
    interface-type interface-number
```

where *access-list-number* is the number of a predefined access list.

IPX

To use EIGRP as the routing protocol for IPX, you must turn on the IPX protocol. Once IPX is enabled, EIGRP is defined as the routing protocol. The commands, along with descriptions and examples, are as follows:

```
ipx routing

ipx router [eigrp autonomous-system-number | rip | nlsp]

Router_A#conf t
Enter configuration commands, one per line. End with⏎
    CNTL/Z.
Router_A(config)#ipx routing
Router_A(config)#ipx router eigrp 400
Router_A(config-ipx-router)#^Z
Router_A#
```

As you can see by the command syntax, it is possible to use RIP, NLSP, and EIGRP as the routing protocols. You're going to use EIGRP at this time. The preceding example first initializes IPX routing and then defines EIGRP 400 as the routing protocol that IPX will use.

The Novell networks should be added to the IPX-EIGRP session. Networks are added with the same network command that was used in IP EIGRP configuration. Here is an example and the resulting configuration. The IPX networks are seen under the IPX-routing EIGRP 400 session:

```
Router_A#config t
Router_A(config)#ipx router eigrp 400
Router_A(config-ipx-router)network 10
Router_A(config-ipx-router)network 20
Router_A(config-ipx-router)exit
Router_A(config)ipx-router rip
Router_A(config-ipx-router)no network 10
Router_A(config-ipx-router)no network 20
Current configuration:
!
version 11.3
no service password-encryption
!
hostname Router_A
!
ipx routing 0010.7bd9.2880
!
router eigrp 100
 network 10.0.0.0
 network 172.16.0.0
!
ip classless
!
ipx router eigrp 400
 network 10
 network 20
!
ipx router rip
no network 10
no network 20
```

Just as IP interfaces can be configured to allow or disallow routing updates or portions thereof, so can IPX interfaces. SAP updates can be controlled with the `incremental update` command. This command tells the router that SAP updates are to be sent only when there is a change in the information, and then, only the change is advertised. The command is not issued under the IPX-EIGRP session, but on the interface itself. Another router running IPX-EIGRP should be on the opposite end of the link for this command to work properly. If no IPX peer exists, SAP updates are sent periodically. The command syntax is as follows:

```
ipx sap-incremental eigrp autonomous-system-number
    [rsup-only]
```

The `rsup-only` option is used when RIP is used as the routing protocol. It indicates to the router that SAP updates are sent via EIGRP only incrementally.

WAN links have this feature turned on by default; LAN interfaces have this feature turned off by default.

AppleTalk

EIGRP also supports AppleTalk. To enable AT-EIGRP on a router, you must first initialize AppleTalk routing on the router. This is done with the following command:

```
appletalk routing eigrp router-number
```

Once this command is entered, AppleTalk route redistribution is turned on as well. Other commands relating to AT-EIGRP can be issued directly from the interface. The following options are available:

`eigrp-bandwidth-percent`	Sets EIGRP bandwidth limit
`eigrp-splithorizon`	Enables split-horizon processing, generating AT-EIGRP updates
`eigrp-timers`	Sets AT-EIGRP hello and hold-down timers

Summary

This chapter began by discussing the difference between routed and routing protocols, and then reviewed the design implications of different routing protocols. We discussed the differences between distance-vector and link-state protocols and explored several protocols in depth, including RIP, IGRP, and Enhanced IGRP.

RIP is a distance-vector routing algorithm that only uses hop count to find the best path to a remote network. It uses broadcasts for route updates, and no formal neighbor relationships are established, so it is often referred to as "routing by rumor."

IGRP is also a distance-vector routing algorithm. IGRP uses bandwidth and delay of the line to determine the best path to an internetwork. It can also be configured to use MTU, load, and reliability.

EIGRP is an enhanced version of IGRP. It uses both distance-vector algorithms and link-state properties to build an internetwork route table with support for IP, IPX, and AppleTalk. It establishes formal neighbor relationships and maintains both topology and route tables.

Exam Essentials

Understand the scalability limitations of routing protocols. Network convergence can take longer than desired with distance-vector routing protocols because of their update interval. More complex configuration is the only real scalability issue with link-state routing protocols.

Understand how distance-vector routing protocols prevent routing loops. Counting to infinity is used to prevent routing loops by setting the maximum hop count to 15. Split horizon enforces the rule that routing information cannot be sent back to the direction from which it came. Route poisoning, along with triggered updates, prevents a route from propagating by entering a hop count of 16; notification updates will occur once the network is up by triggered updates.

Understand the advantages of hybrid routing protocols. Hybrid routing protocols such as EIGRP support multiple routed protocols: IP, IPX, and AppleTalk. EIGRP and IS-IS allow for equal-cost load balancing, incremental routing updates, and formal relationships, combining the best of distance-vector and link-state routing.

Understand the features and operation of Cisco's EIGRP. EIGRP uses DUAL for metric calculation and supports multiple routed protocols and classless routing. Hello packets are used to form neighbor relationships with acknowledgment, and topology databases are created and route calculations are made.

Know how to configure EIGRP. EIGRP configuration requires an autonomous system number for all routers in the same domain along with `network`, `bandwidth`, `passive-interface` and `distribute-list` commands for proper configuration.

Understand the routing protocol types. RIP, IGRP, and RTMP are distance-vector routing protocols. EIGRP and IS-IS are hybrid protocols, and OSPF and NLSP are link-state protocols.

Key Terms

Before you take the exam, be certain you are familiar with the following terms:

adjacencies	link-state routing
autonomous system (AS)	NLSP
classfull routing	OSPF
classless routing	poison reverse
convergence time	prefix routing
counting to infinity	RIP
distance-vector routing	route poisoning
Enhanced IGRP (EIGRP)	routing loops
gateway of last resort	routing protocols
hold-down	ships-in-the-night routing
hybrid routing	split horizon
IGRP	update intervals
IS-IS	

Case Studies

Complete the following exercises for the three case study companies. You may wish to refer back to Chapter 4, "Pre-Design Procedures," to review the complete overview of each company. Once you have completed these exercises, you may compare your solutions with those in the back of the book. Realize that even though your answers may differ from those answers, that does not necessarily mean that one is right and the other is wrong.

Have-A-Seat

Case study exercises for Have-A-Seat's routing protocols will be covered in Chapter 9, "Link-State and Bridging Protocols."

MPS Construction

1. MPS Construction has decided to standardize on TCP/IP as a communications protocol. Would you recommend a distance-vector or link-state routing protocol?

2. Assuming that MPS construction will use only Cisco equipment, which routing protocol would you recommend?

Willow Creek School District

Case study exercises for the Willow Creek School District's routing protocols will be covered in Chapter 9.

Review Questions

1. What are two benefits of using a link-state routing protocol?

   A. It uses the Hello protocol to establish adjacencies.

   B. It uses several components to calculate the metric of a route.

   C. Updates are sent only when changes occur in the network.

   D. It has a longer convergence time than distance-vector protocols.

2. Which of the following metrics are used by IGRP by default when selecting a route? (Choose all that apply.)

   A. Bandwidth

   B. Load

   C. Delay

   D. Reliability

3. Which of the following are *not* features of EIGRP? (Choose all that apply.)

   A. Incremental updates

   B. Only one route per destination

   C. Support for IP, IPX, and AT

   D. Hybrid distance-vector and link-state protocol

   E. Not a scalable protocol

   F. Hello protocol used to establish adjacencies

4. By default, which of the following metrics are used by EIGRP when selecting a route? (Choose all that apply.)

   A. Load

   B. Bandwidth

   C. Reliability

   D. MTU

   E. Delay

5. What is the routing algorithm used by RIP?

   A. Routed information

   B. Link together

   C. Link-state

   D. Distance-vector

6. What is the routing algorithm used by IGRP?

   A. Routed information

   B. Link together

   C. Link-state

   D. Distance-vector

7. What is the routing metric used by IP RIP?

   A. Counting to infinity

   B. Hop count

   C. TTL

   D. Bandwidth, reliability, MTU, delay, and load

8. Which of the following protocols send out incremental updates by default? (Choose all that apply.)

   A. RIP

   B. IGRP

   C. OSPF

   D. EIGRP

9. What does a metric of 16 hops represent in a RIP routing network?

   A. 16 ms

   B. Number of routers in the internetwork

   C. Number of hops

   D. 16 hops—unreachable

10. What are hold-downs used for?

    A. To hold down the protocol from going to the next hop

    B. To prevent regular update messages from reinstating a route that has gone down

    C. To prevent regular update messages from reinstating a route that has just come up

    D. To prevent irregular update messages from reinstating a route that has gone down

11. What is split horizon?

    A. Split horizon is information received from a router that can't be sent back to that originating router.

    B. Split horizon is when you have a large bus (horizon) physical network and as a result, the routing protocol splits the traffic.

    C. Split horizon holds the regular updates from broadcasting to a down link.

    D. Split horizon prevents regular update messages from reinstating a route that has gone down.

12. What is poison reverse?

    A. Poison reverse sends back the protocol received from a router as a poison pill, which stops the regular updates.

    B. Poison reverse is information received from a router that can't be sent back to that originating router.

    C. Poison reverse prevents regular update messages from reinstating a route that has gone down.

    D. Poison reverse is when a router sets the metric for a down link to infinity.

13. Which of the following are distance-vector protocols? (Choose all that apply.)

    A. IGRP

    B. RIP

    C. OSPF

    D. NLSP

14. What is convergence time?

   A. The hold-down update time

   B. The time it takes for all routers to update their route table when a change takes place

   C. The time it takes for a packet to get from a destination host to a receiving host

   D. The time it takes to boot a router

15. Which of the following protocols send out periodic updates by default? (Choose all that apply.)

   A. RIP

   B. IGRP

   C. OSPF

   D. EIGRP

16. What are the metrics used by IPX RIP? (Choose all that apply.)

   A. Bandwidth

   B. Delay

   C. Hop count

   D. Ticks

17. When do the IGRP timers remove a network route from the route table?

   A. When the update timer expires

   B. When the invalid timer expires

   C. When both the invalid and flush timers expire

   D. When both the update and flush timers expire

18. What methods are used to stop routing loops with IGRP? (Choose all that apply.)

   A. Split horizon

   B. Spanning tree

   C. Infinite reply

   D. Poison reverse

19. Which of the following statements are true about the routing process of a router? (Choose all that apply.)

    A. Path desirability is determined by routing metrics.

    B. All paths must be assigned by a network administrator.

    C. It is the process of determining the most desirable path through an internetwork.

    D. Once a router has determined a path for a transmission, any intermediary routers simply functions as repeaters.

20. What happens during convergence time in an internetwork?

    A. The routers exchange manual updates.

    B. The routers exchange routing metrics.

    C. The routers exchange topology alerts.

    D. The routers exchange routing updates.

Answers to Review Questions

1. **A, C.**   Adjacencies and link-state updates provide for much more reliable routing protocol updates.

2. **A, C.**   Metrics of bandwidth and delay create a more defined routing update.

3. **B, E.**   EIGRP uses DUAL to create multiple best route destinations and is scalable to large routing domains.

4. **B, E.**   Load, reliability, and MTU can be configured as metrics for the EIGRP routing process.

5. **D.**   RIP is a distance-vector routing protocol and uses hop count as a routing metric.

6. **D.**   IGRP is a distance-vector routing protocol and uses bandwidth and delay as routing metrics.

7. **B.**   RIP is a distance-vector routing protocol and uses hop count as a routing metric.

8. **C, D.**   Both OSPF and EIGRP use incremental updates to notify neighbors of link-state changes.

9. **D.**   RIP uses hop count as a metric, and 16 is deemed unreachable.

10. **B.**   When routes have gone down, hold-downs prevent the routes from being reinstated until the next triggered update.

11. **A.**   Split horizon is commonly used with distance-vector routing protocols to prevent route updates from being sent back the direction from which they came.

12. **D.**   Poison reverse is used to prevent downed route updates from propagating through the network.

13. **A, B.**   IGRP and RIP are both examples of distance-vector routing protocols.

14. **B.**   Network convergence is the time from the first update to the final update when all routers have the same routing information.

15. **A, B.**   Both RIP and IGRP use broadcast-type routing updates at specific intervals.

16. C, D. IPX RIP uses the hop count and tick metric for best path determination.

17. C. IGRP removes the downed route from the route table only after both the invalid and flush timers have expired.

18. A, D. IGRP uses both split horizon and poison reverse to prevent network routing loops.

19. A, C. The routing process is to determine the best path using the respective routing metric.

20. D. Convergence is the time in which route tables are processing updates.

Chapter

9

Link-State and Bridging Protocols

CCDA EXAM TOPICS COVERED IN THIS CHAPTER:

✓ Given a network design or a set of requirements evaluate
a solution that meets routing protocol needs.

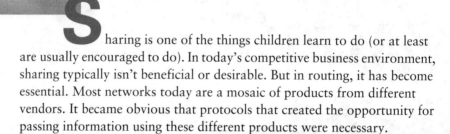

Sharing is one of the things children learn to do (or at least are usually encouraged to do). In today's competitive business environment, sharing typically isn't beneficial or desirable. But in routing, it has become essential. Most networks today are a mosaic of products from different vendors. It became obvious that protocols that created the opportunity for passing information using these different products were necessary.

OSPF and IS-IS are open standard routing protocols that allow Cisco routers to share routing information with other Cisco routers and with non-Cisco routers.

This chapter will introduce and discuss design implications for link-state routing using OSPF, Novell Link-State Protocol (NLSP), and IS-IS. This chapter will also explain the concept of bridging protocols.

Cisco has traditionally supported an extremely rich set of both routing and bridging functionality using a variety of Cisco proprietary and other protocols. Chapter 8, "Routing Protocols," discussed the differences between distance-vector and link-state routing protocols, and then described several specific examples of each. This chapter will go into detail about OSPF, NLSP, and IS-IS. Then we will look at five types of bridging protocols and the situations where each would apply.

Topics covered in this chapter include:

- The purpose and operation of routing protocols, including OSPF, NLSP, and IS-IS

- The operation and implementation of source-route bridging, transparent bridging, and mixed media bridging

Open Shortest Path First (OSPF)

Open Shortest Path First (OSPF) differs from IGRP and Enhanced IGRP (EIGRP) in that it is a pure *link-state routing* technology. Link-state routing protocols only send updates when the topology of the network changes. Also, OSPF is an open standard routing protocol, which means that it was not developed solely by Cisco. OSPF was designed and developed by the IETF to provide a scalable, quickly converging, and efficient routing protocol that could be used by all routing equipment. Complete details for OSPF are found in RFC 1247. You can implement several types of OSPF areas—each of these types will be discussed in detail. Configuration examples and information specific to OSPF such as metrics, redistribution, and filtering will be explained.

OSPF supports several features that RIP version 1 does not; for example, VLSM and route summarization are supported by OSPF but not by RIP.

The hop count was eliminated with OSPF, thus giving it limitless reachability. RIP was limited to 16 hops. Due to the algorithm used to calculate and advertise routes, network *convergence*, or the time it takes for the network routers to update their route tables, is fast with OSPF. OSPF is like EIGRP in that it sends route updates only when changes occur in the network. A formal *neighbor* relationship is established with all adjacent OSPF routers.

Areas are used within OSPF to define a group of routers and networks belonging to the same OSPF session. Links connect routers, and the information about each link is defined by its link state. On each broadcast or multi-access network segment, two routers must be assigned the responsibilities of *designated router (DR)* and *backup designated router (BDR)*. Designated routers are OSPF routers that generate *link-state advertisements (LSAs)* for a multi-access network and have other special responsibilities in running OSPF. Each multi-access OSPF network that has at least two attached routers has a designated router that is elected by the OSPF Hello protocol. The designated router enables a reduction in the number of *adjacencies* required on a multi-access network, which in turn reduces the amount of routing protocol traffic and the size of the topology database.

Like EIGRP, OSPF maintains three databases: adjacency, topology, and route. The adjacency database is similar to the neighbor database used by EIGRP. It contains all information about OSPF neighbors and the links connecting them. The topology database maintains *all* route information. The best routes from the topology database are placed in the route database, also known as the *route table*.

That was a billboard summary of OSPF. Now that you have a general understanding of how OSPF is set up, let's move on and discuss its features and operation in detail.

OSPF Features and Operation

OSPF operation can be divided into several categories. Let's start with how OSPF initializes and creates a peering relationship with adjacent routers. After an OSPF area is defined, we will discuss how the DR and BDR are chosen and what their responsibilities are. Once the area is established and functioning, routing information must be learned and shared.

Initializing OSPF

The Hello protocol is used to establish peering sessions between routers. Hello packets are multicast out every interface. The information that is multicast includes

- The router ID

- Timing intervals

- Existing neighbors

- Area identification

- Router priority

- Designated and backup router information

- Authentication password

- Stub area information

All this information is used when establishing new peers. Table 9.1 contains descriptions of each of these elements.

TABLE 9.1 OSPF Multicast Information

Information	Description
Router ID	The highest active IP address on the router or the loopback interface IP address (even if it is lower).
Time intervals	Contains intervals between Hello packets and the dead time interval.
Existing neighbors	Addresses for any existing OSPF neighbors.

TABLE 9.1 OSPF Multicast Information *(continued)*

Information	Description
Area identification	OSPF area number and link information must be the same for a peering session to be established.
Router priority	This value is used when choosing the DR and BDR.
DR and BDR	If they have already been chosen, their information is contained in the Hello packet.
Authentication password	All peers must have the same authentication password if authentication is enabled.
Stub area flag	This is a special area—two routers must share the same stub information. This is not necessary to initiate a regular peering session with another OSPF router.

Figure 9.1 displays a flowchart that depicts each step of the initialization process. The process starts by sending out Hello packets. Every *listening* router will then add the originating router to the adjacency database. The responding routers will reply with all of their Hello information so that the originating router can add them to its adjacency table.

Once adjacencies have been established, the DR and BDR need to be chosen before route information and link-state information can be exchanged. After the DR and BDR are chosen, route information is exchanged, and the OSPF peers continue to multicast Hello packets every 10 seconds to determine if neighbors are still reachable.

Before proceeding further with peer initialization, let's discuss several terms specific to OSPF. These terms are important for understanding OSPF and how it functions.

The easiest way to understand OSPF is to build from what you already know about EIGRP. In Chapter 8 you learned that EIGRP uses autonomous system (AS) numbers to specify routing processes and the routing process to which individual routers belong. OSPF uses areas in addition to autonomous systems. OSPF areas participate within a single AS and consist of a group of routers or interfaces on a router that are assigned to a common area.

FIGURE 9.1 OSPF peer initialization

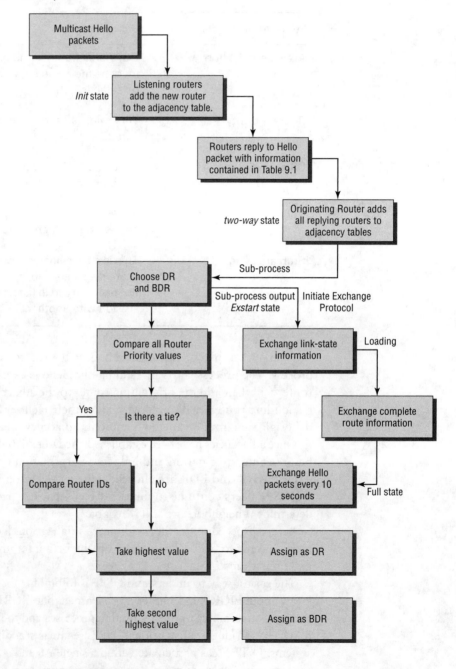

OSPF also allows and uses different area types. When deploying OSPF, there must be a *backbone area*. The standard and stub areas connect to the backbone area. Here is a list of each router type, followed by a short description of the area type:

Backbone   The backbone area accepts all LSAs and is used to connect multiple areas.

Stub   The stub area will not accept any external routing update, but it will accept summary LSAs.

Totally stub   The totally stub areas are closed off from accepting external or summary advertisements.

Standard   The standard area is the normal area that accepts internal and external LSAs and summary information.

From the previous area descriptions, you probably noticed the frequent use of the term LSA. LSAs are the heart of OSPF's information exchange. LSAs distribute a list of active links to neighbor routers. Different types of LSAs represent different types of route information. Table 9.2 summarizes all of the LSA types.

TABLE 9.2   OSPF LSA Types

LSA Type	Description
1. Router link entry	This LSA is broadcast only within its defined area. The Type 1 LSA contains all of the default link-state information.
2. Network entry	This LSA is multicast to all area routers by the DR. This update contains network-specific information.
3./4. Summary entry	Type 3 LSAs contain route information for internal networks and are sent to backbone routers. Type 4 LSAs contain information about Autonomous System Boundary Routers (ASBRs). Summary information is multicast by the Area Border Router (ABR), and the information reaches all backbone routers.
5. Autonomous system entry	As the name indicates, these advertisements originate from the ASBR. These packets contain information about external networks.

Different LSA types represent the type of route that is being advertised and assist in restricting the number and types of routes that are accepted by a given area. As shown in Table 9.2, an LSA of Type 5 is sent only by the ASBR.

Multiple router types can exist within an OSPF area. Table 9.3 lists all of the OSPF router types and the role that each plays within the area.

TABLE 9.3   OSPF Router Types

Router Type	Description
Internal	All interfaces are defined on the same area. All internal routers have an identical link-state database.
Backbone	Backbone routers have at least one interface assigned to area 0.
Area border router (ABR)	Interfaces are connected to multiple OSPF areas. Information specific to each area is stored on ABRs.
Autonomous system boundary router (ASBR)	An ASBR has an interface connected to an external network or to a different AS.

In addition to the listed responsibilities, a router can also be assigned additional responsibilities. These responsibilities are assumed when a router is assigned the role of DR or BDR.

Designated and Backup Designated Routers

The DR and BDR are focal points within each multi-access network segment. These special routers act something like switchboards for information. Routers on any given segment will exchange link-state information with the DR and BDR instead of with each other. After a router has updated the DR and BDR with its information, the DR or BDR multicasts this information to all other routers on this segment. The DR and BDR are also in charge of making sure that all routers have the same version of link-state information. The BDR listens to all updates, but it sends OSPF information on a segment only when the DR fails.

Once a DR and BDR have been established, new routers will establish adjacencies only with the DR and BDR.

Initializing and Maintaining Route Information

Routes are discovered via the Exchange Protocol, as illustrated in Figure 9.1. The Exchange Protocol commences only after the DR and BDR have been chosen. The Exstart state depicted in Figure 9.1 creates peering relationships with the DR, BDR, and each individual router within the area.

The following steps are taken when route information is exchanged (also known as *database synchronization*):

1. Master-slave relationships are established between routers; the router with the highest router ID is the master. And just like master-slave relationships of the human kind, the slave does most of the work.

2. Master and slaves exchange database description packets (called DBDs or DDPs). These packets contain LSA information, which consists of the IP address of the advertising router, cost, and sequence number or data that indicates how recent the link-state information is.

3. After the slave router receives the DBD or DDP, it sends back an LSAck (link-state acknowledgment) packet. It also compares new information to the existing information. If the information provided by the DBD is newer than the existing information, an LSR (link-state request) is sent back to the master router. The LSR tells the master router to send complete information. The sending of LSRs occurs in the *loading* state.

4. The master responds with a *link-state update (LSU)*.

5. The slave replies with another LSAck packet.

6. All routers within the area receive the link-state information via the DR.

7. A router will continue to send LSRs until it receives all the information that it needs. Once it has all of the information it needs, it will change to the *full* state.

8. Once a router is in full state, it can route traffic. At this point in the exchange, all routers should have the same link-state database.

Look at the example in Figure 9.2. This is a protocol trace from a network. Look at the final exchange between the master sending out the LSU and other routers replying with LSAck packets. Note that the destination address of all the LSUs and LSAck packets are multicast addresses.

FIGURE 9.2 OSPF LSU and LSAck exchange

Packet	Source	Destination	Flag	Size	Time-Stamp	Protocol
541	00:10:7b:53:a7:b2	01:80:c2:00:00:00	*	64	13:04:42.139000	802.1
542	IP-131.31.194.141	IP-224.0.0.5		94	13:04:42.586000	OSPF LSU
543	IP-131.31.194.129	IP-224.0.0.6		94	13:04:42.594000	OSPF LSU
544	IP-131.31.194.141	IP-224.0.0.5		94	13:04:42.596000	OSPF LSU
545	IP-131.31.194.142	IP-224.0.0.5		94	13:04:42.773000	OSPF Hlo
546	IP-131.31.194.129	IP-224.0.0.5		94	13:04:42.839000	OSPF Hlo
547	AT-1105.179	AT-0.255	*	64	13:04:42.901000	RTMP Data
548	00:10:7b:a4:4a:a1	00:10:7b:a4:4a:a1		64	13:04:43.413000	Loopback
549	00:10:7b:53:a7:b0	01:80:c2:00:00:00	*	64	13:04:44.138000	802.1
550	00:10:7b:53:a7:b1	01:80:c2:00:00:00	*	64	13:04:44.138000	802.1
551	00:10:7b:53:a7:b2	01:80:c2:00:00:00	*	64	13:04:44.138000	802.1
552	00:10:7b:a4:4a:a1	Ethernet Brdcast	*	178	13:04:44.169000	NW SAP
553	IP-131.31.194.129	IP Broadcast		110	13:04:44.598000	UDP RIP
554	IP-131.31.194.140	IP-224.0.0.6		102	13:04:45.087000	OSPF LSA
555	IP-131.31.194.129	IP-224.0.0.6		82	13:04:45.087000	OSPF LSA
556	IP-131.31.194.142	IP-224.0.0.5		102	13:04:45.088000	OSPF LSA

Now that you have seen the trace, let's look at the actual packets. First, you'll see the LSU packet, and then you'll see the LSAcks after the LSUs have been sent:

```
IP Header - Internet Protocol Datagram
     Version:              4
     Header Length:        5
     Precedence:           6
     Type of Service:      %000
     Unused:               %00
     Total Length:         76
     Identifier:           14145
     Fragmentation Flags:  %000
     Fragment Offset:      0
     Time To Live:         1
     IP Type:              0x59  OSPF
     Header Checksum:      0x5ba6
     Source IP Address:    131.31.194.141
     Dest. IP Address:     224.0.0.5
     No Internet Datagram Options
OSPF - Open Shortest Path First Routing Protocol
     Version:                  2
     Type:                     4  Link State Update
```

```
Packet Length:              56
Router IP Address:          153.53.193.1
Area ID:                    1
Checksum:                   0x6aa5
Authentication Type:        0  No Authentication
Authentication Data:
........             00 00 00 00 00 00 00 00
# Of Advertisements:        1
Link State Advertisement Header
   Age:                     3600   seconds
   Options:                 %00100010
        No AS External Link State Advertisements
   Type:                    3  Summary Link (IP Network)
   ID:                      0x90fb6400
   Advertising Router:      153.53.193.1
   Sequence Number:         2147483708
   Checksum:                0x3946
   Link State Length:       28
Summary Links Advertisement (IP Network)
   Network Mask:            0xffffff00
   Type Of Service:         0
   Metric:                  0xffffff
Frame Check Sequence:   0x20536f66
```

From this packet decoding, you can see that the IP type is OSPF. From there, skip down to the OSPF header information; it indicates that the packet is an LSU. Also in the packet decoding, you can find the IP address of the advertising router and the LSA header. The LSA includes summary information.

Now let's look at just one of the acknowledgments to the LSU:

```
IP Header - Internet Protocol Datagram
   Version:                 4
   Header Length:           5
   Precedence:              6
   Type of Service:         %000
   Unused:                  %00
   Total Length:            84
```

```
        Identifier:            1285
        Fragmentation Flags:   %000
        Fragment Offset:       0
        Time To Live:          1
        IP Type:               0x59  OSPF
        Header Checksum:       0x8dda
        Source IP Address:     131.31.194.140
        Dest. IP Address:      224.0.0.6
        No Internet Datagram Options
OSPF - Open Shortest Path First Routing Protocol
        Version:               2
        Type:                  5  Link State Acknowledgment
        Packet Length:         64
        Router IP Address:     142.42.193.1
        Area ID:               1
        Checksum:              0x6699
        Authentication Type:   0  No Authentication
        Authentication Data:
        ........        00 00 00 00 00 00 00 00
Link State Advertisement Header
        Age:                   3600  seconds
        Options:               %00100010
                No AS External Link State Advertisements
        Type:                  3  Summary Link (IP Network)
        ID:                    0x90fb6400
        Advertising Router:    153.53.193.1
        Sequence Number:       2147483708
        Checksum:              0x3946
        Link State Length:     28
Link State Advertisement Header
        Age:                   3600  seconds
        Options:               %00100010
                No AS External Link State Advertisements
        Type:                  3  Summary Link (IP Network)
        ID:                    0x90fb6400
        Advertising Router:    131.31.193.1
```

Sequence Number:	2147483650
Checksum:	0x25c0
Link State Length:	28
Frame Check Sequence:	0x00000000

This decoding shows you that the packet is an LSAck. The IP address is the IP address of the responding router. Other LSAs were also picked up on the trace, because each router responds to the LSU.

Link-state protocols choose their routes differently than *distance-vector routing algorithms* do. Bandwidth is one of the most important metrics for route selection within OSPF. The Dijkstra algorithm (discussed in Chapter 8) is used to choose the lowest cost link for route selection.

The costs of the local router are added to the cost required to reach the destination. The route with the lowest cost is selected as the primary route. Just as with EIGRP, OSPF can hold six equal-cost routes for each destination. Changes in link-state status change the cost of the link.

Every time a link state changes, LSUs are sent to the DR and BDR. The DR relays the information to all other routers within the segment, causing the route table to be recalculated. You have already seen the trace and decoding for this process during the discussion of the route initialization process. If there are many link-state changes within a short period, network convergence may never be reached. OSPF prevents this problem by using *hold-down* times. The default hold-down time for route calculation is 10 seconds.

Let's summarize how route information is calculated and shared between other routers:

1. A link-state change occurs.

2. An LSU packet with the new LSA attached is sent to all DRs. The multicast address 224.0.0.6 is used by a router to send to all DRs and BDRs.

3. The DR then notifies all other adjacent routers by multicasting an LSU on the address 224.0.0.5.

4. Each adjacent router responds with an LSAck.

5. Other networks receive updates via LSUs sent by the other network's DR.

6. The receiving router updates the link-state database.

7. The SPF algorithm is used to calculate the new route table and to control when the router begins to use the new table.

OSPF Metrics

The metrics associated with OSPF are different from those associated with IGRP and EIGRP. OSPF uses bandwidth as the main metric in selecting a route. The cost is calculated using the bandwidth for the link. The equation is 10^8 divided by the bandwidth. You may change bandwidth on the individual interface.

The cost is manipulated by changing the value to a number within the range of 1 to 65,535. Since the cost is assigned to each link, the value must be changed on each interface. The command to do this is as follows:

```
ip ospf cost
```

Cisco bases link cost on bandwidth. Other vendors may use other metrics to calculate the link's cost. In other words, you may have to compare apples to oranges or bananas. When connecting links between routers from different vendors, you may have to adjust the cost to match the other router. Both routers must assign the same cost to the link (in apples, oranges, or bananas) for OSPF to work.

You can configure the OSPF distance with the following command:

```
distance ospf [external | Intra-area | Inter-area] distance
```

This command allows the distance metric to be defined for external OSPF and for intra-area and inter-area routes.

Intra-area and inter-area routes are discussed later in this chapter.

Distance values range from 1 to 255, and the lower the distance, the better. Connected interfaces have a distance of 0.

Other values important to OSPF's operation are not actually metrics, but they can be configured as well. Values such as the router ID and router priority are important in router initialization and DR and BDR selection. You can change these values with some minor configuration changes.

To change the router priority, use the following command on the desired interface:

```
ip ospf priority number
```

The *number* can range from 0 to 255; the higher value indicates a higher priority when choosing the DR and BDR for the area.

A loopback interface must be added to the router to change the router ID. The IP address of the loopback can be a private address or a fake address. If the IP address is to be announced, a private IP address should be used. To implement a loopback interface on the router, use the following command:

```
interface loopback number
 ip address A.B.C.D
```

You can inject the address used on the loopback interface into OSPF by using the `network area` command.

Configuring OSPF

The initial configuration for OSPF is simple and straightforward, but for connectivity to be established between routers from different vendors, other configuration commands may have to be issued.

Configuration can be broken down into two groups. The first group is for *internal routers*, or routers within an area; the second group is for routers that connect different areas.

Internal Routers

When you're initializing OSPF on a router, the session is defined by a process identification. Unlike EIGRP's AS number, the process identification number does not have to be uniform across all the routers within the OSPF area. Instead of using the process ID to identify the OSPF area, the networks that are added to the session are assigned to an OSPF area. This means that all networks assigned to a given area make up that area. Okay, I admit that is probably obvious!

To initiate OSPF on a router, the first step is to assign the routing protocol with the process ID. After that is done, networks are added and assigned to the desired OSPF area. The commands to do this are as follows:

```
router ospf process-id
network address wildcard-mask area area-id
```

The *process-id* is an integer from 1 to 65,535; the *area-id* is an integer from 0 to 4,294,967,295.

Let's look at a configuration example:

```
Router_A#conf t
Enter configuration commands, one per line.  End with↵
   CNTL/Z.
Router_A(config)#router ospf 1
```

```
Router_A(config-router)#network 172.16.20.0 0.0.0.255↵
    area 20
Router_A(config-router)#network 10.1.2.0 0.0.0.255 area↵
    20
Router_A(config-router)#^Z
Router_A#

Router_A#show running-config
Building configuration...
Current configuration:
!
version 11.3
no service password-encryption
!
hostname Router_A
!
enable password aloha
!
interface Ethernet0/0
 ip address 172.16.10.1 255.255.255.0
!
interface Serial0/0
 ip address 172.16.20.5 255.255.255.252
 no ip mroute-cache
 no fair-queue
!
interface Ethernet0/1
 ip address 10.1.2.1 255.255.255.0
!
router ospf 1
 network 10.1.2.0 0.0.0.255 area 20
 network 172.16.20.0 0.0.0.255 area 20
!
ip classless
!
line con 0
line aux 0
```

```
line vty 0 4
 password aloha
 login
!
end
Router_A#
```

This example shows that the OSPF process was defined as *one*. Two networks were added to OSPF area 20. As you can see, the configuration is quite simple. Again, this configuration is the simplest form of OSPF implementation.

Area Configuration and Wildcard Masks

OSPF configurations can get complicated really fast. It is important to understand the networks your router is attached to before attempting configuration. In this section, we will use a sample router configuration and use the network command with a *wildcard mask*.

The sample router has three interfaces. Interface Ethernet 0 is connected to 172.16.10.0/24 area 0. Serial 0 is connected to 172.16.4.0/22, and Serial 1 is connected to 172.16.8.0/22, both connected to area 1. Notice that we are using a different mask for the WANs than we are for the LANs. This is a benefit of using OSPF; it allows variable-length subnet masks (VLSMs). The router configuration should then look like this:

```
Router ospf 1
Network 172.16.10.0 0.0.0.255 area 0
Network 172.16.4.0 0.0.3.255 area 1
Network 172.16.8.0 0.0.3.255 area 1
```

Notice that the backbone connection is defined first. The wildcard mask was simple since a whole subnet was specified. To figure out a wildcard mask, use all 1s minus the network mask. Here is an example:

```
255.255.255.255 (all 1s)
255.255.255.0   (the mask)
0  .0  .0  .255 (the answer)
```

For the serial interfaces connected to area 1, remember that the mask was not 24 bits, but 22 bits. The mask would then be as follows:

```
255.255.255.255 (all 1s)
255.255.252.0   (our mask)
0  .0  .3  .255 (the answer)
```

OSPF uses areas to group routers. This area, and the topology of the routers, is hidden from the rest of the AS. This allows routing traffic to be reduced, which saves bandwidth.

An OSPF network must have a backbone, or area 0. All other areas must connect to the backbone. Virtual links can be configured for areas that do not, or cannot, connect to the backbone.

To configure area 0, for example, 0 or 0.0.0.0 say the same thing. After the area number, you apply a wildcard mask, which is the same type of wildcard mask used in access lists. By using wildcard masks, OSPF gives you a granular control over the OSPF routing process.

Consider the following example:

```
Network 172.16.16.0 0.0.7.255 area 0
```

This command tells the router that only interfaces addressed with subnets 172.16.16.0 will participate in OSPF area 0. Any other interface on the router that is not part of that subnet range will not be part of area 0. Try that with RIP!

To figure out what wildcard mask to use, minus all 1s from the mask. For example, the network 172.16.0.0 in the preceding example is using a /21 network, or 255.255.248.0. The wildcard mask would be configured like so:

```
255.255.255.255 (all 1s)
255.255.248.0   (the mask)
  0.  0.  7.255 (the answer)
```

Since $256 - 248$ equals 8, then you know the subnets are 8, 16, 24, ..., 240. If you place a 16 in the third octet, then you are saying you want to use only subnets 16–23.

Wildcard masks can also be used to reference only a certain number of subnets. In this example,

```
Network 172.16.64.0 0.0.63.255 area 1
Network 172.16.32.0 0.0.31.255 area 2
```

the first network command tell the OSPF routing process to only let networks defined in the third octet as 64–127 participate in area 1 routing. The second network command tells the OSPF routing process to only let subnets defined in the third octet as 32–63 participate in area 2 routing.

In the first network command example, only two bits are used in the third octet. To figure this out, take eight binary bits and then count up 63. The result is 00111111. This means that the 0s are used to define the networks, and 1s are wild, or can be anything. The zero bits can be all on or all off, hence the addresses of 0 and 192.

In the second `network` command example, 31 in binary is 00011111. This leaves three bits to define the networks and five bits to be wild. Since the zero bits can be all on or all off, eight subnets can be defined.

Let's take a look at one more example. This is important to really understand.

Multi-Area Example

This next example has a router with three interfaces:

- Ethernet 0 (E0) is connected to network 172.16.17.0/20.

- Serial 0 (S0) is connected to network 172.16.9.0/21.

- Serial 1 (S1) is connected to network 172.16.7.0/30.

Here's how the configuration would look:

```
Router(config)#router ospf 172
Router(config-router)#exit
Router(config)#int e0
Router(config-if)#ip address 172.16.17.1 255.255.240.0
Router(config-if)#no shut
Router(config-if)#int s1
Router(config-if)#ip address 172.16.9.1 255.255.248.0
Router(config-if)#no shut
Router(config-if)#int s0
Router(config-if)#ip address 172.16.7.1 255.255.252.0
Router(config-if)#no shut
Router(config-if)#router ospf 172
Router(config-router)#network 172.16.17.0 0.0.15.255↵
    area 0
Router(config-router)#network 172.16.9.0 0.0.7.255 area 1
Router(config-router)#network 172.16.7.0 0.0.3.255 area 2
```

Notice that the first command is the `router ospf 172` command. If you do not type this command, then you cannot configure VLSM interfaces; you would get an error from the router.

Notice the wildcard addresses. Let's work through the wildcard mask of each command:

- Network 172.16.17.0 0.0.15.255 area 0:

```
255.255.255.255  (all 1s)
255.255.240.0    (the subnet mask)
0.0.15.255       (the answer)
```

- Network 172.16.9.0 0.0.7.255 area 1:

  255.255.255.255 (all 1s)
  255.255.248.0   (the subnet mask)
  0.0.7.255   (the answer)

- Network 172.16.7.0 0.0.3.255 area 2:

  255.255.255.255 (all 1s)
  255.255.252.0   (the subnet mask)
  0.0.3.255   (the answer)

Route Summarization

Route summarization in OSPF is used for the same reasons that other routing protocols use it. When a route table becomes large, it taxes the router in multiple ways: CPU utilization, and bandwidth and memory consumption.

OSPF supports two types of route summarization: *inter-area* and external. As with many inter-area functions, the *area border router (ABR)* is in charge of summarizing inter-area routes. External summarization is exactly that—only external routes are summarized by the *autonomous system border router (ASBR)*.

The summarization commands must be issued on the respective routers. Inter-area summarization must be configured on the ABR with the following command within the OSPF routing session:

```
area area-id range address mask
```

The *area-id* is the OSPF area number. The *address* and *mask* define the range of IP addresses that will be summarized for the specified area. To configure external summarization, the following command must be entered within the OSPF routing session on the ASBR:

```
summary-address address mask
```

Notice that the area ID was not used in the second command. This is because only external routes will be summarized. The address and mask define the range of external IP addresses that will be summarized.

Stub Areas

When the route tables and link-state databases grow too large and can't be remedied with route summarization alone, the area may be configured as a *stub area* or a *totally stub area*.

The difference between a stub area and a normal area is that intra-area and inter-area routes are the only routes allowed inside the stub area. To communicate with networks that are not present in the route table, the stub area relies on a default route of 0.0.0.0. This means that when a router does not have a route to the destination address, it will forward the packet to the ABR from which it learned the default network 0.0.0.0. The ABR will then do the route lookup and forward the packet accordingly.

A stub area contains all routes from its area and other areas that are connected via the backbone and ABRs. It does not contain any external routes.

To further shrink a route table for an area, you can make the route table totally stubby. A totally stub area contains an even smaller route table, because the only routes it knows are the routes from within its own area. To contact networks outside the area, the default route 0.0.0.0 is used as well. The ABR is responsible for *forwarding* packets to the correct destination.

Configuring Stub Areas

To configure a stub area, the following command should be implemented on an internal router that is not an ASBR and not connected to the backbone. It is also important to issue this command on every router within the stub or totally stub area:

```
area area-id stub
```

The command is self-explanatory—the *area-id* simply defines the stub area.

To make an area totally stubby, the same command is used, with one modification. It must be issued on the ABR for the area:

```
area area-id stub no-summary
```

You cannot configure routers as stub routers if they belong to the backbone. An area cannot be defined as a stub area if an ASBR is part of the area.

Redistribution

OSPF supports *redistribution* (the movement of networks from one protocol into another protocol) for many protocols. The following listing directly from a router lists the protocols supported:

```
Router_A(config-router)#redistribute ?
  bgp           Border Gateway Protocol (BGP)
```

```
connected   Connected
egp         Exterior Gateway Protocol (EGP)
eigrp       Enhanced Interior Gateway Routing Protocol⤵
  (EIGRP)
igrp        Interior Gateway Routing Protocol (IGRP)
isis        ISO IS-IS
iso-igrp    IGRP for OSI networks
mobile      Mobile routes
odr         On Demand stub Routes
ospf        Open Shortest Path First (OSPF)
rip         Routing Information Protocol (RIP)
static      Static routes
```

Just as with EIGRP, new metrics must be assigned to route information that is injected into the OSPF session. The command to do this is much simpler than the command used when assigning metrics for EIGRP or IGRP— it is almost the same, but only one metric is assigned. The value of the metric is the cost for the route:

```
default-metric cost
```

OSPF Filtering Considerations

Normal methods of route *filtering* done by distribution lists are effective when filtering route information. The most effective method of filtering OSPF is to implement the filters on the ASBR as outbound filters. Inbound filters are effective in filtering routes, but since they are inbound filters, LSA packets are still propagated.

Cisco recommends that you filter within other protocols and that you don't filter OSPF if possible. This is accomplished by implementing outbound filters on other protocols, which keeps unwanted networks from even entering the OSPF area.

Novell Link-State Protocol (NLSP)

Novell *Link-State Protocol (NLSP)* is used exclusively to route IPX traffic. It is a link-state routing protocol, not a distance-vector protocol like IPX RIP. The current version of NLSP, version 1.1, supports a multitude of advanced routing features, such as:

- Multiple areas
- Route aggregation
- Hierarchical addressing
- Network summarization

NLSP is similar to IS-IS and OSPF in that it defines areas. NLSP offers solutions to many of the problems that we discussed with RIP and SAP, and it can actually work as a replacement for all RIP and SAP communication between servers (or routers). Every NLSP router (remember that NLSP-enabled NetWare servers are NLSP routers) builds and maintains three databases:

- Adjacency
- Link-state
- Forwarding

These three databases are listed in the order in which they are built. The adjacency database can be unique on every router. Each router will, on each of its NLSP-enabled interfaces, meet every other NLSP router on that network segment. On an Ethernet interface, for example, there can be several other NLSP-enabled devices (other routers, servers, etc.). On a point-to-point WAN interface, there is only one other device. All of this information goes into the adjacency database, and once it is built, each router knows all of its NLSP neighbors on all connected networks.

The information in the adjacency database is used to create the link-state database. Once the routers know all of their adjacencies, they share that information with every other router in what is called the *area* (we will cover this process and define an area in the next section). At that point, every router knows not only its own adjacencies, but every other router's adjacencies as well. From this, each router builds a link-state database that represents every router in the area and every path between them. Since every router builds this database with the same information (all unique adjacency databases from all routers), the link-state database will be identical on every router in the area.

Once the link-state database is built and all routers agree upon it, each router builds from the link-state database a forwarding database. This is really just a route table. It lists all networks and the best path for each individual router to take to get to these networks. Because each router can occupy a unique position in the area, each router will have a unique forwarding database.

Intermediate System–to–Intermediate System (IS-IS)

In recent years, the *Intermediate System–to–Intermediate System (IS-IS)* routing protocol has become increasingly popular, with widespread usage among ISPs. IS-IS is a link-state protocol that enables very fast convergence with large scalability.

Features of IS-IS include

- Hierarchical routing
- Classless behavior
- Rapid flooding of new information
- Flexible timer tuning

IS-IS uses a two-level hierarchy to support large routing domains. A large domain may be administratively divided into areas. Each system resides in exactly one area. Routing within an area is referred to as *Level 1 routing*. Routing between areas is referred to as *Level 2 routing*. A Level 2 Intermediate System (IS) keeps track of the paths to destination areas. A Level 1 IS keeps track of the routing within its own area. For a packet destined for another area, a Level 1 IS sends the packet to the nearest Level 2 IS in its own area, regardless of what the destination area is. Then the packet travels via Level 2 routing to the destination area, where it may travel via Level 1 routing to the destination. Figure 9.3 shows how with IS-IS, an individual router is in only one area and the border between areas is on the link that connects two routers that are in different areas. This is in contrast to OSPF in which the area borders are within the ABRs.

A Level 1/Level 2 (L1/L2) router may have neighbors in any area. It has two link-state databases: a Level 1 link-state database for *intra-area* routing and a Level 2 link-state database for inter-area routing. A Level 1/Level 2 router runs two SPFs and may require more memory and processing power.

FIGURE 9.3 IS-IS areas with Level 1 and Level 2 routing

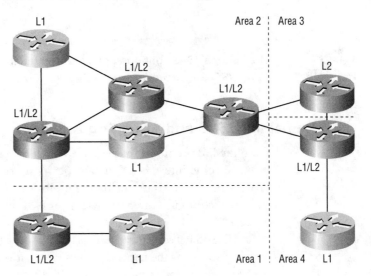

When designing a network, care should be taken to choose the correct setting: Level 1, Level 2, or Level 1/Level 2. When IS-IS is configured on a Cisco router, the default setting is Level 1/Level 2.

Configuring IS-IS for IP on Cisco Routers

IS-IS is an International Organization for Standardization (ISO) dynamic routing specification described in ISO 10589. The Cisco implementation of IS-IS allows you to configure IS-IS as an IP routing protocol.

To configure IS-IS, you need to consider the following list of tasks. Enabling IS-IS and assigning areas is required; the remaining tasks are optional, although you might need them depending upon your specific application:

- Enabling IS-IS and assigning areas (required)

- Enabling IP routing for an area on an interface (optional)

- Configuring IS-IS interface parameters (optional)

- Configuring miscellaneous IS-IS parameters (optional)

- Monitoring IS-IS (optional)

In addition, you can filter routing information and specify route redistribution.

> **NOTE**
> The optional IS-IS configurations are covered in much more depth in *CCNP/ CCIP: BSCI Study Guide,* also by Sybex.

Enabling IS-IS and Assigning Areas

Enabling IS-IS requires that you create an IS-IS routing process and assign it to a specific interface. You can specify more than one IS-IS routing process per Cisco router using the multi-area IS-IS configuration syntax. You then configure the parameters for each instance of the IS-IS routing process.

Small IS-IS networks are built as a single area that includes all the routers in the network. As the network grows larger, it is usually reorganized into a backbone area made up of the connected set of all Level 2 routers from all areas, which in turn is connected to the local areas. Within a local area, routers know how to reach all system IDs. Between areas, routers know how to reach the backbone, and the backbone routers know how to reach other areas.

Routers establish Level 1 adjacencies to perform routing within a local area (intra-area routing). Routers establish Level 2 adjacencies to perform routing between Level 1 areas (inter-area routing).

Cisco routers are used to interconnect each area to the Level 2 backbone. In general, each routing process corresponds to an area. By default, the first instance of the routing process configured performs both Level 1 and Level 2 routing. You can configure additional router instances, which are automatically treated as Level 1 areas. You can configure a process to perform Level 1 routing at the same time. If Level 2 routing is not desired for a router instance, remove the Level 2 capability using the `is-type` command. Use the `is-type` command also to configure a different router instance as a Level 2 router.

You must configure the parameters for each instance of the IS-IS routing process individually. *Network entity titles (NETs)* define the area addresses for the IS-IS area and the system ID of the router.

Table 9.4 lists the commands you use to enable IS-IS and to specify the area for each instance of the IS-IS routing process.

TABLE 9.4   Enabling IS-IS and Assigning Areas

Command	Purpose
Router(config)#router isis [*area tag*]	Enables IS-IS routing for the specified routing process and places the router in configuration mode. Use the *area tag* to identify the area to which this IS-IS router instance is assigned. A value for *tag* is required if you are configuring multiple IS-IS areas.
Router(config)# net *network-entity-title*	Configures NETs for the routing process.

IS-IS allows you to alter certain interface-specific parameters. Most interface configuration commands can be configured independently from other attached routers. The isis password command should configure the same password on all routers on a network. The settings of other commands (isis hello-interval, isis hello-multiplier, isis retransmit-interval, isis retransmit-throttle-interval, isis csnp-interval, and so on) can be different on different routers or interfaces. However, if you decide to change certain values from the defaults, it makes sense to configure them on multiple routers and interfaces. Referring to the following example and to Figure 9.4, you can see how IS-IS configuration is performed:

```
Router_A(config)router isis
Router_A(config-router)net 49.0001.0000.0000.000a.00
Router_A(config-router)interface ethernet 0
Router_A(config-if)ip router isis
Router_A(config-if)interface serial 0
Router_A(config-if)ip router isis

Router_B(config)router isis
Router_B(config-router)net 49.0001.0000.0000.000b.00
Router_B(config-router)interface ethernet 0
Router_B(config-if)ip router isis
Router_B(config-if)interface ethernet 1
Router_B(config-if)ip router isis
```

```
Router_B(config-if)interface serial 0
Router_B(config-if)ip router isis

Router_C(config)router isis
Router_C(config-router)net 49.0001.0000.0000.000c.00
Router_C(config-router)interface ethernet 1
Router_C(config-if)ip router isis
Router_C(config-if)interface ethernet 2
Router_C(config-if)ip router isis
```

FIGURE 9.4 IS-IS area and NET configuration

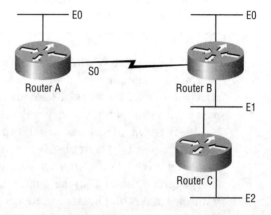

Bridging Protocols

*B*ridging is a method of connecting individual network segments so that they look like a single LAN. Bridging takes place at Layer 2 of the OSI model, as opposed to routing, which takes place at Layer 3. In Figure 9.5, you can see that bridging occurs at Layer 2 and routing at Layer 3.

There are situations where traffic must be bridged rather than routed. For starters, some network protocols cannot be routed and must be bridged. We will take a look at several of those shortly. With Ethernet networks, bridging is a common method of controlling collisions and reducing contention for the media. If you haven't heard of Ethernet switches over the last few years, you must not have been paying attention, because they're everywhere! But that flashy Ethernet switch is really nothing more than a multi-port bridge (on steroids, of course). Its operation is similar to that of the transparent bridges (discussed shortly).

FIGURE 9.5 OSI-model bridge routing

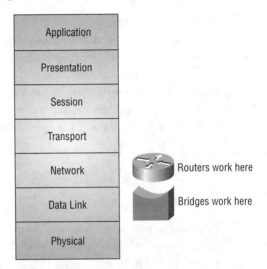

Since bridges operate at Layer 2 rather than Layer 3 of the OSI model, they don't see all of the protocol-dependent traffic that routers have to deal with. For example, IP and IPX packets are really indistinguishable to a bridge. IP and IPX are Layer 3 specifications, and the bridge really doesn't care about their differences. The bridge simply focuses on the Layer 2 frames and avoids the hassle of looking any further.

Bridging creates a single, extended, data-link network. This is often referred to as a *flat* network. With Cisco IOS, all routable protocols can be bridged. However, don't think that this is an easy shortcut to avoid routing. Bridging creates its own special concerns. For example, bridges forward broadcasts while routers block them, which means that while 1,500 workstations will work nicely in a routed network, they may melt the wire with broadcasts alone in a bridged one.

Let's take a quick look at some situations where you have to bridge. Some protocols cannot be routed. In their specifications, they simply do not provide for Layer 3 network addressing. That means they must share a common data-link network (Layer 2) to communicate, which calls for bridging. These non-routable protocols are

- LAT (Local Area Transport)

- MOP (Maintenance Operation Protocol)

- NetBIOS

Transparent Bridging

A *transparent bridge* can connect two or more network segments into a single data-link LAN. It is called a transparent bridge because the devices on the network are unaware that the bridge is even there. The bridge simply listens to frames and passes them along. It does not address, modify, or receive frames. The bridge really is transparent to the devices on the network.

Transparent bridging is generally used with Ethernet. To be transparent to network devices, the bridge performs three functions:

- Learning MAC addresses
- Forwarding packets
- Filtering packets

These functions allow the bridge to act transparently. Additionally, with multiple bridges, there is the possibility of an endless loop, so the bridge is required to perform a fourth function:

- Avoiding loops

Let's discuss each of these functions in detail.

Learning MAC Addresses

When you hook a transparent bridge to an Ethernet segment, it will actually receive all frames transmitted on that segment (remember the *MA—Multiple Access* in CSMA/CD). Now, suppose you have the bridge illustrated in Figure 9.6.

FIGURE 9.6 Transparent bridge

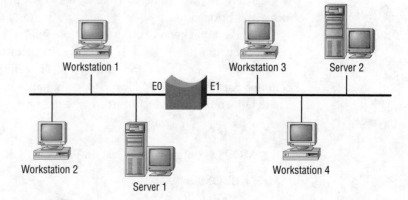

When Workstation 1 is communicating with Server 1, the bridge overhears all of this traffic on its E0 interface. It quietly notes the source MAC address of each frame received on E0 and enters those addresses into a table as originating from E0. It does the same for all traffic received by its E1 interface. Pretty soon, the bridge will have a fairly comprehensive database of all attached devices (their MAC addresses) out each of its interfaces. The bridge updates the database each time it receives a frame to keep the database current. If the bridge does not see a frame from a device for some predetermined period of time (typically five minutes), the entry for that device is removed from the database.

In this sense, a transparent bridge can accurately be called a *learning bridge*. By simply listening to traffic, it can quickly learn the location of all network devices on those segments to which it is attached. By continuously updating the database and discarding stale entries, the map of the network remains accurate.

Forwarding Packets

Suppose that in the previous figure (Figure 9.6), you have just turned on the bridge, so it has an empty database. It will immediately begin populating its database with MAC addresses from frames that it receives. Now, suppose that the first frame the bridge receives is the one shown in Figure 9.7.

FIGURE 9.7   Workstation 1–to–Server 1 frame

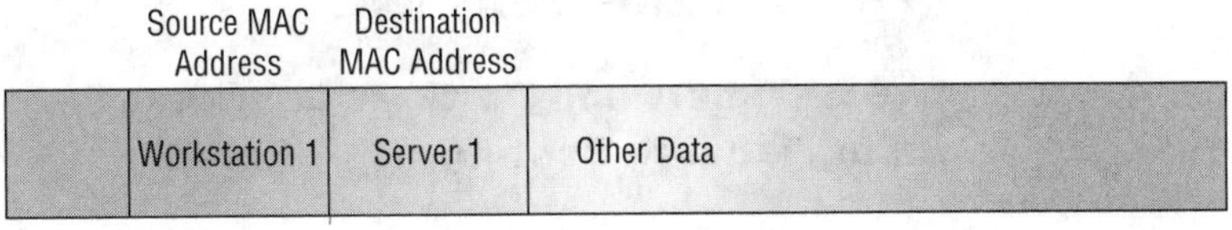

	Source MAC Address	Destination MAC Address	
	Workstation 1	Server 1	Other Data

The bridge now knows that Workstation 1 is out its E0 interface and makes an appropriate entry into its database. However, it still does not know where Server 1 is. The bridge will *flood* the frame—it will forward the frame out all interfaces except the one on which the frame was received. This ensures that no matter where Server 1 is (and the bridge still does not know where Server 1 is), Server 1 will still receive the frame addressed to it. You know from the Figure 9.4 diagram that this is not necessary, but the bridge does not know that (yet). However, consider what happens next. Server 1 receives the frame from Workstation 1 and generates a reply, as pictured in Figure 9.8.

FIGURE 9.8 Server 1–to–Workstation 1 frame

	Source MAC Address	Destination MAC Address	
	Server 1	Workstation 1	Other Data

The bridge receives this frame on its E0 interface, makes an entry for Server 1 in its database, and now knows that both of these devices are located on the same segment. At this point, the transparent bridge can begin the next step: filtering.

Some frames must always be flooded by the bridge; whenever they are received, they must be forwarded to all interfaces (other than the one on which they were received). They include the following types:

- Frames destined for unknown MAC addresses
- Broadcast frames
- Multicast frames

The ramifications of this requirement are discussed in the "Avoiding Loops" section.

 Real World Scenario

STP Timers and PortFast Configuration for Network Booting

Spanning-Tree PortFast is a Cisco enhancement to the *Spanning-Tree Protocol (STP)* that alters the STP port transition phases, allowing a port to forward data during the listening and learning phases (as opposed to *blocking* data during this time). If a loop is detected, the switch will immediately block the port. However, there is a danger that it could be too late, because the switch may already be overwhelmed by a broadcast storm. For this reason, PortFast should only ever be used on ports that are connected to a single host, because this ensures that a loop could never occur.

The PortFast configuration is a required solution if you have clients that boot from the network, such as Microsoft's RIS (Remote Installation Services) clients for operating system imaging. These clients use their network card to search for a Microsoft DHCP, Active Directory, and RIS server immediately upon power-up. The clients will not locate the Microsoft servers if PortFast is not configured on their connected switch ports because of the typical 50-second delay from blocking to forwarding on a Cisco switch.

PortFast is configured using the following commands:

- CatOS: `set spantree portfast` *mod/port* `{enable | disable}`

- Cisco IOS: `(config-if)# spanning-tree portfast`

If you are absolutely certain that all PortFast ports are connected to a single host, you can also implement a Cisco feature called *PortFast BPDU Filter*, which prevents any PortFast port from *sending* bridge protocol data units (BPDUs). This prevents the connected host from having to process each BPDU transmitted.

Filtering Packets

Let's continue with the preceding example in Figure 9.8. Now that the bridge knows the MAC address of Workstation 1 and Server 1 and knows that they are on the same segment (i.e., out the same bridge interface), it no longer needs to flood packets exchanged between those two machines out its other interfaces.

Suppose that now Workstation 1 sends out a packet to Server 2. If the bridge does not recognize the MAC address of Server 2, it will flood the packet. However (assuming that Server 2 is running), it will immediately learn Server 2's location when it responds to Workstation 1's request. From that point forward, the bridge will filter (drop) packets between Workstation 1 and Server 1, because they are on the same segment and do not require the bridge's help to communicate. The bridge will forward frames between Workstation 1 and Server 2, because without the bridge's help, these two devices would not be able to communicate. Finally, if Workstation 2 addresses a frame to an unknown device, the bridge will flood the frame and hopefully learn the new device's location when it responds.

The bridge has the following three options whenever it receives a frame:

- Filter

- Forward

- Flood

The MAC address database is kept in cache on the bridge to speed up the decision-making process.

Avoiding Loops

Loops can be good or bad. When they work correctly, redundant paths provide fault tolerance for certain failures. However, when loops do not work correctly, they can cause complete network failure. Consider the network shown in Figure 9.9.

FIGURE 9.9 Redundant bridges

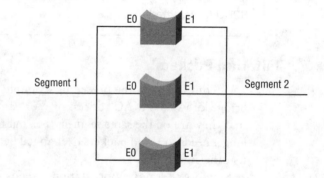

Three bridges connect Segment 1 and Segment 2. All three bridges hear all frames on each segment; all three bridges also build MAC address databases. However, what if all three bridges forward frames? Suppose a frame on Segment 1 is destined for a device on Segment 2, and all three bridges forward the frame. How will the destination device react when it receives three identical frames? It will probably be a bit confused and require counseling (just kidding).

There is, however, a worse case. Suppose that a *broadcast* is issued on Segment 1. All three bridges pick it up and flood it to Segment 2. But now, each bridge hears two broadcasts on Segment 2 (one from each of the other two bridges). They are actually copies of the same broadcast, but since these are transparent bridges, there is no way to know that. Each bridge floods the two broadcasts it received on Segment 2 back to Segment 1. Now there are six frames on Segment 1, which becomes 12 frames on Segment 2, which becomes 24 frames on Segment 1. This is called a *broadcast storm*, and it is a real problem with topological loops and bridges. As this example shows, a single broadcast frame can cause a broadcast storm that will consume all available bandwidth in seconds.

This problem results from the transparent nature of the bridges. Routers tear apart and rebuild packets, and therefore can address issues such as TTL, number of hops, etc. They also handle broadcasts much differently from bridges. However, transparent bridges by definition do not modify packets. They just filter, forward, or flood. Of course, there is a solution.

The Spanning-Tree Protocol (STP) solves this problem. It allows multiple paths to exist for fault tolerance, yet creates a loop-free topology to reduce the risk of broadcast storms. It does this by turning off (blocking) unnecessary interfaces until they are needed. For example, using STP in the preceding example, you may end up with the situation illustrated in Figure 9.10.

FIGURE 9.10   Spanning-Tree Protocol implemented

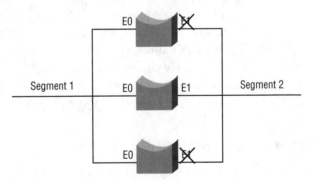

STP turns off (blocks) the interfaces, which can cause loops, and then re-enables the interfaces when necessary for fault tolerance (in case another active path fails, for example).

Cisco supports two STPs for transparent bridging: DEC and IEEE 802.1D. They are not compatible—they will not communicate with each other. The *IEEE 802.1D* protocol was actually derived from work done by DEC, but nevertheless, they are not compatible.

Spanning-Tree Protocol and bridging are covered in much more depth in *CCNP: Switching Study Guide*, also by Sybex.

STP works in the following manner:

- All bridges in the Spanning-Tree environment agree on a *root* bridge. The root bridge is chosen based on the bridge id (a combination of the lowest MAC address and bridge id value).

- Each bridge discovers all possible paths to the root and then selects the lowest-cost path.

- Each bridge blocks all other interfaces to prevent loops.

Integrated Routing and Bridging

Integrated routing and bridging (IRB) is an IOS 11.2 feature that allows you to route and bridge the same protocol within a single router. Normally, you cannot have packets cross a single router between routed and bridged interfaces. However, with IRB, you can.

This is accomplished by creating a bridge-group virtual interface (BVI), which represents the bridge group in the routed environment. The interface number of the BVI must correspond to the bridge-group number you wish to include in IRB. The BVI can then be configured and will act just like any other routed interface.

This type of configuration can be useful when you have to connect bridged and routed networks, or perhaps when you need to preserve network addresses (such as IP) yet still route those protocols to a larger internetwork.

Source-Route Bridging

IBM created *source-route bridging (SRB)* in the mid-1980s to connect corporate Token Rings to their IBM mainframes. With SRB, the source knows the entire route to a destination before any data are transmitted. It is called source-route bridging because the source device gets to choose the entire route to the destination device. SRB is part of the IEEE 802.5 Token Ring specification.

SRB was not designed for large internetworks. The specifications for IBM Token Ring define a maximum of eight rings and seven bridges. The 802.5 specification defines up to 14 rings and 13 bridges.

Types of Explorer Packets

A source device determines the best path to a destination device by sending explorer packets. There are three types of explorer packets:

Local explorer packets   Local explorer packets are used to find local destination devices.

Spanning explorer packets   Spanning explorer packets are used to find the best route to the final destination.

All-routes explorer packets   All-routes explorer packets are used to find all routes to a destination host by checking all rings.

All-routes explorer packets are also known as *all-rings explorer packets*, and spanning explorer packets are also known as *single-route* and *limited-route explorer packets*.

The following steps describe how the three types of explorer packets work together to find a route to a destination device:

1. A NetBIOS or SNA device generates a local explorer packet to determine if the destination device is connected to the local ring.

2. If the destination device is not located on the local ring, the transmitting device sends either a spanning or an all-routes explorer packet. (A NetBIOS device sends a spanning explorer packet; an SNA device sends an all-routes explorer packet.)

3. The destination device responds to the explorer packets, which then return to the originating device. By examining the RIF (route information field), the source can determine the route to take to the destination.

From that point forward, the source determines the path, hence the name source-route bridging.

Source-Route Transparent Bridging

Source-route transparent bridging (SRT) was introduced by IBM in 1990. In SRT, both SRB and transparent bridging occur within the same device. You can use SRT on Token Ring networks where some devices are doing SRB, but some are not. SRT does not translate between two bridging domains—the SRB and transparent bridging systems do not communicate via the SRT. If the traffic arrives with SRB routing information, SRB is used. If not, transparent bridging is used. Token Ring–to–Ethernet communication is not provided by SRT.

Source-Route Translational Bridging

Source-route translational bridging (SR/TLB) is used when bridging domains must be crossed. With SRT, it was possible to do both SRB and transparent bridging. With SR/TLB, SRB and transparent bridging domains can now communicate. With SRT, communication from Ethernet to Token Ring was not supported. With SR/TLB, that issue can be addressed. SRB generally runs on a Token Ring network, while transparent bridging is generally associated with Ethernet. (Note that SR/TLB is a Cisco IOS feature; it is not an industry standard.)

The STP packets used to prevent loops in transparent bridging environments will *not* cross SRB environments. It is crucial that no redundant paths are configured between the two domains, because STP will not be able to detect and thus disable them.

When bridging between Ethernet and Token Ring, a number of issues must be addressed:

- MTU size
- Lack of support for RIF in Ethernet frames
- Different systems for MAC addresses

There are significant technical challenges when bridging between dissimilar media. Cisco has documented problems with bridging Novell IPX, DECnet Phase IV, AppleTalk, VINES, XNS, and IP from Token Ring to other media and recommends that these protocols be routed rather than bridged whenever possible.

Summary

This chapter took off from where Chapter 8 left off. We covered link-state routing protocols in detail for the protocols OSPF, NLSP, and IS-IS. All three protocols are similar in many respects with intra-area routing, inter-area routing, hierarchical routing, fast convergence, and scalable support.

OSPF defines its areas as backbone, stub, totally stubby, and standard. LSA types are used to define the exchange of route table updates. The OSPF routing process uses designated routers (DRs) and backup designated routers (BDRs) as central points for information. The router types (internal, backbone, area border router, and autonomous system boundary router) are defined in and between OSPF areas.

NLSP is a replacement to RIP for IPX developed by Novell. Using adjacency, link-state, and forwarding tables, NLSP creates its route tables for exchanging data between routers of intra-area and inter-area routes.

IS-IS is a preferred routing protocol used by ISPs. A two-level hierarchy is used to support large routing domains. Routing within an area is referred to as Level 1 routing; routing between areas is referred to as Level 2 routing. Routers establish Level 1 adjacencies to perform routing within a local area (intra-area routing). Routers establish Level 2 adjacencies to perform routing between Level 1 areas (inter-area routing).

Finally, this chapter introduced bridging and the Spanning-Tree Protocol (STP). We discussed five specific types of bridging and their applications: transparent bridging, source-route bridging, integrated routing and bridging, source-route transparent bridging, and source-route translational bridging. Bridging works at OSI Layer 2 using MAC addresses forwarding and filtering frames. Loop avoidance is managed by the Spanning-Tree Protocol as defined by the IEEE 802.1d.

Exam Essentials

Understand the operation of OSPF.   OSPF areas are defined by the network designer and established using the multicast Hello protocol, which includes such things as the router ID, timing intervals, existing neighbors, area identification, and so on. Adjacency tables are built, and the DR and BDR are chosen before link-state information is updated and exchanged. LSAs are used to designate the types of updates, and router types are used to control the exchange of route tables.

Know the configuration of OSPF.   OSPF internal, ABR, and ASBR routers require different configuration. All routers must be configured with a process ID and an area ID. During the `router ospf process-id` configuration, wildcard masks are used along with network statements for the networks and areas to advertise. Route summarization is configured on the ABR for inter-area routing, and external summarization is configured on the ASBR.

Remember the use of NLSP. NLSP can be used by Novell servers or Cisco routers to exchange and maintain a link-state database or route table of IPX network routes. The three databases are adjacency, link-state, and forwarding. The link-state database is derived from the adjacency database, which maintains neighbor relationships, and the forwarding database, also known as the route table, is built.

Understand the operation of IS-IS. Larger IS-IS networks are organized into a backbone area made up of the connected set of all Level 2 routers from all areas, which in turn is connected to local areas. Between areas, routers know how to reach the backbone, and the backbone routers know how to reach other areas. Routers establish Level 1 adjacencies to perform routing within a local area (intra-area routing). Routers establish Level 2 adjacencies to perform routing between Level 1 areas.

Know how to configure IS-IS. You must configure the parameters for each instance of the IS-IS routing process individually. Network entity titles (NETs) define the area addresses for the IS-IS area and the system ID of the router. To enable IS-IS and specify the area for each instance of the IS-IS routing process, the following commands in global configuration mode are used:

- `router`

- `isis [area tag]`

- `net network-entity-title`

Understand the use and operation of bridging protocols. Transparent bridging doesn't modify, address, or receive frames but is responsible for listening, learning, filtering, and forwarding of packets. Loop avoidance is also dealt with at the OSI Layer 2 with the Spanning-Tree Protocol. STP finds the loops between bridges and switches at Layer 2 and elects a root bridge, which is then used by all other bridges and switches to calculate the shortest path to the root bridge and disable any ports that create a loop.

Key Terms

Before you take the exam, be certain you are familiar with the following terms:

adjacencies	Level 1 routing
area border router (ABR)	Level 2 routing
autonomous system border router (ASBR)	link-state advertisements (LSAs)
backbone area	link-state routing
backup designated router (BDR)	link-state update (LSU)
blocking	listening
bridging	neighbors
broadcast storm	network entity titles (NETs)
convergence	Novell Link-State Protocol (NLSP)
designated router (DR)	Open Shortest Path First (OSPF)
distance-vector routing algorithms	redistribution
filtering	Route summarization
forwarding	source-route bridging (SRB)
IEEE 802.1D	Spanning-Tree Protocol (STP)
inter-area	stub area
Intermediate System–to–Intermediate System (IS-IS)	totally stub area
internal routers	transparent bridge
intra-area	wildcard mask
learning bridge	

Case Studies

Complete the following exercises for the three case study companies. You may wish to refer back to Chapter 4, "Pre-Design Procedures," to review the complete overview of each company. Once you have completed these exercises, you may compare your solutions with those in the back of the book. Realize that even though your answers may differ from those, that does not necessarily mean one is right and the other is wrong.

Have-A-Seat

1. Since Have-A-Seat is just installing their TCP/IP network, you have the opportunity to recommend a routing protocol. Would you recommend distance-vector or link-state routing protocols (or even static routing)? Which protocol?

2. Have-A-Seat will have both Ethernet and Token Ring at the company's Atlanta headquarters. Will you need to configure bridging between Ethernet and Token Ring? Why or why not?

MPS Construction

Case study exercises for MPS Construction's routing protocols were covered in Chapter 8.

Willow Creek School District

Scott has informed you that he will be running TCP/IP, IPX, and AppleTalk traffic all across his WAN.

1. Which routing protocol would you select for TCP/IP at the Willow Creek School District? For IPX? For AppleTalk?

Review Questions

1. What is the purpose of LSAs?

   A. They elect DRs and BDRs.

   B. They broadcast a link-state change.

   C. They distribute a list of active links to neighbor routers.

   D. They distribute a list of network services provided by links.

2. Which protocols do not use a topology table? (Choose all that apply.)

   A. EIGRP

   B. IGRP

   C. RIP1

   D. OSPF

3. Which route type must be redistributed by a routing protocol if other routers are to learn about it?

   A. RIP

   B. Default routes

   C. Connected routes

   D. Static routes

4. Why are passive interfaces used within routing protocols such as RIP and IGRP?

   A. To stop unwanted route information from entering the specified interface

   B. To allow route information to be filtered by an access list

   C. To allow routes to be sent out the specified interface, but deny route information to enter the interface

   D. To allow routes to enter the interface, but deny any route information to exit the specified interface

5. How is a feasible successor chosen when a route fails?

   A. The route with the next lowest metric is chosen.

   B. If a router doesn't have a feasible successor, queries are multicast to neighboring routers in search of a feasible successor.

   C. The route is removed from the route table.

   D. The route is flagged as an active state.

6. What configuration option changes a stub area to a totally stub area?

   A. `area area-id stub no-summary`

   B. `area area-id total stub`

   C. `area process-id stub`

   D. `area process-id stub no-summary`

7. Which OSPF initialization states allow routers to actually exchange route information? (Choose all that apply.)

   A. The loading state

   B. The two-way state

   C. The full state

   D. The exchange state

8. What two characteristics distinguish a stub area from a totally stub area? (Choose all that apply.)

   A. A totally stub area accepts summary routes.

   B. A totally stub area is Cisco proprietary.

   C. A totally stub area contains only intra-area routes.

   D. A totally stub area contains only inter-area routes.

9. What three enhancements were made to OSPF to make it better than RIP version 1? (Choose all that apply.)

   A. No hop-count limit

   B. Use of distance-vector algorithm

   C. Use of classfull routing

   D. Incremental routing updates

   E. Route tables are calculated after the change has been propagated.

10. Which commands are used to verify correct operation of OSPF? (Choose all that apply.)

    A. show ip ospf *area-id*

    B. show ospf database

    C. show ip ospf border-routers

    D. show ip ospf *process-id*

    E. show ip ospf *links*

    F. show ip ospf database [network | summary | asbr-summary | external | database-summary]

    G. show ip ospf virtual-links

11. What are the commands needed to implement OSPF on a router? (Choose two.)

    A. router ip ospf *area-id*

    B. router ospf *area-id*

    C. router ospf *process-id*

    D. network *address mask* area-id

    E. network *address wildcard-mask area-id*

    F. network *address wildcard-mask* area *area-id*

12. What is the difference between an ABR and an ASBR?

   A. An ABR is the border router between two or more defined areas, and an ASBR is a border router between an OSPF area and external autonomous system.

   B. An ASBR is the border router between two or more defined areas, and an ABR is a border router between an OSPF area and external autonomous system.

   C. An ABR is the area backbone router that connects the backbone routers, and an ASBR borders different autonomous systems.

   D. An ASBR is the autonomous system backbone router that connects the backbone to other autonomous systems, and the ABR is the area border router.

13. What is true about link-state networks? Choose the best answer.

   A. They maintain a more complex table than distance-vector-based networks.

   B. They maintain a less complex table than distance-vector-based networks.

   C. They don't use convergence.

   D. They use RIP timers.

14. What is the metric for OSPF?

   A. Bandwidth

   B. Delay

   C. Hop count

   D. Cost

15. Have-a-Seat has specified that the IP routing protocol must adhere to recent industry standards and must scale to support a large network. Which routing protocol should you recommend to Have-a-Seat?

A. RIP

B. EGP

C. IGRP

D. OSPF

16. Scott from the Willow Creek School District has informed you that he has Bay and 3Com routers that he wants you to include in your network design. Since he wants to keep them, what routing protocol should you use?

A. RIP

B. IGRP

C. OSPF

D. EIGRP

17. What is IS-IS routing within a single area referred to as?

A. Level 2 routing

B. Level 3 routing

C. Level 1 routing

D. inter-area routing

18. Which of the following IS-IS configuration is required?

A. Enabling IS-IS and assigning areas

B. Enabling IP routing for an area on an interface

C. Configuring IS-IS interface parameters

D. Configuring miscellaneous IS-IS parameters

19. IS-IS routers establish Level 2 adjacencies to perform routing between _____ areas.

    A. Level 3

    B. Level 2

    C. inter-area

    D. Level 1

20. What does EIGRP use to find the best path to a remote network by default?

    A. Hop count

    B. Bandwidth

    C. Load

    D. Delay

    E. MTU

Answers to Review Questions

1. C.   There are five primary types of LSAs that are used between OSPF routers to distribute the list of active network links.

2. B, C.   IGRP and RIP1 do not use a topology table to calculate route updates because they are distance-vector protocols.

3. D.   Static routes must be redistributed, but all other types are sent automatically in route updates.

4. D.   To prevent route updates from being sent to an unknown or unneeded router, the passive interface command can be used.

5. A.   OSPF chooses a feasible successor when a primary route becomes unavailable; the metric value is used to determine the best route.

6. A.   The IOS command to configure an OSPF area as totally stubby is `area` *area-id* `stub no-summary`.

7. A, C.   During the OSPF loading state, routers send link-state request packets. Full state indicates that all routers have the same link-state database and can begin the state of exchange.

8. B, C.   Cisco routers support OSPF totally stub areas, which contain only intra-area routes because there are no other networks within.

9. A, D, E.   OSPF supports an unlimited number of network hops, incremental routing updates, and topology tables that include link-state updates.

10. C, D, F, G.   The IOS command `show ip ospf border-routers` verifies ABR and ASBR operation. The `show ip ospf` *process-id* can be used to verify correct configuration. The other two commands are also used to verify the correct operation of the OSPF database updates and calculations.

11. C, F.   The required OSPF IOS configuration commands are `router ospf` *process-id* and `network` *address wildcard-mask* `area` *areaid*.

12. A.   The ABR includes the link-state updates for its connected areas, and the ASBR is configured with autonomous system areas to advertise externally.

13. A.   Link-state routing protocols include adjacency, link-state, and forwarding tables and use more complex calculations to determine the best route.

14. D.   OSPF uses cost as a routing metric in which bandwidth is one of the most important metrics for route selection. The Dijkstra algorithm is used to choose the lowest cost link for route selection, and the cost of the local router is added to the cost required to reach the destination.

15. D.   OSPF is an industry-standard routing protocol and is very scalable.

16. C.   OSPF is supported by most vendors' routers and is very scalable.

17. C.   IS-IS routing in a single area is called Level 1 routing.

18. A.   Enabling IS-IS and assigning areas is required for IS-IS routing configuration. The other tasks are optional with IS-IS.

19. D.   IS-IS level 2 routers establish adjacencies to route between Level 1 areas.

20. B, D.   Enhanced IGRP uses bandwidth and delay of the line by default to find the best path to a remote network. MTU, reliability, and load can be configured by the administrator, but they are not used by default.

Chapter

10

Cisco IOS Software

CCDA EXAM TOPICS COVERED IN THIS CHAPTER:

✓ Identify the features and functions of the Cisco Internetwork Operating System.

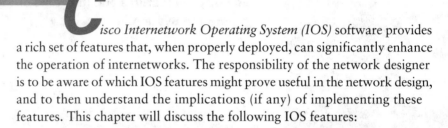

*C*isco Internetwork Operating System (IOS) software provides a rich set of features that, when properly deployed, can significantly enhance the operation of internetworks. The responsibility of the network designer is to be aware of which IOS features might prove useful in the network design, and to then understand the implications (if any) of implementing these features. This chapter will discuss the following IOS features:

- Access lists

- Proxy services

- Compression

- Queuing

- Traffic shaping

- Resource Reservation Protocol (RSVP)

Although there are no Cisco objectives that map directly to this chapter, it is nevertheless important for you to understand the components and functions of Cisco's IOS software that are described in this chapter.

Access Lists

*A*ccess lists are essentially lists of conditions that control packet flow across router interfaces. They're powerful tools that control access both to and from network segments. They can be used for many purposes, but the two most common (and perhaps powerful) are

- Limit or control the amount of traffic on network segments by filtering unwanted or unnecessary packets.

- Implement basic security by preventing packets disallowed by policy from being forwarded or received.

With the right combination of access lists, a network manager is armed with the power to enforce nearly any access policy he or she can invent.

All access lists work similarly—they are packet filters that packets are compared to, categorized by, and acted upon by. Once the lists are built, they can be applied to either inbound or outbound traffic on any interface. Applying an access list causes the router to analyze every packet crossing that interface in the specified direction and to take action accordingly.

There are a few important rules that a packet follows when it's being compared to an access list:

- It is always compared to each line of the access list in sequential order; it starts with line 1, then line 2, then line 3, and so on.

- It is compared to lines of the access list only until a match is made. Once the packet matches a line of the access list, it's acted upon, and no further comparisons take place.

- There is an implicit *deny* at the end of each access list. This means that if a packet doesn't match up to any lines in the access list, it will be denied.

Access lists can permit or deny packets based on a number of criteria. The most common reasons to allow or deny a packet are

- Protocol type

- Source address

- Destination address

- Upper layer protocol port or socket

Individual types of access lists may have additional specific capabilities to filter on additional criteria. For example, extended IP access lists can filter any of the following IP protocols:

```
RouterA(config)#access-list 110 permit ?
  <0-255>  An IP protocol number
  ahp      Authentication Header Protocol
  eigrp    Cisco's EIGRP routing protocol
  esp      Encapsulation Security Payload
  gre      Cisco's GRE tunneling
  icmp     Internet Control Message Protocol
```

```
igmp      Internet Gateway Message Protocol
igrp      Cisco's IGRP routing protocol
ip        Any Internet Protocol
ipinip    IP in IP tunneling
nos       KA9Q NOS compatible IP over IP tunneling
ospf      OSPF routing protocol
pcp       Payload Compression Protocol
tcp       Transmission Control Protocol
udp       User Datagram Protocol
```

If you wish, you can permit all TCP traffic and deny all Internet Control Message Protocol (ICMP) traffic. To get even more granular in your control, you could permit or deny specific TCP ports, as follows:

RouterA(config)#access-list 110 permit tcp host⤶
172.16.50.2 host 172.16.10.2 eq ?

```
<0-65535>    Port number
bgp          Border Gateway Protocol (179)
chargen      Character generator (19)
cmd          Remote commands (rcmd, 514)
daytime      Daytime (13)
discard      Discard (9)
domain       Domain Name Service (53)
echo         Echo (7)
exec         Exec (rsh, 512)
finger       Finger (79)
ftp          File Transfer Protocol (21)
ftp-data     FTP data connections (used infrequently,⤶
    20)
gopher       Gopher (70)
hostname     NIC hostname server (101)
ident        Ident Protocol (113)
irc          Internet Relay Chat (194)
klogin       Kerberos login (543)
kshell       Kerberos shell (544)
login        Login (rlogin, 513)
lpd          Printer service (515)
nntp         Network News Transport Protocol (119)
pim-auto-rp  PIM Auto-RP (496)
```

pop2	Post Office Protocol v2 (109)
pop3	Post Office Protocol v3 (110)
smtp	Simple Mail Transport Protocol (25)
sunrpc	Sun Remote Procedure Call (111)
syslog	Syslog (514)
tacacs	TAC Access Control System (49)
talk	Talk (517)
telnet	Telnet (23)
time	Time (37)
uucp	Unix-to-Unix Copy Program (540)
whois	Nicname (43)
www	World Wide Web (HTTP, 80)

As you can see, access lists give you a great deal of control over IP traffic. Access lists for protocols other than IP offer similar features.

As mentioned earlier, access lists can apply to either outbound or inbound traffic on any given interface. This means that you can have separate policies for packets leaving and entering your network. For example, consider an Ethernet network with both users and servers. You can implement an access list that prevents your users from accessing web servers on the Internet (inbound traffic), but allows users on the Internet to access your web servers on the Ethernet network (outbound traffic).

This outbound and inbound terminology can get a bit confusing. It helps to remember that the command is being applied to the router, not to the network, so the *outbound* and *inbound* designations refer to the router's perspective, not that of the nodes on the network. To the router, *outbound* means packets leaving their interface(s) and going out to the network; *inbound* means packets arriving at the router's interface(s) from the network.

Access lists can be optimized by moving the most frequently used lines to the top of the access list. This means that fewer comparisons are necessary before a packet matches a specific line. This can save CPU cycles, but be careful when optimizing lists. It is possible to significantly change the function of an access list by simply changing the order of the statements.

It is also possible to enable the logging of individual lines in some access lists. This function is useful if you are using access lists for security purposes, because it provides a log of attempts to violate your security policy. These logs contain several pieces of useful information about the packet, including

- Access list number
- Time

- Protocol
- Source address
- Source port
- Destination address
- Destination port
- Number of packets

By default, the log files will be directed to the router console. However, all of this log information could be redirected to the Syslog server and stored for security purposes.

There are many types of access lists available in Cisco's IOS. In IOS versions 11.2 and later, you can use text names for IP access lists. In earlier IOS versions, and with other protocols, access lists are numbered, and the number of the access list indicates the protocol and type of the access list. Here is a list of access list numbers:

```
RouterA(config)#access-list ?
  <1-99>        IP standard access list
  <100-199>     IP extended access list
  <1000-1099>   IPX SAP access list
  <1100-1199>   Extended 48-bit MAC address access list
  <1200-1299>   IPX summary address access list
  <200-299>     Protocol type-code access list
  <300-399>     DECnet access list
  <600-699>     Appletalk access list
  <700-799>     48-bit MAC address access list
  <800-899>     IPX standard access list
  <900-999>     IPX extended access list
```

Proxy Services

There are situations where a Cisco router can act as a proxy for another network device. This *proxy services* function can help preserve bandwidth and can also help in situations where workstations would otherwise be *isolated* in the internetwork. This section describes a few of these situations.

IPX Proxy Services

Still have a bit of IPX on your network? Many large networks have not yet migrated completely to IP and have a few, well, cobwebs in the corners to sweep away. While you're waiting for that last NetWare 3.12 server to die, here are a few IPX Proxy services you may find useful:

GNS Requests

When IPX clients need to access any resource, they transmit an IPX broadcast called a *Get Nearest Server (GNS)*, assuming that it will be both heard and answered by a Novell server. The servers that receive the GNS check their SAP tables to find a NetWare server that matches the client's request, and then respond to the client with another GNS, which includes the address of the server that the client can contact for the resource it requested. If none of the servers hearing the client's GNS broadcast have a server in their SAP tables that hosts the requested resource, they simply don't respond, leaving the requesting client without access.

All is not lost. Cisco routers build SAP tables and can respond to client GNS requests just as if they were NetWare servers. (This doesn't mean they *offer* the services that NetWare servers do, just that their responses are identical when it comes to locating services.) So a GNS response to a client can come from a local NetWare server, from a remote NetWare server, or from a Cisco router. If any local NetWare servers are present, they'll usually respond to the client. However, if none are present, a local Cisco router that is connected to the client's segment can respond to its GNS request instead.

IPX Watchdog Spoofing

NetWare servers like to keep track of their clients. They do this by periodically sending a watchdog packet to their attached clients and waiting for a response. If the client does not respond, the server will terminate the client's connection. This leaves the client hanging when it goes to resume the connection.

Cisco routers can *spoof* these watchdog packets, meaning that when a NetWare server sends a watchdog to a client, the router will respond to the server as if it were the client. The router will not actually forward the packet. However, since it receives a response to its watchdog request, the NetWare server assumes that the client is all right, and as a result, the client's connection does not get terminated.

Proxy ARP

Proxy ARP is a method of providing dynamic default router addresses to IP clients. The clients must first be configured to Address Resolution Protocol (ARP) whenever they need to communicate with a remote IP device, regardless of whether the device is on their subnet or not. Then, when a router receives an ARP request (for a device on a different network), it can respond with its own MAC address. This allows the workstation to simply ARP for a device not on its own subnet and dynamically receive back the equivalent of a default gateway through the router.

This can be useful when there are several routers providing a path out of a network. Should one of the routers go down, the other one could always respond to the ARP requests, thus providing a fault-tolerant path out to the internetwork.

IP Helper Address

Cisco routers can be configured with IP addresses to assist workstations in communicating with remote servers. For example, a Cisco router can use an *IP helper address* to forward Dynamic Host Configuration Protocol (DHCP) requests from a segment without a DHCP server to the actual DHCP server. The DHCP server would then respond back to the router, which forwards the lease offer just as if the DHCP server were local to that segment. This is all transparent to the workstation.

This configuration makes deploying DHCP significantly easier. First, it saves having to bridge traffic to get LAN-based broadcasts to the appropriate servers, which ultimately saves on bandwidth. Second, it saves having to install or configure specialized devices, such as DHCP servers, on every subnet. You can run multiple subnets on a single DHCP server, all without having to configure bridging of DHCP requests to your server.

Compression

Compression is the act of making data smaller, thus saving space on a network. By default, Cisco routers transmit data across serial links in an uncompressed format, but by using Cisco serial compression techniques, you can make more efficient use of your available bandwidth. It's true that any compression method will cause overhead on the router's CPU, but the benefits of compression on slower links can outweigh that disadvantage.

Three types of compression are used in a Cisco internetworking environment:

Header compression   Cisco uses the Van Jacobson algorithm to compress the headers of IP packets before sending them out onto WAN links. This method leaves the data intact, compressing only the header information, and can be used for applications (e.g., Telnet) and HDLC or X.25 encapsulation. However, it doesn't allow for protocol independence.

Payload compression   The payload compression approach compresses the data, but leaves the header intact. Because the packet's header isn't changed, it can be switched through a network. As a result, this method is the one generally used for switching services such as X.25, SMDS, Frame Relay, and ATM.

Link compression   The link compression method is a combination of both header and payload compression, and for you to be able to use it, the data must be encapsulated in either Point-to-Point Protocol (PPP) or Link Access Procedure, Balanced (LAPB). Link compression allows for protocol independence.

Software compression can significantly affect router CPU performance, and the Cisco rule of thumb is that the routers' CPU load must not exceed 65 percent when running software compression. If it does, you're better off just disabling any compression method.

Queuing Methods

Bandwidth has to be available for time-sensitive applications, because if it isn't, packets will be dropped, and retransmit requests will be sent back to the originating host. Time-sensitive applications aren't the only type of traffic needing to access bandwidth—it's just flat-out important that bandwidth is there when it's needed.

Since trying to increase bandwidth capacity can be an expensive pursuit, it might be wise to explore alternatives—such as queuing—first. The Cisco IOS allows for several different types of queuing:

- First in, first out (FIFO)
- Weighted fair

- Priority

- Custom

Each queuing algorithm provides a solution to different routing problems, so have a clear picture of your desired result before you configure queuing on an interface.

Queuing generally refers to several different criteria to define the priority of incoming or outgoing packets:

- TCP port number

- Packet size

- Protocol type

- MAC address

- Logical Link Control (LLC) SAP

After the packet's priority is determined by the router, the packet is assigned to a buffered queue. Each queue has a priority globally assigned to it and is processed according to that priority and the algorithm it's using. Because each algorithm has specific features intended to solve specific traffic problems, and because solidly understanding queuing features will make it easier to make decisions regarding which management technique will really solve a given problem, we'll explain each algorithm's features in detail.

But first, understand that you should take certain steps before you select a queuing algorithm:

1. Accurately assess the network need. Thoroughly analyze the network to determine the types of traffic present and isolate any special needs that need to be met.

2. Know which protocols and traffic sessions can be delayed, because once you implement queuing, any traffic assigned a higher priority status will push other traffic offline if necessary.

3. Configure and then test the appropriate queuing algorithm.

FIFO Queuing

This is the most basic form of queuing—*FIFO* stands for first in, first out. Strangely enough, FIFO does not help much with time-sensitive traffic. Working chronologically, all it does is send the oldest packet in the queue out first.

Weighted Fair Queuing

Weighted fair queuing provides equal amounts of bandwidth to each conversation that traverses the interface using a process that refers to the timestamp found on the last bit of a packet as it enters the queue.

Assigning Priorities

Weighted fair queuing assigns a high priority to all low-volume traffic. Figure 10.1 demonstrates how the timing mechanism for priority assignment occurs. The weighted fair algorithm determines which frames belong to either a high-volume or low-volume conversation and forwards out the low-volume packets from the queue first. Through this timing convention, the remaining packets can be assigned an exiting priority. In Figure 10.1, packets are labeled A through H. As depicted in the diagram, Packet A will be forwarded out first because it's part of a low-volume conversation, even though the last bit of Packet B arrived before the last bit of the packets associated with Packet A did. The remaining packets are divided between the two high-traffic conversations, with their timestamps determining the order in which they will exit the queue. (A more detailed picture of how bandwidth is shared among conversations will be shown in Figure 10.2.)

FIGURE 10.1   Priority assignment using weighted fair queuing

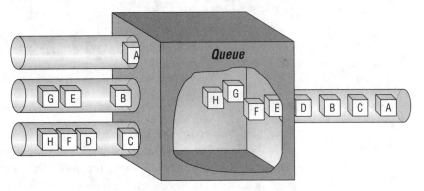

Assigning Conversations

You've learned how priority is assigned to a packet or conversation, but it's also important to understand the type of information the processor needs to associate a group of packets with an established conversation.

The most common elements used to establish a conversation are as follows:

- Source and destination IP addresses
- MAC addresses
- Port numbers
- Type of service
- The data-link connection identifier (DLCI) number assigned to an interface

Figure 10.2 shows two conversations. The router, using some or all of the preceding factors to determine which conversation a packet belongs to, allocates equal amounts of bandwidth for the conversations. Each of the two conversations receives half of the available bandwidth.

FIGURE 10.2 Bandwidth allocation with weighted fair queuing

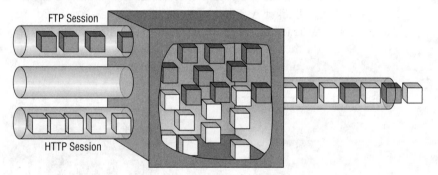

Priority Queuing

Priority queuing happens on a packet basis instead of on a session basis and is ideal in network environments that carry time-sensitive applications or protocols. When congestion occurs on low-speed interfaces, priority queuing guarantees that traffic assigned a high priority will be sent first. In turn, if the queue for high-priority traffic is always full, monopolizing bandwidth, then packets in the other queues will be delayed or dropped.

Assigning Priorities

The header information that priority queuing uses consists of either the TCP port or the protocol being used to transport the data. When a packet enters the router, it's compared against a list that will assign a priority to it and forward it to the corresponding queue.

Priority queuing has four different priorities it can assign to a packet: high, medium, normal, and low, with a separate dispatching algorithm to manage the traffic in all four. Figure 10.3 illustrates how these queues are serviced; you can see that the algorithm starts with the high-priority queue processing all of the data there. When that queue is empty, the dispatching algorithm moves down to the medium-priority queue, and so on down the priority chain, performing a cascade check of each queue before moving on. So if the algorithm finds packets in a higher priority queue, it will process them first before moving on; this is where problems can develop. Traffic in the lower queues could be totally neglected in favor of the higher ones if the higher queues are continually busy with new packets arriving.

FIGURE 10.3 Dispatching algorithm in priority queuing

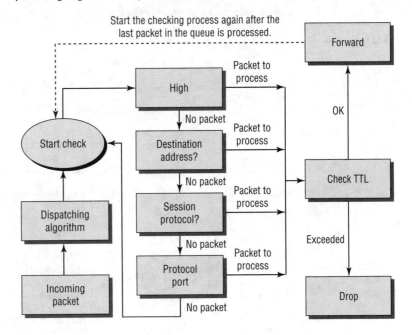

Custom Queuing

Cisco's *custom queuing* functions are based on the concept of sharing bandwidth among traffic types. Instead of assigning a priority classification to a specific traffic or packet type, custom queuing forwards traffic in the different queues by referencing FIFO. Custom queuing offers the ability to customize the amount of actual bandwidth used by a specified traffic type.

While remaining within the limits of the physical line's capacity, virtual pipes are configured through the custom queuing option. Varying amounts of the total bandwidth are reserved for various specific traffic types, and if the bandwidth isn't being fully utilized by its assigned traffic type, other types can access it. The configured limits go into effect during high levels of utilization or when congestion on the line causes different traffic types to compete for bandwidth.

Figure 10.4 shows each queue being processed, one after the other. Once this begins, the algorithm checks the first queue, processes the data within it, then moves to the next queue. If the algorithm comes across an empty queue, it simply moves on without hesitating. The amount of data that will be forwarded is specified by the *byte count* for each queue, which directs the algorithm to move to the next queue once the byte count has been attained. Custom queuing permits a maximum of 16 configurable queues.

FIGURE 10.4 Custom queuing algorithm

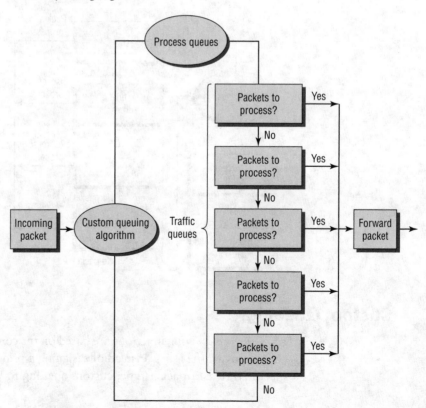

Traffic Shaping

Traffic shaping is a tool available to network designers working with Cisco equipment. The basic purpose of traffic shaping is to allow an administrator to manage and control network traffic to avoid bottlenecks and meet quality of service (QoS) requirements.

Traffic shaping eliminates bottlenecks by throttling back traffic volume at the source or outbound end. It reduces source traffic to a configured bit rate and queues traffic bursts for that flow.

Administrators can configure traffic shaping by using access lists to select the traffic they want to shape and then applying the access list to an interface. You can use traffic shaping with Frame Relay, ATM, SMDS, and Ethernet.

Frame Relay can use traffic shaping to throttle dynamically to available bandwidth using the backward explicit congestion notification (BECN) mechanism. BECN is a bit set by a Frame Relay network in frames traveling in the opposite direction of frames encountering a congested path.

 Real World Scenario

QoS Design Considerations

Quality of Service is an issue in networks due to the bursty nature of network traffic and the possibility of buffer overflow and packet loss. In fact, it's buffering more than bandwidth that is the issue in the network design. QoS tools are required to manage these buffers to minimize loss, delay, and delay variation.

Transmit buffers have a tendency to fill to capacity in high-speed networks due to the bursty nature of data. If an output buffer fills, ingress interfaces are not able to place new flow traffic into the output buffer. Once the ingress buffer fills, packet drops will occur.

In Voice over IP (VoIP) networks, packet loss causes voice clipping and skips. If two successive voice packets are lost, voice quality begins to degrade. Using multiple queues on transmit interfaces is the only way to eliminate the potential for dropped traffic caused by buffers operating at 100 percent capacity. By separating voice and video (which are both sensitive to delays and drops) into their own queues, you can prevent flows from being dropped at the ingress interface, even if data flows are filling up the data transmit buffer.

Priority queuing is a solution for this problem. Regardless of whether the VoIP traffic is using any of its queue buffers, the dropped packets of lower priority traffic cause each of these applications to send the data again. If this same scenario is configured with a single queue but with multiple thresholds used for congestion avoidance, the default traffic would share the entire buffer space with the VoIP traffic. Only during periods of congestion, when the entire buffer memory approaches saturation, would the lower priority traffic (HTTP and e-mail) be dropped.

RSVP

Traditional data traffic is relatively tolerant of delays and retransmissions. When you are ftp'ing a file down from a server, of course you want it to go as fast as possible. However, if a few frames get delayed along the way, they will eventually either arrive or be retransmitted, and in the end you will have your file. This type of traffic is defined as *elastic*, meaning that it is tolerant of delay. Now, consider a video or voice transmission. If you are watching a video and one of the frames gets delayed, you don't really want it later. You either have it in time to show in the video transmission, or you skip it and don't want it later. This type of traffic is defined as *inelastic*, meaning that it is not tolerant of transmission delays.

Resource Reservation Protocol (RSVP) allows end stations to communicate with routers and routers to communicate with each other to guarantee passage of these inelastic transmissions. This guarantee is secured by reserving bandwidth on every link between the source and destination of the transmission. Of course, data traffic will likely still be using these same links, which can lead to a conflict. Part of the RSVP design should include defining just how much (what percentage) of a particular link can be reserved for inelastic transmission. By default, 75 percent of the bandwidth on an interface is reservable by RSVP, although this can be changed.

Another design consideration when deploying RSVP is the type of interface or network. RSVP works better across some data-link networks than across others. Serial line interfaces generally work very well, but some LAN interfaces pose more of a challenge. A router with Ethernet interfaces, for example, may not be able to reliably deliver a set bandwidth across the

Ethernet LAN. As you recall, with Ethernet, all devices have an equal chance to use the network (CSMA/CD), and the router has no special advantage in this competition. Therefore, RSVP across Ethernet is less reliable than a serial line, simply because the router does not directly control the traffic on Ethernet the same way it controls the traffic on a serial connection.

Summary

This chapter described many IOS features that go significantly beyond the basic function of routing packets. These features are available on all routers capable of running the current IOS. These features include access lists that provide both security services and bandwidth utilization and proxy services that allow the router to respond to LAN-based queries on behalf of devices on remote segments.

Compression can be used to save bandwidth at the expense of router CPU utilization. Queuing allows time-sensitive traffic to be prioritized. RSVP allows for bandwidth reservation across an internetwork.

Exam Essentials

Remember the different IOS traffic-management control features.   Access lists, proxy services, compression, encryption, and queuing are IOS traffic-management control features. Access lists are the primary control method for traffic flow. Proxy services allow Cisco routers to respond on behalf of network services. Compression can save bandwidth at the expense of the router CPU. Queuing is required when priority traffic must get through.

Understand the types of access lists.   Access lists offer many different types for traffic control. Their primary use is often security.

Know the different types of compression available with the Cisco IOS. Header, payload, and link are all types of compression. Header compression only affects the IP header, whereas payload compression compresses only the data. Link compression affects both the IP header and the data payload.

Understand the different queuing methods. FIFO, weighted fair, priority, and custom queuing are all methods of traffic queuing. FIFO does not help with time-sensitive traffic, because there is no priority placed on the data. Weighted fair queuing provides equal amounts of bandwidth to each conversation but places a higher priority on low-volume traffic. Priority queuing works on a packet-by-packet basis, and custom queuing allows for the customization of traffic types.

Understand the traffic-shaping techniques used to meet QoS requirements. RSVP allows for bandwidth reservation and traffic shaping. RSVP allows the network designer to reserve up to 75 percent of the available bandwidth for time-sensitive traffic and works best when applied to serial WAN links.

Key Terms

Before you take the exam, be certain you are familiar with the following terms:

access lists	priority queuing
Cisco Internetwork Operating System (IOS)	proxy ARP
compression	proxy services
custom queuing	Resource Reservation Protocol (RSVP)
FIFO	spoof
Get Nearest Server (GNS)	traffic shaping
IP helper address	weighted fair queuing
IPX watchdog spoofing	

Case Studies

Complete the following exercises for the three case study companies. You may wish to refer back to Chapter 4, "Pre-Design Procedures," to review the complete overview of each company. Once you have completed these exercises, you may compare your solutions with those in the back of the book. Realize that even though your answers may differ from those, that does not necessarily mean one is right and the other is wrong.

Have-A-Seat

1. Describe where access lists would be used in Have-A-Seat's network.

2. Dave is concerned about bandwidth utilization in the switch from terminal-based to web-based communications. Would you recommend data compression as a possible solution?

MPS Construction

There are no exercises for MPS Construction in this chapter.

Willow Creek School District

1. Scott is concerned about his Novell servers at the high schools and junior high schools being accessed from other schools. He wants everyone (including the high schools and junior high schools) to be able to access the Novell servers at the District Office, but he only wants local access to the servers located in schools. How can he use access lists to accomplish this?

2. Scott is concerned about security when faculty members access the NT server at the District Office to store grade and attendance information. He would like to encrypt those sessions only. How would you respond?

Review Questions

1. Which of the following statements is true regarding traffic shaping?

   A. Traffic shaping eliminates bottlenecks by throttling back traffic volume at the source end.

   B. Traffic shaping only works at Layer 3.

   C. Traffic shaping cannot be used with Frame Relay or Switched Multimegabit Data Service (SMDS).

   D. Traffic shaping only works on Cisco switch technology.

2. Which of the following might be logged when IP access list logging is enabled? (Choose all that apply.)

   A. Source address

   B. Source port

   C. Destination address

   D. Destination port

   E. Time

   F. Protocol

   G. Access list line number

   H. Access list number

3. Which of the following are reasons why access lists are used? (Choose all that apply.)

   A. To improve security

   B. To reduce routing protocols

   C. To save bandwidth

   D. To speed convergence

4. Which of the following will allow IP devices to simply ARP for remote devices and receive the MAC address of a default gateway?

   A. IPX Watchdog ARP

   B. Proxy ARP

   C. Spoofed ARP

   D. DDR

   E. None of the above

5. Which of the following would be most useful on a subnet without a DHCP server that required DHCP services?

   A. IPX watchdog spoofing

   B. Responding to IPX GNS requests

   C. Proxy ARP

   D. IP helper address

   E. None of the above

6. In which of the following situations would compression be most useful?

   A. Insufficient bandwidth

   B. Time-sensitive traffic

   C. Multiple routing protocols

   D. High router CPU utilization

7. Which of the following are valid types of compression?

   A. Header compression

   B. Data compression

   C. Payload compression

   D. Link compression

8. When using numbered access lists, which range of numbers is used for extended IP access lists?

   A. 0–99

   B. 100–199

   C. 800–899

   D. 900–999

9. To which type of traffic does weighted fair queuing assign the highest priority?

   A. SNA

   B. IPX

   C. High volume

   D. Low volume

10. When should weighted fair queuing be used?

    A. To provide priority to interactive traffic

    B. To provide priority to file transfers

    C. To allow all traffic to be forwarded

    D. A and C

    E. A and B

11. Where is the most effective place to implement queuing?

    A. High-speed LAN links

    B. T1/E1 links only

    C. Any WAN link whose capacity is 2Mbps and slower

    D. All interfaces

12. When should priority queuing be used?

    A. When traffic has a hierarchical order of importance

    B. When delay doesn't matter

    C. When all traffic must be forwarded

    D. None of the above

13. When should custom queuing be used?

   A. When traffic has a hierarchical order of importance

   B. To overcome the possible problem that is introduced with priority queuing

   C. When trying to provide bandwidth sharing for all traffic

   D. When delay is not important

14. Which step is *not* part of configuring custom queuing?

   A. Defining the custom queuing filter

   B. Assigning a default queue

   C. Configuring the transfer rate per queue

   D. Assigning a priority queue list to the interface

15. Which statement best describes weighted fair queuing?

   A. The queues are based on the source and destination of the packets.

   B. Bandwidth is shared among all traffic types, giving priority to low-volume traffic.

   C. Bandwidth is shared among high-priority traffic only.

   D. The queues use FIFO.

16. Which statement best describes priority queuing?

   A. It processes all queues in a round-robin fashion.

   B. The queues are based on the destination address of the packet.

   C. The queues are based on the traffic type; all queues are processed equally.

   D. The queues are based on the traffic type; the highest priority traffic is always processed first.

17. Which of the following statements is true regarding traffic shaping?

   A. Frame Relay can use traffic shaping to adapt dynamically to available bandwidth using the BECN mechanism.

   B. IP can use traffic shaping to adapt dynamically to available bandwidth using the BECN mechanism.

   C. Traffic shaping does not work with Layer 2 technologies.

   D. Traffic shaping processes packets based on the destination address.

18. In which of the following situations would RSVP be useful? (Choose all that apply.)

   A. Insufficient bandwidth

   B. Time-sensitive traffic

   C. Multiple routing protocols

   D. High router CPU utilization

19. What is the maximum router CPU utilization for enabling compression?

   A. 10 percent

   B. 100 percent

   C. 50 percent

   D. 65 percent

20. Named access lists are available since which IOS revision?

   A. 10.2

   B. 10.3

   C. 11.2

   D. 11.3

Answers to Review Questions

1. A.   Access lists, along with the Frame Relay BECN mechanism, can be used for traffic shaping to help eliminate network bottlenecks.

2. A, B, C, D, E, F, H.   All items are logged either to the console or to a Syslog server for later review except for access list line number.

3. A, C.   The primary uses of access lists are traffic control. Security and bandwidth are methods of traffic control.

4. B.   Proxy ARP can minimize the need for client reconfiguration of default router addresses.

5. D.   IP helper addresses can be configured on the Cisco router and allow for central services network designs.

6. A.   Traffic compression is best applied to WAN links where bandwidth is at a premium.

7. A, C, D.   Header, payload, and link compression are supported by the Cisco IOS. Header compression only affects the IP header, payload compression only affects the data, and link compression works on both the IP header and data.

8. B.   Extended IP access lists are numbered using numbers between 100 and 199.

9. D.   Weighted fair queuing assigns the highest priority to low-volume traffic.

10. A.   Interactive traffic is time-sensitive and is sensitive to delay.

11. C.   Queuing is most effective on WAN links.

12. A.   Priority queuing guarantees that higher priority traffic will get sent first.

13. B.   Custom queuing allows the network designer to classify traffic at the router interface.

14. D.   Defining the filter, assigning the queue, and configuring the transfer rate are all configurations required to configure custom queuing.

15. B.   Weighted fair queuing assigns a higher priority to low-volume traffic.

16. D.   Traffic type (i.e., high-priority), will be processed through the queue first.

17. A.   Frame Relay uses the BECN notification method to dynamically accomplish traffic shaping.

18. A, B.   RSVP is used by end stations and routers to guarantee the passage of time-sensitive traffic.

19. D.   Cisco recommends that compression be disabled on the router if CPU utilization is greater than 65 percent.

20. C.   Named access lists have been available since IOS release 11.2.

Network Management

CCDA EXAM TOPICS COVERED IN THIS CHAPTER:

✓ Given a network design or a set of requirements evaluate a
solution that meets network management needs.

No network design is complete without a network management strategy. After all, even the best-designed internetworks are prone to failure. A well-conceived network management scheme is an essential tool in trouble-shooting connectivity and efficiency issues and in identifying potential areas of trouble and preventing major network outages. As networks have become larger, increasingly complex, and business critical, the ability to easily and efficiently manage them cannot be overestimated.

When designing networks, network management is one of the key factors to the network's overall success. Conversely, a management scheme that is simply dropped into an existing network with little thought to the overall network design can result in many sleepless nights for network support personnel. As with any facet of network design, a well-thought-out management strategy is essential to the overall success of the network. This chapter introduces some of the major factors that should be considered when developing a network management strategy.

This chapter will cover the following topics as they relate to the management of Cisco equipment:

- The benefits derived from industry standard management technologies

- SNMP (Simple Network Management Protocol)

- MIB (Management Information Base)

- RMON (Remote Monitoring)

- CDP (Cisco Discovery Protocol)

- The ISO network management model

- SLM (service-level management)

- Proactive Network Management

The Benefits of Industry Standard Management Technologies

Large networks consist of a large number of networking devices from many different vendors. In the past, network administrators had to use separate network management systems to support equipment from different vendors. The need for a standard means of managing these large, complex, and heterogeneous networks is apparent. Industry standard management technologies provide the following benefits to users:

Multi-vendor support   Industry-adopted standards can all but eliminate the need for a variety of management devices from different vendors. Instead of having to install, utilize, and support technology from many different vendors, industry standards allow users to adopt a single solution (for example, HP OpenView or CiscoWorks2000) as their network management strategy.

Interoperability   In addition to supporting a number of different vendors, industry standards allow network management of many different types of networking devices, including routers, bridges, and switches. Standards also provide an efficient and homogeneous interface for these devices, making troubleshooting that much easier.

Flexibility   The standards-based approach to network management technology allows ease of growth as new devices are deployed in the network. Since most manufacturers now support industry standards, network designers have greater flexibility in selecting networking equipment that is compatible with their network management solution.

Cost reduction   Perhaps the biggest value to a customer is the reduction in overall network management costs that industry standards can provide. By decreasing dependence on a variety of vendors and simplifying the addition of networking devices, companies can decrease their networking costs.

These four benefits of industry standards provide a compelling argument for the adoption of network management solutions that include these non-proprietary open standards over the more proprietary methods used in the past.

This chapter discusses three network management industry standards:

- SNMP (Simple Network Management Protocol)
- MIB (Management Information Base)
- RMON (Remote Monitoring)

Simple Network Management Protocol (SNMP)

*S*imple Network Management Protocol (SNMP) is the *de facto* standard network management protocol for the IP protocol suite. Developed in the late 1980s by the IETF (Internet Engineering Task Force), SNMP provides a simple means for vendors to provide management capabilities to their networking devices. The SNMP protocol is actually a grouping of standards, defined by several RFCs (Requests For Comments), including the following:

RFC 1155 Structure and Identification of Management Information for TCP/IP-Based Internets

RFC 1157 A Simple Network Management Protocol (SNMP)

RFC 1212 Concise MIB Definitions

RFC 1213 Management Information Base for Network Management of TCP/IP-Based Internets: MIB-II

A *Management Information Base (MIB)* is a database of network management objects that are used and maintained by the SNMP protocol.

SNMPv2 and SNMPv3 also include the following additional RFCs:

RFC 1901 Introduction to Community-Based SNMPv2

RFC 1902 Structure of Management Information for Version 2 of the Simple Network Management Protocol (SNMPv2)

RFC 1903 Textual Conventions for Version 2 of the Simple Network Management Protocol (SNMPv2)

RFC 1904 Conformance Statements for Version 2 of the Simple Network Management Protocol (SNMPv2)

RFC 1905   Protocol Operations for Version 2 of the Simple Network Management Protocol (SNMPv2)

RFC 1906   Transport Mappings for Version 2 of the Simple Network Management Protocol (SNMPv2)

RFC 1907   Management Information Base for Version 2 of the Simple Network Management Protocol (SNMPv2)

RFC 1908   Coexistence Between Version 1 and Version 2 of the Internet-Standard Network Management Framework

RFC 2574   User-Based Security Model (USM) for Version 3 of the Simple Network Management Protocol (SNMPv3)

RFC 2575   View-Based Access Control Model (VACM) for the Simple Network Management Protocol version 3 (SNMPv3)

An RFC can go through several stages of review and refinement before the Internet community adopts it as a standard.

One of the SNMP's greatest assets is its extendibility—vendors can enhance SNMP to encompass the proprietary features of their products and technologies. This frees vendors from having to build proprietary solutions and instead allows them to develop SNMP-based solutions to carry their product-specific information. In a Cisco environment, for example, *Cisco Discovery Protocol (CDP)* information can be queried utilizing SNMP, even though CDP is a proprietary Cisco protocol.

All Cisco equipment that supports IOS (Internetworking Operating System) supports SNMP. SNMP's successors, SNMP2 and SNMP3, were developed in the early and late 1990s to incorporate security and improved protocol operations and management.

SNMPv2 was supported as of IOS 10.2, and SNMPv3 is supported in versions 12.0(3)T and beyond.

SNMP Functionality

SNMP defines a manager/agent relationship for network management. A manager device essentially has two functions: monitor and control. It monitors network devices (agents) by sending queries for performance, configuration, and status information. It controls agents by sending directives to change configuration parameters.

An example of an SNMP manager is an NMS (network management station) running CiscoWorks2000, while an agent might be a Cisco 7500 router. The NMS, acting as manager, communicates with the 7500, acting as agent, for information about its performance. SNMP is the protocol they use to communicate.

An NMS can manage systems that include hosts, servers, routers, switches, hubs, UPSs, or most any network-attached device. The NMS runs the network management applications, such as CiscoWorks2000, that present management information to network managers and other users. The processing of SNMP is mostly performed by the NMS.

SNMP Communications

Since SNMP is a simple, request/reply protocol, the messages between the manager and agent are "carried" in the *protocol data unit (PDU)*. SNMP uses the UDP (User Datagram Protocol) as its Transport layer protocol for IP. PDUs essentially transmit messages between agents and managers.

As mentioned earlier, there have been three versions of SNMP. These versions do not replace the previous versions; rather, they expand on the functionality of the earlier versions. SNMP1 and SNMP2 define the messages or methods available in SNMP. SNMP3 adds security that was sorely needed. Let's summarize the major features in each of the SNMP versions:

SNMP1

The following messages are defined in SNMP1:

GetRequest   A GetRequest message retrieves information from a networking device's SNMP agent.

GetResponse   A GetResponse message is a response from the SNMP agent to the SNMP manager's GetRequest and GetNextRequest messages.

GetNextRequest   A GetNextRequest message retrieves the next object instance from the networking device's SNMP agent.

SetRequest   A SetRequest message is sent by an SNMP manager to perform remote configuration on a networking device.

Trap   A Trap message is issued by the SNMP agent to inform the SNMP manager about a significant event (called a trigger) on the networking device.

There are rules governing how these messages can be used. Only certain messages can be sent by certain devices in the managed environment. The NMS (manager) may send a request for information to a router (agent), in this case a GetRequest. The router responds with a message of its own containing the requested information, the GetResponse. The SetRequest is used when the NMS needs to change the configuration of the agent. An agent can respond only to requests and cannot initiate requests of its own. The only message initiated by an agent is the *Trap message*.

SNMP2

The following additional messages are added in SNMP2:

GetBulkRequest   The GetBulkRequest message enables an SNMP manager to access large chunks of data. GetBulkRequest allows an agent to respond with as much information as will fit in the response PDU. Agents that cannot provide values for all variables in a list will send partial information.

InformRequest   The InformRequest message allows NMS stations to share trap information. (Traps are issued by SNMP agents when a device change occurs.) InformRequest messages are generally used between NMS stations, not between NMS stations and agents.

SNMP3

And finally, SNMP version 3. Some have joked that SNMP really stands for "Security is Not My Problem." That should change with SNMP3. SNMP3 adds three methods to secure the transmission of potentially sensitive or critical data between agent and NMS. These methods are combinations of authentication and encryption:

NoAuthNoPriv   Authentication is based only on the username provided.

AuthNoPriv   Authentication is based on HMAC-MD5 or HMAC-SHA.

AuthPriv   In addition to authentication, CBC-DES-56 is used to encrypt the data.

These three methods provide mechanisms to better control the authentication between network devices and to protect the data crossing the network carried by SNMP.

Management Information Base (MIB)

A MIB is nothing more than a database of objects. The MIB has a tree-like structure, similar to a file system. Each leaf object represents a parameter on the managed device. A common understanding of the MIB between NMS and agent is what allows SNMP communications to work.

For example, an NMS may need to query a router for interface errors on a particular interface. These requests do not take place in English, but by referencing a particular object identifier (OID) in the MIB for that device. The NMS may request the current value of object 1.3.6.1.2.1.2.2.1.20.0, which according to the MIB for that device is interface errors for a particular interface. When the NMS goes to ask a server about available disk space on a particular volume, it sends a different OID request to the server, which references an object in a MIB common to the NMS and the server.

OIDs are almost infinitely scaleable, and there are controls in place to make sure that OIDs from different vendors do not overlap. There are RFCs that define public MIBs, such as TCP/IP and Token Ring MIBs. There are also private MIBs, where vendors can create their own MIBs specific to their equipment and its functions.

MIBs can grow to tens of thousands of objects in size, and dealing with MIBs is a part of working with any NMS. Operators of the NMS frequently need to compile MIBs into the NMS. This allows outputs to have descriptive variable names rather than rather cryptic OIDs. Cisco maintains its private MIB definitions under the Cisco MIB subtree (1.3.6.1.4.1.9).

Remote Monitoring (RMON)

L ike SNMP, *RMON (Remote Monitoring)* was developed by the IETF. Originally proposed in 1992, RMON was officially adopted as a draft standard in 1995, as RFC 1757. At its core, RMON is an SNMP MIB, which defines a set of objects available to an RMON probe.

RMON works on a manager/agent basis, but while SNMP retrieves information about a specific network device's status, RMON polls probes for information about network segments. One of the biggest advantages of RMON probes is what is referred to as *offline operation*, whereby a probe can continuously monitor a network segment in lieu of the RMON console device. This is especially beneficial when the segment is not in continual contact with the console device, such as when a link on the network has failed. This also can substantially reduce overhead CPU usage for the NMS itself, because the probe can handle the segment-specific monitoring duties.

Groups

RMON defines a number of statistics (referred to as *groups*), each of which delivers specific sets of data. Each group is optional, and vendors can support as many or as few of the groups as they like. Currently, there are two versions of RMON defined by the IETF: RMON1 and RMON2. RMON1 includes 10 groups, and RMON2 adds 9 more. RMON2 does not replace RMON1; instead, it adds onto it. RMON1 is limited to data-link visibility, that is, it only sees Layers 1 and 2 of the OSI model. RMON2 gives visibility into upper layer protocols for better visibility in application and protocol-monitoring situations.

Let's take a look at the RMON1 and RMON2 groups.

RMON1

RMON1 contains the following groups:

Statistics   The Statistics group contains statistics measured by the probe for each monitored interface on the network, for example, broadcast packets, multicast packets, CRC errors, etc.

History   The History group records periodic statistical samples and stores them for later analysis.

Alarm   The Alarm group periodically collects statistical samples from variables in the probe and compares them with previously configured thresholds. If these variables cross a threshold, an event is generated. (See also the description of the Events group.)

Host   The Host group collects information about each host on the network, for example, host MAC address, packets received and transmitted, etc.

HostTopN   The HostTopN group is used to prepare reports that describe the hosts that top a list ordered by one of their statistics.

Matrix   The Matrix group stores statistics for conversations between sets of two addresses. As the probe detects new conversations, new table entries are created.

Filters   The Filters group allows packets to be matched by a filter equation. These matched packets from a data stream may be captured for later analysis, or they may generate events. Associated with each filter is a channel, a specific path along which data flows.

Packet Capture   The Packet Capture group allows packets to be captured after they flow through a channel.

Events   The Events group controls the generation and notification of events from the probe. An event can generate an SNMP trap, or generate a log entry, or both.

Token Ring   The Token Ring group contains Token Ring extensions, including ring station, ring station order, and source routing information.

RMON2

RMON2 contains the following groups:

Protocol Directory   The Protocol Directory group provides a list of protocols supported by the RMON device.

Protocol Distribution   The Protocol Distribution group contains the traffic statistics for each Layer 3 and above supported protocol.

Address Mapping   This group contains the mappings of Network layer addresses to Layer 2 or MAC addresses.

Network Layer Host   The Network Layer Host group contains information on Network layer traffic to and from individual hosts.

Network Layer Matrix   This group contains statistics for Network layer conversations between pairs of hosts.

Application Layer Host   The Application Layer Host group contains statistics on the Application layer traffic to or from individual hosts.

Application Layer Matrix   The Application Layer Matrix group contains statistics for Application layer conversations between pairs of hosts.

User History Collection   This group contains periodic samples of user-specified variables.

Probe Configuration   This group allows for probe configuration issues, such as trap destinations or OBM (out-of-band management).

CDP (Cisco Discovery Protocol)

The proprietary protocol CDP (Cisco Discovery Protocol) allows you to access configuration information on other Cisco routers and switches with a single command. By analyzing CDP data, you can characterize the topology of an existing network. CDP uses SNAP (Subnetwork Access Protocol) frames at the Data Link layer, so two devices running different Network layer protocols can still communicate and learn about each other. These devices can include all LANs and most WANs.

CDP starts by default on any router version 10.3 or later and discovers neighboring Cisco routers running CDP by doing a Data Link broadcast. It doesn't matter which protocol is running at the Network layer.

Once CDP has discovered a router, it can then display information about the upper layer protocols such as IP and IPX. A router caches the information it receives from its CDP neighbors. Any time a router receives updated information that a CDP neighbor has changed, it discards the old information in favor of the new broadcast.

 Real World Scenario

The Pros and Cons of CDP

CDP is a very useful protocol and feature of Cisco routers and switching for collecting, analyzing, and documentation purposes. But CDP can also be a security risk in today's networks.

CDP allows you to collect information from neighboring Cisco devices, depending on your perspective in the Cisco network. With collected CDP data you can display the platform, IOS version, and configured interfaces of neighbors. With the commands show cdp, show cdp entry, show cdp interface, and show cdp neighbors, you can gather plenty of information.

One of the more useful features of CDP is the collection of neighboring device interface IP numbers. With this information, you can telnet further into the network and manage these devices. You can disable CDP on a Cisco router or switch globally or disable it per interface.

> CDP is enabled by default on Cisco devices. This means that at a specified interval, each device sends valuable information out each and every port to any other CDP listening device. This information can be intercepted or captured, researched, and exploited. The global configuration command no cdp run will globally disable the CDP announcements. You can also disable CDP per interface in the interface configuration with no cdp enable. You can type **show cdp** to verify if CDP is enabled and running.

The ISO Network Management Model

The International Organization for Standardization (ISO) defines the types of network management applications that reside on the NMS. Just as the seven-layer OSI model defines function but not implementation for data communications, the *ISO network management model* defines five areas of network management without specifying specific implementations. Those five areas are as follows:

Fault management Fault management is concerned with the detection, isolation, and correction of any and all non-normal network conditions. The architecture consists of event collectors and event producers. Collectors consist of NMS and Syslog servers. Producers are SNMP agents, RMON probes, etc.

Configuration management Configuration management is concerned with network configuration consistency, change control, and documentation. Granular detail on items such as descriptions on interfaces, IP address control, DHCP and DNS controls, and other policies and procedures are covered. The end results are higher network availability and reduced network operation cost.

Accounting management Accounting management targets the regulation of network resources. Network utilization and actions can be tracked on a per-user basis, and the costs for those resources can be allocated as well.

Performance management Performance management is the management of network response time, quality, and consistency for all services. Baselining and trending lead to SLAs with network "customers." Performance management is closely related to network capacity planning.

Security management   Security management is concerned with the application of security policies regarding network resources. The distribution of security policies, tracking of security-related events, and accounting of access to network resources are included topics. The intentions are to prevent network sabotage, whether intentional or otherwise.

As was mentioned earlier, each of these specifications is meant to be a framework for necessary network management components, not a specification of those components. There are many Cisco (and other) products that fit into one or more of these five categories. The ISO network management model provides a reasonable checklist that can help you identify areas of network management that may be lacking in an enterprise.

SLM (Service-Level Management)

Many network design projects today require a *service-level contract (SLC)*. This contract may be between two separate enterprises, for example, a customer and a telecommunications provider, or it may be internal to a single enterprise. For example, the IT department may have an SLC to provide services at pre-arranged levels to internal customers, such as other departments that use the IT infrastructure.

The SLC will likely consist of multiple *SLAs (service-level agreements)*. The most common SLA metrics include

- Network availability
- Network delay
- Network delay variation (jitter)
- Packet loss

Regardless of which metrics are used in the SLAs, they should be mapped to application-specific network conditions. The SLC should specify penalties for missed SLAs, as well as specify reporting mechanisms for SLA compliance or non-compliance.

Creation and management of the SLC, as with many other aspects of network design, require skill in both business and technical arenas. While technically adept persons can quickly fabricate SLA criteria such as availability, packet loss, etc., it requires deeper business-impact skills to successfully select

SLA criteria and thresholds. Communication between the service provider and the customer regarding actual business needs and agreement upon measurable metrics and agreeable penalty for missed metrics are paramount.

Cisco has a number of tools available that assist in the monitoring of SLAs. For further information, you may want to look into the IPM component of CiscoWorks on Cisco's website.

Proactive Network Management

As stated earlier, no network is completely fault-tolerant. Problems inevitably arise, interfaces go down, and bottlenecks occur. During times like these, a network management solution is often a network administrator's best friend, allowing easy identification and resolution of network outages.

Network management is more than troubleshooting problem spots on a network, however. Today's network management solutions provide a host of tools that can perform detailed analysis on a network's performance and status, providing valuable information to network managers. In addition, these tools can identify potential trouble spots (faulty interfaces, data bottlenecks, etc.) before they threaten network up time.

To utilize these tools in a proactive manner, network managers should initiate the following actions to better gauge the performance of their systems:

Set goals Considering the amount and types of equipment on your network, as well as the configurations of each, it is wise to set a network performance goal based on a number of different metrics. Metrics can include link reliability, route optimization, effective use of bandwidth, router CPU usage, or any number of measurable variables.

Generate reports Reports are the lifeblood of any well-maintained network management scheme. Using data gathered from the network management solution, network managers can compose reports that provide as detailed a summary as needed of network performance. These reports should be weighed against the stated performance goals, and the collection of information used in network reports should certainly reflect the metrics that define the design goals. In other words, knowing what to look for can eliminate sifting through mounds of unneeded data.

Identify problems   Perhaps the most vital feature of network management is the ability to identify not only severe problems (i.e., network outages), but also potential bottlenecks and/or irregularities. In this way, performance reports generated from data analysis can be used for future upgrades and improvements in a network before they become a problem.

Respond to change   A network is an ever-changing entity, with components being removed and added often. A seemingly innocent change on a large internetwork can create a ripple effect that can dramatically alter a network's performance. Network management trend analysis provides summaries of network status over set periods of time. As the network grows, trends may require that you rethink the report metrics. For example, the manager of a small network using only static IP routes might consider implementing a routing protocol such as RIP or IGRP as the network grows and adds a number of links.

Summary

A data network is the lifeblood of thriving modern businesses. Because advanced networks are critical to corporations, data network technology evolves rapidly. Hand in hand with the leaps in technology and size come corresponding leaps in complexity.

When designing a computer network, it is essential to consider a network management strategy to be used once the network has been implemented. A proper network management design will include a number of different factors, including the types of protocols and equipment used to monitor the network. Factors to be considered should be (but are not limited to) network size, bandwidth, and protocols. Although two standard protocols (SNMP and RMON) dominate network management, their feature sets and equipment-specific applicability call for a wide variety of solutions.

SNMP is a management protocol for IP and provides a simple means for administrators to manage their network devices while RMON allows network managers to poll entire network segments and upper layer protocol information.

Proper selection of network management tools is almost as vital as the selection of the networking equipment. Without the tools to manage the network after it has been deployed, discovering and diagnosing network failures can become much more difficult.

Yet, as valuable as state-of-the-art technology is, network management equipment is merely a tool to help you achieve the kind of detailed data analysis that can reap performance rewards (maximizing performance and minimizing down time). That said, a network management strategy should also include a number of proactive procedures for quantifying network performance goals. You should define a baseline that can evolve as the company's data needs change over time.

Good management strategy is the result of an accurate assessment of resources and technology and careful planning from the start of a network design process. These steps help ensure that the design becomes a functional, efficient network reality.

Exam Essentials

Be familiar with the network management protocols.   For managing Cisco internetworks, you can use SNMP, RMON, CDP, and other vendor equipment. All of these management tools allow you to gather, collect, evaluate, and analyze network statistics and other information about your network.

Know the functions of SNMP.   SNMP uses a series of Get and Set responses and requests to query and configure network devices. Traps are issued by SMNP agents when a device change occurs.

Know the benefits of SNMPv2 and v3.   SNMPv2 provides for bulk responses and requests but offers no security. SNMPv3 offers message authentication and integrity.

Understand the ISO network management model.   There are five components of the ISO network management model: fault management, configuration management, accounting management, performance management, and security management.

Understand the uses of CDP.   CDP is enabled by default on all Cisco devices and can be used to collect information from Cisco neighbors. CDP can also be used to troubleshoot internetworks with the information collected.

Key Terms

Before you take the exam, be certain you are familiar with the following terms:

Cisco Discovery Protocol (CDP)	protocol data unit (PDU)
groups	RMON (Remote Monitoring)
ISO network management model	service-level contract (SLC)
Management Information Base (MIB)	Simple Network Management Protocol (SNMP)
Network management	SLAs (service-level agreements)
offline operation	Trap message

Case Studies

Complete the following exercises for the case study companies. You may wish to refer back to Chapter 4, "Pre-Design Procedures," to review the complete overview of Have-A-Seat and Willow Creek School District. Once you have completed these exercises, you may compare your solutions with those in the back of the book. Realize that even though your answers may differ from those, that does not necessarily mean one is right and the other is wrong.

Have-A-Seat

1. Dave will be installing both routers and switches in his network. Which of the ISO network management areas do you think he needs to be most concerned with? Which products would you recommend for each of these areas?

MPS Construction

There are no case studies for MPS Construction in this chapter.

Willow Creek School District

1. Scott needs to manage his network from the District Office. He wants to manage all devices across his network, including non-Cisco devices. What advice would you offer him concerning his network management requirements?

2. Which network management products would you recommend for Scott?

3. Scott is aware that technology in education is changing rapidly and is concerned about his bandwidth requirements and network responsiveness when technologies such as video, audio, and multimedia are introduced into the classroom. What recommendations would you have for him in analyzing these changing requirements?

Review Questions

1. Industry standards are developed to

  A. Enable interoperability between different vendors' equipment.

  B. Solve common problems.

  C. Allow vendors to develop products that support other vendors' equipment.

  D. All of the above.

2. SNMP was designed to

  A. Allow different vendors' routers and switches to communicate with each other using TCP/IP.

  B. Provide a means to monitor user activity.

  C. Allow a standard interface to access propriety network management protocols.

  D. Provide a standard means to manage networking devices.

3. Which networking management entity can send an SNMP GetRequest?

  A. Agent

  B. Manager

  C. Client

  D. None of the above

4. An SNMP Trap message is sent to inform

  A. The manager that a change of state has occurred on the device.

  B. The manager to start capturing network traffic.

  C. The agent that a change of state has occurred on the device.

  D. That an RMON event has occurred.

  E. Both A and D.

5. SNMP PDUs are carried in which of the following protocols?

   A. TCP

   B. UDP

   C. SMTP

   D. RDP

6. RMON was developed to

   A. Allow network analyzers to interoperate.

   B. Provide a more detailed view than SNMP of a device's internal status.

   C. Obtain detailed information about a network segment's traffic.

   D. Provide a means to control remote NMS stations.

7. Which of the following ISO network management model areas is concerned with the detection, isolation, and correction of any and all non-normal network conditions?

   A. Fault management

   B. Configuration management

   C. Accounting management

   D. Performance management

   E. Security management

8. Which of the following ISO network management model areas is concerned with baselining and trending?

   A. Fault management

   B. Configuration management

   C. Accounting management

   D. Performance management

   E. Security management

9. Which of the following ISO network management model areas is concerned with the allocation of costs for network utilization?

   A. Fault management

   B. Configuration management

   C. Accounting management

   D. Performance management

   E. Security management

10. Which of the following ISO network management model areas intends to prevent network sabotage, whether intentional or otherwise.

   A. Fault management

   B. Configuration management

   C. Accounting management

   D. Performance management

   E. Security management

11. Which feature did SNMP3 add that was not previously specified in earlier versions of SNMP?

   A. TCP transport

   B. RMON

   C. Secure transmission

   D. MIB

   E. All of the above

12. When configuring an SLA, which of the following must be provided?

   A. Thresholds for SLA metrics

   B. Actions or remedies should the SLA be violated

   C. Reports showing compliance with the SLA

   D. All of the above

13. Which SNMP message does the NMS use to get the next record from a managed device?

   A. GetRequest

   B. GetMIBRequest

   C. SetRequest

   D. GetNextRequest

14. In SNMPv2, which message allows you to get multiple records from a MIB?

   A. Trap

   B. GetRequest

   C. GetBulkRequest

   D. SetRequest

15. Which of the following may be considered as SLA metrics?

   A. Network availability

   B. Network jitter

   C. Network delay

   D. Packet loss

   E. All of the above

16. If your network includes two routers, 20 PCs, three Unix workstations, a single server, and a dedicated NMS, which devices can support SNMP agents?

   A. All devices (except the NMS)

   B. All devices (including the NMS)

   C. Only network devices such as the router

   D. Only end nodes such as workstations and hosts

17. When are SNMP Trap messages sent from the agents to the NMS?

    A. When the NMS requests them using a GetRequest

    B. When the agents have items to report to the NMS

    C. Every five minutes

    D. Never

18. Which of the following SNMP messages are sent from the agent to the management station? (Choose all that apply.)

    A. Trap

    B. GetRequest

    C. GetResponse

    D. GetNextRequest

    E. SetRequest

19. Which of the following SNMP messages are sent from the management station to the agent? (Choose all that apply.)

    A. Trap

    B. GetRequest

    C. GetResponse

    D. GetNextRequest

    E. SetRequest

20. What of the following are the features of SNMPv3? (Choose all that apply.)

    A. Community authentication

    B. Message integrity

    C. Message authentication

    D. Groups

Answers to Review Questions

1. D. Industry standards are usually defined by a series of RFCs.

2. D. SNMP is a popular choice for a network management protocol.

3. B. The SNMP manager is responsible for the SNMP GetRequest and GetNextRequest messages.

4. E. SNMP relies on SNMP Trap messages sent by SNMP agents for changes. RMON defines events that can generate SNMP Trap messages.

5. B. SNMP PDUs are carried in UDP segments.

6. C. RMON polls probe for information about network segments.

7. A. Fault management is concerned with the detection, isolation, and correction of non-normal network conditions.

8. D. Performance management is concerned with baselining and trending.

9. C. Accounting management is concerned with the allocation of costs for utilization.

10. E. Security management intends to prevent network sabotage.

11. C. SNMP3 added the ability to secure the transmission between the agent and the NMS.

12. D. Any SLA should include agreed-upon thresholds, remedies for non-compliance, and reporting mechanisms.

13. D. GetNextRequest is used by SNMP to query the managed device for the next available record.

14. C. GetBulkRequest is used with SNMPv2 to query the managed device for the next available set of records.

15. E. These are all common metrics when implementing SLAs.

16. B. The NMS cannot also act as an SNMP agent.

17. B. Trap messages are the only type of unsolicited communication from agents to the NMS; they take place whenever the agent has items to report.

18. A, C.   The Trap message is triggered at the agent to notify the management station of a change. The GetResponse message is triggered by a GetRequest.

19. B, D, E.   The GetRequest and GetNextRequest allow queries to be sent to the agent and the SetRequest allows for configuration of the agent or network device.

20. B, C.   SNMPv3 uses message integrity and authentication to detect tampering and verification of the source.

Chapter

12

Post-Design Issues

✓ Given a network design or a set of requirements evaluate a solution to incorporate equipment and technology within a Campus design.

✓ Given a network design or a set of requirements evaluate a solution to incorporate equipment and technology within the Enterprise Edge design.

✓ Evaluate solutions for compliance with SAFE architecture.

✓ Develop a prototype testing plan.

✓ Develop a verification plan.

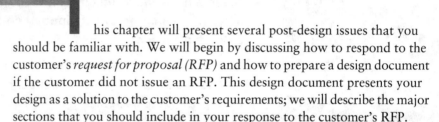

This chapter will present several post-design issues that you should be familiar with. We will begin by discussing how to respond to the customer's *request for proposal (RFP)* and how to prepare a design document if the customer did not issue an RFP. This design document presents your design as a solution to the customer's requirements; we will describe the major sections that you should include in your response to the customer's RFP.

We will also discuss how to implement either a pilot or a prototype of your proposed internetwork. These can be powerful tools in proving to your customer that your designs will actually work in the real world. We will review the steps required to complete both pilots and prototypes.

Finally, this chapter will discuss the Cisco Enterprise Composite Network model (ECN), which allows you to take a modular approach to securing your network.

Preparing a Design Document

As you finalize your network design and prepare to present it to your customer, there are a few steps you should take to ensure that all of your hard work is presented in the best way possible. You want to emphasize the strengths of Cisco's solutions along with your company's ability to implement these solutions.

The two methods you can use to present your work are

- Respond to a customer's RFP.

- Prepare a *design document*.

If the customer issued an RFP, they likely specified in the RFP the format in which you need to respond. You should prepare your documentation accordingly. However, if the customer did not issue an RFP, then you need to prepare a design document to present your proposed solution. Cisco recommends that you include the following five sections in your design document:

- Executive summary
- Design requirements
- Design solution
- Summary
- Appendixes

Let's take a look at each of these sections in more detail.

Section 1: Executive Summary

As the name implies, the *executive summary* is a summary of your design. The actual design will come later; at this point you are trying to create the big picture. Keep this section brief—one or two pages should be adequate. The target audience for this section is specified in the name of this section: the *executives* of the company. Emphasize solutions that will be provided by both you and Cisco. Be specific, but don't get too caught up in details. That will come later.

Cisco has made some recommendations for items that you could include in the executive summary. You might include one to two paragraphs on any of the following:

- The purpose of the project, especially how the project will help your customer's company achieve its strategic objectives.

- Your network design—more specifically, how your design fulfills the purpose of the project. Tie this information to helping the company achieve its strategic objectives.

- Implementation issues. Mention both technical constraints as well as business constraints.

- Benefits offered by your solution. Once again, these should be tied to the customer's strategic objectives.

Notice that the emphasis is on the customer and the customer's objectives. It is crucial to keep in mind that even after all the work that you have invested thus far, this is the *customer's* network. The customer likely has specific reasons for making the decision to install it. If you have done your homework, you will know these reasons (the strategic objectives), and you can orient your solution towards fulfilling these objectives. After all the work you have done, this is where you can really show your customer that your design *solves their problems*.

Section 2: Design Requirements

The *design requirements* of your design document lays out the information that you gathered before the design process began. You may recall that Chapter 4, "Pre-Design Procedures," discussed gathering information on the customer's current network, and then meeting with the customer to evaluate their needs and expectations for the new network. This section is where you present this information. You are not presenting your design yet, but you are discussing the customer's current network and what the customer wants to accomplish. Therefore, the administrative or technical data that you gathered when completing the steps in Chapter 4 can be included here.

As you describe the customer's current network, you may wish to include any of the following:

- A high-level topology map of the customer's current network

- Current applications, protocols, hardware, network management systems, etc.

- Router status, network utilization statistics, bottlenecks, reliability issues, and network health

- Business constraints such as budgets, training issues, staffing, scheduling of installation, etc.

As you move on to discuss the customer's needs and expectations, you may wish to include the following:

- A high-level topology map of the customer's proposed network

- Requirements for security, reliability, performance, and manageability

- Any new business constraints identified by the customer

Section 3: Design Solution

The *design solution* section is where you (finally) get to propose your solution in detail. All of the work completed during Chapters 5 through 11 can be included here. However, as with the executive summary, you do not want to focus on your design; emphasize *how your design solves the customer's requirements!* Remember, the preceding section presented an analysis of the customer's current network and the customer's requirements and expectations. Now, you want to present a design solution that meets the objectives described in the design requirements section.

As mentioned, any of the information gathered in Chapters 5 through 11 can be described here, including

- Topology issues, such as using the three-part firewall or hierarchical design.

- Hardware recommendations for LAN and WAN devices. Be thorough in discussing any new technologies you introduce, such as ISDN, ATM, or switching. Discuss specific Cisco model numbers for the devices that you are deploying.

- Network addressing scheme, including the use of private addressing and NAT if applicable. You may also want to describe a network-naming standard.

- Routing protocols to be used. You may need to include details on items such as redistribution or DDR.

- Bridging protocols, if they will be used.

- Any special IOS software features that you will be using such as access lists, encryption, compression, traffic shaping, or queuing.

- Network management solutions.

Section 4: Summary

Your *summary* needs to be brief, like the executive summary. You want to summarize how your solutions (presented in the design solution section) solve the customer's requirements (presented in the design requirements section). You may also wish to point out the specific advantages of deploying a Cisco solution over other solutions, as well as any specific advantages offered by your company.

Section 5: Appendixes

You may wish to include *appendixes* in your design document to provide additional information. However, these appendixes should supplement the material in the preceding sections; that is, your presentations in those sections should not depend on these appendixes to make their point. Tempted as you may be to include volumes of information, answer the following question honestly before you do it:

When was the last time you read the appendixes of a book?

Of course, this question does not apply to *this* book, as I am sure that you will absolutely devour the appendixes. However, you get the point.

Should you choose to include appendixes, the following are Cisco recommended topics:

- A contact list, including e-mail, telephone, and mailing information for any contacts at your customer's company, your company, or even Cisco

- A proposed schedule for implementing the network

- Any additional details on your design

- The results of your prototype (covered next)

Pilot or Prototype Implementation

A *pilot* or *prototype* of your proposed internetwork may be necessary to prove that your design actually meets the customer's requirements. The data produced by a pilot or prototype can be a powerful tool as you present your design and (hopefully) win the customer's business. The saying that "talk is cheap" certainly applies here. Anyone can *claim* that their design will work; here is where you *prove* that your design actually works.

The idea behind a pilot or prototype is that you do not need to build the entire internetwork to prove that your design works. Many times that simply isn't feasible. Instead, you can select key components of the internetwork, implement them, and then test them under simulated real-world conditions. The difference between a pilot and prototype is largely one of scale. These differences can be summarized as follows:

- A pilot is smaller in scale, and thus requires less money and time to implement. It is useful to prove small portions of your design.

- A prototype is larger than a pilot in scale, but smaller than the finished internetwork; you don't just order the internetwork and set it up, complete in a warehouse somewhere. A prototype can be used to prove sections or entire modules of your design.

Your customer will likely drive the choice between implementing a pilot or prototype. There are costs involved in completing either one. Your customer should be involved in deciding just how extensive your testing needs to be. The following sections describe the steps you need to take to implement either a pilot or prototype.

Steps Required for a Pilot Implementation

As mentioned, a pilot is simply a small test. It is useful for a small network design, or if only a small component of a larger design needs to be demonstrated. At a minimum, Cisco recommends the following steps for implementing a pilot:

Test the design.   You should test your design and verify that it will work before proceeding with the pilot. A pilot is not an ad-lib, preliminary test in front of the customer. You do not want any surprises when you go in front of the customer with your pilot, so verify your design with actual testing before proceeding with the pilot. If your design fails at this point, re-evaluate your design and retest it.

Investigate what the competitors will be proposing.   Cisco recommends you be aware of what the competition will propose. If you know what the competition is doing, you can prepare to present reasons why your design is superior. You may wish to outline the features of your design that are not supported by other vendors and demonstrate these as part of your pilot. For example, if you are aware of specific IOS features that are useful to the customer, but not available in products proposed by other vendors, use this time to demonstrate those features.

Remember, the focus is still on the customer's needs.

Write a script for the demonstration.   Prepare a script of your presentation before you actually give it. This will keep you focused as you present. Your script should focus on several issues. First and foremost, your test should prove that your design will satisfy the customer's requirements. Your test is also an opportunity to showcase your company's technical expertise and the power and scalability of Cisco's solutions. Don't be afraid to demonstrate any potential problems with the competition's solutions at this point. As mentioned earlier, talk is cheap. However, if you script side-by-side comparisons, be able to demonstrate both the acceptability of your solution and any problems with the competition's solutions.

Practice the demonstration.   As mentioned, a pilot is not a first shot. It is a scripted, practiced, real-time demonstration of a solution. Make sure to practice the demonstration ahead of time. Of course, this is no guarantee that nothing will go wrong. However, your confidence level will be significantly higher if you are not wondering how your demonstration will turn out.

Schedule time with the customer and present the pilot.   Finally, set up a time and present the pilot to the customer. If you have prepared well, your confidence level should be high and your presentation should go smoothly. Be courteous of the customer's time and be prepared to answer any questions the customer may have after you complete your demonstrations.

Steps Required for a Prototype Implementation

A prototype is larger in scale than a pilot, so there is more work to do to prepare for a prototype. Cisco recommends the following steps for a prototype implementation:

Review the customer requirements.   To complete this step, go back to the customer requirements that you extracted at the end of Chapter 4. Armed with those requirements, note which of the customer's concerns are most likely to be met by a prototype. Make sure to consider any aspects of your design that the customer may be uncomfortable or unfamiliar with.

Define the scale of the prototype.   Decide just how extensive the test needs to be. For example, you do not need to purchase 1,000 PCs to test the load that 1,000 PCs would cause on an Ethernet switch. There is testing software available for this purpose. In this example, you may only need a few PCs and the switch. Identify any available tools that would allow you to simplify your prototype.

Investigate what the competitors will be proposing.   As with a pilot, you can better tailor your demonstrations if you know your competition. For example, if you believe that your competition is going to critique some aspect of your design, that is an excellent item to demonstrate as part of your prototype (assuming your competition is wrong, of course!).

Develop a test plan.   Be thorough in developing a test plan. First of all, develop a list of tests you intend to run. This list should focus on demonstrating how your solutions meet the customer's requirements. Next, prepare a topology map of your test environment, including any specialized testing equipment that you will be using. Finally, prepare (as with the pilot) a script for each demonstration you will be performing.

Purchase and configure all the necessary equipment.   Once you know exactly what you intend to demonstrate, you can go about acquiring the necessary equipment.

Practice the prototype demonstration.   No one likes surprises during a presentation. Make sure to practice your prototype demonstration so that everything will (hopefully) go smoothly.

Conduct final tests and demonstrations.   Be sure to gather all relevant data during your tests. For example, you may use a protocol analyzer to place a load on a network segment and then gather buffer or utilization statistics from the networking equipment on that segment. Be thorough in gathering information about all aspects of your prototype. Use the guidelines from the section "Overall Health of Existing Network" in Chapter 4 on the current network to show how your prototype has resolved these issues. Those guidelines are:

- Ethernet segments should not exceed 40 percent network utilization.

- Token Ring segments should not exceed 70 percent network utilization.

- WAN links should not exceed 70 percent network utilization.

- Response time should be less than 1/10 of a second, or 100 milliseconds.

- Broadcasts/multicasts should not be more than 20 percent of overall traffic.

- On Ethernet, there should be no more than one CRC error per one million bytes of data on any network segment.

- No Cisco router CPU utilization should exceed 75 percent.

Summary

In responding to a request for proposal (RFP) or when presenting a design document to showcase your design, include five sections in your presentation. First, your executive summary should be brief and should target the company executives. Your design requirements address the customer's needs and the current network. The design solution section is where you describe your new network design. The summary is where you summarize your design solutions. Finally, the appendixes contain contact information and any additional details the customer might need.

Pilot and prototype implementations are partial implementations of the overall internetwork that you can use to prove your concepts to your customer. There are five steps to a pilot implementation, which is smaller in scale than a prototype. These steps include testing the design, investigating what your competitors will be proposing, writing a script for the demonstration, practicing the demonstration, and scheduling time with the customer and presenting the demonstration.

There are seven steps to a prototype implementation, which is larger than a pilot but smaller than the overall internetwork. These seven steps are reviewing customer requirements, defining the scale of the prototype, investigating what your competitors will be proposing, developing a test plan, purchasing and configuring all the necessary equipment, practicing the prototype demonstration, and conducting final tests and demonstrations.

Cisco's ECN (Enterprise Composite Network) model is a design philosophy developed by Cisco that includes the SAFE (*Secure Blueprint for Enterprise Networks*) using Cisco switches, routers, VPN concentrators, access servers, firewalls, and so on. The principle behind Cisco's ECN model is a modular approach to security design.

Exam Essentials

Understand the five sections included in a response to an RFP or in a design document.   A response to an RFP or design document includes the executive summary, design requirements, design solution, summary, and appendixes.

Identify the purpose of the response to an RFP or design document's executive summary.   The executive summary section should be at a higher level than most other sections of the response to RFP or design document. It should include a brief description of the purpose, the proposed design, the implementation, and the benefits to the customer.

Know the difference between a pilot and a prototype.   A pilot is smaller in scale, requires fewer resources, and generally is used to prove smaller portions of a design. A prototype is larger in scale and can be used to prove sections or modules of network design.

Understand Cisco's ECN model design modules.   Using a layered approach, modular security design allows the designer to address the security relationship of the network design security on a module-by-module basis.

Know the typical devices found in the modules of Cisco's ECNM.   The Network Edge module contains firewalls, DMZs, access servers, VPNs, and routers. The Network Campus module contains network devices, servers, users, and resources.

Key Terms

Before you take the exam, be certain you are familiar with the following terms:

appendixes	Network Campus
design document	Network Edge
design requirements	pilot
design solution	prototype
Enterprise Composite Network model (ECN)	request for proposal (RFP)
executive summary	Secure Blueprint for Enterprise Networks (SAFE)
modular blocks	summary

Case Studies

There are no case study exercises in this chapter. However, some of the review questions are related to the three case studies. You may wish to refer back to Chapter 4 to refresh your memory on the three case studies before proceeding to the review questions.

Review Questions

1. When responding to an RFP or preparing a design document, which section would you use to discuss the customer's current network, the customer's needs, and the expectations for the new network?

   A. Executive summary

   B. Design requirements

   C. Design solution

   D. Summary

   E. Appendixes

2. When responding to an RFP or preparing a design document, which sections would you keep brief (a few pages)? (Choose all that apply.)

   A. Executive summary

   B. Design requirements

   C. Design solution

   D. Summary

   E. Appendixes

3. When responding to an RFP or preparing a design document, which section would you use to discuss your proposed design in detail?

   A. Executive summary

   B. Design requirements

   C. Design solution

   D. Summary

   E. Appendixes

4. When responding to an RFP or preparing a design document, which sections would you use to describe your design briefly? (Choose all that apply.)

   A. Executive summary

   B. Design requirements

   C. Design solution

   D. Summary

   E. Appendixes

5. When responding to an RFP or preparing a design document, which of the following should you emphasize with respect to your design?

   A. How brilliant and insightful it is

   B. How it meets the customer's requirements

   C. How much it will cost to implement

   D. Why it is the best design

6. If you choose to include a list of contacts for the project, where should you include this information in your design document?

   A. Executive summary

   B. Design requirements

   C. Design solution

   D. Summary

   E. Appendixes

7. When implementing a pilot implementation, which of the following are not required steps? (Choose all that apply.)

   A. Review customer requirements.

   B. Test the design.

   C. Investigate what competitors will be proposing.

   D. Write a script for the demonstration.

   E. Practice the demonstration.

   F. Schedule time with the customer and present the demonstration.

   G. Define the scale of the prototype.

8. When implementing a prototype implementation, which of the following are not required steps?

   A. Review customer requirements.

   B. Define the scale of the prototype.

   C. Investigate what the competitors will be proposing.

   D. Develop a test plan.

   E. Identify business constraints.

   F. Purchase and configure all necessary equipment.

   G. Practice the demonstration.

   H. Conduct final tests and demonstrations.

9. Suppose that you do a prototype for Have-A-Seat. Which of the following would indicate a successful prototype? (Choose all that apply.)

   A. The overall project can be completed for the specified budget.

   B. The Token Ring network can support sufficient web traffic for Have-A-Seat's network.

   C. Testing for the Ethernet-to-Token Ring solution.

   D. The Macintosh computers will be able to communicate across the WAN.

10. Which of the following tests would you use in your prototype to demonstrate to Have-A-Seat that the Ethernet switches in Atlanta will successfully protect the data?

A. Implement VLANs on a switch and use a protocol analyzer to demonstrate that packets are not crossing VLANs.

B. Implement VLANs on a router and use three users and a server to demonstrate that packets are not crossing VLANs.

C. Install the equipment in the customer's production network and test for security.

D. Bring your customer's servers into the prototype lab for security testing.

11. Suppose that you do a prototype for MPS Construction. Which of the following would indicate a successful prototype?

A. Only e-mail traffic can leave the internal network.

B. Alpha running NT is under 75 percent utilization.

C. The mainframe can send packets across Token Ring to Ethernet.

D. 40 laptops are unable to dial in.

12. Which of the following tests would you use in your prototype to demonstrate to MPS Construction that the access servers will successfully allow incoming calls to access the NT servers?

A. Download a white paper from Microsoft on remote access to NT.

B. Install a T1 into the prototype lab and use it to access the NT server.

C. Install the access router and a phone line and dial in using a laptop.

D. Use a protocol analyzer to capture the packets between the access router and the authentication server.

13. When responding to an RFP or preparing a design document, which of the following is not one of the recommended sections? (Choose all that apply.)

A. Executive summary

B. Specification

C. Design solution

D. Competitive analyses

E. Design requirements

14. When preparing the design requirements section of a design document or response to an RFP, which of the following should be included? (Choose all that apply.)

    A. High-level topology map of the customer's current network

    B. Listing of business constraints

    C. Routing protocols to be used

    D. Addressing schemes

    E. High-level topology map of the customer's proposed network

    F. LAN/WAN hardware to be used on the new network

15. When preparing the design solution section of a design document or response to an RFP, which of the following should be included? (Choose all that apply.)

    A. High-level topology map of the customer's current network

    B. Listing of business constraints

    C. Routing protocols to be used

    D. Addressing schemes

    E. High-level topology map of the customer's proposed network

    F. LAN/WAN hardware to be used on the new network

16. Suppose that you are responding to an RFP issued by Scott at the Willow Creek School District. What format should you use for your design document?

    A. Use the RFP template provided by your word processor.

    B. Respond in the format specified in Scott's RFP.

    C. Respond using the five sections described in this chapter for a design document.

    D. Don't respond; arrange a pilot to demonstrate your design's viability.

17. Suppose that you arrange a pilot for MPS Construction. When should you complete the pilot?

    A. Before submitting the design document

    B. After submitting the design document

    C. Before the prototype

    D. After the prototype

18. Suppose that you are arranging a pilot demonstration for a customer. Which of the following should you do in preparation for the pilot? (Choose all that apply.)

    A. Test your design.

    B. Research the competition.

    C. Practice your presentation.

    D. All of the above.

19. Suppose that you are doing a prototype for the Willow Creek School District to demonstrate your LAN design for the high schools. Which of the following would indicate that your prototype was successful?

    A. An Ethernet switch is able to handle the simulated traffic of 250 computers and two servers.

    B. An Ethernet switch is not able to handle the simulated traffic of 250 computers and two servers.

    C. An Ethernet switch is able to handle the actual production traffic of 250 computers and two servers.

    D. Your prototype indicates that the customer should migrate away from Macintoshes and install PCs.

20. When should you consider what your competition might be doing?

    A. When preparing for a pilot implementation

    B. When preparing for a prototype implementation

    C. Both A and B

    D. None of the above

Answers to Review Questions

1. **B.** The design requirements section should include a discussion of the customer's current network and needs.

2. **A, D.** Summaries are brief and are often used to open and close a design document.

3. **C.** The design solution section should describe the new network design.

4. **A, D.** The design solution and summary sections should be brief and generally don't include design details.

5. **B.** Keeping the customer's needs in focus, you can respond to an RFP or present a design document that meets their requirements.

6. **E.** The appendixes include contact information and any additional details relating to scheduling and the results of your prototype.

7. **A, G.** A review of customer's requirements should be completed prior to a pilot. Defining the scale of a prototype is considered after the pilot.

8. **E.** Business constraints can have a big impact on the prototype and should be considered prior to the prototype.

9. **B, C.** The Have-A-Seat prototype should include testing for the Token Ring network and a solution for Ethernet-to-Token Ring connectivity.

10. **A.** VLANs provide security, and without a network router, data will be confined to each VLAN.

11. **A.** One of the MPS Construction's customer requirements is that e-mail is the only traffic that enters and leaves the network.

12. **C.** The MPS Construction prototype should allow testing for remote user access to the NT server.

13. **B, D.** A response to an RFP or design document includes five sections: executive summary, design requirements, design solution, summary, and appendixes.

14. A, B, E.   The design requirements section of a response to an RFP or design document should discuss the customer's current network, business constraints, and the proposed network.

15. C, D, F.   The design solution section of a response to an RFP or design document should include the routing protocols used, addressing schemes, and network hardware.

16. B.   A response to an RFP or design document should be in the customer's requested format.

17. A.   A pilot should always be completed prior to the design document, which includes the new design proposal. A prototype may or may not always be necessary.

18. D.   A successful pilot always includes testing, researching the competition, and practicing the presentation.

19. A.   The Willow Creek School District customer requirements include the need to support up to 250 users and two servers in each location.

20. C.   For a successful pilot and prototype, research what your competition plans to present.

Designing Networks for Integrated Security and Voice Transport

CCDA EXAM TOPICS COVERED IN THIS CHAPTER:

- ✓ Evaluate solutions for compliance with SAFE architecture.

- ✓ Evaluate solutions addressing the issues of delivering voice traffic over a data network.

Modern networks must consider modern issues and technologies. Two contemporary issues in network design are security and voice transport. As your network grows and voice becomes a more integral part of your intranetworks, security is so important that it can be considered part of the voice implementation. This chapter will introduce the topic of network security and voice integration, building on the information presented thus far. Our focus on both of these technologies will be those aspects relevant to network design. In addition, this chapter will explain how you can use Cisco's SAFE architecture design blueprint to help you design security policies and manage your network.

Designing Secure Networks

Security has certainly become a critical issue in recent years for networks. Increasing the interconnection of enterprise networks with both public and private external networks, along with other growth issues, has turned network security into a career instead of just a skill set! Indeed, a quick look at Cisco's (and other) certifications reveals multiple recent security certifications, including a CCIE in security. While we cannot cover this immense topic in half a chapter, this chapter will introduce the topic of network security and its relevance in the network design process.

NOTE   Todd Lammle highly recommends the *CCSP: Securing Cisco IOS Networks Study Guide*, also by Sybex, for a fuller discussion of Cisco security strategies and technologies.

Traditional Three-Part Firewall

Security is a top concern of network designers today. However, many designers may not be aware that security can actually be engineered into the network topology at design time, or perhaps more accurately, the network topology can be designed to be readily secured. Designing secure networks from the inside out and using a layered-defense approach is the best plan.

A *firewall* is really just a filter between your network and another and is placed in the Enterprise Edge functional area of a SAFE security architecture design. The firewall can be configured by the network administrator to protect sensitive resources on the internal network while still providing communication with the larger internetwork.

In the example shown in Figure 13.1, the internal network is connected via a router to the external network. The logical place for firewall placement is at the router, which places it between the internal network and the external, untrusted internetwork. However, what if there are resources on the internal network that the external internetwork requires access to, perhaps a DNS or WWW server? Access to those machines would have to be provided through the firewall. Now, what if one of the available services on those machines is hacked? That's certainly a problem, because that machine is part of your internal network and behind your firewall. Now the *hackers* have not only penetrated the firewall, but they have accessed your internal network!

FIGURE 13.1   Firewall placement

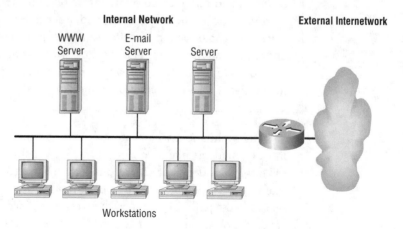

Real World Scenario

A Defense-in-Depth Approach to Network Security

Securing today's networks requires much more than a firewall. A combination of router access lists, multi-part firewall designs, intrusion detection systems (IDSs), and anti-virus products, to name a few, provide for a defense-in-depth strategy. Many network administrators still believe what they were sold several years ago by the firewall vendors: a firewall will protect your network from the Internet. Today's network designs must include all of the aforementioned items, along with well-written and enforced security policies with designer, administrator, and user compliance. There are many vendor-neutral recommendations for creating the baselines of security in your network.

For Cisco Internet-facing routers, the NSA (National Security Agency) has published a detailed guide available for free download from www.nsa.gov. You can also download the two-page executive summary, which includes many to-the-point configuration settings and access lists that must be implemented today.

The Cisco PIX firewall can be used to create the multi-part design with its multi-port options. The 506 and 515 PIX offer a minimum of three ports for internal, DMZ, and external connections to your network. You could also stack two firewalls back to back, with a DMZ in the middle for added protection. In addition, Cisco offers intrusion detection systems for your routers, *switches*, network, hosts, and firewall. However, your IDS doesn't always have to be vendor-specific. Anti-virus products come in many flavors and from many vendors. Your best bet when shopping for an anti-virus solution is to ask around or read the reviews in the popular network trade magazines for the right solution at the right price.

In those situations where internal networks must be protected yet resources must be made available, a *three-part firewall* system is the most suited to the task. Consider Figure 13.2. Rather than having a single router between the internal network and the untrusted external internetwork, two routers are placed in the path. The segment between these two routers becomes what is called the *DMZ* (de-militarized zone), or the *isolation LAN*. It is physically a buffer or protection between the internal and external networks! On this segment you can place servers that the external internetwork needs to access. These servers might include

- WWW servers

- FTP servers

- SMTP (e-mail) servers

- DNS servers

These are all examples of servers that untrusted hosts from the external internetwork could appropriately access. This allows external users to view your web pages, exchange e-mail with the local network, etc. However, unlike the topology in Figure 13.1, in Figure 13.2, servers are not located on the internal network but on the isolation LAN, which is a completely different network segment. Therefore, if the web server is somehow compromised, the hacker has not penetrated the firewall, as he or she would have in the network in Figure 13.1.

FIGURE 13.2   A three-part firewall system

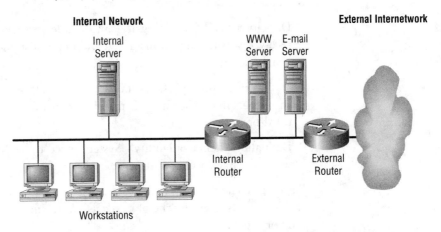

There are many techniques in the three-part firewall to ensure that the internal network is protected. Access lists are used to ensure that inappropriate access is not permitted. In Figure 13.2, the external router has an access list that permits access to certain ports on specific servers in the DMZ, thus allowing web and e-mail traffic to flow. That access list can also include a line to permit only established TCP sessions to the internal network and then to deny all other traffic. In addition, the internal router can be configured to permit only established TCP connections to the internal network. At this point, workstations on the internal network can initiate TCP sessions with devices on the external internetwork, but external devices are not permitted to initiate TCP connections with hosts on the internal network.

If you need to take this a step further, you can install application proxies in the DMZ and configure all workstations on the internal network to use the proxies whenever they communicate with the external internetwork. At this point, the external router only needs to advertise the address of the DMZ LAN out to the external internetwork. As a result, on the external internetwork, routers do not even have routing table entries for the internal network's address!

Network Security: The Targets

Modern networks are, well, target rich to would-be hackers. Increasing complexity, increased interconnectivity, the gravitation of many applications towards a common protocol (IP), the complexity of systems, and other factors make network security a never-ending challenge. At a high level, you are concerned with three factors:

Data integrity Data integrity can include verification that the data received was the data transmitted and might also include controls on changing data.

Data confidentiality Only those who are authorized to access the data should be able to see it. This may include encrypting data to prevent third-party interception.

Data and system availability Systems need to be "hardened" so that a would-be hacker cannot disrupt vital services.

The first two factors deal with protecting data. The third factor considers the problem that sometimes the objective is not to steal or alter, but simply to deny or break.

With this high-level view, let's look at some of the specific components on your network and their particular vulnerabilities.

Routers and Switch Security

Router security is a critical element in any security design. By their nature, routers pass all internetwork traffic. An attack on a router can be an attack on data integrity and certainly can affect network and application availability. It is essential to secure routers to reduce the likelihood that they can be compromised. Many documents provide details on the following router security topics:

- Locking down Telnet access to a router

- Locking down Simple Network Management Protocol (SNMP) access to a router

- Controlling access to a router through the use of *Terminal Access Controller Access Control System Plus (TACACS+)*

- Turning off unneeded services

- Logging at appropriate levels as well as at a Syslog server

- Secure routing protocols

The most current Cisco document on router security is available at http://www.cisco.com/warp/public/707/21.html. Additional security guides are available from the National Security Agency at http://www.nsa.gov/snac/cisco/index.html.

Switches have their own set of security considerations. As Layer 2 devices, switches are a logical target to intercept data and can also be targets to disrupt services. There are several tactics that can harden these devices. Ports without any need to trunk should have any *trunk* settings set to off, as opposed to auto. This setup prevents a host from becoming a trunk port and receiving all traffic that normally resides on a trunk port. Disable all unused ports; this prevents hackers from plugging in to unused ports and communicating with the rest of the network. You may want to consider enabling port security for added protection.

Network Security

Networks in general can be targets of attacks. There are several areas of exposure to networks beyond those risks to their individual components:

Reconnaissance attacks   Reconnaissance attacks attempt to gather information about devices on a network that can be used in further attacks. The mapping of particular system weaknesses, taking inventory of devices and operating systems, and taking inventory of available services (port scanning) are all examples of reconnaissance attacks.

Traffic attacks   Traffic attacks involve intercepting data as it traverses network segments. This can be for the purpose of eavesdropping, or perhaps to change data en route.

Denial-of-service attacks   Just as the name indicates, *denial-of-service (DoS) attacks* are an attempt to deny access to services on the network. They can include sending a malformed packet to a particular host, which causes the host to become unstable and halt. It can also include brute traffic generation, essentially monopolizing available network resources with irrelevant "noise" and thereby preventing legitimate network traffic access.

 Real World Scenario

Distributed Denial-of-Service Attacks (DDoS)

The worst type of attack is the one that is extremely difficult to stop. When performed properly, a *distributed denial-of-service (DDoS)* attack is just such an attack. DDoS works by causing tens or hundreds of machines to simultaneously send spurious data to a single destination IP address. The goal of such an attack is generally not to shut down a particular host, but rather to make the entire network unresponsive. For example, consider an organization with a T1 (1.5Mbps) connection to the Internet that provides e-commerce services to its web site users. Such a site is very security conscious and has intrusion detection, firewalls, logging, and active monitoring. Unfortunately, none of these security devices helps when a hacker launches a successful DDoS attack.

Consider 100 devices around the world, each with DSL (500Kbps) connections to the Internet. By programming these distributed systems to flood the e-commerce organization's Internet connection, they can overwhelm the T1. Even if each host generates only 100Kbps of traffic, this amount is still almost 10 times the amount of traffic that the e-commerce site can handle. As a result, legitimate web requests are discarded, and the site appears to be down for most users.

Only through cooperation with the ISP can this fictitious e-commerce company hope to thwart such an attack. One approach to limiting this sort of attack is to follow filtering guidelines for networks outlined in RFC 1918 and RFC 2827.

When implemented at the ISP, this filtering prevents DDoS attack packets that use these addresses as sources from crossing the WAN link, potentially saving bandwidth during the attack. Implementation of the guidelines described in RFC 2827 by ISPs worldwide greatly reduces source address spoofing. Although this strategy does not directly prevent DDoS attacks, it does prevent such attacks from masking their source, making traceback to the attacking networks much easier.

Hosts and Application Security

The most likely target during an attack, the host presents some of the most difficult challenges from a security perspective. There are numerous hardware platforms, operating systems, and applications, all of which have updates, patches, and fixes available at different times. Because of these security challenges, hosts are also the most successfully compromised devices. For example, a given web server on the Internet might run a hardware platform from one vendor, a network card from another, an operating system from still another vendor, and a web server from yet another vendor. Additionally, the same web server might run applications that are freely distributed, and thus well known, via the Internet.

Applications coded by human beings are subject to errors. These errors can be benign—for example, an error that causes your document to print incorrectly. Or, they can be more serious errors that make credit card numbers on your database server available to unauthorized persons or services. Ensuring that both commercial and public domain applications are up-to-date with the latest security fixes is essential.

Components of Network Security

Every security plan should proceed from an enterprise security policy. Whether this is provided by the customer or created by the customer and network designer, this document guides the security decisions that must be made as part of the design process.

This section will examine some of the components that can be used as part of the network design. Selection and provisioning of these components should be based on the enterprise security policy.

Physical Security

Physical security is frequently overlooked, yet it can be one of the easiest ways to compromise a network. Consider for a moment just what *physical access* to a device means. Can you break it? Of course. Can you plug into a console port or perhaps into an open switch port? Of course. Can you listen to a wire that you can touch? Of course.

There are solutions to these issues. Good old-fashioned locks can do a lot; access methods that are logged are even better. Console ports can require TACACS+, and data can be encrypted should it be intercepted on physical devices beyond your control.

Access Control

Cisco devices using AAA (Authentication, Authorization, and Accounting) give you the capability to tightly control access. You can control who gets access to the devices, what they can do to the device once they have access, and keep logs of everything they do while logged into the device. This is done through the use of a centralized security server, and it allows enterprise-wide policy changes or security modifications at a single point. Have you ever had an engineer leave and had to change hundreds (or more) of passwords by hand? If so, AAA is for you.

Intrusion Detection Systems

An *intrusion detection system (IDS)* acts like an alarm system. When an IDS detects something that it considers a host or network attack, it can either take corrective action itself or notify a management system for actions by the administrator. Some systems are equipped to recognize and respond to specific attacks. Host-based intrusion detection systems work by intercepting operating system and application calls on an individual host. They can also operate by after-the-fact analysis through log files. The former approach allows better attack prevention, whereas the latter approach dictates a more passive response role. *Host-based IDS (HIDS)* systems are often better at preventing specific attacks than *network IDS (NIDS)* systems, which usually issue only an alert upon discovery of an attack. Ideally, a combination of the two systems would be deployed: HIDS on critical hosts and NIDS watching over the entire network.

Secure Device Management

In the *out-of-band (OOB)* environment, each network device and host has its own dedicated management interface, which is connected to a separate, private management network. This setup mitigates the risk of passing management protocols such as Telnet, TFTP, SNMP, and Syslog over the production network. In the SAFE architecture, management traffic flows (*in-band*) and becomes as secure as possible using tunneling protocols and secure variants to insecure management protocols. For example, use *Secure Shell Protocol (SSH)* whenever possible instead of Telnet.

Device Reporting

Most networking devices can send Syslog data to a centralized server. Sending this data to your Syslog analysis host from devices whose logs you wish to view is an effective reporting method. The data can be viewed in real time or via on-demand and scheduled reports. You can choose various logging levels to ensure that the Syslog messages are relevant but do not become overly verbose. To ensure that log messages are time-synchronized to one another, clocks on the hosts and on the network devices must be in sync. For devices that support it, *Network Time Protocol (NTP)* provides a way to ensure accurate time-keeping on all devices.

The Cisco SAFE Blueprint

Cisco's *SAFE (Security Blueprint for Enterprise Networks)* model addresses a defense-in-depth approach to secure network design. SAFE serves as a guide to network designers to meet the security requirements and threats of their network. It is built on top of the Enterprise Composite Networking Modules; that is, it takes a modular approach to security. One central concept of SAFE is defense in depth, that is, a multi-layered approach to security. With defense in depth, failure or breach of security on one device in a network does not lead to failure or breach of security on successive devices.

Today's network designers who understand these threats can better decide where and how to deploy secure technologies. Without a full understanding of the threats involved in network security, there is a tendency to incorrectly configure deployments. Also, network designers focus on security appliances or lack threat response options. By taking a threat-mitigation approach, network designers, armed with this information, can make sound network security choices.

SAFE is a security architecture, and it prevents most attacks from successfully affecting network resources. SAFE must accurately detect the attacks that succeed in penetrating the first line of defense. Additionally, these attacks must be quickly contained to minimize their effect on the rest of the network. However, in being secure, the network must continue to provide critical services that users expect. It is essential to provide network security and network functionality at the same time.

At many points in the network design process, designers need to choose between using integrated functionality in a network device versus using a specialized functional appliance. The integrated functionality is often attractive because designers can implement it on existing equipment, or because the features can interoperate with the rest of the device to provide a functional solution. Appliances are often used when the depth of functionality required is very advanced or when needs require using specialized hardware. Designers should make decisions based on the capacity and functionality of the appliance versus the integration advantage of the device. For example, sometimes designers choose an integrated, higher capacity router with IOS firewall software as opposed to a smaller IOS router with a separate firewall such as the Cisco PIX. When the design requirements do not dictate a specific choice, the designer can opt for integrated functionality in order to reduce the overall cost of the solution.

In the following sections, I'll define the aspects of a SAFE architecture–designed network and explain securing specific device types. I'll also discuss security tools for management.

Module Concept

Cisco's *Enterprise Composite Network Modules (ECNM)* are the building blocks of Cisco's SAFE architecture design model, and they offer two main advantages: First, ECNM allows the architecture to address the security relationship between the various modular blocks of the network. Second, it permits the designer to evaluate and implement security on a module-by-module basis, instead of attempting the complete architecture in a single phase.

For the most part, dissecting a network into clear-cut modules is not an easy task. However, this approach provides a guide for implementing different security functions throughout the network. Figure 13.3 shows how the modules of SAFE create a modular approach to a secure network design.

FIGURE 13.3 Modules of a SAFE network design

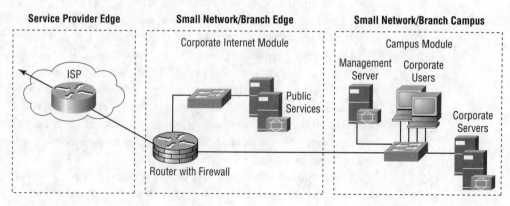

The Service Provider Edge functional area is not usually under the control of the private network administrators. Usually, the ISP secures it with a security agreement provided to administrators. The Corporate Internet module provides internal users with connectivity to Internet services and Internet users with access to information on public servers. Also, remote locations and telecommuters receive VPN access. The Service Provider Edge functional area does not serve e-commerce–type applications.

The Campus functional area contains end-user workstations, corporate intranet servers, management servers, and the associated Layer 2 infrastructure required to support the devices. In this small network design, a single switch controls this Layer 2 functionality.

SAFE is well documented by Cisco via white papers and other content. It does not apply in all network situations and is not necessarily the best or easiest solution to apply to given situations. Let's look at SAFE and how it applies to some of the ECNM modules.

Internet Connectivity module   The Internet Connectivity module is where the enterprise network touches the Internet. This module has traditionally received the most attention in security. A common problem is to be strong on security here and weak elsewhere. There are many threats at the Internet Connectivity module: DoS attacks, reconnaissance, and compromised hosts attempting to penetrate deeper into the enterprise network. Countermeasures such as IDS, host hardening, DMZ networks, and firewall deployment all help to secure this most vulnerable point.

E-Commerce module   Common threats at the E-Commerce module include compromised hosts and/or applications and DoS attacks. Many of the same countermeasures of the Internet Connectivity module listed previously also apply here; host hardening, IDS, DMZ networks, firewalls, and access controls all are effective tools.

Remote Access and VPN module   By definition, the Remote Access and VPN modules are the places where you securely enter the enterprise network. Risks in this module include spoofing (stealing or lying) identity and gaining access to a remote access point or VPN connection. Also at risk are the legitimate clients that access these services. "If I can hack your laptop, I don't need to attack your VPN; the laptop has legitimate access through the VPN." Countermeasures include strong authentication, cryptography, and personal firewalls on remote clients.

WAN module   Security threats in the WAN module include the potential for data transmission to be intercepted (since you cannot control physical access to media) and the potential for service-provider error. What would happen if your telecommunications provider accidentally mapped one of your PVCs to another enterprise customer, one running the same routing protocol as you? Security countermeasures include data encryption and peer authentication across the WAN.

Network Management module   Potential security issues in the Network Management module include the manipulation of management protocols, host compromise, and device misconfiguration (accidental or otherwise). Countermeasures include using secure network management protocols (TACACS+, SNMP v3), AAA (Authentication, Authorization, and Accounting), and firewalls to protect network management hosts.

Server Farm module   Security risks in the Server Farm module include compromised hosts and applications. Host hardening, IDS, and firewalls may all be appropriate here.

As previously mentioned, further documentation on the SAFE blueprint is available directly from Cisco. We've only scratched the surface of network security here, yet that completes our whirlwind introduction to network security and SAFE. Our next topic is IP telephony and the network design issues associated with that technology.

Voice Solutions

Remember earlier in this chapter when we mentioned that security is an extremely large topic? Well, the convergence of modern data and voice networks is not far behind in scale. Cisco voice certifications? Check. Entire books on IP telephony? Check. Entire *careers* in IP telephony? Check. Once again, we'll be scratching the surface of a very deep topic. Once again, we'll be discussing this technology in light of how it impacts modern network design.

Let's begin by discussing some of the traditional ways voice traffic has been handled. Then we'll look at the implications on the design process of integrating voice and data networks.

Traditional Voice Technologies

As humans, our voice communications are analog. Our vocal cords and ears are preconfigured to produce and receive analog voice communications and work quite well. However, there are distance limitations in our natural equipment, so the telephone has emerged over the last hundred or so years to help us communicate at greater distances.

Analog communications are not as desirable on telephone networks as they are to human ears. Analog communications are subject to distortion when amplified and are not efficient users of transmission media. Converting analog conversations to digital (and back again) allows digital signals to cross the telephone network, and this overcomes the previously listed issues with analog communications.

Analog signals are generally converted into PCM (pulse code modulation) digital format signals. This analog-to-digital conversion process requires several steps, including filtering (eliminating sounds outside standard frequencies) and sampling (at a consistent interval).

PBXs and PSTN Switches

There are two types of telephone switches. They have many features in common such as the ability to connect multiple telephones and route calls between them. However, there are some differences as well.

Private branch exchanges (PBXs) are essentially telephone switches used by private enterprises, where public telephone switches are owned and operated by telephone companies. PBXs are used to implement many features within an enterprise such as voice mail, call hold and music on hold, call transfer, call parking, conference calling, and call history. Within an enterprise, multiple PBXs may be interconnected, and internal calling and telephone services will work without any connection to the *public switched telephone network (PSTN)* at all!

PSTN switches are more, well, public than PBXs, and fill a different role. First of all, where PBXs generally support thousands of phones, a PSTN switch supports hundreds of thousands of phones. PSTN switches are used to connect individual telephones, PBXs, and other PSTN switches.

PSTN switches are generally located at a central office (CO). For example, you most likely have a telephone in your home. That phone is connected to a PSTN switch in a CO via a local loop. The local loop is the physical cable between your home and the CO and is used to provide your phone line. There are connections between other types of devices. Tie trunks connect

PBXs, CO trunks connect a PSTN switch to a PBX, and PSTN switch trunks connect PSTN switches.

All of these devices must have ways of talking to each other; that's called *signaling*. In the broadest sense, there are two types of signaling: that between a switch and subscriber (subscriber signaling) and that between multiple switches (trunk signaling).

PSTN Services

Modern PSTNs offers a variety of services to home and business users. We mention a few here that are relevant in converged data and voice networks:

Voice mail   Ah, who doesn't have a love/hate relationship with voice mail? As a service, it truly is an indispensable part of business voice systems today.

Centrex   *Centrex* services are essentially having the PSTN act as if it is your private PBX. There are numerous advantages to this over actually purchasing and installing a PBX. Centrex is an outsourced service, so there is no infrastructure to buy, house, and maintain. Service is provided based on monthly fees. Services such as call forwarding and transfer, three-way calling, and closed dial plans are available.

Call center   The *call center* concept is based on the *automatic call distribution (ACD)* system. Most people have called a call center and experienced the customer perspective of ACD. Incoming calls are accepted; if no agents are available, the incoming calls are "buffered" and music is played while you wait for an agent.

Interactive voice response (IVR)   Did you cringe? If not, you have never called into an *interactive voice response (IVR)*. IVR systems are responsible for that endless cycle of "Select 1 for support, select 2 for sales, ..." A very efficient system, it allows information to be retrieved via telephone lines without anyone on the other end of the line. Certainly a vital business feature, but in the author's humble opinion, a bit overused by some.

That is a quick introduction to the infrastructure and services available on traditional telephone networks. It is only recently that people have been converging voice networks and data networks effectively, and there are many choices available. Most new data networks need to be evaluated for the possibility of supporting voice traffic, if not immediately then eventually.

Now let's look at some of the issues that arise when we migrate this mature voice technology to the rough-and-tumble world of data networking.

Integrated Voice and Data Networks

So what is the big deal with converged networks? There is no single answer to that question, but if there were, it would likely be cost. Consider a medium-sized enterprise with multiple sites. It is not uncommon in such an example to have multiple PBXs, connected by leased *tie-lines*. It is also not uncommon to have multiple routers connected by WAN circuits. Two separate networks. Two bills. Two teams of engineers to support them. This is one area where convergence really shines. The ability to get a single network leads to cost savings in the long run. There is really nothing wrong with PSTN, but if data, voice, and video are going to converge onto a single network, it can't be the PSTN—it must be the data network.

Security and application delivery are other issues in converging voice and data. There are many options for security available on IP networks, and it is easier to secure a single network than multiple networks. Application delivery to voice solutions on data networks can move quicker than on traditional voice networks.

Certainly the most popular technology to integrate voice and data onto the same network is *voice over IP (VoIP)*. As the name implies, voice traffic is digitized, placed in IP packets for transport across IP internetworks, and then converted back to sound when it reaches its destination.

However, VoIP traffic crossing a Frame Relay link is not the same as *Voice over Frame Relay (VoFR)*. With VoFR, a voice-enabled router might be directly attached to a PBX. The router takes a voice feed from the PBX and converts it to Frame Relay frames (no IP) for transport. The same applies to *Voice over ATM (VoATM)*.

H.323

H.323 is an ITU-T defined protocol capable of carrying audio, video, and even data across IP networks. H.323-compliant devices are theoretically capable of interoperation. H.323 established standards for compression and decompression (codec) of voice (and video) traffic, allowing devices from separate manufacturers to interoperate. Since it runs on IP, H.323 is capable of traversing the Internet as well as private IP networks without regard to implementation details.

IP Telephony

While H.323 is a specific protocol used to carry voice traffic across IP networks, IP telephony is the structure and service that facilitates this communication.

Essentially, the IP telephony architecture defines how to remove a PBX and replace the services and functionality using IP networks. IP telephony includes four components:

Infrastructure   The infrastructure is the component required to interconnect all devices. Phones (endpoints) are connected through IP-enabled routers and Layer 2 switches to the broader IP network, as well as with the PSTN network.

Call processing   The call processor is the "brain" or central component. Operating much as the PBX does, it handles, well, call processing. Cisco CallManager (CCM) is Cisco's call processing offering.

Applications   Applications are the functions similar to the PSTN services discussed earlier. No one wants to lose functionality, and migrating to a converged voice and data network requires the replacement of existing services on IP. IVR, call center (ICD), voice mail, and automated attendants are all available applications.

Client devices   These are the phones. Cisco has both hard phones (real handsets) and soft phone offerings. Soft phones run on a PC as software.

Voice Issues

Let's face it, data networks were not initially designed with voice transport in mind. While they do work quite well, managing data networks with voice traffic requires attention to a few details that typically fell "below the radar" when managing data traffic. Let's discuss several of these issues.

Delay

Delay is a major stumbling block for voice traffic and needs to be addressed with the various QoS mechanisms discussed later. Distance is usually the major contributor to delay in existing voice networks. In a phone call to a friend across town, the delay due to distance is imperceptible as the electrical signals travel at the speed of light. In a phone call to someone 8,000 miles away, however, the delay can be noticeable. Propagation delay is the time required for the signal carrying voice traffic to travel the distance across the physical network medium. When distances are short, propagation delay is negligible. As distances increase, delay increases also.

In integrated networks, delay can be a voice-quality problem. Voice information has a characteristic *timing*. A user will utter a particular syllable of a word with an interval of time between it and the following syllable.

Since this tiny pause is as much a part of speech as the verbalized parts, preserving its timing is essential. In traditional voice networks, the voice channel is a synchronized bit stream that preserves the timing of all speech elements precisely. However, in data networks, inserting delay due to congestion or handling corrupts the speech.

Constant delay should not exceed 150ms in one direction. Anything above 400ms renders the network unusable for voice traffic. Constant delays can be caused by processing delay, *serialization* delay, or propagation delay. However, not all delays are constant. Next, let's look at variable delay.

Jitter

Jitter is inconsistent delay, and it can be very annoying. It is caused by a number of factors, including high network utilization and queuing problems. Jitter can be compensated for to some degree through the buffering of packets. Since packets are received at an irregular rate, they are buffered and played back at a constant rate. The dejitter buffer handles this task.

Packet Loss

A voice conversation on a network is a stream of packets. Each packet represents a small time slice of the voice conversation (20ms). Each lost packet represents a "skip" or "blank" in the conversation. While codecs (compressor/decompressor) can generally deal with the loss of a single packet, the loss of multiple packets can cause audible gaps. With data traffic an upper layer protocol would simply notice the lost packet and retransmit, but this is simply not an option when the payload is voice.

QoS

QoS stands for Quality of Service. While broad in its implementation, the basic concept is that of marking voice traffic as "important," and then letting "important" traffic have a right-of-way through network devices. When implemented, QoS can allow voice traffic to speed through normal data network congestion. In order to work, the voice packets must be marked or "colored" to indicate that their content is time-sensitive. Intermediate network devices must be configured to look for this mark and then queue the packet appropriately. QoS is an effective tool in dealing with delay.

That introduction brings us to the end of our voice discussion. As mentioned previously, and like security, this is a very deep field and we haven't begun to explore it here. However, we've covered the concepts of legacy voice and its migration onto the data network. For more details, check out CCO at www.cisco.com.

Summary

Cisco's SAFE architecture design blueprint allows network designers to use a modular approach to creating secure network designs. Network devices and appliances are deployed within the modules of the SAFE blueprint to support security policies and management and reporting needs.

Each and every piece of the network is a target for attack and thus needs to be designed, secured, and monitored to prevent attacks from successfully penetrating or to help minimize the effects.

As converged networks become more and more common, network designers must consider the implications of voice traffic on data networks and create a network design that accommodates voice traffic. Legacy telephone systems had many applications and features, which have now been largely replicated on IP over data networks. Convergence is not without its challenges and issues, but in the end, it can provide significant cost savings over running separate infrastructures for voice and data.

Exam Essentials

Know the reasons for migrating voice from a traditional to integrated architecture. Cost, security, and additional services all contribute to the reasons for migrating to an integrated voice network solution. A unified group of designers and administrators is also a benefit of migration.

Know the traditional voice network devices. Traditional voice network devices include a PBX switch or Centrex line, tie-lines, and trunks.

Know the benefits of Cisco's SAFE architecture design. SAFE helps prevent some of the most common type of network attacks with a defense-in-depth approach using modular design.

Remember the network targets of a SAFE architecture. Routers and switches share common security design considerations such as controlling management access and disabling unused services or ports. Secure your hosts and networks by keeping them up-to-date with security-related patches. Additionally, monitor them with IDSs. Secure code and applications are the foundation to secure computing.

Key Terms

Before you take the exam, be certain you are familiar with the following terms:

automatic call distribution (ACD)

call center

Centrex

denial-of-service (DoS) attacks

distributed denial-of-service (DDoS)

DMZ

Enterprise Composite Network Modules (ECNM)

firewall

hackers

host-based IDS (HIDS)

in-band

interactive voice response (IVR)

intrusion detection system (IDS)

isolation LAN

jitter

network IDS (NIDS)

Network Time Protocol (NTP)

out-of-band (OOB)

private branch exchanges (PBXs)

public switched telephone network (PSTN)

SAFE (Security Blueprint for Enterprise Networks)

Secure Shell Protocol (SSH)

serialization

switches

Terminal Access Controller Access Control System Plus (TACACS+)

three-part firewall

tie-lines

timing

trunk

Voice over ATM (VoATM)

Voice over Frame Relay (VoFR)

voice over IP (VoIP)

Review Questions

1. Traditional voice networks typically include which of the following devices or protocols? (Choose all that apply.)

   A. VoATM

   B. PBX switches

   C. Centrex switches

   D. H.323 application support

2. Subscriber signaling is used between which voice network devices?

   A. PBX and trunk line

   B. Trunk line and tie-line

   C. PBX to PBX

   D. PBX and telephone

3. Centrex lines offer which additional services beyond those of a PBX switch? (Choose all that apply.)

   A. Call transfer

   B. Three-way calling

   C. Closed-user dialing plans

   D. Signaling System 7

4. Which of the following methods best handles delay in VoIP networks?

   A. Addressing

   B. QoS

   C. Routing

   D. Hardware

5. What is the responsibility of the codec in voice networks? (Choose all that apply.)

A. It encrypts the voice traffic.

B. It decrypts the voice traffic.

C. It compresses the voice traffic.

D. It decompresses the voice traffic.

6. Which of the following best describes variable delay?

A. Delay

B. Jitter

C. QoS

D. Packet loss

7. Which solution can help smooth voice traffic that has been affected by jitter?

A. Codec

B. IP telephony

C. Dejitter buffer

D. None of the above

8. Cisco's SAFE architecture blueprint design model addresses what network requirements?

A. Performance

B. Equipment

C. Security

D. Administration

9. Which devices would you expect to find in the Corporate Internet module of a SAFE-designed network? (Choose all that apply.)

A. End-user workstations

B. Intranet servers

C. VPN access

D. Internet services

10. Which devices would you expect to find in the Campus functional area of a SAFE-designed network? (Choose all that apply.)

    A. E-Commerce servers

    B. Management servers

    C. VPN access

    D. Intranet servers

11. Where would you typically find a firewall in a SAFE-designed network?

    A. Internet Connectivity module

    B. Campus

    C. Service Provider Edge

    D. None of the above

12. Which devices of a network are targets for security exploitation? (Choose all that apply.)

    A. Hubs

    B. Servers

    C. Routers and switches

    D. Applications

13. What can be placed on a host or network to act like an alarm system if security issues should arise?

    A. TFTP server

    B. IDS

    C. FTP server

    D. Syslog server

14. When designing security for the E-Commerce module, which of the following are common countermeasures to typical security issues in this module? (Choose all that apply.)

    A. IDS

    B. Firewalls

    C. Host hardening

    D. DMZ networks

    E. All of the above

    F. None of the above

15. Which type of server can be used to log security-related information from network devices?

    A. TFTP

    B. Telnet

    C. FTP

    D. Syslog

16. When capturing security-related information to a Syslog server, which protocol provides accurate time reporting?

    A. NTP

    B. FTP

    C. IDS

    D. HTTP

17. Which of the following is an outsourced service?

    A. PSTN

    B. Centrex

    C. PBX

    D. QoS

18. Which SAFE technology is most effective at preserving data confidentiality?

    A. IDS

    B. Encryption

    C. Authentication

    D. QoS

19. What is the first step in any secure network security design?

    A. Cisco's SAFE architecture blueprint

    B. Security policy

    C. Education

    D. Manager's approval

20. This type of network attack can render a host unreachable by valid requests.

    A. IDS

    B. DoS

    C. SNMP

    D. Flood

Answers to Review Questions

1. B, C.   Traditional voice networks typically include PBX and Centrex switches. They also include tie-lines and trunks.

2. D.   Subscriber signaling is used between the PBX and the telephone.

3. A, B, C.   Centrex lines offer additional services such as call transfer, three-way calling, and closed-user plans.

4. B.   Delay in VoIP networks is handled by QoS.

5. C, D.   The codec is responsible for compressing and decompressing voice traffic. Codec choice determines the transfer rate.

6. B.   Jitter is defined as variable delay.

7. C.   Dejitter buffers can receive packets at an irregular rate and send them out at a more consistent rate.

8. C.   The purpose of Cisco's SAFE architecture blueprint design model is to address the network's security requirements.

9. C, D.   Cisco's SAFE architecture design blueprint recommends that VPN access and Internet services be placed in the Corporate Internet module.

10. B, D.   Cisco's SAFE architecture design blueprint recommends that management and intranet servers, along with end-user workstations, be placed in the Campus functional area.

11. A.   Cisco's SAFE architecture design blueprint recommends that firewalls be placed in the Internet Connectivity module.

12. B, C, D.   Servers, routers, switches, and applications are all targets for security exploitation. Hubs are not generally a risk because of their lack of management features.

13. B.   Although a Syslog server is typically used to log security data, only the IDS actually acts like an alarm system.

14. E.   E-Commerce modules are similar to Internet Connectivity modules; both employ IDS, firewalls, host hardening, and DMZ networks.

15. D.   A Syslog server is the preferred server to log security-related information from network devices and IDSs.

16. A.   The NTP (Network Time Protocol) provides for accurate time reporting when configured on each network device and a central server.

17. B.   Centrex is a service purchased, generally on a monthly fee, to provide services commonly provided by a PBX.

18. B.   Encryption can help keep data confidential.

19. B.   Every secure network security design starts with a security policy relevant to the organization.

20. B.   A DoS (denial-of-service) attack can render a host unreachable by valid requests and cause network slowdowns.

Appendix A

Solutions to Case Studies

Chapter 4

Have-A-Seat

1. Mainframe-based software to control inventory, production, shipping, accounting, and payroll, Office suite applications, terminal emulation software.

2. Note that this map does not include the Ethernet LANs in the office/warehouse facilities.

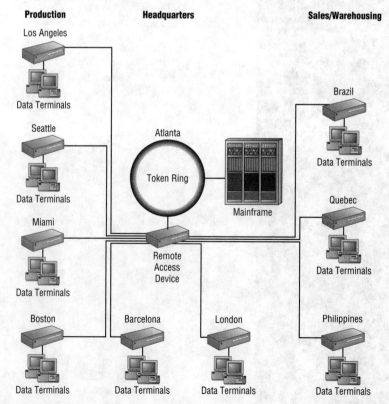

3.

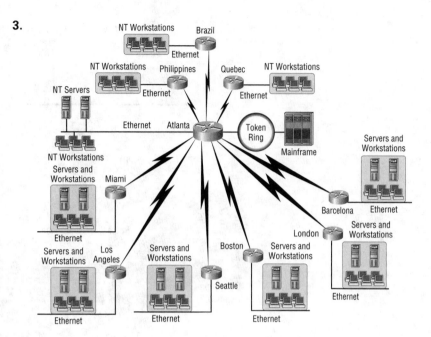

MPS Construction

1.

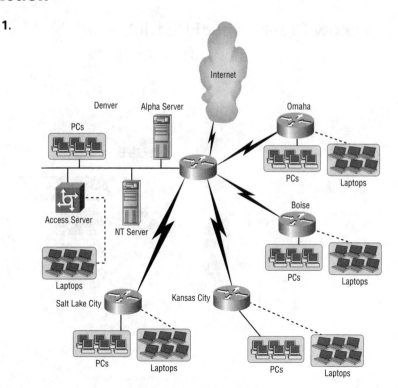

2.

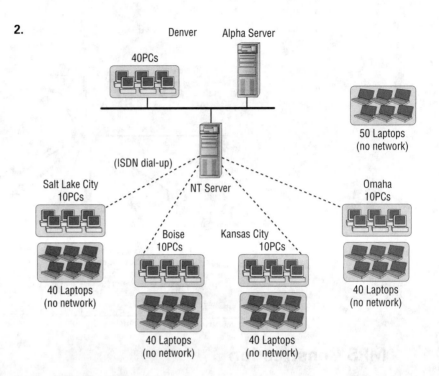

Willow Creek School District

1. TCP/IP, IPX, and AppleTalk

2.

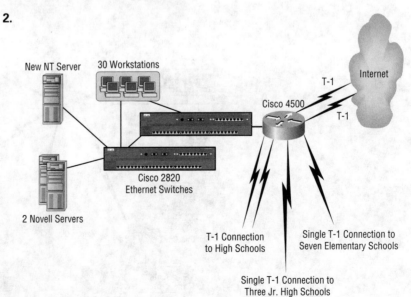

Chapter 5

Have-A-Seat

1. DDR could be configured to dial up Atlanta from the three production facilities and provide a backup should a primary link fail. This solution would be most cost-effective as the backup lines would only be used in situations where the primary lines were unavailable. Dedicated, redundant connections could be used. They would be more expensive, and you would want to address the issue of load balancing should they be deployed.

MPS Construction

1. By deploying the three-part firewall, Mike is able to place the e-mail server in a secure location on the DMZ outside of MPS's internal network. By using access lists on the routers, Mike is able to ensure that the only traffic leaving MPS's internal network is to their mail server, thus denying access to other less-productive Internet resources. Mike needs to be concerned with the Enterprise Campus and the Enterprise Edge functional areas. MPS Construction's Internet connection is shown below.

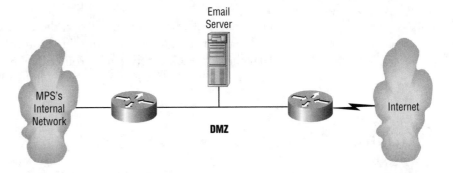

2. By using hierarchical design, Mike is able to simply add additional access-layer and distribution-layer devices as necessary. He will still keep the core of his network in Denver, and that will not expand or change. As new sites are added, they add into the hierarchy without having to change the existing network, which is a major benefit. Addressing issues and routing protocol configurations is also simplified.

Willow Creek School District

1. In this instance, the core layer is represented by the hub router at the District office, the distribution layer by the routers in the individual schools, and the access layer by the switches installed in the schools. As a school's network grows, additional access layer devices are added (switches). As new schools come on line, additional distribution layer devices are added (routers). Expanding any part of the network will not require the entire internetwork to be re-engineered. A diagram of Willow Creek's network is shown below.

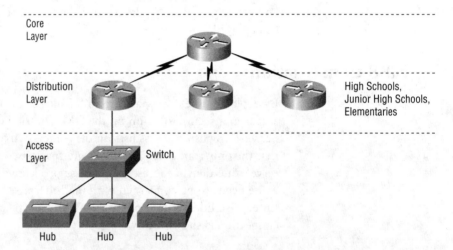

2. Since Scott will be running TCP/IP over these two connections, he will need to ensure that he is using a routing protocol that supports load balancing like EIGRP between his routers and his ISP. Should one of the lines go down, the routing protocol will handle the failover.

Chapter 6

Have-A-Seat

There are no case study exercises for Have-A-Seat in this chapter.

MPS Construction

1. Mike could consider installing ISDN BRI, and using DDR to allow connections to be made between sites only when traffic that he defined as interesting in an access list needed to pass.

2. The AS5200 access server will provide up to 48 asynchronous dial-in connections. This solution actually provides better than a one-to-one ratio of remote users and dial-in connections, guaranteeing that remote users will always have access to the network.

Willow Creek School District

1. One possible solution would be to have three T1s at the district office, each with multiple PVCs on sub-interfaces. Scott could connect the two high schools to one physical interface, the three junior high schools to another physical interface, and the six elementary schools to the third interface. He would not want to connect his two Internet connections to the same physical interface, but would connect them to two separate physical interfaces. The Cisco 7000 router would be an excellent choice.

Chapter 7

Have-A-Seat

1. I would recommend the use of private addressing by Have-A-Seat. They can use them whether or not they connect to the Internet, so that is not an issue. Deployment will be simpler, as there is no application or delay process involved in using private addresses. I would also recommend the use of NAT, but only if they connect to the Internet. If they do not connect to the Internet, there is little advantage to running NAT internally.

2.

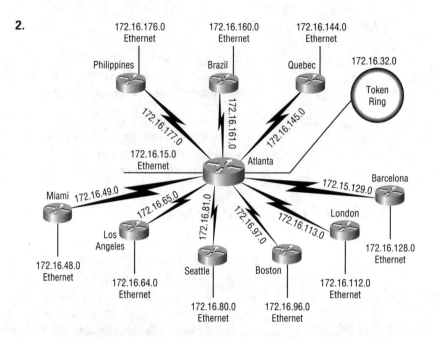

This graphic, showing a high-level topology map with IP addresses, assumes the use of private addressing using 172.16.0.0 and subnetting using 255.255.255.0 as a subnet mask. There is plenty of address space left for future growth both at the remote locations as well as across the entire enterprise.

3. Given the size of their network and their use of private addressing, there would appear to be little advantage in using route summarization. However, you may notice that the IP addressing scheme proposed would support route summarization should significant changes be made in the future.

4.

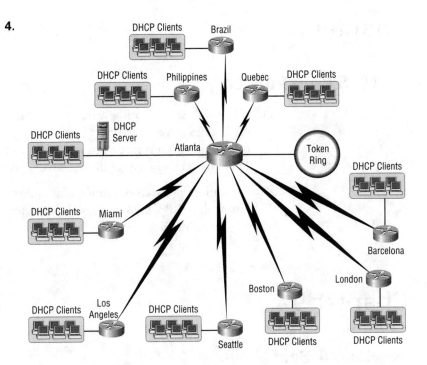

You will need to make sure that you enable IP forwarding on all routers, so that the remote workstation's broadcasts of DHCP requests will be forwarded to the DHCP server. Since servers and networking devices are statically assigned, there will be no DHCP on the Token Ring interface in Atlanta.

MPS Construction

In speaking with Mike, you find that he is willing to use TCP/IP as his exclusive communications protocol. You agree to help him with this transition.

1. We would definitely use private addressing for MPS Construction. As Mike has specified that the only Internet traffic is to be e-mail, there is no reason to run NAT. NAT would only enable workstations to communicate with the Internet, which they are not supposed to do. The workstations do not need translated addresses to speak to the e-mail server in the DMZ, and they also do not need to speak to any device other than the e-mail server to send and receive e-mail.

Chapter 8

MPS Construction

1. While link-state routing protocols do offer more scalability, MPS really does have a relatively small network and thus most of the problems with distance-vector routing protocols would not apply. They could choose either distance-vector or link-state protocols.

2. Assuming that MPS is comfortable running a Cisco proprietary protocol, IGRP would be a good choice for MPS Construction. It recognizes metrics beyond hop count and will easily handle MPS Construction's needs.

Chapter 9

Have-A-Seat

1. For Have-A-Seat, a link-state routing protocol would be preferable to a distance-vector routing protocol for a number of reasons. First of all, faster convergence time is always an issue. Dave has mentioned that he wants redundant links in case of failure for the production facilities, and this indicates the importance of availability. Static routing would be difficult to maintain should the network change at all.

2. Either EIGRP (technically a hybrid) or OSPF would be best. Since Have-A-Seat has no experience running IP routing protocols, their staff thus would have to be trained to use either one. If the customer had reservations about using a proprietary routing protocol, which would hinder interoperability should the customer introduce non-Cisco routing devices to the internetwork, OSPF would be a better choice.

3. Have-A-Seat will not need bridging configured in Atlanta. True, they do have both Ethernet and Token Ring, but they are switching all of their devices to TCP/IP for communications (including their mainframe). TCP/IP will route just fine between Ethernet and Token Ring. If they were not migrating away from SNA, bridging would be an issue. However, here it is not.

Willow Creek School District

1. In this case, EIGRP may well be the best choice. It is the only routing protocol capable of routing all three of Scott's routed protocols. You could recommend OSPF to Scott for IP routing, and NLSP for IPX routing, but you would probably need to recommend EIGRP for AppleTalk routing. In this case, it may well be simpler to standardize on EIGRP for all three routed protocols. Of course, EIGRP is proprietary so you will need to educate the customer to this issue. Also, you will need to support SAP/RIP (IPX) and RTMP (AppleTalk) in the LAN environments for the customer's clients. However, you would only need EIGRP on the WAN.

Chapter 10

Have-A-Seat

1. As discussed in Chapter 5, Have-A-Seat would use access lists on the routers that border their DMZ should they choose to implement a firewall. Those would allow access to their web server and e-mail server, but not allow direct access into Have-A-Seat's internal network.

2. Yes, you could use compression to save bandwidth. Be sure that CPU utilization on affected routers is below 65 percent, though.

Willow Creek School District

1. Scott can use SAP filters at the high schools and junior high schools to prevent their local server's services from being advertised out.

2. Cisco IOS supports encryption between routers, not between hosts. A better solution might be to either use security between the web server and client, or to use switches and VLANs to ensure that administrative traffic could not be overheard on student workstations.

3. Cisco IOS supports GNS Proxy, whereby the router in the elementary school will build its own SAP table and respond to local GNS requests. There is no need to configure bridging, and the workstations will never care that there is not actually a Novell server present.

Chapter 11

Have-A-Seat

1. First of all, Dave should be concerned with configuration as well as Security management in the four ISO network management modules. Dave could consider CiscoWorks as a management platform for his routers. This will allow him a simplified interface to configurations, as well as a powerful interface to monitor his routers. Dave should also consider CWSI for his switched environment. Dave mentioned that he may be deploying VLANs, and using CWSI would simplify both his management and monitoring capabilities.

2. Certainly the Sniffer by Network Associates would be a good choice. This would allow Dave to troubleshoot problems and monitor segments.

Willow Creek School District

1. Scott should strongly consider the use of standards-based management solutions. In particular, SNMP-based solutions would be a good choice as he would be able to monitor a wide variety of devices using a single method.

2. Certainly CiscoWorks would be helpful for working with the Cisco routers that Scott will be deploying. Scott may also want to consider using CWSI to manage his switches.

3. Cisco's NetSys would allow Scott to not only define and monitor service levels, but to view the effects of equipment additions and configuration changes without actually performing them. This would allow Scott to be proactive in anticipating and solving service issues.

Glossary

A

A&B bit signaling   Used in T1 transmission facilities and sometimes called "24th channel signaling." Each of the 24 T1 subchannels in this procedure uses one bit of every sixth frame to send supervisory signaling information.

AAL   ATM Adaptation Layer: A service-dependent sublayer of the Data Link layer, which accepts data from other applications and brings it to the ATM layer in 48-byte ATM payload segments. CS and SAR are the two sublayers that form AALs. Currently, the four types of AAL recommended by the ITU-T are AAL1, AAL2, AAL3/4, and AAL5. AALs are differentiated by the source-destination timing they use, whether they are CBR or VBR, and whether they are used for connection-oriented or connectionless mode data transmission. *See also: AAL1, AAL2, AAL3/4, AAL5, ATM, and ATM layer.*

AAL1   ATM Adaptation Layer 1: One of four AALs recommended by the ITU-T, it is used for connection-oriented, time-sensitive services that need constant bit rates, such as isochronous traffic and uncompressed video. *See also: AAL.*

AAL2   ATM Adaptation Layer 2: One of four AALs recommended by the ITU-T, it is used for connection-oriented services that support a variable bit rate, such as voice traffic. *See also: AAL.*

AAL3/4   ATM Adaptation Layer 3/4: One of four AALs (a product of two initially distinct layers) recommended by the ITU-T, supporting both connectionless and connection-oriented links. Its primary use is in sending SMDS packets over ATM networks. *See also: AAL.*

AAL5   ATM Adaptation Layer 5: One of four AALs recommended by the ITU-T, it is used to support connection-oriented VBR services primarily to transfer classical IP over ATM and LANE traffic. This least complex of the AAL recommendations uses SEAL, offering lower bandwidth costs and simpler processing requirements but also providing reduced bandwidth and error-recovery capacities. *See also: AAL.*

AARP   AppleTalk Address Resolution Protocol: The protocol in an AppleTalk stack that maps data-link addresses to network addresses.

AARP probe packets   Packets sent by the AARP to determine whether a given node ID is being used by another node in a nonextended AppleTalk network. If the node ID is not in use, the sending node appropriates that node's ID. If the node ID is in use, the sending node will select a different ID and then send out more AARP probe packets. *See also: AARP.*

ABM   Asynchronous Balanced Mode: When two stations can initiate a transmission, ABM is an HDLC (or one of its derived protocols) communication technology that supports peer-oriented, point-to-point communications between both stations.

ABR   Area Border Router: An OSPF router that is located on the border of one or more OSPF areas. ABRs are used to connect OSPF areas to the OSPF backbone area.

Access layer   The layer at which user workstations and servers connect in the Cisco three-layer hierarchical design model.

access list   An itemization kept by routers that determines access to and from the router for various services on the network.

access method   The way network devices approach gaining access to the network itself.

access server   Also known as a "network access server," it is a communications process connecting asynchronous devices to a LAN or WAN through network and terminal emulation software, providing synchronous or asynchronous routing of supported protocols.

acknowledgment   Verification sent from one network device to another signifying that an event has occurred. May be abbreviated as ACK. *Contrast with: NAK.*

ACR   Allowed Cell Rate: A designation defined by the ATM Forum for managing ATM traffic. Dynamically controlled using congestion control measures, the ACR varies between the minimum cell rate (MCR) and the peak cell rate (PCR). *See also: MCR and PCR.*

active monitor   The mechanism used to manage a Token Ring. The network node with the highest MAC address on the ring becomes the active monitor and is responsible for management tasks such as preventing loops and ensuring tokens are not lost.

address mapping   By translating network addresses from one format to another, this methodology permits different protocols to operate interchangeably.

address mask   A bit combination descriptor identifying which portion of an address refers to the network or subnet and which part refers to the host. Sometimes simply called the mask. *See also: subnet mask.*

address resolution   The process used for resolving differences between computer addressing schemes. Address resolution typically defines a method for tracing Network layer (Layer 3) addresses to Data Link layer (Layer 2) addresses. *See also: address mapping.*

adjacency   The relationship made between defined neighboring routers and end nodes, using a common media segment, to exchange routing information.

administrative distance   A number between 0 and 225 that expresses the value of trustworthiness of a routing information source. The lower the number, the higher the integrity rating.

administrative weight   A value designated by a network administrator to rate the preference given to a network link. It is one of four link metrics exchanged by PTSPs to test ATM network resource availability.

ADSU   ATM Data Service Unit: The terminal adapter used to connect to an ATM network through an HSSI-compatible mechanism. *See also: DSU.*

advertising   The process whereby routing or service updates are transmitted at given intervals, allowing other routers on the network to maintain a record of viable routes.

AEP   AppleTalk Echo Protocol: A test for connectivity between two Apple-Talk nodes where one node sends a packet to another and receives an echo, or copy, in response.

AFI   Authority and Format Identifier: The part of an NSAP ATM address that delineates the type and format of the IDI section of an ATM address. *See also: IDI and NSAP.*

AFP   AppleTalk Filing Protocol: A presentation-layer protocol, supporting AppleShare and Mac OS File Sharing, that permits users to share files and applications on a server.

AIP ATM Interface Processor: Supporting AAL3/4 and AAL5, this interface for Cisco 7000 series routers minimizes performance bottlenecks at the UNI. *See also: AAL3/4 and AAL5.*

algorithm A set of rules or process used to solve a problem. In networking, algorithms are typically used for finding the best route for traffic from a source to its destination.

alignment error An error occurring in Ethernet networks, in which a received frame has extra bits; that is, a number not divisible by eight. Alignment errors are generally the result of frame damage caused by collisions.

all-routes explorer packet An explorer packet that can move across an entire SRB network, tracing all possible paths to a given destination. Also known as an all-rings explorer packet. *See also: explorer packet, local explorer packet, and spanning explorer packet.*

AM Amplitude Modulation: A modulation method that represents information by varying the amplitude of the carrier signal. *See also: modulation.*

AMI Alternate Mark Inversion: A line-code type on T1 and E1 circuits that shows zeros as "01" during each bit cell, and ones as "11" or "00," alternately, during each bit cell. The sending device must maintain ones density in AMI but not independently of the data stream. Also known as binary-coded, alternate mark inversion. *Contrast with: B8ZS. See also: ones density.*

Amplitude An analog or digital waveform's highest value.

Analog transmission Signal messaging whereby information is represented by various combinations of signal amplitude, frequency, and phase.

ANSI American National Standards Institute: The organization of corporate, government, and other volunteer members that coordinates standards-related activities, approves U.S. national standards, and develops U.S. positions in international standards organizations. ANSI assists in the creation of international and U.S. standards in disciplines such as communications, networking, and a variety of technical fields. It publishes over 13,000 standards, for engineered products and technologies ranging from screw threads to networking protocols. ANSI is a member of the IEC and ISO. *See also: IEC and ISO.*

anycast An ATM address that can be shared by more than one end-system, allowing requests to be routed to a node that provides a particular service.

AppleTalk   Currently in two versions, the group of communication protocols designed by Apple Computer for use in Macintosh environments. The earlier Phase 1 protocols support one physical network with only one network number that resides in one zone. The later Phase 2 protocols support more than one logical network on a single physical network, allowing networks to exist in more than one zone. *See also: zone.*

Application layer   Layer 7 of the OSI reference network model, supplying services to application procedures (such as electronic mail or file transfer) that are outside the OSI model. This layer chooses and determines the availability of communicating partners along with the resources necessary to make the connection, coordinates partnering applications, and forms a consensus on procedures for controlling data integrity and error recovery.

ARA   AppleTalk Remote Access: A protocol for Macintosh users establishing their access to resources and data from a remote AppleTalk location.

area   A logical, rather than physical, set of segments (based on either CLNS, DECnet, or OSPF) along with their attached devices. Areas are commonly connected to others using routers to create a single autonomous system. *See also: autonomous system.*

ARM   Asynchronous Response Mode: An HDLC communication mode using one primary station and at least one additional station, in which transmission can be initiated from either the primary or one of the secondary units.

ARP   A protocol within TCP/IP (Transmission Control Protocol/Internet Protocol) and AppleTalk networks that allows a host to find the physical address of a node on the same network when it knows only the target's logical or IP address.

   Under ARP, a network interface card contains a table (known as the address resolution cache) that maps logical addresses to the hardware addresses of nodes on the network. When a node needs to send a packet, it first checks the address resolution cache to see if the physical address information is already present. If so, that address is used, and network traffic is reduced; otherwise, a normal ARP request is made to determine the address. *See also: RARP.*

ASBR   Autonomous System Boundary Router: An area border router placed between an OSPF autonomous system and a non-OSPF network that operates both OSPF and an additional routing protocol, such as RIP. ASBRs must be located in a non-stub OSPF area. *See also: ABR, non-stub area, and OSPF.*

ASCII   American Standard Code for Information Interchange: An eight-bit code for representing characters, consisting of seven data bits plus one parity bit.

application-specific integrated circuit   Abbreviated ASIC. A computer chip developed for a specific purpose, designed by incorporating standard cells from a library rather than created from scratch. Also known as gate arrays, ASICs are found in all sorts of appliances, including modems, security systems, digital cameras, and even microwave ovens and automobiles.

ASN.1   Abstract Syntax Notation One: An OSI language used to describe types of data that is independent of computer structures and depicting methods. Described by ISO International Standard 8824.

ASP   AppleTalk Session Protocol: A protocol employing ATP to establish, maintain, and tear down sessions, as well as sequence requests. *See also: ATP.*

AST   Automatic Spanning Tree: A function that supplies one path for spanning explorer frames traveling from one node in the network to another, supporting the automatic resolution of spanning trees in SRB networks. AST is based on the IEEE 802.1 standard. *See also: IEEE 802.1 and SRB.*

asynchronous transmission   Digital signals sent without precise timing, usually with different frequencies and phase relationships. Asynchronous transmissions generally enclose individual characters in control bits (called start and stop bits) that show the beginning and end of each character. *Contrast with: isochronous transmission and synchronous transmission.*

ATCP   AppleTalk Control Protocol: The protocol for establishing and configuring AppleTalk over PPP, defined in RFC 1378. *See also: PPP.*

ATDM   Asynchronous Time-Division Multiplexing: A technique for sending information, it differs from normal TDM in that the time slots are assigned when necessary rather than preassigned to certain transmitters. *Contrast with: FDM, statistical multiplexing, and TDM.*

ATG   Address Translation Gateway: The mechanism within Cisco DECnet routing software that enables routers to route multiple, independent DECnet networks and to establish a user-designated address translation for chosen nodes between networks.

ATM   Asynchronous Transfer Mode: The international standard, identified by fixed-length 53-byte cells, for transmitting cells in multiple service systems, such as voice, video, or data. Transit delays are reduced because the fixed-length cells permit processing to occur in the hardware. ATM is designed to maximize the benefits of high-speed transmission media, such as SONET, E3, and T3.

ATM ARP server   A device that supplies logical subnets running classical IP over ATM with address-resolution services.

ATM endpoint   The initiating or terminating connection in an ATM network. ATM endpoints include servers, workstations, ATM-to-LAN switches, and ATM routers.

ATM Forum   The international organization founded jointly by Northern Telecom, Sprint, Cisco Systems, and NET/ADAPTIVE in 1991 to develop and promote standards-based implementation agreements for ATM technology. The ATM Forum broadens official standards developed by ANSI and ITU-T and creates implementation agreements before official standards are published.

ATM layer   A sublayer of the Data Link layer in an ATM network that is service independent. To create standard 53-byte ATM cells, the ATM layer receives 48-byte segments from the AAL and attaches a 5-byte header to each. These cells are then sent to the Physical layer for transmission across the physical medium. *See also: AAL.*

ATMM   ATM Management: A procedure that runs on ATM switches, managing rate enforcement and VCI translation. *See also: ATM and VCI.*

ATM user-user connection   A connection made by the ATM layer to supply communication between at least two ATM service users, such as ATMM processes. These communications can be uni- or bidirectional, using one or two VCCs, respectively. *See also: ATM layer and ATMM.*

ATP   AppleTalk Transaction Protocol: A transport-level protocol that enables reliable transactions between two sockets, where one requests the other to perform a given task and to report the results. ATP fastens the request and response together, assuring a loss-free exchange of request-response pairs.

attenuation   In communication, weakening or loss of signal energy, typically caused by distance.

AURP   AppleTalk Update-based Routing Protocol: A technique for encapsulating AppleTalk traffic in the header of a foreign protocol that allows the connection of at least two noncontiguous AppleTalk internetworks through a foreign network (such as TCP/IP) to create an AppleTalk WAN. The connection made is called an AURP tunnel. By exchanging routing information between exterior routers, the AURP maintains routing tables for the complete AppleTalk WAN. *See also: AURP tunnel and exterior router.*

AURP tunnel   A connection made in an AURP WAN that acts as a single, virtual link between AppleTalk internetworks separated physically by a foreign network such as a TCP/IP network. *See also: AURP.*

authority zone   A portion of the domain-name tree associated with DNS for which one name server is the authority. *See also: DNS.*

automatic call reconnect   A function that enables automatic call rerouting away from a failed trunk line.

autonomous confederation   A collection of self-governed systems that depend more on their own network accessibility and routing information than on information received from other systems or groups.

autonomous switching   The ability of Cisco routers to process packets more quickly by using the ciscoBus to switch packets independently of the system processor.

autonomous system (AS)   A group of networks under mutual administration that share the same routing methodology. Autonomous systems are subdivided by areas and must be assigned an individual 16-bit number by the IANA. *See also: area and IANA.*

autoreconfiguration   A procedure executed by nodes within the failure domain of a Token Ring, wherein nodes automatically perform diagnostics, trying to reconfigure the network around failed areas.

B

B8ZS   Binary 8-Zero Substitution: A line-code type, interpreted at the remote end of the connection, that uses a special code substitution whenever eight consecutive zeros are transmitted over the link on T1 and E1 circuits.

This technique assures ones density independent of the data stream. Also known as bipolar 8-zero substitution. *Contrast with: AMI. See also: ones density.*

backbone   The basic portion of the network that provides the primary path for traffic sent to and initiated from other networks.

back end   A node or software program supplying services to a front end. *See also: client, front end, and server.*

bandwidth   The gap between the highest and lowest frequencies employed by network signals. More commonly, it refers to the rated throughput capacity of a network protocol or medium.

baseband   A feature of a network technology that uses only one carrier frequency, for example Ethernet. Also named "narrowband." *Compare with: broadband.*

baud   Synonymous with bits per second (bps), if each signal element represents one bit. It is a unit of signaling speed equivalent to the number of separate signal elements transmitted per second.

Bc   Committed Burst. Negotiated tariff in Frame Relay networks. The maximum amount of data (in bits) that a Frame Relay network is committed to accept and transmit at the CIR. See also CIR.

B channel   Bearer channel: A full-duplex, 64Kbps channel in ISDN that transmits user data. *Compare with: D channel, E channel, and H channel.*

beacon   An FDDI device or Token Ring frame that points to a serious problem with the ring, such as a broken cable. The beacon frame carries the address of the station thought to be down. *See also: failure domain.*

BDR   (Backup Designated Router) OSPF elects a designated router and a backup designated router for route updates.

BECN   Backward Explicit Congestion Notification: BECN is the bit set by a Frame Relay network in frames moving away from frames headed into a congested path. A DTE that receives frames with the BECN may ask higher-level protocols to take necessary flow control measures. *Compare with: FECN.*

BGP4   BGP Version 4: Version 4 of the interdomain routing protocol most commonly used on the Internet. BGP4 supports CIDR and uses route-counting mechanisms to decrease the size of routing tables. *See also: CIDR.*

binary   A two-character numbering method that uses ones and zeros. The binary numbering system underlies all digital representation of information.

binding   The process of establishing communications between the protocol device driver and the network interface card driver.

BIP   Bit Interleaved Parity: A method used in ATM to monitor errors on a link, sending a check bit or word in the link overhead for the previous block or frame. This allows bit errors in transmissions to be found and delivered as maintenance information.

BISDN   Broadband ISDN: ITU-T standards created to manage high-bandwidth technologies such as video. BISDN presently employs ATM technology along SONET-based transmission circuits, supplying data rates between 155Mbps and 622Mbps and beyond. *Contrast with N-ISDN. See also: BRI, ISDN, and PRI.*

bit-oriented protocol   Regardless of frame content, the class of Data Link layer communication protocols that transmits frames. Bit-oriented protocols, as compared with byte-oriented, supply more efficient and trustworthy, full-duplex operation. *Compare with: byte-oriented protocol.*

border gateway   A router that facilitates communication with routers in different autonomous systems.

BPDU   Bridge Protocol Data Unit: A Spanning Tree Protocol initializing packet that is sent at definable intervals for the purpose of exchanging information among bridges in networks.

BRI   Basic Rate Interface: The ISDN interface that facilitates circuit-switched communication between video, data, and voice; it is made up of two B channels 64Kbps each) and one D channel (16Kbps). *Compare with: PRI. See also: BISDN, ISN.*

bridge   A device for connecting two segments of a network and transmitting packets between them. Both segments must use identical protocols to communicate. Bridges function at the Data Link layer, Layer 2 of the OSI reference model. The purpose of a bridge is to filter, send, or flood any incoming frame, based on the MAC address of that particular frame.

broadband   A transmission methodology for multiplexing several independent signals onto one cable. In telecommunications, broadband is classified as any channel with bandwidth greater than 4kHz (typical voice grade). In LAN terminology, it is classified as a coaxial cable on which analog signaling is employed. Also known as wideband. *Contrast with: baseband.*

broadcast   A data frame or packet that is transmitted to every node on a network. Broadcasts are known by their broadcast address, which is a destination address with all the bits turned on.

broadcast domain   A group of devices receiving broadcast frames initiating from any device within the group. Because they do not forward broadcast frames, broadcast domains are generally surrounded by routers.

broadcast storm   An undesired event on the network caused by the simultaneous transmission of any number of broadcasts across all network segments. Such an occurrence can overwhelm network bandwidth, resulting in time-outs.

buffer   A storage area dedicated to handling data while in transit. Buffers are used to receive/store sporadic deliveries of data bursts, usually received from faster devices, compensating for the variations in processing speed. Incoming information is stored until everything is received prior to sending data on. Also known as an information buffer.

bus topology   A linear LAN architecture in which transmissions from various stations on the network are reproduced over the length of the medium and are accepted by all other stations. *Compare with: ring, star, and tree topologies.*

bus   Any physical path, typically wires or copper, through which a digital signal can be used to send data from one part of a computer to another.

BUS   Broadcast and Unknown Server: In LAN emulation, the hardware or software responsible for resolving all broadcasts and packets with unknown (unregistered) addresses into the point-to-point virtual circuits required by ATM. *See also: LEC, LECS, LES, and LANE.*

BX.25   AT&T's use of X.25. *See also: X.25.*

bypass mode   An FDDI and Token Ring network operation that deletes an interface.

bypass relay   A device that enables a particular interface in the Token Ring to be closed down and effectively taken off the ring.

byte-oriented protocol   Any type of data-link communication protocol that, in order to mark the boundaries of frames, uses a specific character from the user character set. These protocols have generally been superseded by bit-oriented protocols. *Compare with: bit-oriented protocol.*

C

cable range   In an extended AppleTalk network, the range of numbers allotted for use by existing nodes on the network. The value of the cable range can be anywhere from a single to a sequence of several touching network numbers. Node addresses are determined by their cable range value.

CAC   Connection Admission Control: The sequence of actions executed by every ATM switch while connection setup is performed in order to determine if a request for connection is violating the guarantees of QoS for established connections. Also, CAC is used to route a connection request through an ATM network.

call admission control   A device for managing of traffic in ATM networks, determining the possibility of a path containing adequate bandwidth for a requested VCC.

call center   The call center concept is based on the ACD (automatic call distribution) system. Incoming calls are accepted; if no agents are available, the incoming calls are "buffered" and music is played while you wait for an agent.

call priority   In circuit-switched systems, the defining priority given to each originating port; it specifies in which order calls will be reconnected. Additionally, call priority identifies which calls are allowed during a bandwidth reservation.

call set-up time   The length of time necessary to effect a switched call between DTE devices.

CAS   (Channel Associated Signaling) used in voice signaling to carry the signal from the trunk to the PBX.

CBR   Constant Bit Rate: An ATM Forum QoS class created for use in ATM networks. CBR is used for connections that rely on precision clocking to guarantee trustworthy delivery. *Compare with: ABR and VBR.*

CBWFQ (Class Based Weighted Fair Queuing) extends the standard WFQ functionality to provide support for user-defined traffic classes. For CBWFQ, you define traffic classes based on match criteria including protocols, access control lists (ACLs), and input interfaces. Packets satisfying the match criteria for a class constitute the traffic for that class. A queue is reserved for each class, and traffic belonging to a class is directed to the queue for that class.

CCS A common link is used to carry voice signaling information for a number of trunks to the PBX switch. This form of signaling is cheaper, supports faster connect times, and is more flexible than CAS.

CD Carrier Detect: A signal indicating that an interface is active or that a connection generated by a modem has been established.

CDP Cisco Discovery Protocol: Cisco's proprietary protocol that is used to tell a neighbor Cisco device about the type of hardware, software version, and active interfaces that the Cisco device is using. It uses a SNAP frame between devices and is not routable.

CDVT Cell Delay Variation Tolerance: A QoS parameter for traffic management in ATM networks specified when a connection is established. The allowable fluctuation levels for data samples taken by the PCR in CBR transmissions are determined by the CDVT. *See also: CBR and PCR.*

cell In ATM networking, the basic unit of data for switching and multiplexing. Cells have a defined length of 53 bytes, including a 5-byte header that identifies the cell's data stream and 48 bytes of payload. *See also: cell relay.*

cell payload scrambling The method by which an ATM switch maintains framing on some medium-speed edge and trunk interfaces (T3 or E3 circuits). Cell payload scrambling rearranges the data portion of a cell to maintain the line synchronization with certain common bit patterns.

cell relay A technology that uses small packets of fixed size, known as cells. Their fixed length enables cells to be processed and switched in hardware at high speeds, making this technology the foundation for ATM and other high-speed network protocols. *See also: cell.*

cell switching A term that describes how a cellular telephone system switches from one cell to the next as the signal strength fades. The switch takes about 300 milliseconds to complete and is not noticeable by the user.

Centrex   A local exchange carrier service, providing local switching that resembles that of an on-site PBX. Centrex has no on-site switching capability. Therefore, all customer connections return to the CO. *See also: CO.*

CER   Cell Error Ratio: The ratio in ATM of transmitted cells having errors to the total number of cells sent in a transmission within a certain span of time.

channelized E1   Operating at 2.048Mpbs, an access link that is sectioned into 29 B-channels and one D-channel, supporting DDR, Frame Relay, and X.25. *Compare with: channelized T1.*

channelized T1   Operating at 1.544Mbps, an access link that is sectioned into 23 B-channels and 1 D-channel of 64Kbps each, where individual channels or groups of channels connect to various destinations, supporting DDR, Frame Relay, and X.25. Also known as fractional T1. *Compare with: channelized E1.*

CHAP   Challenge Handshake Authentication Protocol: Supported on lines using PPP encapsulation, it is a security feature that identifies the remote end, helping keep out unauthorized users. After CHAP is performed, the router or access server determines whether a given user is permitted access. It is a newer, more secure protocol than PAP. *Compare with: PAP.*

checksum   A test for ensuring the integrity of sent data. It is a number calculated from a series of values taken through a sequence of mathematical functions, typically placed at the end of the data from which it is calculated, and then recalculated at the receiving end for verification. *Compare with: CRC.*

choke packet   When congestion exists, it is a packet sent to inform a transmitter that it should decrease its sending rate.

CIDR   Classless Interdomain Routing: A method supported by BGP4 and based on route aggregation that enables routers to combine routes in order to minimize the routing information that needs to be conveyed by the primary routers. It allows a group of IP networks to appear to other networks as a unified, larger entity. In CIDR, IP addresses and their subnet masks are written as four dotted octets, followed by a forward slash and a two-digit subnet mask. *See also: BGP4.*

CIP   Channel Interface Processor: A channel attachment interface for use in Cisco 7000 series routers that connects a host mainframe to a control unit. This device eliminates the need for an FBP to attach channels.

CIR Committed Information Rate: Averaged over a minimum span of time and measured in bps, a Frame Relay network's agreed-upon normal rate of transferring information.

Cisco CNS Network Registrar Network Registrar automates enterprise IP address management. It includes Domain Name System (DNS), Dynamic Host Configuration Protocol (DHCP), and Trivial File Transfer Protocol (TFTP) servers. You can control these servers using the Network Registrar graphical user interface (GUI) or command-line interface (CLI). These user interfaces can control server clusters that run on different platforms.

Cisco FRAD Cisco Frame-Relay Access Device: A Cisco product that supports Cisco IPS Frame Relay SNA services, connecting SDLC devices to Frame Relay without requiring an existing LAN. May be upgraded to a fully functioning multiprotocol router. Can activate conversion from SDLC to Ethernet and Token Ring, but does not support attached LANs. *See also: FRAD.*

Cisco Express Forwarding (CEF) CEF evolved to best accommodate the changing network dynamics and traffic characteristics resulting from increasing numbers of short duration flows typically associated with web-based applications and interactive type sessions.

CiscoFusion Cisco's name for the internetworking architecture under which its Cisco IOS operates. It is designed to "fuse" together the capabilities of its disparate collection of acquired routers and switches.

Cisco IOS software Cisco Internetwork Operating System software. The kernel of the Cisco line of routers and switches that supplies shared functionality, scalability, and security for all products under its CiscoFusion architecture. *See also: CiscoFusion.*

CiscoView GUI-based management software for Cisco networking devices, enabling dynamic status, statistics, and comprehensive configuration information. Displays a physical view of the Cisco device chassis and provides device-monitoring functions and fundamental troubleshooting capabilities. May be integrated with a number of SNMP-based network management platforms.

CiscoWorks2000 CiscoWorks2000 Server provides a unified desktop environment for managing a network of Cisco network devices.

classfull   Each of the commercial IP address classes has a classfull network mask. The network mask defines which bits out of the 32 bits of the address are defined as the network portion and which are the host portion.

classless   Some routing protocols do not assume the network mask as with classfull routing protocols and hence the network mask is always sent with the network number in routing updates.

classical IP over ATM   Defined in RFC 1577, the specification for running IP over ATM that maximizes ATM features. Also known as CIA.

CLP   Cell Loss Priority: The area in the ATM cell header that determines the likelihood of a cell being dropped during network congestion. Cells with CLP = 0 are considered insured traffic and are not apt to be dropped. Cells with CLP = 1 are considered best-effort traffic that may be dropped during congested episodes, delivering more resources to handle insured traffic.

CLR   Cell Loss Ratio: The ratio of discarded cells to successfully delivered cells in ATM. CLR can be designated a QoS parameter when establishing a connection.

CO   Central Office: The local telephone company office where all loops in a certain area connect and where circuit switching of subscriber lines occurs.

collapsed backbone   A nondistributed backbone where all network segments are connected to each other through an internetworking device. A collapsed backbone can be a virtual network segment at work in a device such as a router, hub, or switch.

collision   The effect of two nodes sending transmissions simultaneously in Ethernet. When they meet on the physical media, the frames from each node collide and are damaged. *See also: collision domain.*

collision domain   The network area in Ethernet over which frames that have collided will spread. Collisions are propagated by hubs and repeaters, but not by LAN switches, routers, or bridges. *See also: collision.*

compression   Often used with data. Data compression eliminates unnecessary data and uses markers to compress the data.

committed information rate (CIR)   Frame Relay providers allow customers to buy a lower amount of bandwidth than what they really might need. This is called the committed information rate (CIR). This means that the customer can buy bandwidth of, for example, 256k, but it is possible to burst up to T1 speeds.

community string Used with SNMP, a community string defines the community an SNMP management station and agent reside within.

configuration register A 16-bit configurable value stored in hardware or software that determines how Cisco routers function during initialization. In hardware, the bit position is set using a jumper. In software, it is set by specifying a hexadecimal value with configuration commands.

congestion Traffic that exceeds the network's ability to handle it.

congestion avoidance To minimize delays, the method an ATM network uses to control traffic entering the system. Lower-priority traffic is discarded at the edge of the network when indicators signal it cannot be delivered, thus using resources efficiently.

congestion collapse The situation that results from the retransmission of packets in ATM networks where little or no traffic successfully arrives at destination points. It usually happens in networks made of switches with ineffective or inadequate buffering capabilities combined with poor packet discard or ABR congestion feedback mechanisms.

connectionless Data transfer that occurs without the creating of a virtual circuit. No overhead, best effort delivery, not reliable. *Contrast with: connection-oriented. See also: virtual circuit.*

connection-oriented Data transfer method that sets up a virtual circuit before any data is transferred. Uses acknowledgments and flow control for reliable data transfer. *Contrast with: connectionless. See also: virtual circuit.*

control direct VCC One of three control connections defined by Phase I LAN Emulation—a bidirectional virtual control connection (VCC) established in ATM by an LEC to an LES. *See also: control distribute VCC.*

control distribute VCC One of three control connections defined by Phase 1 LAN Emulation—a unidirectional virtual control connection (VCC) set up in ATM from an LES to an LEC. Usually, the VCC is a point-to-multipoint connection. *See also: control direct VCC.*

convergence   A measurement of the time required for all routers in an internetwork to update their routing tables. No data is passed during a convergence time.

Core layer   The layer at which high-speed routing and switching occur in the Cisco three-layer hierarchical design model.

cost   Also known as path cost, an arbitrary value, based on hop count, bandwidth, or other calculation, that is typically assigned by a network administrator and used by the routing protocol to compare different routes through an internetwork. Routing protocols use cost values to select the best path to a certain destination: the lowest cost identifies the best path. Also known as path cost. *See also: routing metric.*

count to infinity   A problem occurring in routing algorithms that are slow to converge where routers keep increasing the hop count to particular networks. To avoid this problem, the network administrator fixes an arbitrary hop count limit.

CPCS   Common Part Convergence Sublayer: One of two AAL sublayers that is service-dependent, it is further segmented into the CS and SAR sublayers. The CPCS prepares data for transmission across the ATM network; it creates the 48-byte payload cells that are sent to the ATM layer. *See also: AAL and ATM layer.*

CPE   Customer Premises Equipment: Items, such as telephones, modems, and terminals, installed at customer locations and connected to the telephone company network.

crankback   In ATM, a correction technique used when a node somewhere on a chosen path cannot accept a connection setup request, blocking the request. The path is rolled back to an intermediate node, which then uses GCAC to attempt to find an alternate path to the final destination.

CRC   Cyclic Redundancy Check: A methodology that detects errors, whereby the frame recipient makes a calculation by dividing frame contents with a prime binary divisor and compares the remainder to a value stored in the frame by the sending node. *Contrast with: checksum.*

CSMA/CD   Carrier Sense Multiple Access Collision Detect: A technology defined by the Ethernet IEEE 802.3 committee. Each device senses the cable for a digital signal before transmitting. Also, CSMA/CD allows all devices on the network to share the same cable, but one at a time. If two devices transmit at the same time, they will stop transmitting, wait a predetermined amount of time, and then try to transmit again.

CSU   Channel Service Unit: A digital mechanism that connects end-user equipment to the local digital telephone loop. Frequently referred to along with the data service unit as CSU/DSU. *See also: DSU.*

CTD   Cell Transfer Delay: For a given connection in ATM, the time period between a cell exit event at the source user-network interface (UNI) and the corresponding cell entry event at the destination. The CTD between these points is the sum of the total inter-ATM transmission delay and the total ATM processing delay.

custom queuing   For networks that need to provide a guaranteed level of service for all traffic, Cisco offers custom queuing. Custom queuing allows a customer to reserve a percentage of bandwidth for specified protocols.

cut-through packet switching   A packet-switching technique that flows data through a switch so that the leading edge exits the switch at the output port before the packet finishes entering the input port. Packets will be read, processed, and forwarded by devices that use cut-through packet switching as soon as the destination address is confirmed and the outgoing port is identified.

D

data direct VCC   A bidirectional point-to-point virtual control connection (VCC) set up between two LECs in ATM and one of three data connections defined by Phase 1 LAN Emulation. Because data direct VCCs do not guarantee QoS, they are generally reserved for UBR and ABR connections. *Compare with: control distribute VCC and control direct VCC.*

datagram   A logical collection of information transmitted as a Network layer unit over a medium without a previously established virtual circuit. IP datagrams have become the primary information unit of the Internet. At various layers of the OSI reference model, the terms cell, frame, message, packet, and segment also define these logical information groupings.

data link control layer   Layer 2 of the SNA architectural model, it is responsible for the transmission of data over a given physical link and compares somewhat to the Data Link layer of the OSI model.

Data Link layer   Layer 2 of the OSI reference model, it ensures the trustworthy transmission of data across a physical link and is primarily concerned with physical addressing, line discipline, network topology, error notification, ordered delivery of frames, and flow control. The IEEE has further segmented this layer into the MAC sublayer and the LLC sublayer. Also known as the link layer. Can be compared somewhat to the data link control layer of the SNA model. *See also: Application layer, LLC, MAC, Network layer, Physical layer, Presentation layer, Session layer, and Transport layer.*

DCC   Data Country Code: Developed by the ATM Forum, one of two ATM address formats designed for use by private networks. *Compare with: ICD.*

DCE   Data Communications Equipment (as defined by the EIA) or Data Circuit-terminating Equipment (as defined by the ITU-T): The mechanisms and links of a communications network that make up the network portion of the user-to-network interface, such as modems. The DCE supplies the physical connection to the network, forwards traffic, and provides a clocking signal to synchronize data transmission between DTE and DCE devices. *Compare with: DTE.*

D channel   1. Data channel: A full-duplex, 16kbps (BRI) or 64kbps (PRI) ISDN channel. *Compare with: B channel, E channel, and H channel.*
    2. In SNA, anything that provides a connection between the processor and main storage with any peripherals.

DDP   Datagram Delivery Protocol : Used in the AppleTalk suite of protocols as a connectionless protocol that is responsible for sending datagrams through an internetwork.

DDR   Dial-On-Demand Routing: A technique that allows a router to automatically initiate and end a circuit-switched session per the requirements of the sending station. By mimicking keep-alives, the router fools the end station into treating the session as active. DDR permits routing over ISDN or telephone lines via a modem or external ISDN terminal adapter.

default route   The routing table entry used to direct frames whose next hop is not spelled out in the routing table.

delay   The time elapsed between a sender's initiation of a transaction and the first response they receive. Also, the time needed to move a packet from its source to its destination over a path. *See also: latency.*

demarc   The demarcation point between the customer premises equipment (CPE) and the telco's carrier equipment.

demodulation   A series of steps that return a modulated signal to its original form. When receiving, a modem demodulates an analog signal to its original digital form (and, conversely, modulates the digital data it sends into an analog signal). *See also: modulation.*

demultiplexing   The process of converting a single multiplex signal, comprising more than one input stream, back into separate output streams. *See also: multiplexing.*

denial of service   (DoS) A type of network attack that can cause the receiving device to be non-responsive.

designated bridge   In the process of forwarding a frame from a segment to the route bridge, the bridge with the lowest path cost.

designated router   An OSPF router that creates LSAs for a multiaccess network and is required to perform other special tasks in OSPF operations. Multiaccess OSPF networks that maintain a minimum of two attached routers identify one that is chosen by the OSPF Hello protocol, which makes possible a decrease in the number of adjacencies necessary on a multiaccess network. This in turn reduces the quantity of routing protocol traffic and the physical size of the database.

destination address   The address for the network devices that will receive a packet.

DHCP   (Dynamic Host Configuration Protocol) A system based on network interface card addresses that is used to allocate IP addresses and other configuration information automatically for networked systems. DHCP is an update of the Bootstrap Protocol.

digital subscriber line (DSL)   DSL is a technology that allows ordinary PSTN copper to be used for high-speed data communications. In essence, it is a new way of using the existing infrastructure.

discontiguous addressing   Some routing protocols support the use of discontiguous addressing where different major network numbers are supported in a single network design.

discovery mode   Also known as dynamic configuration, this technique is used by an AppleTalk interface to gain information from a working node about an attached network. The information is subsequently used by the interface for self-configuration.

distance vector routing algorithm   In order to find a shortest-path spanning tree, this group of routing algorithms repeats on the number of hops in a given route, requiring each router to send its complete routing table with each update, but only to its neighbors. Routing algorithms of this type tend to generate loops, but they are fundamentally simpler than their link-state counterparts. *See also: link-state routing algorithm and SPF.*

distributed denial of service   (DDoS) A type of network attack that can cause the receiving device, devices or network to be non-responsive.

Distribution layer   The layer at which routing redistribution, network policies, and firewalls are placed and Internet access occurs in the Cisco three-layer hierarchical design model.

DLCI   Data-Link Connection Identifier: Used to identify virtual circuits in a Frame Relay network.

DMZ   (Demilitarized Zone) Used in many network designs and implementations, the DMZ usually includes publicly accessible servers.

DNS   Domain Name System: Used to resolve host names to IP addresses.

downtime   The amount of time during which a computer system is not available to users, because of a hardware or software failure.

DSAP   Destination Service Access Point: The service access point of a network node, specified in the destination field of a packet. *See also: SSAP and SAP.*

DSCP   Used by voice over IP QoS to define the Type of Service field of the IP packet as voice traffic.

DSR Data Set Ready: When a DCE is powered up and ready to run, this EIA/TIA-232 interface circuit is also engaged.

DSU Data Service Unit: This device is used to adapt the physical interface on a data terminal equipment (DTE) mechanism to a transmission facility such as T1 or E1 and is also responsible for signal timing. It is commonly grouped with the channel service unit and referred to as the CSU/DSU. *See also: CSU.*

DTE Data Terminal Equipment: Any device located at the user end of a user-network interface serving as a destination, a source, or both. DTE includes devices such as multiplexers, protocol translators, and computers. The connection to a data network is made through data channel equipment (DCE) such as a modem, using the clocking signals generated by that device. *See also: DCE.*

DTR Data Terminal Ready: An activated EIA/TIA-232 circuit communicating to the DCE the state of preparedness of the DTE to transmit or receive data.

DUAL Diffusing Update Algorithm: Used in Enhanced IGRP, this convergence algorithm provides loop-free operation throughout an entire route's computation. DUAL grants routers involved in a topology revision the ability to synchronize simultaneously, while routers unaffected by this change are not involved. *See also: Enhanced IGRP.*

DVMRP Distance Vector Multicast Routing Protocol: Based primarily on the Routing Information Protocol (RIP), this Internet gateway protocol implements a common, condensed-mode IP multicast scheme, using IGMP to transfer routing datagrams between its neighbors. *See also: IGMP.*

DXI Data Exchange Interface: Described in RFC 1482, DXI defines the effectiveness of a network device such as a router, bridge, or hub to act as an FEP to an ATM network by using a special DSU that accomplishes packet encapsulation.

dynamic addressing A network interface device that receives its IP addresses and other configuration information automatically for networked systems.

dynamic routing Also known as adaptive routing, this technique automatically adapts to traffic or physical network revisions.

E

E1   Generally used in Europe, a wide-area digital transmission scheme carrying data at 2.048Mbps. E1 transmission lines are available for lease from common carriers for private use.

E.164   1. Evolved from standard telephone numbering system, the standard recommended by ITU-T for international telecommunication numbering, particularly in ISDN, SMDS, and BIISDN.
2. Label of field in an ATM address containing numbers in E.164 format.

E channel   Echo channel: A 64Kbps ISDN control channel used for circuit switching. Specific description of this channel can be found in the 1984 ITU-T ISDN specification, but was dropped from the 1988 version. *See also: B, D, and H channels.*

ECNM   (Enterprise Composite Network Module) Cisco's Enterprise Composite Network Modules approach has two main advantages: First, it allows the architecture to address the security relationship between the various modular blocks of the network. Second, it permits the designer to evaluate and implement security on a module-by-module basis, instead of attempting the complete architecture in a single phase.

edge device   A device that enables packets to be forwarded between legacy interfaces (such as Ethernet and Token Ring) and ATM interfaces based on information in the Data Link and Network layers. An edge device does not take part in the running of any Network layer routing protocol; it merely uses the route description protocol in order to get the forwarding information required.

EFCI   Explicit Forward Congestion Indication: A congestion feedback mode permitted by ABR service in an ATM network. The EFCI may be set by any network element that is in a state of immediate or certain congestion. The destination end-system is able to carry out a protocol that adjusts and lowers the cell rate of the connection based on value of the EFCI. *See also: ABR.*

EIGRP   *See: Enhanced IGRP.*

EIP   Ethernet Interface Processor: A Cisco 7000 series router interface processor card, supplying 10Mbps AUI ports to support Ethernet Version 1 and Ethernet Version 2 or IEEE 802.3 interfaces with a high-speed data path to other interface processors.

ELAN   Emulated LAN: An ATM network configured using a client/server model in order to emulate either an Ethernet or Token Ring LAN. Multiple ELANs can exist at the same time on a single ATM network and are made up of an LAN emulation client (LEC), an LAN emulation server (LES), a broadcast-and unknown server (BUS), and an LAN emulation configuration server (LECS). ELANs are defined by the LANE specification. *See also: LANE, LEC, LECS, and LES.*

ELAP   EtherTalk Link Access Protocol: In an EtherTalk network, the link-access protocol constructed above the standard Ethernet Data Link layer.

encapsulation   The technique used by layered protocols in which a layer adds header information to the protocol data unit (PDU) from the layer above. As an example, in Internet terminology, a packet would contain a header from the Physical layer, followed by a header from the Network layer (IP), followed by a header from the Transport layer (TCP), followed by the application protocol data.

encryption   The conversion of information into a scrambled form that effectively disguises it to prevent unauthorized access. Every encryption scheme uses some well-defined algorithm, which is reversed at the receiving end by an opposite algorithm in a process known as decryption.

Enhanced IGRP   Enhanced Interior Gateway Routing Protocol: An advanced routing protocol created by Cisco, combining the advantages of link-state and distance-vector protocols. Enhanced IGRP has superior convergence attributes, including high operating efficiency. *See also: IGP, OSPF, and RIP.*

Enterprise Campus   A layer found in the Enterprise Composite Network Model, this layer contains four major modules. It applies to a single campus and can easily be replicated campus to campus.

Enterprise Edge   A layer found in the Enterprise Composite Network Model, this layer includes four modules. Each of these modules is connected to the Edge Distribution module of the Enterprise Campus functional area. This bridges the gap between the campus site and WAN connectivity.

enterprise network   A privately owned and operated network that joins most major locations in a large company or organization.

EPROM   Erasable Programmable Read-Only Memory: Programmed after their manufacture, these nonvolatile memory chips can be erased if necessary and reprogrammed. *See also: PROM.*

ESF Extended Superframe: Made up of 24 frames with 192 bits each, with the 193rd bit providing other functions including timing. This is an enhanced version of SF. *See also: SF.*

Ethernet A baseband LAN specification created by the Xerox Corporation and then improved through joint efforts of Xerox, Digital Equipment Corporation, and Intel. Ethernet is similar to the IEEE 802.3 series standard and, using CSMA/CD, operates over various types of cables at 10Mbps. *See also: 10BaseT, Fast Ethernet, and IEEE.*

EtherTalk A data-link product from Apple Computer that permits Apple-Talk networks to be connected by Ethernet.

excess rate In ATM networking, traffic exceeding a connection's insured rate. The excess rate is the maximum rate less the insured rate. Depending on the availability of network resources, excess traffic can be discarded during congestion episodes. *Compare with: maximum rate.*

expansion The procedure of directing compressed data through an algorithm, restoring information to its original size.

expedited delivery An option that can be specified by one protocol layer, communicating either with other layers or with the identical protocol layer in a different network device, requiring that identified data be processed faster.

explorer packet A packet transmitted by a source device to find the path through a source-route-bridged network.

F

failure domain The region in which a failure has occurred in a Token Ring. When a station gains information that a serious problem, such as a cable break, has occurred with the network, it sends a beacon frame that includes the station reporting the failure, its NAUN, and everything between. This defines the failure domain. Beaconing then initiates the procedure known as autoreconfiguration. *See also: autoreconfiguration and beacon.*

fallback In ATM networks, this mechanism is used for scouting a path if it's not possible to locate one using customary methods. The device relaxes requirements for certain characteristics, such as delay, in an attempt to find a path that meets a certain set of the most important requirements.

Fast Ethernet   Any Ethernet specification with a speed of 100Mbps. Fast Ethernet is 10 times faster than 10BaseT, while retaining qualities like MAC mechanisms, MTU, and frame format. These similarities make it possible for existing 10BaseT applications and management tools to be used on Fast Ethernet networks. Fast Ethernet is based on an extension of IEEE 802.3 specification. *Compare with: Ethernet. See also: 100BaseT, 100BaseTX, and IEEE.*

fast switching   A Cisco feature that uses a route cache to speed packet switching through a router. *Contrast with: process switching.*

fault tolerance   A design method that ensures continued system operation in the event of individual failures by providing redundant elements.

At the component level, the design includes redundant chips and circuits and the capability to bypass faults automatically. At the computer-system level, any elements that are likely to fail, such as processors and large disk drives, are replicated.

Fault-tolerant operations often require backup or UPS (uninterruptible power supply) systems in the event of a main power failure. In some cases, the entire computer system is duplicated in a remote location to protect against vandalism, acts of war, or natural disaster.

FDM   Frequency-Division Multiplexing: A technique that permits information from several channels to be assigned bandwidth on one wire based on frequency. *See also: TDM, ATDM, and statistical multiplexing.*

FDDI   Fiber Distributed Data Interface: An LAN standard, defined by ANSI X3T9.5, that can run at speeds up to 200Mbps and uses token-passing media access on fiber-optic cable. For redundancy, FDDI can use a dual-ring architecture.

FECN   Forward Explicit Congestion Notification: A bit set by a Frame Relay network that informs the DTE receptor that congestion was encountered along the path from source to destination. A device receiving frames with the FECN bit set can ask higher-priority protocols to take flow-control action as needed. *See also: BECN.*

FEIP   Fast Ethernet Interface Processor: An interface processor employed on Cisco 7000 series routers, supporting up to two 100Mbps 100BaseT ports.

FIFO   (First In First Out) Often used with queuing, FIFO uses a first in first out method.

flat network   A term for describing a Layer 2 network that is one large broadcast domain.

filtering   One of the five states of a network switch is filtering. The others are blocking, listening, learning, and forwarding.

firewall   A barrier purposefully erected between any connected public networks and a private network, made up of a router or access server or several routers or access servers, that uses access lists and other methods to ensure the security of the private network.

flash memory   Developed by Intel and licensed to other semiconductor manufacturers, it is nonvolatile storage that can be erased electronically and reprogrammed. Flash memory permits software images to be stored, booted, and rewritten as needed. Cisco routers and switches use flash memory to hold the IOS by default.

flooding   When traffic is received on an interface, it is then transmitted to every interface connected to that device with exception of the interface from which the traffic originated. This technique can be used for traffic transfer by bridges and switches throughout the network.

flow control   A methodology used to ensure that receiving units are not overwhelmed with data from sending devices. Pacing, as it is called in IBM networks, means that when buffers at a receiving unit are full, a message is transmitted to the sending unit to temporarily halt transmissions until all the data in the receiving buffer has been processed and the buffer is again ready for action.

forwarding   One of the five states of a network switch is forwarding. The others are blocking, listening, learning, and filtering.

FRAD   Frame Relay Access Device: Any device affording a connection between a LAN and a Frame Relay WAN. *See also: Cisco FRAD, FRAS.*

fragment   Any portion of a larger packet that has been segmented into smaller pieces.

FragmentFree   A LAN switch type that reads into the data field before forwarding to make sure that no fragmentation has taken place.

fragmentation   The process of segmenting a packet into smaller pieces when sending data over a network medium that cannot support the larger packet size.

frame   A logical unit of information sent by the Data Link layer over a transmission medium. The term often refers to the header and trailer, employed for synchronization and error control, that surround the data contained in the unit.

frame filtering   A LAN switch function that reads the destination hardware address and only forwards the frame out the correct port. This process filters the frame from going out unneeded ports.

Frame Relay   A more efficient replacement of the X.25 protocol, Frame Relay is the industry-standard, switched Data Link layer protocol that services multiple virtual circuits using HDLC encapsulation between connected mechanisms.

Frame Relay bridging   Defined in RFC 1490, this bridging method uses the identical spanning-tree algorithm as other bridging operations but permits packets to be encapsulated for transmission across a Frame Relay network.

FRAS   Frame Relay Access Support: A feature of Cisco IOS software that enables SDLC, Ethernet, Token Ring, and Frame Relay–attached IBM devices to be linked with other IBM mechanisms on a Frame Relay network. *See also: FRAD.*

frequency   The number of cycles of an alternating current signal per time unit, measured in hertz (cycles per second).

FRTS   (Frame Relay Traffic Shaping) A combination of techniques used to efficiently shape network traffic on a Frame Relay circuit.

FSIP   Fast Serial Interface Processor: The Cisco 7000 routers' default serial interface processor, it provides four or eight high-speed serial ports.

FTP   File Transfer Protocol: The TCP/IP protocol used for transmitting files between network nodes, it supports a broad range of file types and is defined in RFC 959. *See also: TFTP.*

full duplex   The capacity to transmit information between a sending station and a receiving unit at the same time. *See also: half duplex.*

full mesh   A type of network topology where every node has either a physical or a virtual circuit linking it to every other network node. A full mesh supplies a great deal of redundancy but is typically reserved for network backbones because of its expense. *See also: partial mesh.*

G

gateway   A shared connection between a LAN and a larger system, such as a mainframe computer or a large packet-switching network, whose communications protocols are different. Usually slower than a bridge or router, a gateway is a combination of hardware and software with its own processor and memory used to perform protocol conversions.

GNS   Get Nearest Server: On an IPX network, a request packet sent by a customer for determining the location of the nearest active server of a given type. An IPX network client launches a GNS request to get either a direct answer from a connected server or a response from a router disclosing the location of the service on the internetwork to the GNS. GNS is part of IPX and SAP. *See also: IPX and SAP.*

GRE   Generic Routing Encapsulation: A tunneling protocol created by Cisco with the capacity for encapsulating a wide variety of protocol packet types inside IP tunnels, thereby generating a virtual point-to-point connection to Cisco routers across an IP network at remote points. IP tunneling using GRE permits network expansion across a single-protocol backbone environment by linking multiprotocol subnetworks in a single-protocol backbone environment.

guard band   The unused frequency area found between two communications channels, furnishing the space necessary to avoid interference between the two.

H

H.323   A videoconferencing standard developed by the International Telecommunication Union (ITU) that defines videoconferencing from the desktop over LANs, intranets, and the Internet.

H.323 specifies techniques for compressing and transmitting real-time voice, video, and data between a pair of videoconferencing workstations. It also describes signaling protocols for managing audio and video streams, as well as procedures for breaking data into packets and synchronizing transmissions across communications channels.

hacker   In the programming community, where the term originated, this term describes a person who pursues knowledge of computer systems for its own sake—someone willing to "hack through" the steps of putting together a working program.

More recently, in popular culture at large, the term has come to mean a person who breaks into other people's computers with malicious intent (what programmers call a "cracker"). Many countries now treat convicted crackers in the same way that they treat conventional breaking-and-entering criminals.

half duplex   The capacity to transfer data in only one direction at a time between a sending unit and receiving unit. *See also: full duplex.*

handshake   Any series of transmissions exchanged between two or more devices on a network to ensure synchronized operations.

hardware address   The address assigned to a network interface card (NIC) by the original manufacturer or by the network administrator if the interface card is configurable.

This address identifies the local device address to the rest of the network and allows messages to find the correct destination. Also known as the physical address, media access control (MAC) address, or Ethernet address.

H channel   High-speed channel: A full duplex, ISDN primary rate channel operating at a speed of 384Kbps. *See also: B, D, and E channels.*

HDLC   High-Level Data Link Control: Using frame characters, including checksums, HDLC designates a method for data encapsulation on synchronous serial links. HDLC is a bit-oriented synchronous Data Link layer protocol created by ISO and derived from SDLC. *See also: SDLC.*

helper address   Used to send multicast addresses to a server on a remote network.

hierarchical addressing   Any addressing plan employing a logical chain of commands to determine location. IP addresses are made up of a hierarchy of network numbers, subnet numbers, and host numbers to direct packets to the appropriate destination.

HIP   HSSI Interface Processor: An interface processor used on Cisco 7000 series routers, providing one HSSI port that supports connections to ATM, SMDS, Frame Relay, or private lines at speeds up to T3 or E3.

holddown   The state a route is placed in so that routers can neither advertise the route nor accept advertisements about it for a defined time period.

Holddown is used to surface bad information about a route from all routers in the network. A route is generally placed in holddown when one of its links fails.

hop The movement of a packet between any two network nodes. *See also: hop count.*

hop count A routing metric that calculates the distance between a source and a destination. RIP employs hop count as its sole metric. *See also: hop and RIP.*

host-based IDS (HIDS) Installed locally on a host network device, host-based IDS systems are often better at preventing specific attacks than *network IDS* (NIDS) systems.

HSCI High-Speed Communication Interface: Developed by Cisco, a single-port interface that provides full-duplex synchronous serial communications capability at speeds up to 52Mbps.

HSRP Hot Standby Router Protocol: A protocol that provides high network availability and makes network topology changes without administrator intervention. It generates a Hot Standby router group, including a lead router that lends its services to any packet being transferred to the Hot Standby address. If the lead router fails, it will be replaced by any of the other routers—the standby routers—that monitor it.

HSSI High-Speed Serial Interface: A network standard for high-speed serial linking over a WAN at speeds of up to 52Mbps.

hub A device used to extend a network so that additional workstations can be attached. There are two main types of hubs:
Active hubs amplify transmission signals to extend cable length and ports.
Passive hubs split the transmission signal, allowing additional workstations to be added, usually at a loss of distance.
In some star networks, a hub is the central controlling device.

hybrid network A network that uses a collection of different technologies, such as frame relay, leased lines, and X.25.

I

ICD International Code Designator: Adapted from the subnetwork model of addressing, this assigns the mapping of Network layer addresses to ATM addresses. HSSI is one of two ATM formats for addressing created by the ATM Forum to be utilized with private networks. *See also: DCC.*

ICMP   Internet Control Message Protocol: Documented in RFC 792, it is a Network layer Internet protocol for the purpose of reporting errors and providing information pertinent to IP packet procedures.

IEEE   Institute of Electrical and Electronics Engineers: A professional organization that, among other activities, defines standards in a number of fields within computing and electronics, including networking and communications. IEEE standards are the predominant LAN standards used today throughout the industry. Many protocols are commonly known by the reference number of the corresponding IEEE standard.

IEEE 802.1D   The IEEE specification for STP (Spanning Tree Protocol). The STP uses SPA (Spanning Tree Algorithm) to find and prevent network loops in bridged networks.

IEEE 802.3   The IEEE committee specification that defines Ethernet 10BaseT. Ethernet is a LAN protocol that specifies physical layer and MAC sublayer media access. IEEE 802.3 uses CSMA/CD to provide access for many devices on the same network. FastEthernet is defined as 802.3u, and Gigabit Ethernet is defined as 802.3q. *See also: CSMA/CD.*

IEEE 802.5   IEEE committee that defines Token Ring media access.

IGMP   Internet Group Management Protocol: Employed by IP hosts, the protocol that reports their multicast group memberships to an adjacent multicast router.

IGP   Interior Gateway Protocol: Any protocol used by the Internet to exchange routing data within an independent system.

IGRP   (Interior Gateway Routing Protocol) A distance-vector routing protocol from Cisco Systems for use in large heterogeneous networks.

ILMI   Integrated (or Interim) Local Management Interface. A specification created by the ATM Forum, designated for the incorporation of network-management capability into the ATM UNI. Integrated Local Management Interface cells provide for automatic configuration between ATM systems. In LAN emulation, ILMI can provide sufficient information for the ATM end station to find an LECS. In addition, ILMI provides the ATM NSAP (network service access point) prefix information to the end station.

in-band management   In-band management is the management of a network device "through" the network using Simple Network Management Protocol (SNMP) or Telnet.

insured burst   In an ATM network, it is the largest, temporarily permitted data burst exceeding the insured rate on a PVC and not tagged by the traffic policing function for being dropped if network congestion occurs. This insured burst is designated in bytes or cells.

interactive voice response (IVR)   A very efficient system, IVR allows information to be retrieved via telephone lines without anyone on the other end of the line.

interarea routing   Routing between two or more logical areas. *Contrast with: intra-area routing. See also: area.*

interface processor   Any of several processor modules used with Cisco 7000 series routers. *See also: AIP, CIP, EIP, FEIP, HIP, MIP, and TRIP.*

Internet   The global "network of networks," whose popularity has exploded in the last few years. Originally a tool for collaborative academic research, it has become a medium for exchanging and distributing information of all kinds. The Internet's need to link disparate computer platforms and technologies has led to the development of uniform protocols and standards that have also found widespread use within corporate LANs. *See also: TCP/IP and MBONE.*

internet   Before the rise of the Internet, this lowercase form was shorthand for "internetwork" in the generic sense. Now rarely used. *See also: internetwork.*

Internet protocol   Any protocol belonging to the TCP/IP protocol stack. *See also: TCP/IP.*

internetwork   Any group of networks interconnected by routers and other mechanisms, typically operating as a single entity.

internetworking   Broadly, anything associated with the general task of linking networks to each other. The term encompasses technologies, procedures, and products. When you connect networks to a router, you are creating an internetwork.

intra-area routing   Routing that occurs within a logical area. *Contrast with: interarea routing.*

Intrusion Detection System   (IDS) A software package designed to detect specific actions on a network that are typical of an intruder or that might indicate an act of corporate espionage.

An IDS package monitors the network or the server for specific "attack signatures" that might indicate an active intruder is attempting to gain access to the network; such actions are carefully documented by the system.

Specific actions, such as opening or renaming certain important files, opening specific applications, downloading large amounts of data from key documents, or sending classified documents out as e-mail attachments, are also monitored by the IDS software.

Inverse ARP   Inverse Address Resolution Protocol: A technique by which dynamic routes are constructed in a network, allowing an access server to locate the network address of a mechanism affiliated with a permanent virtual circuit (PVC).

IOS Network Management Model   The International Organization for Standardization (ISO) defines the types of network management applications that reside on the NMS. Just as the seven-layer OSI model defines function but not implementation for data communications, the ISO network management model defines five areas of network management without specifying specific implementations.

IP   Internet Protocol: Defined in RFC 791, it is a Network layer protocol that is part of the TCP/IP stack and allows connectionless service. IP furnishes an array of features for addressing, type-of-service specification, fragmentation and reassembly, and security.

IP unnumbered command   When you use the `ip unnumbered` command, a serial interface is not on a separate network, as all router interfaces tend to be. Instead, the serial port "borrows" an IP address from another interface.

IP v4 address   Often called an Internet address, this is an address uniquely identifying any device (host) on the Internet (or any TCP/IP network). Each address consists of four octets (32 bits), represented as decimal numbers separated by periods (a format known as "dotted-decimal"). Every address is made up of a network number, an optional subnetwork number, and a host number. The network and subnetwork numbers together are used for routing, while the host number addresses an individual host within the network or subnetwork. The network and subnetwork information is extracted from the IP address using the subnet mask. There are five classes of IP addresses (A–E), which allocate different numbers of bits to the network, subnetwork, and host portions of the address. *See also: CIDR, IP, and subnet mask.*

IP v6 address   With the growth of the Internet since the early 1990s, the IETF, IANA, IAB, and many networking vendors have realized the need for an expanded IP address space. RFC 2373 defines the IP version 6 addressing architecture. IP version 6 addresses are 128 bits in length and are globally unique.

IPCP   IP Control Protocol: The protocol used to establish and configure IP over PPP. *See also: IP and PPP.*

ip forward protocol   A broadcast-based protocol such as DHCP, DNS, and WINS that is forwarded across the router when configured with the `ip helper-address` command.

ip helper address   A Cisco IOS command for specifying that broadcast-based protocols are forwarded across the router.

IP multicast   A technique for routing that enables IP traffic to be reproduced from one source to several endpoints or from multiple sources to many destinations. Instead of transmitting only one packet to each individual point of destination, one packet is sent to a multicast group specified by only one IP endpoint address for the group.

IP Security   (IPSec) A suite of protocols under development by the Internet Engineering Task Force (IETF) designed to add security provisions to the Internet Protocol (IP).

The Authentication Header (AH) ensures that the datagram has not been tampered with during transmission, and the Encapsulating Security Payload (ESP) defines encryption methods for IP data.

IPSec operates in two modes:

Transport mode: AH or ESP is placed immediately after the original IP datagram header and provides security between two end systems such as a server and a workstation.

Tunnel mode: The original IP datagram is placed inside a new datagram, and AH and ESP are inserted between the IP header of the new packet and the original IP datagram. The new header points to the tunnel endpoint, and the original header points to the final destination of the datagram. Tunnel mode is best suited to Virtual Private Network (VPN) use, securing remote access to your corporate network through the Internet.

IPX Internetwork Packet Exchange: Network layer protocol (Layer 3) used in Novell NetWare networks for transferring information from servers to workstations. Similar to IP and XNS.

IPX address A logical address used to send packets through a Novell intranetwork.

IPXCP IPX Control Protocol: The protocol used to establish and configure IPX over PPP. *See also: IPX and PPP.*

IPXWAN Protocol used for new WAN links to provide and negotiate line options on the link using IPX. After the link is up and the options have been agreed upon by the two end-to-end links, normal IPX transmission begins.

ISDN Integrated Services Digital Network: Offered as a service by telephone companies, a communication protocol that allows telephone networks to carry data, voice, and other digital traffic. *See also: BISDN, BRI, and PRI.*

IS-IS Intermediate System–to–Intermediate System, or IS-IS, is an interior routing protocol or an Interior Gateway Protocol (IGP). Developed in the 1980's, IS-IS was intended to be the routing protocol for OSI in an attempt to produce a standards protocol suite that could allow internetworks generous scalability.

isochronous transmission Asynchronous data transfer over a synchronous data link, requiring a constant bit rate for reliable transport. *Compare with: asynchronous transmission and synchronous transmission.*

isolation LAN Also called DMZ but can be a stand-alone LAN within a campus LAN for security purposes.

ITU-T International Telecommunication Union Telecommunication Standardization Sector: This is a group of engineers that develops worldwide standards for telecommunications technologies.

J

jitter   A type of distortion found on communications lines that results in data-transmission errors.

L

LAN   Local Area Network: Broadly, any network linking two or more computers and related devices within a limited geographical area (up to a few kilometers). LANs are typically high-speed, low-error networks within a company. Cabling and signaling at the physical and Data Link layers of the OSI are dictated by LAN standards. Ethernet, FDDI, and Token Ring are among the most popular LAN technologies. *Compare with: MAN and WAN.*

LANE   LAN emulation: The technology that allows an ATM network to operate as a LAN backbone. To do so, the ATM network is required to provide multicast and broadcast support, address mapping (MAC-to-ATM), and SVC management, in addition to an operable packet format. Additionally, LANE defines Ethernet and Token Ring ELANs. *See also: ELAN.*

LAN switch   A high-speed switching mechanism, transmitting packets between segments of data links, occasionally referred to as a frame switch. LAN switches transfer traffic based on MAC addresses. Multilayer switches are a type of LAN switch. *See also: multilayer switch, cut-through packet switching, and store-and-forward packet switching.*

LAPB   Link Accessed Procedure, Balanced: A bit-oriented Data Link layer protocol that is part of the X.25 stack and has its origin in SDLC. *See also: SDLC and X.25.*

LAPD   Link Access Procedure on the D channel. The ISDN Data Link layer protocol used specifically for the D channel and defined by ITU-T Recommendations Q.920 and Q.921. LAPD evolved from LAPB and is created to comply with the signaling requirements of ISDN basic access.

latency   Broadly, the time it takes a data packet to get from one location to another. In specific networking contexts, it can mean either 1) the time elapsed (delay) between the execution of a request for access to a network by a device and the time the mechanism actually is permitted transmission, or 2) the time elapsed between when a mechanism receives a frame and the time that frame is forwarded out of the destination port.

LCP   Link Control Protocol: The protocol designed to establish, configure, and test data link connections for use by PPP. *See also: PPP.*

leaky bucket   An analogy for the basic cell rate algorithm (GCRA) used in ATM networks for checking the conformance of cell flows from a user or network. The bucket's "hole" is understood to be the prolonged rate at which cells can be accommodated, and the "depth" is the tolerance for cell bursts over a certain time period. *See also: GCRA.*

learning bridge   A bridge that builds a dynamic database of MAC addresses and the interfaces associated with each address to reduce traffic on the network.

LE ARP   LAN Emulation Address Resolution Protocol: The protocol providing the ATM address that corresponds to a MAC address.

LEC   LAN Emulation Client: Software providing the emulation of the Link Layer interface that allows the operation and communication of all higher-level protocols and applications to continue. The LEC client runs in all ATM devices, which include hosts, servers, bridges, and routers. The LANE client is responsible for address resolution, data transfer, address caching, interfacing to the emulated LAN, and driver support for higher-level services. *See also: ELAN and LES.*

LECS   LAN Emulation Configuration Server: An important part of emulated LAN services, providing the configuration data that is furnished upon request from the LES. These services include address registration for Integrated Local Management Interface (ILMI) support, configuration support for the LES addresses and their corresponding emulated LAN identifiers, and an interface to the emulated LAN. *See also: LES and ELAN.*

LES   LAN Emulation Server: The central LANE component that provides the initial configuration data for each connecting LEC. The LES typically is located on either an ATM-integrated router or a switch. Responsibilities of the LES include configuration and support for the LEC, address registration for the LEC, database storage and response concerning ATM addresses, and interfacing to the emulated LAN *See also: ELAN, LEC, and LECS.*

Level 1 routing   Used by the IS-IS routing protocol. An area is a group of contiguous networks and attached hosts that is specified to be an area by a network administrator or manager. A domain is a collection of connected areas. Routing domains provide full connectivity to all end systems within them. Level 1 routing is routing within a Level 1 area.

Level 2 routing   Used by the IS-IS routing protocol. An area is a group of contiguous networks and attached hosts that is specified to be an area by a network administrator or manager. A domain is a collection of connected areas. Routing domains provide full connectivity to all end systems within them. Level 1 routing is routing within a Level 1 area while Level 2 routing is routing between Level 1 areas.

link-state routing algorithm   A routing algorithm that allows each router to broadcast or multicast information regarding the cost of reaching all its neighbors to every node in the internetwork. Link-state algorithms provide a consistent view of the network and are therefore not vulnerable to routing loops. However, this is achieved at the cost of somewhat greater difficulty in computation and more widespread traffic (compared with distance vector routing algorithms). *See also: distance vector routing algorithm.*

listening   One of the five states of a network switch is listening. The others are blocking, learning, forwarding, and filtering.

LLAP   LocalTalk Link Access Protocol: In a LocalTalk environment, the Data Link–level protocol that manages node-to-node delivery of data. This protocol provides node addressing and management of bus access, and it also controls data sending and receiving to assure packet length and integrity.

LLC   Logical Link Control: Defined by the IEEE, the higher of two Data Link layer sublayers. LLC is responsible for error control, flow control, framing, and MAC-sublayer addressing. The predominant LLC protocol, IEEE 802.2, defines both connectionless and connection-oriented operations. *See also: Data Link layer and MAC.*

LLQ   *LLQ* is a feature that provides a PQ to *CBWFQ*. LLQ enables a single PQ within CBWFQ at the class level. With LLQ, delay-sensitive data in the PQ is dequeued and sent first. In a VoIP network with LLQ implementation, voice traffic is placed in the PQ.

LMI An enhancement to the original Frame Relay specification. Among the features it provides are a keep-alive mechanism, a multicast mechanism, global addressing, and a status mechanism.

LNNI LAN Emulation Network-to-Network Interface: In the Phase 2 LANE specification, an interface that supports communication between the server components within one ELAN.

load balancing A technique that distributes network traffic along parallel paths to make the most efficient use of the available bandwidth while also providing redundancy. Load balancing will automatically move a user's job from a heavily loaded network resource to a less-loaded resource.

local explorer packet In an SRB network, a packet generated by an end system to find a host linked to the local ring. If no local host can be found, the end system will produce one of two solutions: a spanning explorer packet or an all-routes explorer packet.

LocalTalk Utilizing CSMA/CD, in addition to supporting data transmission at speeds of 230.4Kbps, LocalTalk is Apple Computer's proprietary baseband protocol, operating at the Data Link and Physical layers of the OSI reference model.

Logical Address A logical address is usually assigned by the administrator and is subject to change. IP and IPX addresses are examples of logical addresses.

LPD LPD is the line printer daemon. It uses the system calls listen and accept to receive requests to print files in the queue, transfer files to the spooling area, display the queue, or remove jobs from the queue. In each case, it forks a child to handle the request so the parent can continue to listen for more requests.

LSA Link-State Advertisement: Occasionally referred to as link-state packets (LSPs), these advertisements are broadcast packets, containing information about neighbors and path costs, that are employed by link-state protocols. Receiving routers use LSAs to maintain their routing tables.

LSU (Link State Update) OSPF uses IP multicast to exchange Hello packets and Link State Update packets or routing updates.

LUNI LAN Emulation User–to–Network Interface: Defining the interface between the LAN Emulation Client (LEC) and the LAN Emulation Server,

LUNI is the ATM Forum's standard for LAN Emulation on ATM networks. *See also: LES and LECS.*

M

MAC   Media Access Control: The lower sublayer in the Data Link layer, it is responsible for hardware addressing, media access, and error detection of frames. *See also: Data Link layer and LLC.*

MAC address   A Data Link layer address that every port or device needs in order to connect to a LAN. These addresses are used by various devices in the network for accurate location of ports, including the creation and revision of routing tables. MAC addresses are defined by the IEEE standard and their length is six characters. Variously called hardware address, physical address, or MAC-layer address.

MacIP   In AppleTalk, the Network layer protocol encapsulating IP packets in Datagram Delivery Protocol (DDP) packets. MacIP also supplies substitute ARP services.

MAN   Metropolitan-Area Network: Any network that encompasses a metropolitan area; that is, an area typically larger than a LAN but smaller than a WAN. *See also: LAN and WAN.*

manageability   Term used when discussing the benefits of a hierarchical network design. One of the benefits of a hierarchical network design is better management of the network.

Manchester encoding   A method for digital coding in which a mid-bit-time transition is employed for clocking, and a 1 (one) is denoted by a high voltage level during the first half of the bit time. This scheme is used by Ethernet and IEEE 802.3.

MAU   (Multi-station Access Unit) sometimes abbreviated MSAU. A multi-port wiring hub for token-ring networks that can connect as many as eight lobes to a ring network. IBM refers to an MAU that can be managed remotely as a Controlled Access Unit.

maximum burst   Specified in bytes or cells, the largest burst of information exceeding the insured rate that will be permitted on an ATM permanent virtual connection for a short time and will not be dropped even if it goes over the specified maximum rate. *Compare with: insured burst. See also: maximum rate.*

maximum rate   The maximum permitted data throughput on a particular virtual circuit, equal to the total of insured and uninsured traffic from the traffic source. Should traffic congestion occur, uninsured information may be deleted from the path. Measured in bits or cells per second, the maximum rate represents the highest throughput of data the virtual circuit is ever able to deliver and cannot exceed the media rate. *Compare with: excess rate. See also: maximum burst.*

MBS   Maximum Burst Size: In an ATM signaling message, this metric, coded as a number of cells, is used to convey the burst tolerance.

MBONE   Multicast Backbone: The multicast backbone of the Internet, it is a virtual multicast network made up of multicast LANs, including point-to-point tunnels interconnecting them.

MCDV   Maximum Cell Delay Variation: The maximum two-point CDV objective across a link or node for the identified service category in an ATM network. The MCDV is one of four link metrics that are exchanged using PTSPs to verify the available resources of an ATM network. Only one MCDV value is assigned to each traffic class.

MCLR   Maximum Cell Loss Ratio: The maximum ratio of cells in an ATM network that fail to transit a link or node, compared with the total number of cells that arrive at the link or node. MCDV is one of four link metrics that are exchanged using PTSPs to verify the available resources of an ATM network. The MCLR applies to cells in VBR and CBR traffic classes whose CLP bit is set to zero. *See also: CBR, CLP, and VBR.*

MCR   Minimum Cell Rate: A parameter determined by the ATM Forum for traffic management of the ATM networks. MCR is specifically defined for ABR transmissions and specifies the minimum value for the allowed cell rate (ACR). *See also: ACR and PCR.*

MCTD   Maximum Cell Transfer Delay: In an ATM network, the total of the maximum cell delay variation and the fixed delay across the link or node. MCTD is one of four link metrics that are exchanged using PNNI topology state packets to verify the available resources of an ATM network. There is one MCTD value assigned to each traffic class. *See also: MCDV.*

MIB   Management Information Base: Used with SNMP management software to gather information from remote devices. The management station can poll the remote device for information, or the MIB running on the remote station can be programmed to send information on a regular basis.

media   The physical connecting wire or cable found in computer networks.

microsegmentation   The division of a network into smaller segments, usually with the aim of increasing bandwidth.

MIP   Multichannel Interface Processor: The resident interface processor on Cisco 7000 series routers, providing up to two channelized T1 or E1 connections by serial cables connected to a CSU. The two controllers are capable of providing 24 T1 or 30 E1 channel groups, with each group being introduced to the system as a serial interface that can be configured individually.

mips   Millions of Instructions Per Second: A measure of processor speed.

MLP   Multilink PPP: A technique used to split, recombine, and sequence datagrams across numerous logical data links.

MMP   Multichassis Multilink PPP: A protocol that supplies MLP support across multiple routers and access servers. MMP enables several routers and access servers to work as a single, large dial-up pool with one network address and ISDN access number. MMP successfully supports packet fragmenting and reassembly when the user connection is split between two physical access devices.

modem   Modulator-demodulator: A device that converts digital signals to analog and vice versa so that digital information can be transmitted over analog communication facilities, such as voice-grade telephone lines. This is achieved by converting digital signals at the source to analog for transmission, and reconverting the analog signals back into digital form at the destination. *See also: modulation and demodulation.*

modem eliminator   A mechanism that makes possible a connection between two DTE devices without modems.

modulation   The process of modifying some characteristic of an electrical signal, such as amplitude (AM) or frequency (FM), in order to represent digital or analog information. *See also: AM.*

MOSPF Multicast OSPF: An extension of the OSPF unicast protocol that enables IP multicast routing within the domain. *See also: OSPF.*

MPOA Multiprotocol over ATM: An effort by the ATM Forum to standardize how existing and future Network-layer protocols such as IP, Ipv6, AppleTalk, and IPX run over an ATM network with directly attached hosts, routers, and multilayer LAN switches.

MTBF (Mean Time Between Failures) The statistically derived average length of time for which a system component operates before failing. MTBF is expressed in thousands or tens of thousands of hours, also called power-on hours, or POH.

MTU Maximum Transmission Unit: The largest packet size, measured in bytes, that an interface can handle.

multicast Broadly, any communication between a single sender and multiple receivers. Unlike broadcast messages, which are sent to all addresses on a network, multicast messages are sent to a defined subset of the network addresses; this subset has a group multicast address, which is specified in the packet's destination address field. *See also: broadcast.*

multicast address A single address that points to more than one device on the network. Identical to group address. *See also: multicast.*

multicast send VCC A two-directional point-to-point virtual control connection (VCC) arranged by an LEC to a BUS, it is one of the three types of informational link specified by phase 1 LANE. *See also: control distribute VCC and control direct VCC.*

multilayer switch A type of LAN switch, the device filters and forwards packets based on their Layer 2 MAC addresses and Layer 3 network addresses. It's possible that even Layer 4 can be read. *See also: LAN switch.*

multiplexing The process of converting several logical signals into a single physical signal for transmission across one physical channel. *Contrast with: demultiplexing.*

N

NAK Negative acknowledgment: A response sent from a receiver, telling the sender that the information it received contained errors. *Compare with: acknowledgment.*

NAT   Network Address Translation: An algorithm instrumental in minimizing the requirement for globally unique IP addresses, permitting an organization whose addresses are not all globally unique to connect to the Internet, regardless, by translating those addresses into globally routable address space.

native VLAN   An access link is part of one VLAN, and that VLAN is referred to as the native VLAN of the port. Any device attached to an access link is unaware of a VLAN membership—the device just assumes it's part of a broadcast domain, but it has no understanding of the physical network.

NBP   Name Binding Protocol: In AppleTalk, the transport-level protocol that interprets a socket client's name, entered as a character string, into the corresponding DDP address. NBP gives AppleTalk protocols the capacity to discern user-defined zones and names of mechanisms by showing and keeping translation tables that map names to their corresponding socket addresses.

NCP   NetWare Core Protocol. In Novell NetWare, a presentation-layer procedure used by a server when responding to workstation requests. It includes routines for manipulating directories and files, opening semaphores, printing, and creating and destroying service connections.

neighboring routers   Two routers in OSPF that have interfaces to a common network. On networks with multiaccess, these neighboring routers are dynamically discovered using the Hello protocol of OSPF.

NetBEUI   NetBIOS Extended User Interface: An improved version of the NetBIOS protocol used in a number of network operating systems including LAN Manager, Windows NT, LAN Server, and Windows for Workgroups, implementing the OSI LLC2 protocol. NetBEUI formalizes the transport frame—not standardized in NetBIOS—and adds more functions. *See also: OSI.*

NetBIOS   Network Basic Input/Output System: The API employed by applications residing on an IBM LAN to ask for services, such as session termination or information transfer, from lower-level network processes.

NetFlow Switching   A feature of some routers that allows them to categorize incoming packets into flows. Because packets in a flow often can be treated in the same way, this classification can be used to bypass some of the work of the router and accelerate its switching operation.

NetView A mainframe network product from IBM, used for monitoring SNA (Systems Network Architecture) networks. It runs as a VTAM (Virtual Telecommunications Access Method) application.

NetWare A widely used NOS created by Novell, providing a number of distributed network services and remote file access.

Network Campus One of the many modules that make up the Cisco ECNM. The network campus module includes private clients, servers, and network devices.

Network Edge One of the many modules that make up the Cisco ECNM. The Network Edge module includes proxy services, firewalls, VPN servers, and publicly accessible servers.

Network IDS (NIDS) looking over the whole network for a complete intrusion detection system, a NIDS is better at preventing general network attacks than a host-based IDS.

Network layer In the OSI reference model, it is Layer 3—the layer in which routing is implemented, enabling connections and path selection between two end-systems. *See also: Application layer, Data Link layer, Physical layer, Presentation layer, Session layer, and Transport layer.*

network management When designing networks, network management is one of the key factors to the network's overall success. Industry standards allow network management of many different types of networking devices, including routers, bridges, and switches.

network operations center (NOC) Usually a central hub of network engineers and administrators who manage enterprise networks.

Network Time Protocol (NTP) provides a way to ensure that accurate time is kept on all devices. When dealing with attacks, seconds matter because it is important to identify the order in which a specified attack occurred.

Network topology The map of a network. Physical topology describes where the cables are run and where the workstations, nodes, routers, and gateways are located. Networks are usually configured in bus, ring, star, or mesh topologies. Logical topology refers to the paths that messages take to get from one user on the network to another.

NFS Network File System: One of the protocols in Sun Microsystems' widely used file system protocol suite, allowing remote file access across a network. The name is loosely used to refer to the entire Sun protocol suite, which also includes RPC, XDR (External Data Representation), and other protocols.

NHRP Next Hop Resolution Protocol: In a nonbroadcast multiaccess (NBMA) network, the protocol employed by routers in order to dynamically locate MAC addresses of various hosts and routers. It enables systems to communicate directly without requiring an intermediate hop, thus facilitating increased performance in ATM, Frame Relay, X.25, and SMDS systems.

NHS Next Hop Server: Defined by the NHRP protocol, this server maintains the next-hop resolution cache tables, listing IP-to-ATM address maps of related nodes and nodes that can be reached through routers served by the NHS.

NIC Network Interface Card: An electronic circuit board placed in a computer. The NIC provides network communication to a LAN.

NLSP NetWare Link Services Protocol: Novell's link-state routing protocol, based on the IS-IS model.

NMP Network Management Processor: A Catalyst 5000 switch processor module used to control and monitor the switch.

node Any device attached to the network capable of communicating with other network devices. In Novell NetWare documentation, a workstation is often called a node.

non-stub area In OSPF, a resource-consuming area carrying a default route, intra-area routes, interarea routes, static routes, and external routes. Non-stub areas are the only areas that can have virtual links configured across them and exclusively contain an anonymous system boundary router (ASBR). *Compare with: stub area. See also: ASBR and OSPF.*

NRZ Nonreturn to Zero: One of several encoding schemes for transmitting digital data. NRZ signals sustain constant levels of voltage with no signal shifting (no return to zero-voltage level) during a bit interval. If there is a series of bits with the same value (1 or 0), there will be no state change. The signal is not self-clocking. *See also: NRZI.*

NRZI Nonreturn to Zero Inverted: One of several encoding schemes for transmitting digital data. A transition in voltage level (either from high to low or vice versa) at the beginning of a bit interval is interpreted as a value of 1; the absence of a transition is interpreted as a 0. Thus, the voltage assigned to each value is continually inverted. NRZI signals are not self-clocking. *See also: NRZ.*

NVRAM Non-Volatile RAM: Random-access memory that keeps its contents intact while power is turned off.

O

OC Optical Carrier: A series of physical protocols, designated as OC-1, OC-2, OC-3, and so on, for SONET optical signal transmissions. OC signal levels place STS frames on a multimode fiber-optic line at various speeds, of which 51.84Mbps is the lowest (OC-1). Each subsequent protocol runs at a speed divisible by 51.84. *See also: SONET.*

offline operation During offline operation, the host or computer is not connected to the Internet or even possibly to the LAN.

100BaseT Based on the IEEE 802.3 standard, 100BaseT is the Fast Ethernet specification of 100Mbps baseband that uses UTP wiring. 100BaseT sends link pulses (containing more information than those used in 10BaseT) over the network when no traffic is present. *See also: 10BaseT, Fast Ethernet, and IEEE 802.3.*

100BaseTX Based on the IEEE 802.3 standard, 100BaseTX is the 100Mbps baseband Fast Ethernet specification that uses two pairs of UTP or STP wiring. The first pair of wires receives data; the second pair sends data. To ensure correct signal timing, a 100BaseTX segment cannot be longer than 100 meters.

optimum switching One of the NetFlow switching types, optimum switching remains the most efficient switching mode and results in the highest throughput when extensive access list processing is not required.

ones density Also known as pulse density, this is a method of signal clocking. The CSU/DSU retrieves the clocking information from data that passes through it. For this scheme to work, the data needs to be encoded to contain at least one binary 1 for each eight bits transmitted. *See also CSU and DSU.*

OSI   Open System Interconnection: International standardization program designed by ISO and ITU-T for the development of data networking standards that make multivendor equipment interoperability a reality.

OSI reference model   Open System Interconnection reference model: A conceptual model defined by the International Standardization Organization (ISO), describing how any combination of devices can be connected for the purpose of communication. The OSI model divides the task into seven functional layers, forming a hierarchy with the applications at the top and the physical medium at the bottom, and it defines the functions each layer must provide. *See also: Application layer, Session layer, Data Link layer, Network layer, Physical layer, Presentation layer, and Transport layer.*

OSPF   Open Shortest Path First: A link-state, hierarchical IGP routing algorithm derived from an earlier version of the IS-IS protocol, whose features include multipath routing, load balancing, and least-cost routing. OSPF is the suggested successor to RIP in the Internet environment. *See also: enhanced IGRP, IGP, and IP.*

out-of-band management (OOBM)   Management "outside" of the network's physical channels using a console connection.

out-of-band signaling   Within a network, any transmission that uses physical channels or frequencies separate from those ordinarily used for data transfer. For example, the initial configuration of a Cisco Catalyst switch requires an out-of-band connection via a console port.

P

packet   In data communications, the basic logical unit of information transferred. A packet consists of a certain number of data bytes, wrapped or encapsulated in headers and/or trailers that contain information about where the packet came from, where it's going, and so on. The various protocols involved in sending a transmission add their own layers of header information, which the corresponding protocols in receiving devices then interpret.

packetizing   Adding equipment to a network for *packetizing* voice, and the delays inherent in the data network, makes managing delay a critical factor in integrating voice and data networks.

packet switch   A physical device that makes it possible for a communication channel to share several connections, its functions include finding the most efficient transmission path for packets.

packet switching   A networking technology based on the transmission of data in packets. Dividing a continuous stream of data into small units—packets—enables data from multiple devices on a network to share the same communication channel simultaneously but also requires the use of precise routing information. *Contrast with: circuit switching.*

PAP   Password Authentication Protocol: In Point-to-Point Protocol (PPP) networks, a method of validating connection requests. The requesting (remote) device must send an authentication request, containing a password and ID, to the local router when attempting to connect. Unlike the more secure CHAP (Challenge Handshake Authentication Protocol), PAP sends the password unencrypted and does not attempt to verify whether the user is authorized to access the requested resource; it merely identifies the remote end. *See also: CHAP.*

parity checking   A method of error-checking in data transmissions. An extra bit (the parity bit) is added to each character or data word so that the sum of the bits will be either an odd number (in odd parity) or an even number (even parity).

partial mesh   A type of network topology in which some network nodes form a full mesh (where every node has either a physical or a virtual circuit linking it to every other network node), but others are attached to only one or two nodes in the network. A typical use of partial-mesh topology is in peripheral networks linked to a fully meshed backbone. *See also: full mesh.*

path determination   Path determination means that the router knows a route that leads to the desired destination address.

PCR   Peak Cell Rate: As defined by the ATM Forum, the parameter specifying, in cells per second, the maximum rate at which a source may transmit.

PDN   Public Data Network: Generally for a fee, a PDN offers the public access to computer communication network operated by private concerns or government agencies. Small organizations can take advantage of PDNs, aiding them creating WANs without investing in long-distance equipment and circuitry.

Peers   Other network devices or nodes of similar type.

per-destination load balancing   Load balancing can be configured in two different modes. Per-destination load balancing is load balancing based on the destination; it is on by default and must be turned off to enable the other mode, per-packet load balancing.

per-packet load balancing   Load balancing can be configured in two different modes. Per-packet load balancing is based on the packet. The other mode, per-destination load balancing, is on by default and must be turned off to enable per-packet load balancing.

PGP   Pretty Good Privacy: A popular public-key encryption application offering protected transfer of files and messages.

phantom   Used in a Hot Standby Routing Protocol (HSRP) network to provide an IP default gateway address to hosts.

Physical layer   The lowest layer—Layer 1—in the OSI reference model, it is responsible for converting data packets from the Data Link layer (Layer 2) into electrical signals. Physical-layer protocols and standards define, for example, the type of cable and connectors to be used, including their pin assignments and the encoding scheme for signaling 0 and 1 values. *See also: Data Link layer, Network layer, Application layer, Session layer, Presentation layer, and Transport layer.*

ping   Packet internet groper: A Unix-based Internet diagnostic tool, consisting of a message sent to test the accessibility of a particular device on the IP network. The acronym (from which the "full name" was formed) reflects the underlying metaphor of submarine sonar. Just as the sonar operator sends out signal and waits to hear it echo ("ping") back from a submerged object, the network user can ping another node on the network and wait to see if it responds.

pinhole congestion   Some routing protocols base cost on the number of hops to a particular destination. These routing protocols load balance over unequal bandwidth paths as long as the hop count is equal. Once a slow link becomes saturated, however higher capacity links cannot be filled.

pleisochronous   Nearly synchronous, except that clocking comes from an outside source instead of being embedded within the signal as in synchronous transmissions.

PLP   Packet Level Protocol: Occasionally called X.25 Level 3 or X.25 Protocol, a Network-layer protocol that is part of the X.25 stack.

PNNI   Private Network-Network Interface: An ATM Forum specification for offering topology data used for the calculation of paths through the network, among switches and groups of switches. It is based on well-known link-state routing procedures and allows for automatic configuration in networks whose addressing scheme is determined by the topology.

point-to-multipoint connection   In ATM, a communication path going only one way, connecting a single system at the starting point, called the "root node," to systems at multiple points of destination, called "leaves." *See also: point-to-point connection.*

point-to-point connection   In ATM, a channel of communication that can be directed either one way or two ways between two ATM end-systems. *See also: point-to-multipoint connection.*

poison reverse updates   These update messages are transmitted by a router in order to overcome large routing loops and offer explicit information when a subnet or network is not accessible (instead of merely suggesting that the network is unreachable by not including it in updates).

polling   The procedure of orderly inquiry, used by a primary network mechanism, to determine if secondary devices have data to transmit. A message is sent to each secondary, granting the secondary the right to transmit.

POP   1. Point Of Presence: The physical location where an interexchange carrier has placed equipment to interconnect with a local exchange carrier.

2. Post Office Protocol: A protocol used by client e-mail applications for recovery of mail from a mail server.

port number   The default identifier for a TCP/IP (Transmission Control Protocol/Internet Protocol) or Internet process.

For example, ftp (File Transport Protocol), HTML (HyperText Markup Language), and Telnet are all available at preassigned unique port numbers so that the computer knows how to respond when it is contacted on a specific port; Web servers use port 80, and SMTP (Simple Mail Transfer Protocol) e-mail is always delivered to port 25. You can override these defaults by specifying different values in a URL, but whether they will work depends on the configuration on the target system.

A total of 65,535 port numbers are available for use with TCP, and the same number are available for UDP (User Datagram Protocol).

PPP   Point-to-Point Protocol: The protocol most commonly used for dial-up Internet access, superseding the earlier SLIP. Its features include address notification, authentication via CHAP or PAP, support for multiple protocols, and link monitoring. PPP has two layers: the Link Control Protocol (LCP) establishes, configures, and tests a link; and then any of various Network Control Protocols (NCPs) transport traffic for a specific protocol suite, such as IPX. *See also: CHAP, PAP, and SLIP.*

Presentation layer   Layer 6 of the OSI reference model, it defines how data is formatted, presented, encoded, and converted for use by software at the Application layer. *See also: Application layer, Data Link layer, Network layer, Physical layer, Session layer, and Transport layer.*

PRI   Primary Rate Interface: A type of ISDN connection between a PBX and a long-distance carrier, which is made up of a single 64Kbps D channel in addition to 23 (T1) or 30 (E1) B channels. *See also: ISDN.*

priority queueing   A routing function in which frames temporarily placed in an interface output queue are assigned priorities based on traits such as packet size or type of interface. Also referred to as PQ.

private addresses   IP addresses that are reserved and blocked on the Internet so they can be used on private networks. *See also: IP address.*

private branch exchange (PBX)   A private branch exchange (PBX) is essentially a telephone switch used by private enterprises, where public telephone switches are owned and operated by telephone companies.

Private IP v4 addresses   According to RFC1918, IP addresses that should be used in private networks. 10.0.0.0/8, 172.16.0.0 to 172.16.31.255/16 and 192.168.0.0/16

process switching   As a packet arrives on a router to be forwarded, it's copied to the router's process buffer, and the router performs a lookup on the Layer 3 address. Using the route table, an exit interface is associated with the destination address. The processor forwards the packet with the added new information to the exit interface, while the router initializes the fast-switching cache. Subsequent packets bound for the same destination address follow the same path as the first packet.

PROM   Programmable read-only memory: ROM that is programmable only once, using special equipment. *Compare with: EPROM.*

protocol analyzer   A hardware or combined hardware and software product used to analyze the performance data of the network and to find and troubleshoot network problems.

Protocol analyzers vary greatly in complexity. Some use dedicated hardware and can decode as many as 150 protocols; others convert an existing networked PC into a network-specific analyzer.

propagation delay   The time it takes data to traverse a network from its source to its destination.

protocol   In networking, the specification of a set of rules for a particular type of communication. The term is also used to refer to the software that implements a protocol.

protocol data unit (PDU)   The processes at each layer of the OSI model. PDUs at the Transport layer are called *segments*, PDUs at the Network layer are called *packets* or *datagrams*, and PDUs at the Data Link layer are called *frames*. The Physical layer uses bits.

protocol stack   A collection of related protocols.

Proxy ARP   Proxy ARP means that a particular machine (such as a router) will respond to ARP requests for hosts other than itself. This can be used to make a router disappear from the workstations on a network and eliminate configuration of the workstations.

proxy services   A software package running on a server positioned between an internal network and the Internet. The proxy server filters all outgoing connections so that they appear to be coming from the same machine, in an attempt to conceal the underlying internal network structure from any intruders. By disguising the real structure of the network, the proxy server makes it much more difficult for an intruder to mount a successful attack.

A proxy server will also forward your requests to the Internet, intercept the response, and then forward the response to you at your network node. A system administrator can also regulate the external sites to which users can connect.

PSE   Packet Switch Exchange: The X.25 term for a switch.

PSN   Packet-switched Network: Any network that uses packet-switching technology. Also known as packet-switched data network (PSDN). *See also: packet switching.*

public switched telephone network (PSTN)   Colloquially referred to as plain old telephone service (POTS). A term that describes the assortment of telephone networks and services available globally.

PVC   Permanent Virtual Circuit: In a frame-relay network, a logical connection, defined in software, that is maintained permanently. *Compare with: SVC. See also: virtual circuit.*

PVP   Permanent Virtual Path: A virtual path made up of PVCs. *See also: PVC.*

PVP tunneling   Permanent Virtual Path Tunneling: A technique that links two private ATM networks across a public network using a virtual path, wherein the public network transparently trunks the complete collection of virtual channels in the virtual path between the two private networks.

Q

QoS   Quality of Service: A set of metrics used to measure the quality of transmission and service availability of any given transmission system.

queue   Broadly, any list of elements arranged in an orderly fashion and ready for processing, such as a line of people waiting to enter a movie theater. In routing, it refers to a backlog of information packets waiting in line to be transmitted over a router interface.

R

RARP   Reverse Address Resolution Protocol: The protocol within the TCP/IP stack that maps MAC addresses to IP addresses. *See also: ARP.*

rate queue   A value, assigned to one or more virtual circuits, that specifies the speed at which an individual virtual circuit will transmit data to the remote end. Every rate queue identifies a segment of the total bandwidth available on an ATM link. The sum of all rate queues should not exceed the total available bandwidth.

RCP   Remote Copy Protocol: A protocol for copying files to or from a file system that resides on a remote server on a network, using TCP to guarantee reliable data delivery.

redistribution   Command used in Cisco routers to inject the paths found from one type of routing protocol into another type of routing protocol. For example, networks found by RIP can be inserted into an IGRP network.

redundancy   In internetworking, the duplication of connections, devices, or services that can be used as a backup in the event that the primary connections, devices, or services fail.

reload   An event or command that causes Cisco routers to reboot.

repeater   A simple hardware device that moves all packets from one local-area network segment to another by regenerating, retiming, and amplifying the electrical signals.
   The main purpose of a repeater is to extend the length of the network transmission medium beyond the normal maximum cable lengths.

RIF   Routing Information Field: In source-route bridging, a header field that defines the path direction of the frame or Token (left to right or right to left). It is also defined as part of a MAC header for source-routed frames, which contains path information. This bit is used in an explorer frame to notify computers that it is on its return path.

ring   Two or more stations connected in a logical circular topology. In this topology, which is the basis for Token Ring, FDDI, and CDDI, information is transferred from station to station in sequence.

ring topology   A network logical topology comprising a series of repeaters that form one closed loop by connecting unidirectional transmission links. Individual stations on the network are connected to the network at a repeater. Physically, ring topologies are generally organized in a closed-loop star. *Compare with: bus topology and star topology.*

RFP   (Request for Purchase) A document issued by a customer to the network designer who then creates a design document.

RIP   Routing Information Protocol: The most commonly used interior gateway protocol in the Internet. RIP employs hop count as a routing metric. *See also: Enhanced IGRP, IGP, OSPF, and hop count.*

RMON   Remote Monitoring is a standard monitoring specification that enables various network monitors and console systems to exchange network-monitoring data. RMON provides network administrators with more freedom in selecting network-monitoring probes and consoles with features that meet their particular networking needs.

routed protocol   Routed protocols (such as IP and IPX) are used to transmit user data through an internetwork. By contrast, routing protocols (such as RIP, IGRP, and OSPF) are used to update routing tables between routers.

route summarization   In OSPF and IS-IS, the consolidation of publicized addresses so that a single summary route is advertised to other areas by an area border router.

router   A Network-layer mechanism, either software or hardware, using one or more metrics to decide on the best path to use for transmission of network traffic. Sending packets between networks by routers is based on the information provided on Network layers. Historically, this device has sometimes been called a gateway.

routing   The process of locating a path to the destination host. In large networks, the numerous intermediary destinations a packet might travel before reaching its destination can make routing very complex.

routing domain   Any collection of end systems and intermediate systems that operate under an identical set of administrative rules. Every routing domain contains one or several areas, all individually given a certain area address.

routing loops   Routing algorithms that converge slowly can cause routing loops or network outages whereby routers continue to send updates after a route has gone down.

routing metric   Any value that is used by routing algorithms to determine whether one route is superior to another. Metrics include such information as bandwidth, delay, hop count, path cost, load, MTU, reliability, and communication cost, all of which is stored in routing tables. *See also: cost.*

routing protocol   Any protocol that defines algorithms to be used for updating routing tables between routers. Examples include IGRP, RIP, and OSPF.

routing table   A table kept in a router or other internetworking mechanism that maintains a record of routes to certain network destinations and the metrics associated with those routes.

RP   Route Processor: Also known as a supervisory processor, a module on Cisco 7000 series routers that holds the CPU, system software, and most of the memory components used in the router.

RSP   Route/Switch Processor: A processor module combining the functions of RP and SP used in Cisco 7500 series routers. *See also: RP and SP.*

RSVP   (Resource Reservation Protocol) An Internet protocol designed to deliver data on time and in the right order over TCP/IP networks. RSVP is a control and signaling protocol, not a routing protocol, and it works by reserving bandwidth from one end system to another; this reduces the bandwidth available to other users.

RTP   (Real-time Transport Protocol) creates a priority queue on a Frame PVC for a set of RTP packet flows.

RTS   Request To Send: An EIA/TIA-232 control signal requesting permission to transmit data on a communication line.

S

SAA   (Service Assurance Agents) used by Cisco's service level management suite for such things as software and hardware probes, and to track service levels for a broad range of network services.

SAFE   Cisco's (security blueprint for enterprise networks) is a recommended guideline used by network designers and engineers to secure data networks.

sampling rate   The rate at which samples of a specific waveform amplitude are collected.

SAP   1. Service Access Point: A field specified by IEEE 802.2 that is part of an address specification.

2. Service Advertisement Protocol: The Novell NetWare protocol that supplies a way to inform network clients of resources and services availability on network, using routers and servers. *See also: IPX.*

scalability   The ability of an operating system to add system resources to provide faster processing or to handle increased loads in anticipation of future needs.

In practice, this usually means that an operating system is available on a range of increasingly capable hardware, with only modest increases in price at each level.

SCR   Sustainable Cell Rate: An ATM Forum parameter used for traffic management, it is the long-term average cell rate for VBR connections that can be transmitted.

SDLC   Synchronous Data Link Control: A protocol used in SNA Data Link layer communications. SDLC is a bit-oriented, full-duplex serial protocol that is the basis for several similar protocols, including HDLC and LAPB. *See also: HDLC and LAPB.*

Secure Shell Protocol   (SSH) is a common remote administrative terminal access protocol and is a recommended replacement for Telnet since it does not send passwords in clear text.

Secure Sockets Layer   (SSL) An interface originally developed by Netscape that provides encrypted data transfer between client and server applications over the Internet.

SSL works at the network level and so can be used by any SSL-compliant application. Applications that use SSL use RSA public key encryption and digital signatures to establish the identity of the two parties in the transaction.

seed router   In an AppleTalk network, the router that is equipped with the network number or cable range in its port descriptor. The seed router specifies the network number or cable range for other routers in that network section and answers to configuration requests from nonseed routers on its connected AppleTalk network, permitting those routers to affirm or modify their configurations accordingly. Every AppleTalk network needs at least one seed router.

segmentation   The breaking up of collision and broadcast domains using routers, bridges, and switches.

Serialization   The process of converting data for transport across a WAN serial link, which can cause traffic delays at a router's egress port.

server   Hardware and software that provide network services to clients.

service provider   A term used to define a company that connects your network to the Internet.

Session layer   Layer 5 of the OSI reference model, responsible for creating, managing, and terminating sessions between applications and overseeing data exchange between Presentation layer entities. *See also: Application layer, Data Link layer, Network layer, Physical layer, Presentation layer, and Transport layer.*

SF   Super Frame: A super frame (also called a D4 frame) consists of 12 frames with 192 bits each, with the 193rd bit providing other functions including error checking. SF is frequently used on T1 circuits. A newer version of the technology is Extended Super Frame (ESF), which uses 24 frames. *See also: ESF.*

signaling packet   An informational packet created by an ATM-connected mechanism that wants to establish connection with another such mechanism. The packet contains the QoS parameters needed for connection and the ATM NSAP address of the endpoint. The endpoint responds with a message of acceptance, if it is able to support the desired QoS, and the connection is established. *See also: QoS.*

Signaling System 7   The SS7 protocol uses out-of-band signaling to establish the appropriate path for the call through the carrier network, before establishing the actual transmission path. Many modern PBXs support the SS7 protocol. This enables each PBX to make and process requests from the Telco network.

significant bits   The important bits of a number.

silicon switching   A type of high-speed switching used in Cisco 7000 series routers, based on the use of a separate processor (the Silicon Switch Processor, or SSP). *See also: SSE.*

SLA   (Service Level Agreement) CiscoWorks2000 Service Level Manager allows network administrators to define and monitor service-level agreements (SLAs) specifying traffic type, endpoints, and thresholds against key parameters such as latency, packet loss, and jitter.

SLC   (Service-Level Contract) CiscoWorks2000 includes (*SLCs*) and the service-level agreements (*SLAs*) associated with them, which allows administrators to define the level of service required in a voice network. Business and technical reports can be generated at both detailed and summary levels to demonstrate performance against those SLCs and SLAs.

sliding window   The method of flow control used by TCP, as well as several Data Link layer protocols. This method places a buffer between the receiving application and the network data flow. The "window" available for accepting data is the size of the buffer minus the amount of data already there. This window increases in size as the application reads data from it and decreases as new data is sent. The receiver sends the transmitter announcements of the current window size, and it may stop accepting data until the window increases above a certain threshold.

SLIP   Serial Line Internet Protocol: A variation of TCP/IP used as an industry standard for point-to-point connections. SLIP is the predecessor to PPP. *See also: PPP.*

SLM   (Service Level Manager) CiscoWorks2000 (*SLM*) allows network administrators to define and monitor service-level agreements (SLAs) specifying traffic type, endpoints, and thresholds against key parameters such as latency, packet loss, and jitter.

SMDS   Switched Multimegabit Data Service: A packet-switched, datagram-based WAN networking technology offered by telephone companies that provides high speed.

SMTP   Simple Mail Transfer Protocol: A protocol used on the Internet to provide electronic mail services.

SNA   System Network Architecture: A complex, feature-rich, network architecture similar to the OSI reference model but with several variations; created by IBM in the 1970s and essentially composed of seven layers.

SNAP   Subnetwork Access Protocol: SNAP is a frame used in Ethernet, Token Ring, and FDDI LANs. Data transfer, connection management, and QoS selection are three primary functions executed by the SNAP frame.

SNMP   A standard protocol, part of the TCP/IP protocol suite, used to manage and monitor nodes on a network. SNMP is a communications protocol for collecting information about devices on the network, including hubs, routers, and bridges. Each piece of information to be collected about a device is defined in a Management Information Base (MIB). SNMP uses UDP (User Datagram Protocol) to send and receive messages on the network.

socket   1. A software structure that operates within a network device as a destination point for communications.

2. In AppleTalk networks, an entity at a specific location within a node; AppleTalk sockets are conceptually similar to TCP/IP ports.

SONET   Synchronous Optical Network: The ANSI standard for synchronous transmission on fiber-optic media, developed at Bell Labs. It specifies a base signal rate of 51.84Mbps and a set of multiples of that rate, known as Optical Carrier levels, up to 2.5Gbps.

SP   Switch Processor: Also known as a ciscoBus controller, it is a Cisco 7000 series processor module acting as governing agent for all CxBus activities.

span   A full-duplex digital transmission line connecting two facilities.

SPAN   Switched Port Analyzer: A feature of the Catalyst 5000 switch, offering freedom to manipulate within a switched Ethernet environment by extending the monitoring ability of the existing network analyzers into the environment. At one switched segment, the SPAN mirrors traffic onto a predetermined SPAN port, while a network analyzer connected to the SPAN port is able to monitor traffic from any other Catalyst switched port.

spanning explorer packet   Sometimes called limited-route or single-route explorer packet, it pursues a statically configured spanning tree when searching for paths in a source-route bridging network. *See also: all-routes explorer packet, explorer packet, and local explorer packet.*

spanning tree   A subset of a network topology, within which no loops exist. When bridges are interconnected into a loop, the bridge, or switch, cannot identify a frame that has been forwarded previously, so there is no mechanism for removing a frame as it passes the interface numerous times. Without a method of removing these frames, the bridges continuously forward them—consuming bandwidth and adding overhead to the network. Spanning trees prune the network to provide only one path for any packet. *See also: Spanning Tree Protocol and Spanning Tree Algorithm.*

Spanning Tree Algorithm (STA)   An algorithm that creates a spanning tree using the Spanning Tree Protocol (STP). *See also: spanning tree and Spanning Tree Protocol.*

Spanning Tree Protocol (STP)   The bridge protocol (IEEE 802.1) that enables a learning bridge to dynamically avoid loops in the network topology by creating a spanning tree using the Spanning Tree Algorithm. Spanning tree frames called *bridge protocol data units* (BPDUs) are sent and received by all switches in the network at regular intervals. The switches participating in the spanning tree don't forward the frames; instead, they're processed to determine the spanning tree topology itself. Cisco Catalyst series switches use STP 802.1d to perform this function. *See also: BPDU, learning bridge, MAC address, spanning tree, and Spanning Tree Algorithm.*

SPF   Shortest Path First algorithm: A routing algorithm used to decide on the shortest-path spanning tree. Sometimes called Dijkstra's algorithm and frequently used in link-state routing algorithms. *See also: link-state routing algorithm.*

SPID   Service Profile Identifier: A number assigned by service providers or local telephone companies and assigned by administrators to a BRI port. SPIDs are used to determine subscription services of a device connected via ISDN. ISDN devices use SPID when accessing the telephone company switch that initializes the link to a service provider.

split-horizon updates   Useful for preventing routing loops, a type of distance-vector routing protocol where information about routes is prevented from leaving the router interface through which that information was received.

spoofing   1. In dial-on-demand routing (DDR), where a circuit-switched link is taken down to save toll charges when there is no traffic to be sent, spoofing is a scheme used by routers that causes a host to treat an interface as if it were functioning and supporting a session. The router sends "spoof" replies to keep-alive messages from the host in an effort to convince the host that the session is up and running. *See also: DDR.*

2. The illegal act of sending a packet labeled with a false address, in order to deceive network security mechanisms such as filters and access lists.

spooler   A management application that processes requests submitted to it for execution in a sequential fashion from a queue. A good example is a print spooler.

SPX   Sequenced Packet Exchange: A Novell NetWare transport protocol that augments the datagram service provided by Network layer (Layer 3) protocols, it was derived from the Switch-to-Switch Protocol of the XNS protocol suite.

SQE Signal Quality Error: In an Ethernet network, a message sent from a transceiver to an attached machine that the collision-detection circuitry is working.

SRB Source-Route Bridging: Created by IBM, the bridging method used in Token Ring networks. The source determines the entire route to a destination before sending the data and includes that information in fields within each packet. *Contrast with: transparent bridging.*

SRT Source-Route Transparent bridging: A bridging scheme developed by IBM, merging source-route and transparent bridging. SRT takes advantage of both technologies in one device, fulfilling the needs of all end nodes. Translation between bridging protocols is not necessary. *Compare with: SR/TLB.*

SR/TLB Source-Route Translational Bridging: A bridging method that allows source-route stations to communicate with transparent bridge stations aided by an intermediate bridge that translates between the two bridge protocols. Used for bridging between Token Ring and Ethernet. *Compare with: SRT.*

SSAP Source Service Access Point: The SAP of the network node identified in the Source field of the packet. *See also: DSAP and SAP.*

SSE Silicon Switching Engine: The software component of Cisco's silicon switching technology, hard-coded into the Silicon Switch Processor (SSP). Silicon switching is available only on the Cisco 7000 with an SSP. Silicon-switched packets are compared to the silicon-switching cache on the SSE. The SSP is a dedicated switch processor that offloads the switching process from the route processor, providing a fast-switching solution, but packets must still traverse the backplane of the router to get to the SSP and then back to the exit interface.

Standby Monitor In a Token Ring network, a network node that serves as a backup to the Active Monitor and can take over in the event that the Active Monitor fails.

star topology A LAN physical topology with end points on the network converging at a common central switch (known as a hub) using point-to-point links. A logical ring topology can be configured as a physical star topology using a unidirectional closed-loop star rather than point-to-point links. That is, connections within the hub are arranged in an internal ring. *See also: bus topology and ring topology.*

startup range   If an AppleTalk node does not have a number saved from the last time it was booted, then the node selects from this range of values—from 65280 to 65534.

static addressing   Static addressing provides for a fixed address assigned by an administrator to a network interface.

static route   A route whose information is purposefully entered into the routing table and takes priority over those chosen by dynamic routing protocols.

static VLAN   VLAN port membership assigned to each switch port individually by an administrator.

statistical multiplexing   Multiplexing in general is a technique that allows data from multiple logical channels to be sent across a single physical channel. Statistical multiplexing dynamically assigns bandwidth only to input channels that are active, optimizing available bandwidth so that more devices can be connected than with other multiplexing techniques. Also known as statistical time-division multiplexing or stat mux.

STM-1   Synchronous Transport Module Level 1. In the European SDH standard, one of many formats identifying the frame structure for the 155.52Mbps lines that are used to carry ATM cells.

store-and-forward packet switching   A technique in which the switch first copies each packet into its buffer and performs a cyclic redundancy check (CRC). If the packet is error-free, the switch then looks up the destination address in its filter table, determines the appropriate exit port, and sends the packet.

STP   1. Shielded Twisted Pair: A two-pair wiring scheme, used in many network implementations, that has a layer of shielded insulation to reduce EMI. 2. Spanning Tree Protocol.

stub area   An OSPF area carrying a default route, intra-area routes, and interarea routes, but no external routes. Configuration of virtual links cannot be achieved across a stub area, and stub areas are not allowed to contain an ASBR. *See also: non-stub area, ASBR, and OSPF.*

stub network   A network having only one connection to a router.

STUN   Serial Tunnel: A technology used to connect an HDLC link to an SDLC link over a serial link.

subarea   A portion of an SNA network made up of a subarea node and its attached links and peripheral nodes.

subarea node   An SNA communications host or controller that handles entire network addresses.

subchannel   A frequency-based subdivision that creates a separate broad-band communications channel.

subinterface   One of many virtual interfaces available on a single physical interface.

subnet   *See: subnetwork.*

subnet address   The portion of an IP address that is specifically identified by the subnet mask as the subnetwork. *See also: IP address, subnetwork, and subnet mask.*

subnet mask   Also simply known as mask, a 32-bit address mask used in IP to identify the bits of an IP address that are used for the subnet address. Using a mask, the router does not need to examine all 32 bits, only those selected by the mask. *See also: address mask and IP address.*

subnetting   The process of configuring an IP address network mask to create more usable addresses.

subnetwork   1. Any network that is part of a larger IP network and is identified by a subnet address. A network administrator segments a network into subnetworks in order to provide a hierarchical, multilevel routing structure, and at the same time protect the subnetwork from the addressing complexity of networks that are attached. Also known as a subnet. *See also: IP address, subnet mask, and subnet address.*

2. In OSI networks, the term specifically refers to a collection of ESs and ISs controlled by only one administrative domain, using a solitary network connection protocol.

SVC   Switched Virtual Circuit: A dynamically established virtual circuit, created on demand and dissolved as soon as transmission is over and the circuit is no longer needed. In ATM terminology, it is referred to as a switched virtual connection. *See also: PVC.*

switch   1. In networking, a device responsible for multiple functions such as filtering, flooding, and sending frames. It works using the destination address of individual frames. Switches operate at the Data Link layer of the OSI model.
2. Broadly, any electronic/mechanical device allowing connections to be established as needed and terminated if no longer necessary.

switched LAN   Any LAN implemented using LAN switches. *See also: LAN switch.*

switch fabric   A group of connected switches that share the same VLAN database.

synchronous transmission   Signals transmitted digitally with precision clocking. These signals have identical frequencies and contain individual characters encapsulated in control bits (called start/stop bits) that designate the beginning and ending of each character. *See also: asynchronous transmission and isochronous transmission.*

T

T1   Digital WAN that uses 24 DS0s to create a bandwidth of 1.544Mbps.

T3   Digital WAN that can provide bandwidth of 44.763Mbps.

Terminal Access Controller Access Control System Plus   (TACACS+) Allows network administrators to centrally manage terminal access to Cisco network devices.

tag switching   Based on the concept of label swapping, where packets or cells are designated to defined-length labels that control the manner in which data is to be sent, tag switching is a high-performance technology used for forwarding packets. It incorporates Data Link layer (Layer 2) switching and Network layer (Layer 3) routing and supplies scalable, high-speed switching in the network core.

tagged traffic ATM cells with their cell loss priority (CLP) bit set to 1. Also referred to as discard-eligible (DE) traffic. Tagged traffic can be eliminated in order to ensure trouble-free delivery of higher priority traffic, if the network is congested. *See also: CLP.*

TCP Transmission Control Protocol: A connection-oriented protocol that is defined at the Transport layer of the OSI reference model. Provides reliable delivery of data.

TCP/IP Transmission Control Protocol/Internet Protocol. The suite of protocols underlying the Internet. TCP and IP are the most widely known protocols in that suite. *See also: IP and TCP.*

TDM Time-Division Multiplexing: A technique for assigning bandwidth on a single wire, based on preassigned time slots, to data from several channels. Bandwidth is allotted to each channel regardless of a station's ability to send data. *See also: ATDM, FDM, and multiplexing.*

TE1 A device with a four-wire, twisted-pair digital interface is referred to as terminal equipment type one. Most modern ISDN devices are of this type.

TE Terminal Equipment: Any peripheral device that is ISDN-compatible and attached to a network, such as a telephone or computer.

telco A common abbreviation for the telephone company.

Telnet The standard terminal emulation protocol within the TCP/IP protocol stack. Method of remote terminal connection, enabling users to log in on remote networks and use those resources as if they were locally connected. Telnet is defined in RFC 854.

10BaseT Part of the IEEE 802.3 standard, 10BaseT is the Ethernet specification of 10Mbps baseband that uses two pairs of twisted-pair, Category 3, 4, or 5 cabling—one pair to send data and the other to receive. 10BaseT has a distance limit of about 100 meters per segment. *See also: Ethernet and IEEE 802.3.*

terminal adapter A hardware interface between a computer and an ISDN line. In effect, an ISDN modem.

terminal emulation The use of software, installed on a PC or LAN server, that allows the PC to function as if it were a "dumb" terminal directly attached to a particular type of mainframe.

TFTP   The stripped-down version of FTP, it's the protocol of choice if you know exactly what you want and where it's to be found. TFTP doesn't give you the abundance of functions that FTP does. In particular, it has no directory browsing abilities; it can do nothing but send and receive files.

three-part firewall   The classic firewall system, called a "three-part firewall," has three specialized layers:

An isolation LAN that is a buffer between the corporate internetwork and the outside world. (The isolation LAN is called the DMZ.)

A router that acts as an inside packet filter between the corporate internetwork and the isolation LAN.

Another router that acts as an outside packet filter between the isolation LAN and the outside internetwork.

thrashing   If you have multiple links between switches and are not running the STP protocol, the MAC address filter table of the switch will be totally confused about a source device's location because the switch can receive the same frame from more than one link. The switch can get so caught up in constantly updating the MAC filter table with source hardware address locations that it fails to forward a frame. This is called *thrashing* the MAC table.

Tie-line   A part of traditional voice architecture, tie-lines are the connections between PBX switches.

token   A frame containing only control information. Possessing this control information gives a network device permission to transmit data onto the network. *See also: token passing.*

token bus   LAN architecture that is the basis for the IEEE 802.4 LAN specification and employs token passing access over a bus topology. *See also: IEEE.*

token passing   A method used by network devices to access the physical medium in a systematic way based on possession of a small frame called a token. *Contrast with: circuit switching. See also: token.*

Token Ring   IBM's token-passing LAN technology. It runs at 4Mbps or 16Mbps over a ring topology. Defined formally by IEEE 802.5. *See also: ring topology and token passing.*

ToS   (Type of Service) A field in the IP header that allows traffic to be tagged as voice and payload size to test effectiveness of QoS policies.

totally stubby area   OSPF defines a totally stubby area as one that blocks external routes and summary routes (inter-area routes) from going into the area. This way, intra-area routes and the default of 0.0.0.0 are the only routes injected into that area.

traffic shaping   Often used with Frame Relay, traffic shaping applies to both PVCs and SVCs. This allows network designers and engineers to control the amount of data traffic sent onto a Frame Relay circuit.

transparent bridging   The bridging scheme used in Ethernet and IEEE 802.3 networks, it passes frames along one hop at a time, using routing information stored in tables that associate end nodes within bridge ports. This type of bridging is considered transparent because the source node doesn't need to know the entire route, as it does with source-route bridging. *Contrast with: SRB.*

Transport layer   Layer 4 of the OSI reference model, used for reliable communication between end nodes over the network. The Transport layer provides mechanisms used for establishing, maintaining, and terminating virtual circuits, transport fault detection and recovery, and controlling the flow of information. *See also: Data Link layer, Application layer, Physical layer, Network layer, Presentation layer, and Session layer.*

Trap Message   A function of a SNMP trap, it is used to notify a network management station that an extraordinary event has occurred at an agent. When a trap condition occurs, the SNMP agent sends an SNMP agent trap message to each of the network management stations as specified in the trap receiver table.

TRIP   Token Ring Interface Processor: A high-speed interface processor used on Cisco 7000 series routers. The TRIP provides two or four ports for interconnection with IEEE 802.5 and IBM media with ports set to speeds of either 4Mbps or 16Mbps set independently of each other.

Trunk   A part of traditional voice architecture, trunks are the lines that feed tie-lines.

TTL   Time To Live: A field in an IP header, indicating the length of time a packet is valid.

TUD   Trunk Up-Down: A protocol used in ATM networks for the monitoring of trunks. Should a trunk miss a given number of test messages being sent by ATM switches to ensure trunk line quality, TUD declares the trunk down. When a trunk reverses direction and comes back up, TUD recognizes that the trunk is up and returns the trunk to service.

tunneling   A method of avoiding protocol restrictions by wrapping packets from one protocol in another protocol's packet and transmitting this encapsulated packet over a network that supports the wrapper protocol. *See also: encapsulation.*

U

UDP   User Datagram Protocol: A connectionless Transport layer protocol in the TCP/IP protocol stack that simply allows datagrams to be exchanged without acknowledgments or delivery guarantees, requiring other protocols to handle error processing and retransmission. UDP is defined in RFC 768.

unnumbered frames   HDLC frames used for control management purposes, such as link startup and shutdown or mode specification.

update interval   Typically used with routing protocols, update interval specifies the time between route updates.

uptime   The length or percentage of time during which a computer system is functioning and available for use.

V

VBR   Variable Bit Rate: A QoS class, as defined by the ATM Forum, for use in ATM networks that is subdivided into real time (RT) class and non–real time (NRT) class. RT is employed when connections have a fixed timing relationship between samples. Conversely, NRT is employed when connections do not have a fixed time relationship between samples, but still need an assured QoS.

VCC   Virtual Channel Connection: A logical circuit that is created by VCLs. VCCs carry data between two endpoints in an ATM network. Sometimes called a virtual circuit connection.

VIP   1. Versatile Interface Processor: An interface card for Cisco 7000 and 7500 series routers, providing multilayer switching and running the Cisco IOS software. The most recent version of VIP is VIP2.

2. Virtual IP: A function making it possible for logically separated switched IP workgroups to run Virtual Networking Services across the switch ports of a Catalyst 5000.

virtual circuit   Abbreviated VC, a logical circuit devised to assure reliable communication between two devices on a network. Defined by a virtual path connection (VPC)/virtual path identifier (VCI) pair, a virtual circuit can be permanent (PVC) or switched (SVC). Virtual circuits are used in Frame Relay and X.25. Known as virtual channel in ATM. *See also: PVC and SVC.*

virtual ring   In an SRB network, a logical connection between physical rings, either local or remote.

VLAN   Virtual LAN: A group of devices on one or more logically segmented LANs (configured by use of management software), enabling devices to communicate as if attached to the same physical medium, when they are actually located on numerous different LAN segments. VLANs are based on logical instead of physical connections and thus are tremendously flexible.

VLSM   Variable-Length Subnet Mask: Helps optimize available address space and specify a different subnet mask for the same network number on various subnets.

Voice over ATM   (VoATM) The design and use of voice traffic using ATM networks.

Voice over Frame Relay   (VoFR) The design and use of voice traffic using Frame Relay networks.

VoIP   (Voice over IP) The design and use of voice conversations over IP networks.

W

wide-area network   Abbreviated WAN. A network that connects users across large distances, often crossing the geographical boundaries of cities or states.

wildcard mask   A 32-bit quantity used in conjunction with an IP address to determine which bits in an IP address should be ignored when comparing that address with another IP address. A wildcard mask is specified when setting up access lists.

WinSock   Windows Socket Interface: A software interface that makes it possible for an assortment of applications to use and share an Internet connection. The WinSock software consists of a Dynamic Link Library (DLL) with supporting programs such as a dialer program that initiates the connection.

workgroup switching   A switching method that supplies high-speed (100Mbps) transparent bridging between Ethernet networks as well as high-speed translational bridging between Ethernet and CDDI or FDDI.

X

X.25   An ITU-T standard that defines communication between DTE and DCE network devices. X.25 uses a reliable Data Link layer protocol called LAPB. X.25 also uses PLP at the Network layer. X.25 has mostly been replaced by Frame Relay.

X Window   A windowing environment developed at MIT for Unix workstations. Often referred to simply as X.

X Window is an open and nonproprietary bit-mapped graphics system, designed to be independent of both the display hardware and the underlying operating system. It is supported by all the major workstation vendors.

X Window implements a client/server environment, but with the sense of the terms reversed from today's common usage.

Z

ZIP   Zone Information Protocol: A Session-layer protocol used by AppleTalk to map network numbers to zone names. NBP uses ZIP in the determination of networks containing nodes that belong to a zone. *See also: ZIP storm and zone.*

ZIP storm   A broadcast storm occurring when a router running Apple-Talk reproduces or transmits a route for which there is no corresponding zone name at the time of execution. The route is then forwarded by other routers downstream, thus causing a ZIP storm. *See also: broadcast storm and ZIP.*

zone   A logical grouping of network devices in AppleTalk. *See also: ZIP.*

Index

Note to the reader: Throughout this index **boldfaced** page numbers indicate primary discussions of a topic. *Italicized* page numbers indicate illustrations.

I

J

K

N

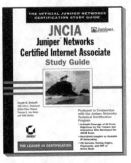
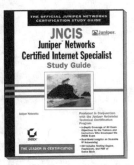
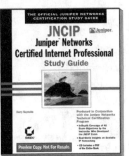
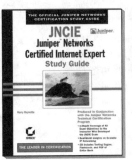

TELL US WHAT YOU THINK!

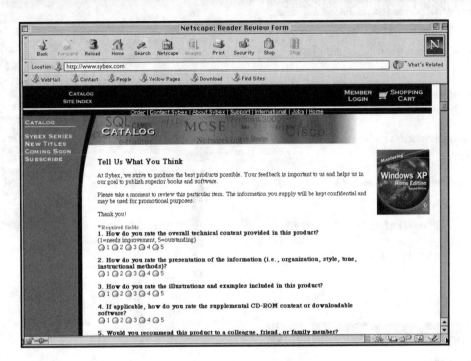

Your feedback is critical to our efforts to provide you with the best books and software on the market. Tell us what you think about the products you've purchased. It's simple:

1. Go to the Sybex website.
2. Find your book by typing the ISBN or title into the Search field.
3. Click on the book title when it appears.
4. Click **Submit a Review.**
5. Fill out the questionnaire and comments.
6. Click **Submit.**

With your feedback, we can continue to publish the highest quality computer books and software products that today's busy IT professionals deserve.

www.sybex.com

SYBEX Inc. • 1151 Marina Village Parkway, Alameda, CA 94501 • 510-523-8233

The Complete Cisco Certification Solution

CCNA: Cisco Certified Networking Associate

For the CCNA Exam, #640-607

CCNA: Cisco Certified Network Associate Study Guide, 3rd Edition
ISBN: 0-7821-4167-6 · $49.99

CCNA: Cisco Certified Network Associate Study Guide, Deluxe Edition,
2nd Edition · ISBN: 0-7821-4169-2 · $89.99

CCNA : Cisco Certified Network Associate Exam Notes
ISBN: 0-7821-4168-4 · $29.99

CCNA Certification Kit, 2nd Edition · ISBN: 0-7821-4170-6
$159.99

CCNA Virtual Lab, Gold Edition · ISBN: 0-7821-3018-6 · $149.99

CCNA Virtual Training Certification Kit · ISBN: 0-7821-3033-X
$139.99

CCNP: Cisco Certified Networking Professional*

*Prerequisite: Valid CCNA certification

CCNP/CCIP: BSCI Study Guide, 2nd Edition · ISBN: 0-7821-4293-1 ·
$49.99
Building Scalable Cisco Internetworks Exam #642-801

CCNP: Switching Study Guide, 3rd Edition · ISBN: 0-7821-4294-X
$49.99   Switching, Exam #642-811

CCNP: Remote Access Study Guide, 3rd Edition · ISBN: 0-7821-4296-6
$49.99   Remote Access, Exam #642-821

CCNP: Support Study Guide, 3rd Edition · ISBN: 0-7821-4295-8
$49.99   Support, Exam #642-831

Also available:
CCNP Study Guide Kit, 3rd Edition · ISBN: 0-7821-4297-4 · $169.96
Covers all four exams

Visit **www.sybex.com** for all of your Cisco certification needs.